Employability Skills

David W G Hind
Stuart Moss

Business Education Publishers Limited

© David W G Hind and Stuart Moss

ISBN 1901888 40 1

First Published 2005

Cover Design Tim Murphy Creative Solutions

Published in Great Britain by
Business Education Publishers Limited
The Teleport
Doxford International
Sunderland
SR3 3XD

Tel: 0191 5252410
Fax: 0191 5201815

British Cataloguing-in-Publications Data
A catalogue record for this book is available from the British Library

Printed in Great Britain by The Alden Group Oxford.

Contents

Chapter Four
Written Communication Skills

Chapter Five
Numeracy Skills

Chapter Six
Career Management Skills

Chapter Seven
Presentation Skills

Chapter Eight
Selling and Negotiation Skills

Chapter Nine
Group Work Skills

Chapter Ten
Information Gathering Skills

Chapter Eleven
Thinking Skills

Chapter Twelve
Project Management

Chapter Thirteen
Consultancy Skills

Chapter Fourteen
Reflective Skills and Personal Development Planning

Preface

The term 'employability skills' is now part of the vocabulary of education. All courses in further and higher education will develop the employability skills of their students. Since the late 1990s great emphasis has been given to this aspect of a student's development and education. One of the reasons for this is that employers, when recruiting new young employees pay careful attention to the personal skills of the candidates they are interviewing. Does the candidate have a well-developed portfolio of personal skills that will enable her or him to make a positive contribution in the workplace. Defining an employability skill is quite easy – it is a skill personal to the individual that can be used in many different situations. A few years ago, before the term was introduced, such skills were often referred to as interpersonal skills or social skills. Since the late 1990s, however, it has been felt that there are other personal skills that the individual needs to master in addition to these in order to help with their personal and career developments.

The view now is that individuals need to be competent at problem solving; decision making; working with, and leading others; expressing their ideas numerically, in written and oral forms of presentation; handling interpersonal encounters such as negotiation sessions or interviews; using technology to communicate; and being able to manage projects. The demand for individuals to become competent in these areas has come primarily from employers.

Surveys have been conducted to establish what employers think about the young people they recruit from colleges and universities. A major and frequently noted finding is that the employers are disappointed with their new recruits' abilities to articulate their ideas, to work effectively with others, to solve problems and to use their initiative. The employers in their recruitment and selection processes now place great store on the applicants' competence with regard to these skills.

In response to these demands from employers, the education sector is now paying great attention to the whole area of employability skills development. The educational validating bodies and the universities, as well as government agencies are actively encouraging universities and colleges to integrate employability skills training into all of their courses.

It is the aim of the education sector to ensure that all young people embarking on their careers have the skills that are sought by employers. While employers' needs for specific areas of subject knowledge vary over time, their demand for young people with competent employability skills will never decline.

At a time when the demand is growing for young people to display competent employability skills, what books are available on the subject? There have been many texts published on communication skills, interpersonal skills, social skills, negotiating, leadership, presentation skills and all the other skills sought by employers. However, each text tends to concentrate on only one or two of these skills, and might adopt a theoretical stance rather than a practical one. This results in a book that is lengthy and necessitates much reading before an understanding is gained of how such skills can be applied in practice. Currently, there are few books that draw together all the skills that have been identified by employers and the educational validating bodies, into a coherent text that is totally practical in nature.

It is with this in mind that this book has been written. The authors in writing the text have tried to make it as 'reader-friendly' as possible. The learner's viewpoint has been firmly considered – what type of book do learners need in order to help them to develop further their employability skills? The assumption that has been made is that learners need a text that is straight-to-the-point; is written in a non-academic way (skills learning is highly practical); that divides each skill into its constituent parts; and provides a series of checklists that can be referred to time and again, to indicate what is good practice with each of the skills that is covered. Thus, a prime purpose of this book is to act as the learner's reference text that can be read whenever a particular employability skill has to be used.

If the reader wishes to investigate the theoretical aspects underpinning employability skills there are many scholarly, refereed books available. However, if the reader wishes to find out how to apply such skills in practice then this text will be of value.

Having set out the purpose of this book, and its style of presentation, who should read it? The book has been written to include a wide variety of different employability skills – those required by employers, educational institutions, and additional ones that will inevitably be of much benefit to the individual learner. The skills covered are highly transferable to different situations and can be used by many different people.

Thus, this book itself is highly transferable, the content discussed means that the readership profile is wide. Students at colleges and universities will find that skills training features prominently in their learning and will benefit from using this book. People in employment wishing to develop further their personal skills will find the points discussed of value to them. Individuals following a self development programme in skills training will learn from reading this text. Teachers and trainers who wish to improve the employability skills of their students will be able to use this text as a reference source to inform them of what constitutes a competent level of skills performance. Indeed, all those who are interested in employability skills development will gain from studying the guidelines in the following chapters.

The content of this book has been gained from the authors' experience as lecturers at Leeds Metropolitan University. A central part of their teaching has been to develop further the employability skills of the students they have been teaching. As a result of carrying out research into skills development much has been learned about this subject. The content of this book is also based on established principles for the implementation of the various skills – thus it draws on 'common knowledge'.

This book, therefore, is written by practitioners of skills training, rather than by academics interested in the theoretical and philosophical issues involved in the subject. It has been written by practitioners whose prime concern is to improve the skills performance of their students in practical settings rather than to equip them to be able to debate the subject in abstract essay questions.

The authors acknowledge that much of what is written is not new, but accepted norms of behaviour. What is novel is the drawing together of all the skills into one book and presenting the content in a totally practical manner.

Each chapter of this book reflects the requirements of Twenty first century education and the personal development needs of students. The opportunity has been taken to ensure that the text reflects modern applications of technology in the presentation and communication of information, and also how to communicate professionally through e-mail – netiquette. In Chapter Nine a team leader/team player matrix has been specifically designed to enable readers to determine how much of a team player or team leader they are.

The authors would like to express their thanks to Andrea Murphy and Moira Page at Business Education Publishers for their help and support in bringing this First Edition of *Employability Skills* to print.

The Authors

David Hind is Head of the Centre for Tourism Management at Leeds Metropolitan University one of the leading providers of tourism education in Europe. His career has been spent entirely in the Service Sector.

Initially he worked for the National Westminster Bank where his responsibilities included organising training courses for new recruits and he spent much of his time developing their personal skills. Following this, David moved into the travel and tourism industry working for specialist adventure tour operators in W. Europe, N. America, and S. E. Asia. These experiences confirmed to him the need for all employees to develop competent employability skills.

Since entering teaching, a major part of David's teaching, research and publications has centred around employability skills training.

Stuart Moss is a Senior Lecturer and the Course Leader for HND Business and the Associate Course Leader for the Certificate in E-Business within the Yorkshire First Foundation – a faculty of Leeds Metropolitan University that specialises in teaching Higher Education courses to non-traditional learners. His career has been spent working within the hospitality, tourism and information communication technology industries.

Originally working for a national hotel chain, he travelled abroad in the mid-nineties to work in Australia within the telecommunications industry, before returning to the UK to work in various ICT roles including web designer for a national tourist attraction. Stuart entered teaching in 2001, and has since specialised in issues associated with using virtual learning environments and e-learning for a flexible approach to the delivery of course materials.

Acknowledgements

In writing this book we would like to express our gratitude to all those friends and colleagues who have provided constructive comments on the content and format of the text. We would also like to thank Moira Page and Andrea Murphy who edited the book.

We would also like to thank Rod and Moira Ashley for permission to use material from *Communication in Practice* and *Core Skills for GNVQ* both published by Business Education Publishers Limited.

DWGH and SM
Leeds

Foreword

In recent years, owing to the growing numbers of graduates and an apparent reduction in the graduate job market, there has been increasing emphasis in Further and Higher Education on enhancing employability and embedding transferable employability skills into the curriculum. These developments have been highlighted and supported by the introduction of Progress Files and the drive from funding and quality assurance bodies to encourage personal development planning as part of the Further Education and Higher Education experience. This process requires students to have an understanding of their skills, attributes and achievements and the ability to reflect on and articulate these.

This book provides students with straightforward, clearly expressed guidance for utilising the wealth of skills which can be developed through Further and Higher Education learning; skills which are transferable to the workplace and invaluable for lifelong learning and employability.

Furthermore, in many institutions teaching staff are finding that they are required to provide support for the personal development planning process and the acquisition of these skills by their students. Many such staff have little or no training for this and will find this book invaluable for their own use as well as for supporting their students.

The authors have extensive experience of learning and teaching activities to develop these skills and attributes. They both work within a vocational area at Leeds Metropolitan University which, for the past decade at least, has been a leader in curriculum enhancement for personal and professional development and for the skills that are useful for academic, personal and working life. Their experience is evident in the way they have developed a readable, user-friendly text.

Jane Stapleford
Principal Lecturer, Employability
Leeds Metropolitan University

Chapter One
Introducing Employability Skills

After reading this chapter you will be able to:

1. Explain in your own words what an employability skill is.

2. Understand why it is important for you to develop further your employability skills.

3. Identify the process that will enable you to develop further your employability skills.

4. Appreciate that the development of your employability skills is a life-long process.

1. What are Employability Skills?

Employability skills (ES) are a set of social behaviours and skills that you can learn to help you interact and work with other people in a variety of different situations. These social behaviours and skills are personal to you, although they do not necessarily come naturally, and once mastered can be applied in a variety of different situations, hence they are transferable.

What constitutes an ES is more difficult to decide as many different types of skill can be identified. In the 1990s, such skills were thought to focus primarily around communication, interpersonal, or social skills. It was felt that individuals ought to be effective oral communicators, or competent team players. The thrust now, though, is for a wider range of skills to be identified, skills which will be of use in many different situations.

The ES discussed in this book include not only the traditional ones of communication, interpersonal and social skills, but also learning and study skills, body language skills, and numeracy skills. The high order, complex ES of working with, and leading other people, problem solving, decision making and critical thinking are covered as are skills in information gathering, consultancy, and undertaking extended projects. Special applications of a variety of skills are drawn together in chapters on making a presentation, being interviewed, and taking part in sales or negotiation sessions.

The reason for including such ES in this book is that these are felt to be the core skills that you will need to master to assist with your career development. All individuals have to be able to communicate with others in a variety of different styles. Oral communication occurs through informal conversation as well as by formal presentation. Business letters and reports have to be written, as do curriculum vitae and application forms. When you are called for an interview you must know how to behave in order to be successful. All individuals are involved with selling and negotiating situations – whether it be 'selling' themselves at interviews or negotiating with colleagues as to who will complete a certain task. In order to influence others assertive skills are required.

Thus, ES extend beyond those skills important to ourselves as individuals, and encompass how we interact and work with other people. Much work is undertaken in groups so group skills need to be developed. Just as it is important for individuals to be able to work harmoniously as group members it is also important for them to be able to analyse problems and to take decisions.

You can improve your problem solving and decision making by following systematic procedures. Information is frequently required to assist the thinking processes involved with problem solving and decision making, and you need to be aware of how to gather valid and reliable information. When undertaking projects for other people, such as gathering information, in which you act as a consultant, a credible working relationship has to be established with the client. Being aware of consultancy skills will help you in this process.

Encompassing all of the above mentioned skills are learning and study skills. ES are not developed overnight but over a considerable period of time. To be able to learn from each new business and social encounter and to be able to structure a self-development programme you must be aware of how learning and studying can be made more effective.

2.   Why are Employability Skills Important?

The demand for individuals to master successfully a wide portfolio of ES is a relatively new trend that is now being fully supported from both the public and private sectors. It has come from a number of different sources: employers, educational validating bodies, and government.

The authors' initial interest in ES development arose from reading an article in the mid-1980s. In April 1986 *The Sunday Times* published the results of a survey conducted by Peter Wilby. The purpose of the research was to establish the level of satisfaction of employers with the young people they recruited from colleges and universities. In total some 450 employers completed the questionnaire. The findings from the research made interesting reading.

While the employers were generally satisfied with the subject knowledge of their new recruits, they explicitly stated that they were dissatisfied with the ES of the young people. The employers were of the opinion that their young recruits were inarticulate, tongue-tied, showed little initiative, and were unable to work effectively with other people. A conclusion that came from the research was that young people, in order to be successful in the career market place, would need to develop competent and effective ES.

This view still holds true today. When an analysis is made of career vacancies advertised in the press it is evident that employers do place considerable importance on the ES of their new recruits. Some career advertisements are very explicit when detailing the profile of the likely candidate for the post:

> The ideal candidate will have a positive outlook and demonstrate the ability to identify problems and produce logical, practical and acceptable solutions. You will be able to manage yourself efficiently whilst showing high levels of creativity. As a team player you

will work cooperatively and flexibly with other members of the team and possess initiative, energy and motivation. You will have excellent interpersonal and presentation skills and the ability to demonstrate strong time management skills within a fast moving, exciting environment.

(World Challenge Expeditions, *The Guardian*, 26 June 2004.)

Such an advertisement leaves no doubt as to the ES that the successful applicant will need to display. Indeed, it could be asserted that employers are now attaching more importance to young recruits' ES than they do to their subject knowledge or technical abilities.

Marks and Spencer, when selecting recruits for its Management Training Programme, is just as interested in selecting individuals who display management aptitude, as well as academic achievement. The selectors look for leadership skills, sensitivity towards other people, decisiveness, and flexibility. British Aerospace, who recruit large numbers of engineers and computer scientists, also look for evidence of the ability to lead, to initiate new ideas, to communicate, and to solve problems when appraising new employees. Unilever is not only interested in recruiting intelligent employees, but looks for people who are able to analyse problems rapidly and accurately, who can work in groups, are able to communicate with other people and to influence them. Indeed, these abilities appear on the 'shopping list' of many major employers from all industrial sectors – engineering, manufacturing, mining, as well as the service sector.

From the above discussion it is apparent that the career market place has changed from being dominated solely by the bright, academically gifted person, to being the domain of the person who has management aptitude, displayed in their ES, in addition to intellectual abilities.

In response to the demands of employers educational institutions are paying much attention to the whole area of ES training. ES development is now featuring prominently on courses validated by universities and courses offered by colleges.

Thus, young people currently studying courses of Further and Higher Education are being required to develop their ES and to use their academic environment as a practice ground for developing abilities that will be appropriate for their future careers. In their assignments students are no longer assessed only on their subject knowledge or technical abilities but also on their ES. To be successful at attaining high grades in this area students need to be aware of what a competent level of performance is for each ES that is being assessed. The chapters in this book will provide such an insight.

There is clearly, therefore, an external justification for you to develop your ES. Additionally, such development will benefit you personally. ES training involves much self-evaluation – analysing and judging your own abilities. This process will inevitably result in you getting to know yourself better. When this has been achieved you will be able to plan your future – which career will be most suited to your skills, which should be avoided. The self-evaluation process will also probably identify any characteristics that might hinder your inter-relationships with other people. When such traits have been identified, steps can be taken to overcome them, making you more 'personable' or sociable.

The training programme will involve much practice and rehearsal of new behaviours and skills. As time progresses and these new behaviours become part of your portfolio of ES, your self-confidence and self-assurance will improve. Situations that once were felt to be daunting, such as interviews or formal presentations, now become enjoyable experiences in which you are happy to display your abilities to other people. For some people these specific personal benefits of ES training are more important than the wider career implications, especially for the more introverted individual who shies away from social encounters.

The discussion in this section indicates that it is most important for you to develop competent ES. From an employment perspective, employers will be looking more closely at the personal skills of applicants when deciding who to recruit for a career vacancy. To prepare young people for their careers, educational institutions are now including ES training into many more courses, and formally assessing the abilities of their students, the grades from which will contribute to the students' overall qualification. Thus, the value of mastering a wide portfolio of ES cannot be understated.

3.   How are Employability Skills Developed?

ES are not developed overnight. In fact the ES learning process is an arduous, life long process with each new business and social encounter offering you the opportunity to develop further your ES. Learning occurs in a variety of ways.

Trial and error of new skills and behaviours will indicate to you which ES are effective in different situations. Reflection on these skills and behaviours will assist the learning process. In addition to learning by trial and error, formal training will also be of value.

Structured learning in a classroom environment will be important, especially if more active learning strategies such as role-playing exercises are used. These allow you to practise new behaviours in a 'safe' and controlled setting, before they are tried out in the real world. Demonstrations, which you can later model, enable good practice to be followed at the outset. Texts, such as this, have a part to play as they can analyse the constituent components of various ES and act as a permanent reference source.

In developing ES each learning strategy mentioned above has to be considered. The challenge for you is to adopt a frame of mind that welcomes each learning strategy and views the development of ES as a process that necessitates using the more active types of learning. A key element when developing new skills is that of practice. Only through active participation in the learning programme will you be able to practise, and hence further develop your abilities.

The nature of ES training is potentially threatening to all learners as much embarrassment and offence could be caused when analysing the behaviour of each participant. Thus, to be successful, the learning has to be implemented in a sensitive way. Both learner and tutor must appreciate this. If an authoritarian approach is adopted by the tutor then the learners will feel reluctant to participate. Sensitivity must be shown to the feelings of all the participants – an ES in its own right.

Chapter Two discusses in more detail how learning occurs. What is important to understand is that you can learn new skills and behaviours. As part of their teaching, the authors always incorporate an element of ES training into the learning activities of their students. Research was conducted to evaluate the effectiveness of this training, the results of which were conclusive. Ninety six per cent of the students who completed a recent ES training programme indicated that they felt that their personal skills had improved as a result of it. All the skills that were included in the programme showed a marked improvement as the programme developed. In addition to improving their skills, ninety eight per cent of the students found the programme to be enjoyable, and ninety four per cent believed the 'quality' of the course had been enhanced because of it.

As a learner, you must appreciate that ES training will not be easy. You will have to learn to evaluate your own ES, where both your strengths and weaknesses are identified. For some learners this might mean self-confrontation, because for the first time in their lives they will see themselves as others do. This is all part of the ES learning process as it is only when you see yourself as other people do that you can start to modify your behaviour so that more effective personal relationships and skills are established.

How, then, can this book help you in the ES learning process?

4.   The Purpose of Employability Skills Training

All learning is concerned with changing behaviour, and ES training is no different. The purpose of the training, though, is not to change your personality, but to allow you to become more competent at using a variety of ES. As a result of the training, however, the learner may become a more 'personable' individual, more self confident or less anxious when thrust into unfamiliar situations.

The implications of this are important. ES training is not designed to force you into conforming to rigid, stereotyped patterns of behaviour. Although guidelines can be given as to what a competent ES is, it is not possible to suggest universal behaviours that can be used in each business or social encounter you will face. This is because each encounter will be different, and each person will bring different abilities to the situation. At its best, ES training will broaden your range of behaviour and increase your awareness of the variety of employability skills available.

Thus, a primary purpose of this book is to make you more aware of the ES that have been identified by employers and educational institutions as being important to young people. As has been stated previously, if you master a variety of ES you will be better placed to succeed in the career market place.

The following chapters look at ES that have been identified as being important. Each ES is outlined and then divided into its constituent parts. Check lists are used to draw your attention to the key components of each skill that is considered. This provides a practical reference guide to the constituent elements of each ES. By this means, you will have close to hand points to be borne in mind when using any of the skills.

This book has been written to be used in two main ways. Firstly, it will be a useful complementary text to a formal period of ES training that is developed by a tutor. When a particular personal skill is being covered in the programme, you can refer to the relevant chapter in this book to gain a knowledge and understanding of the constituent components of the skill under consideration. All the core skills that form the basis of many different types of ES training programmes will be found in this book.

Secondly, this book will allow you to structure your own ES self-development programme. For example, before an interview is attended, the check lists provided will inform you of the preparation stages you should go through in order to succeed at the interview. To learn from the behaviours used during the interview a post-evaluation process is outlined. Likewise, when a formal oral presentation is to be made, similar guidelines are provided.

In writing this book your needs as a learner have been borne firmly in mind. A major emphasis has been placed upon ensuring that all points made have a practical relevance. To achieve this, each chapter includes a series of check lists that you can follow when implementing a particular skill. By adopting this style it is hoped that the text is as practical as possible (ES are only developed by practising them time and again). As a result of this approach little attention is paid to the underpinning theories that suggest why a particular skill should be used in a certain way in order to achieve a competent performance. There are other books that cover these areas of ES development. It is felt that what is important for the reader of this book is to know and understand how ES should be, and can be, used in practical situations.

Please note that to avoid the implication that ES relate to a single sex, the terms he and she are used in alternate chapters to refer to both males and females. In this way we hope to avoid the potential difficulty of sexual stereotyping.

After reading this chapter please complete the following learning activities:

Learning Activities

1. If a friend asked you to define the term employability skills – what would you say?

2. Write down five reasons why it is important for you to develop further your employability skills.

3. Identify five different means by which you can develop further your employability skills.

4. What are the benefits of continuing to develop your employability skills throughout your life long career?

Chapter Two
Learning and Study Skills

After reading this chapter you will be able to:

1. Explain how learning occurs.

2. Define the term study skills.

3. Identify the different study skills that will enable you to become an effective learner.

4. Understand how to manage your time effectively.

You cannot develop ES overnight. In fact it is a life-long process, and each time you meet a new situation in your business or social life it will provide you with the opportunity to try out new behaviours, to reflect on them and to evaluate them. If you are to manage this self-development programme successfully, you need to be aware of how you learn. You will also need study skills to help you learn both in the classroom and from private study in your own time. In this chapter we will examine learning and study skills which should help you with your own self-development. Indeed, learning and studying are ES in their own right as once you have developed such skills they can be used in a wide variety of different settings.

1. Learning

Learning is the gaining over time of skills, knowledge, experience or attitudes. Learning is the process of changing your behaviour so that you will be able to do something that you were unable to do before the learning took place. When you have learnt something, you should be able to see and measure your change in behaviour and this will allow you and your tutors to decide how successful you have been in the learning process.

Learning takes place in a sequence involving three inter-related stages. These are shown in the following learning model diagram.

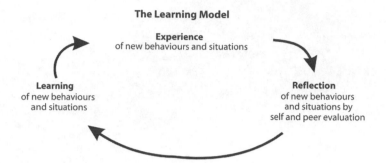

The Learning Model

Your existing experience of different situations in which you have found yourself, and the behaviour of different people which you have seen, form the building blocks for your new learning. From such experiences and observations you can reflect on your own abilities and identify your ES strengths and weaknesses. Once you have done this, you can develop new forms of behaviour that will allow you to overcome your weaknesses and improve your strengths. In the chapters of this book we shall look at each of these three stages, particularly as they relate to ES.

There are a number of different types of learning but for the purpose of this book we shall consider four main types:

- Learning to do something.
- Learning to memorise something.
- Learning to understand something.
- Learning a skill.

We shall look at each of these in turn.

1.1   Learning to do Something

You will face many situations which involve you in learning to do something, whether it is to give an oral presentation, write a report, or to interview an applicant for a job. Whatever the situation there is a simple process involving three steps you can apply:

(i)   determine the purpose of what you are trying to learn;
(ii)   identify the procedures involved;
(iii)   practise the task.

(i)   Determine the Purpose

When learning to do something you must have a clear understanding of the purpose of what you are trying to achieve. You need to understand why you are giving the oral presentation, or the reason for writing the report, or why the interview is taking place.

In the same way, you need to identify the reasons for trying to develop your ES. You can justify it on the grounds that employers now demand a high level of competence in such skills. Employers seek to recruit articulate people who can communicate, who are numerate, and have the ability to work in groups and to solve problems. If you do not possess such skills then you may find it much more difficult to progress in your career.

Therefore it is important that you recognise why you are developing these skills. If you do not, then you might lack motivation towards the ES training programme. If this is the case, you will tend to lose concentration, pay little attention to any advice and information that is given to you, and so reduce the amount of progress that you will make.

(ii)   Identify the Procedures Involved

When you have become clear about why you are learning to do something, you should then identify any procedures that need to be followed in order to complete the task successfully. In a number of situations there are norms or guidelines that you have to follow. For example, when you write a business letter there are conventions that should be followed if you want your letter to be laid out and presented in a professional way so that it will create a favourable impression on the person receiving it.

You should understand these procedures. If there are no norms or guidelines, you will have to use your own judgement to decide the most appropriate procedures to follow.

(iii)   Practise the Task

You will learn to do something successfully only by practising it. Once you have identified the procedures for completing the task, the next stage in the learning process is to practise, following any guidelines that are provided. This part of the cycle is important. You should try to follow all the guidelines correctly and accurately. You have to establish good habits for completing the task at the outset, as it will be difficult to correct bad habits at a later stage.

You will probably find that you have to learn the activities involved in completing the task at a relatively slow pace, practising each individual component until you have mastered it, and frequently referring to the norms or guidelines. As you successfully learn and memorise new tasks you can move on to more complex ones. With practice, your speed in completing the task will increase, and you will not need to refer to the guidelines so frequently.

One of the most commonly used methods of learning to do something is by a tutor giving a demonstration of how to complete a task successfully.

Demonstration of a Task: Often one of the best ways of learning how to do something is to watch someone else doing it. The tutor can demonstrate how a particular task should be completed. For example, the tutor might show you the skills involved in interviewing an applicant for a post, or demonstrate how to use the voice effectively when giving an oral presentation. You will learn from such demonstrations only if you watch and listen to the tutor very carefully:

- Note the body language that is used by the tutor – for example, her hand gestures, her posture, her facial expressions, her eye contact and her appearance and dress.
- Listen carefully to how she uses her voice. When does she use different speeds of speech, and why? How frequently does she vary the tone of her voice, and to what effect?
- What types of speech does she use? For example does she use witticisms or humour? How much jargon does she use? How does she introduce and conclude the speech?
- Does she use special equipment? For example, watch how she switches on and uses the laptop computer and projector. Which disk drive on the personal computer does she use?
- During the demonstration if you do not understand any activities that she demonstrates then you should ask questions until you do understand what is being done, and why it is being done.

You should try to identify and understand the key points in the demonstration. For example, the tutor should draw your attention to the three stages of an oral presentation – the introduction, the development of the argument and the conclusion – and show how linking sentences can be used to add coherence to these stages.

You should make additional notes to help you to memorise the sequence of events, and you should file these notes for future reference.

When the tutor has demonstrated the activity, you should practise it as soon as possible after the demonstration. You should use any equipment or aids that are required to undertake the activity. You should concentrate on doing the key activities slowly until you have achieved a certain level of competence and you are beginning to undertake the sequences in the process almost automatically without having to refer to your notes or other guidelines.

Written Instructions for a Task: Another way of learning to do something is by following written instructions. In some situations all that you will have are written instructions on how to complete the tasks involved. For instance when you buy a personal computer you will be provided with a written instruction manual. The person who wrote the manual has hopefully paid considerable attention to making sure that it is easily understood. In reading such instructions, however, you need to follow certain guidelines:

- Read through the entire document, or at least an entire section, before putting into practice the instructions. Become familiar with all sections in the manual.
- Read through the manual or section again, as it is unlikely that you will understand all the points on the first reading.
- Start at the beginning of the manual, or the relevant section, and read slowly through the instructions, implementing exactly all the directions that are given. If problems arise then start again. Do not hurry the process, but work at a controlled pace.

If you follow these guidelines (providing the instructions have been reasonably well written) then you should complete all the necessary tasks successfully. If you make a mistake then do not worry as this should also be seen as part of the learning process. Sometimes it is the process of making mistakes which turns out to be the most memorable learning experience. If you do make an error, you should analyse it to find out what the problem is, and why it occurred. You should then repeat the correct way of completing the task until you have mastered it.

1.2   Learning to Memorise Something

Much learning requires you to memorise something, whether it be sequences in a process, data, or the content of an oral presentation. Memorising something is the process of acquiring information, retaining it in your brain, and then being able to recall it at a later time. There are three components of your memory:

(i)   the sensory information storage system;
(ii)   the short-term memory store;
(iii) the long-term memory store.

(i)   The Sensory Information Storage System

This stage of the memory process involves you in receiving information from the environment through your senses. This may involve reading instructions from a manual, watching a demonstration given by the tutor, listening to an audio-tape, or touching, tasting or smelling something.

Sensory information is transmitted to your brain via your nervous system, but most of it is only retained for a matter of minutes before it is forgotten.

(ii)   The Short-term Memory Store

Some of the sensory information that your brain receives, however, is transferred to your short-term memory, especially sensory information that is already familiar to you. Here, you interpret the sensory information into a more meaningful form. It can then be recalled immediately, and combined with other knowledge, perceptions or ideas that you already have stored in your memory, helping you to understand what your senses are experiencing. The capacity of your short-term memory, though, is relatively small.

(iii)   The Long-term Memory Store

Your long-term memory has a greater capacity than your short-term memory and can recall information that has been accumulated over quite a long period of time. Thus, it is the most important part of the memory, and also the most complex.

You should aim to commit all the information that you consider to be important and relevant to your long-term memory so that you can recall it and use it at a later time. Information you have retained in your long-term memory can be used for many different purposes, such as recalling facts, helping to solve problems, and critical thinking. When you are learning something new, you do this best if information is transferred into your long-term memory store building upon your previous knowledge and understanding.

You can use a number of techniques to help store information in your long-term memory. The first stage in the process is to translate the information into a form that you can remember more easily. Association techniques are useful:

- Group similar pieces of information together. For example, it costs the same to fly from London to Bangkok as it does to fly from London to Singapore, Los Angeles, San Francisco or Mauritius.
- Pair information or things together – it costs the same to fly from London to Bangkok, Singapore, Los Angeles, San Francisco and Mauritius, and also takes the same flying time.
- You could make up a story linking these pieces of information together – Planet Airways fly from Bangkok to Singapore, then to Mauritius, before arriving in London en route to the west coast of America.
- You could try to visualise the information to be remembered – Bangkok visualised by its temples and palaces, Singapore by skyscrapers, Mauritius as a tropical island paradise, London by Buckingham Palace, Los Angeles by Hollywood and San Francisco by the Golden Gate bridge.

Once you have translated the information you wish to remember into a more memorable form, you should write it down, then read it out loud, and then read it through again, each time trying to commit more of the information to your long-term memory.

If you have to learn a great deal of information, you should break it down into discrete parts which are then the focus of your attention, with the repetition process continuing until you are able to recall all the information without having to refer to your notes. You can help this rote learning process, by using a number of special aids:

- Using rhymes to remember information – 'thirty days hath September, April, June and November...'.
- Using the first letter of key words to remember them – mnemonics, for example the marketing mix is referred to as the 4P's – the product, promotion, price and place.
- Using word associations to differentiate between words which are pronounced the same but spelt differently for example associate stationary with a parked car and stationery with a pile of papers.

The easiest way to remember new things is to connect them with what you already know. This requires conscious efforts to link in the new material to your long-term memory. One way of doing this is to make notes of links with existing knowledge as you gain new information.

You will not help yourself to memorise things if you are mentally or physically tired. A tired mind will be unable to assimilate new information. You will stand a better chance of remembering information that you gain while your mind is fresh. You should avoid prolonged periods memorising information, especially those in excess of two hours. You should take breaks every thirty minutes when you should do something else – make a cup of coffee, or stretch your legs. This will help to refresh your mind and assist your memory process.

When you have completed the memorising period, you should immediately review what you have been studying. This should involve a quick re-read of any notes that you have made, listing again the main points. This should keep your level of recall high for the next twenty four hours. The following day you should undertake a second review. This time it should be a quick review of the previous day's learning to reinforce the memory process, committing the information gained to your long-term memory. At the end of the week, you should review all the material you have learnt in totality, so that you can identify and understand the relationships between the various pieces of information. You should condense further any notes that you have made, but retain the originals for future reference.

After a month has elapsed you should follow the review process again, reading through your condensed notes and seeing how much of the original material you can remember. If you have any problems in recalling the information you should refer back to the original notes and re-read the relevant section until you have committed it to memory.

1.3   Learning to Understand Something

When you understand something you are able to explain it. Understanding something means comprehending it, whether it is a statement, an object, a concept or a principle. When you are learning to do something, it is important to understand the procedures in the process and then to practise them until they have been mastered. Memorising information involves being competent at using a variety of techniques that can assist with its recall. Learning to understand something is different. You will find rote learning (repetitive learning) of little use here and there is little scope for practice as understanding something involves mental processes as opposed to physical ones. How then, can something be understood? The starting point is to ask questions.

(i)   Questions

You should ask questions of yourself as well as of other people. When you are listening to an explanation given by a tutor, or when you read instructions, you should ask yourself what are you listening to, or hearing, and what it means to you. For example after a talk on the nature of 'marketing' you should answer the question:

What does marketing mean to me?

At the same time you should be relating the new information to what you already know, and considering its implications. If you cannot answer the questions that you are asking yourself, then you should try and seek the answers from other people such as your tutors.

You need to ask open questions that demand more than a 'yes' or 'no' answer. You should try and develop a hierarchy of questions that follow the sequence: 'What', 'Where', 'When', 'Who', and 'How'.

Sequencing questions in this way will allow you to take the answer and build the information upon the previous answer given. Your answers to these questions will provide information that will describe what is taking place, and will help further your understanding of the situation under consideration:

What information do I need to solve the problem?

Where is this information to be found?

When should I obtain this information?

Who will be able to provide it for me?

How will I use the information?

If you are trying to find an explanation to something concentrate on questions beginning with 'Why':

Why has this problem developed?

Why can't you help me?

You should ask questions until you understand the situation. This may well require some persistence on your part. If the answers that you are getting are not helping you to understand what you wish to know, then re-phrase the questions until you get a better answer. If persistent questioning still does not provide you with a clearer picture of the situation, however, try making comparisons with similar situations.

(ii)   Comparisons

Look at similar situations and circumstances to see if there are any relationships or patterns which might help you to explain what you are trying to find out. By comparing situations and dividing each into its constituent parts, you can achieve a better understanding of what you are studying. For example, if you are trying to understand what constitutes an effective oral presentation, you might find it useful to analyse the oral presentation of an accomplished public speaker and identify the factors that account for her success. When you have done this you will find that it is possible to develop a checklist of factors that you can use to compare and contrast the oral presentation skills of others. The checklist might look something like this:

The accomplished public speaker will use:

(a)   Different tones of voice.
(b)   Different speeds of speech.
(c)   Inflection in the voice.
(d)   Facial expressions to support her verbal message which will be pleasing to the audience.

(e)   Gestures that are supportive and complementary to the message, rather than distracting and repetitive.

(f)   A posture which displays an air of self-respect and self-confidence.

The unaccomplished public speaker will exhibit characteristics that are the opposite of these.

(iii)   Solving Problems

We shall discuss the topic of problem solving in greater depth later but for the purpose of this section, you need to appreciate that the process of solving problems can help when you are trying to understand something. Solving problems involves transferring knowledge and understanding that you already have stored in your long-term memory to new situations.

By using your current level of knowledge and understanding and applying it to the new situation you might be able to come up with alternative solutions for solving the problem. You can then evaluate these solutions to see which is most appropriate for solving the problem.

To be a successful problem solver you must use your intellectual skills and pose questions that will help you to shed light on the problem you are considering. If you can solve the problem you are in a much better position to understand why it occurred in the first place, and how it can be overcome if it arises again in the future.

When you think you understand a problem, a good test of your understanding will be your ability to explain the solution of the problem to others. If you can do this accurately and without causing confusion you will have demonstrated your understanding.

1.4   Learning a Skill

So far we have discussed how you can learn facts and concepts, and how you can gain a clearer understanding of a given situation. All of these learning approaches are important when you are learning new skills, but there are other aspects to skills development.

All skills, no matter what they are can be learnt. Skills are learnt by dividing the skill into its constituent parts and then rebuilding these parts into the coherent whole. You have to organise and co-ordinate the constituent parts before you can master the skill as a whole. You have to learn lower order skills, or basic skills, before you can progress to the high order ones.

Human beings have the ability to learn a great variety of different skills. From birth onwards, you learn new skills with each new social encounter. As you progress through life and enjoy a challenging career, you have to master fresh skills. The three stage Learning Model that we used to introduce in this section will form the building frame for skills development. You can help your learning process, though, by being aware of how to learn from certain teaching strategies that might form part of the ES training programme. 'Active' teaching strategies such as role-playing exercises might be designed by your tutor, with the exercises being video-recorded. We shall now consider how you can learn most effectively from these strategies.

(i)   Role-play Exercises

A role-play exercise is a situation in which you act out, or perform certain skills and behaviours, in a simulated situation. Each learner is given a certain role to perform and you are free to develop your role as you wish, or according to guidelines that are provided.

Role-play exercises are valuable learning strategies in that they allow you to practise new skills in a controlled, safe setting, before they are used in the real environment.

However, to learn from role-play exercises you should bear in mind the following guidelines:

- You should commit yourself whole-heartedly to the exercise and adopt the role that is required. If you lack commitment then you will not contribute fully and you will not learn as much, and you may hold back other people.
- You should prepare thoroughly beforehand as this will allow you to gain an understanding of the role you have to play, and the behaviours you will have to adopt. Indeed, if you rehearse the role which you have to perform before participating in the role-playing this will increase your confidence.
- If you find this kind of learning strategy 'threatening', you should remember that you are acting out a role, and so you should adopt a frame of mind that recognises this. Indeed, you might find it easier to divorce yourself totally from your own personality and character, and 'step firmly into the shoes' of the role that you have to perform.

You are bound to feel a certain amount of apprehension before a role-playing exercise. This is a positive sign as it shows that you are concerned about what is to take place and it will help to ensure that you contribute to the best of your ability. If you feel complacent towards the exercise then you might not contribute as effectively.

No doubt you will be nervous during the early stages of the role-playing exercise, but as it progresses and your confidence builds, you should become more relaxed. Experience shows that once the initial nervous period has passed, most learners relax and enjoy performing their roles.

Role-playing is not an end in itself. While it is highly beneficial to be able to practise new skills in a controlled and safe setting, you will learn more if there is feedback after the session. A most effective way of providing such feedback is by video-recording the exercise.

(ii)   Being Videoed

You will find that video recording role-playing exercises should greatly improve your learning of skills because the recordings provide 'live' feedback of how you have performed and how others see you. Video recordings can highlight some aspects of your behaviour of which you were previously unaware. Just as role-playing exercises might feel threatening to you, so too might being videoed. Thus, to help you overcome any trepidation about it follow these procedures:

Before the Recording:

- Prepare thoroughly for the exercise which is to be videoed. Rehearse your role and the behaviour you will adopt beforehand.
- If possible rehearse in the room which is to be used for the recording and have a complete run-through of the exercise, with the video-cameras recording this rehearsal. This will familiarise you with the environment and the equipment, and any props that are to be used.
- If a video-recording of the rehearsal is made, watch a play-back of it immediately afterwards. Ideally this should be in private, rather than with the other learners taking part. This will allow you to come to terms with seeing yourself on the screen and also give you an impression of how others see you.

- Identify any distracting mannerisms you might have, such as pulling at your hair, or scratching your nose, as these may detract from the behaviour that you are trying to practise in the exercise.

The Actual Recording:

- The night before the recording, run through again all the behaviours you will employ in the exercise, making sure that you are not using any distracting mannerisms.
- Arrive for the recording in good time so that you can calm your nerves and gather your thoughts and so focus on the exercise ahead.
- When the exercise commences, concentrate one hundred per cent on the role you have to perform. Ignore the cameras, microphones, and lights.
- Look at the other learners participating in the exercise, do not look at the cameras, or touch any of the microphones – these are very sensitive and will pick up the slightest sound.
- Do not be distracted by people entering the room, or other disturbances – 'the show must go on'.
- Do not detract from the serious side of the exercise by giggling. If you cannot control yourself, then quietly leave the recording studio, otherwise everyone else will be distracted.
- Pay careful attention to your dress and grooming. You should wear clothes that will enhance your appearance, and groom yourself in such a way that is pleasing to look at.
- If possible view the tape immediately after the exercise. This will familiarise you with the behaviours you have used and allow you to make more constructive use of the feedback sessions.

The Feedback Session:

You should learn a lot during the feedback session. This session will be most successful if you follow certain guidelines:

- Be totally honest when discussing your behaviour with your peers and the tutor. First identify those aspects of your behaviour that have been successful and say why they are strengths. Then identify those aspects of your behaviour where there is room for improvement and suggest how you can modify them.
- At all times be positive. There will be some skills in which you will be proficient – acknowledge these. At the same time accept that there will be room for improvement in other areas.
- Always focus attention on the skill rather than the person. When providing feedback to other learners never make the comments personal to them, rather refer to the way in which the skill was performed.
- Be objective and constructive when giving feedback to your fellow learners – suggest ways in which their behaviour could be improved.
- When accepting feedback from others, do not take it as a personal criticism. You should not always try to justify your behaviour, or argue with those providing the feedback – listen to their comments, digest them, and acknowledge the validity of what is being said.

If you remember the above points when taking part in video-recorded exercises then you should be more successful in the way you learn skills. All that is required is for you to acknowledge that there is room for improvement and to commit yourself to taking active steps to overcome your weaknesses and turn them into strengths. Without this commitment, you will not improve your ES.

The learning process is complex. You need to appreciate that there are many different types of learning. In this chapter we have considered only four. These, however, have wide transferability and are highly pertinent to ES training. From the discussion so far it is evident that many different approaches are involved in the learning process. You need to be aware of which approaches are most appropriate for you, and for the type of learning that you are seeking to achieve.

A demonstration by a tutor is useful in that you can see a model of correct behaviour provided by the tutor, which you can then imitate. Complex tasks can be divided into discrete stages that can then be demonstrated before you practise and repeat them until you have mastered them. With demonstrations, the tutor is also available to answer any questions that you might have.

If you are trying to learn using written instructions, you have a permanent reference guide which you can refer to time and again, until you have mastered the correct behaviour. Unfortunately, written instructions are not able to answer questions.

In addition to learning by demonstration and written instructions, another common means you could use is trial and error. When you experiment with a new form of behaviour, you should get some form of feedback as to how successful it is. Sometimes it is by making errors that you gain the greatest amount of learning. Once you have mastered a new form of behaviour and have repeated it frequently, you should develop a greater level of competence. Remember that 'practice makes perfect'.

2.   Teaching Resources which help in the Learning Process

To help you in the learning process, your tutor may use a number of different teaching resources. To gain the most from such resources it is important for you to recognise how and why each is being used. These learning resources should motivate and arouse your interest so that you are keen to learn and concentrate on the learning process. If the resources are well prepared and interesting to use they should also help with the retention process and help you to recall information. Carefully designed resources will also enable you to make full use of your time, and help you to apply your learning to real situations in the future. Your tutor might use a great variety of learning resources such as:

- Information handouts – these summarise the main points to be learnt and provide you with background reference material.
- Worksheets – can help to structure the learning process, or can be used to help with the retention and recall of information. With these you are expected to write on the worksheet, filling in missing words, labelling diagrams, correcting errors or filling in the results of an experiment.
- Case studies – these might simulate a real situation and involve you applying your intellectual skills to solve problems. Different approaches can be used for tackling case studies ranging from individual work to group analysis.
- Role-playing exercises – as we have already seen these enable you to practise new behaviours in controlled settings allowing you to make errors which can then be overcome before you face similar situations in the real world.
- Video tapes – again, as we have already noted, these provide recordings of your skills being applied in practice and enable you to evaluate how well you can use the ES in question.

We have not been able to cover every type of learning resource in the above examples. Instead we have tried to show that there are a number of learning resources that you can use to develop further your ES. As technological advances occur a greater variety of learning resources become available. The proliferation of computer simulations that can be used for learning is one such example, providing you with a different learning experience.

3.   e-Learning and Collaborating Online

To put it simply e-learning is the use of information communication technology (ICT) to help facilitate studying and learning. There are very many examples where ICT may be used within education in this way such as:

- The use of the internet to perform information searches using search engines or subject directories.
- The use of technological mediums such as PowerPoint to create and deliver a presentation.
- Using email to contact a tutor or share ideas with other students.

e-Learning can be very useful for people that are studying at a geographical distance to communicate with one another online – this is known as collaborative learning, and is commonly used by universities that have their own Virtual Learning Environment (VLE) such as Blackboard™ or WebCT™. These VLEs are websites that hold and store teaching materials, and also offer communicative tools such as discussion forums. These may be used for people to support each other by sharing resources such as links to useful websites for assignments.It is important for students to understand that studying on a university course does not put an individual in competition with his/her peers – rather students should be supporting one another in their studies. Discussion forums are one facet of VLEs that make this possible.

With advances in technology, more information is being stored online all the time, everything from annual reports, electronic journals, newspapers online and e-books. University libraries are increasingly turning to technology to supplement their traditional paper based information stores. Online libraries are not only more efficient in terms of space saving, but they can be quick to search, and accessible 24 hours a day seven days a week – giving them an obvious advantage over more traditional information stores. See http://www.leedsmet.ac.uk/lis/lss/ – using these information sources is now an essential part of student life.

However, as well as using the range of learning resources available, to be able to learn most efficiently, you need to develop study skills.

4.   Study Skills

You need to develop study skills because much of your learning takes place on an individual basis, perhaps as part of your self-development programme. To make the most of the learning resources that are available, you must be aware of how to take notes from verbal or written messages, you must be able to read efficiently, and you need to be able to structure the learning process.

You will have to make time available for structured learning. No doubt you will have other commitments – family, friends, work, hobbies and other pressures. Not only will you have to accommodate these, but you will also have to find time to study. The key is to establish a balance between each demand on your time. You should not devote all of your time and energy to learning at the expense of your other interests and activities. If you did this, you would not end up as a 'well-rounded' individual, but as someone who has no other interests apart from study.

Time management, therefore, is crucial. Decide on those times of the day which for you are the most conducive to studying, and then schedule your other interests around them. Initially, you should try out different times, until you have established a routine that allows you to find time for studying alongside the other demands on your time. A key ingredient contributing to the success of any learning programme is self-discipline. If you are unable to motivate yourself to undertake regular study periods then you will find that your learning suffers. You require a strong determination to succeed. To reinforce this determination, you need to understand how you will benefit by successfully completing the learning programme.

A further important factor in effective study is to find the right place in which to work. Certain types of learning, for example memorising information require a quiet environment free from distractions. For most individuals a room at home that is quiet and respected by other members of the family as a study room, will be the best study setting. You must have space available for any necessary books or equipment, and a table and chair for writing. You should try and keep noise distractions to a minimum, even to the extent of not listening to the radio, or watching TV. Distractions such as these might make you feel relaxed, but they reduce your concentration and impede the learning process.

When you have found a time and place for studying, they should not be wasted. The approach that you adopt during your study periods will inevitably affect the final outcome.

4.1   Study Timetable

Studying is an ES that you can develop and improve. Some individuals appear naturally studious. They are content to spend hours on end learning. For others, studying requires effort – other interests have to be ignored, distractions removed, and full concentration given to the learning process. To help in this process you should draw up a study timetable. This involves the following steps:

- Set a personal objective that you want to attain as a result of undertaking the learning programme. This might relate to the grade you wish to achieve, or the skills you want to acquire.
- Then, decide how many hours a week you will need to reach that objective. To determine how much study it will require might require consultation with another learner who has experienced the same programme, or with the tutor.
- Allocate these hours to different days of the week, ensuring you achieve a balance during the week, and with other interests – remember not to spend too long on any one session e.g. set aside two hours on Monday afternoon and one hour on Monday evening; two hours on Tuesday evening; two hours on Wednesday afternoon etc.
- Start to schedule the work and topics you have to cover over a period of weeks to make sure that they can be learnt in the time available.
- Prepare a formal study timetable for the duration of the learning programme. On the timetable set target dates for completing certain topics or assignments.
- Make sure that the timetable allows for periods of relaxation in and around the study periods. Have at least one day free from study each week, and also a few longer breaks of a couple of days, or a week, at times during the learning programme.
- Try to adhere to the timetable and try not to fall behind. If this occurs then you might have to make sacrifices elsewhere in your sphere of interests – for example you might have to miss out on a visit to the cinema. Keep a continuous check on the progress you have made to-date so that you do not fall behind.
- If pressures from studying build up, do not panic – it will be inevitable. Discuss the pressure with fellow learners or the tutor. Calm down and take an objective view of

the work you have to cover in the time available. Indeed, write a new timetable, but take seriously the commitment of completing the study programme. Remember, never let your studies 'get on top of you' always 'keep on top of them'.

One characteristic of studying that affects all learners is the tendency to accumulate a great wealth of written material during a programme of study – books, handouts, photo-copies of articles, newspaper and magazine cuttings and notes. If you are not careful all of this information can become highly disorganised, or even lost. It is vital, therefore, that you devise a system for filing and organising all of the material that is collated, so that you can find relevant notes quickly.

We can give you a few suggestions for organising the accumulated material:

- Collate all material as soon as possible.
- Keep all material that you collect in ring binders, box files, or pocket files. Label all files or use different coloured files for different topics or subjects. As you collate new material put it immediately into a file for safe storage.
- Number and index all material that is collated. A common method is to set-up a computer database where each piece of material is given a title, a brief synopsis of its content, its page number, the author, where it was obtained and its publication date. The database is then used as a speedy reference guide for you. A computer database can undertake searching and sorting tasks, to help you find the information you need quickly and efficiently.

An important point to bear in mind is that you must be quite discriminating when collecting information. You should question the relevance of all information before it is stored, otherwise you may have a tendency to accumulate too much. At regular intervals you should review the material that you have collected and remove that which is irrelevant to your needs. Remember when using a computer database to always keep a back-up copy of your file.

A systematic approach to allocating time for study and the storing of information will help your learning process.

4.2   Reading Skills

Learning often requires you to read a great deal of written material. Many people are concerned as whether or not they will be able to read all that the tutor recommends. You can reduce such a concern by developing competent reading skills. You should try to make your reading more rapid by developing the technique of speed reading. This does not mean reading the text as quickly as possible and ignoring its content. When reading for learning purposes, it is essential that you grasp the meaning of the material and understand the ideas that are presented. Therefore, it is important not to become obsessed just with the speed of reading. You should not sacrifice understanding simply to get to the end of a passage. Despite these cautionary words, it is possible for you to increase the speed of your reading and its effectiveness. However, this requires effort and practice on your part. You will have to adopt a new attitude to reading and learn new techniques of reading.

(i)   A New Approach to Reading

When learning to read at school, children are encouraged to read aloud. As your reading skills develop, there is no longer a need to pronounce each word verbally, and you are able to read in silence. However, many people continue to say each word in their head. This is known as subvocalisation. It is possible though, to read without doing this. Your brain is quite capable of understanding the written word without the need for constant pronunciation. Words are merely symbols for expressing the writer's thoughts. For example, consider the analogy of two friends waving to each other in the street. It is not necessary for either to say consciously 'there's my friend waving to me' as each knows that the wave is a sign of greeting and friendship. An effective reader does the same with words. A group of words have a collective meaning and it is this meaning which you need to know, rather than each individual word in the phrase.

Developing such a skill is not always easy. You should try and look for the meaning of phrases rather than attempt to pronounce each word in your head. As the speed of your reading increases you will find that you are not pronouncing each word. The true sign of success will be when you can not only read quickly, but also understand what has been read.

So, this is a new approach to reading that you could adopt if you have to read and understand a great deal of written material. Techniques can be followed that enable you to master such an approach.

(ii)   Techniques for Increasing the Speed of Reading

As you are reading this sentence, your eyes are moving across the page until the end of each line is reached. Then your eyes will be switched back to the beginning of the next line and the process repeated. Your eyes move in a manner similar to that given in the following illustration:

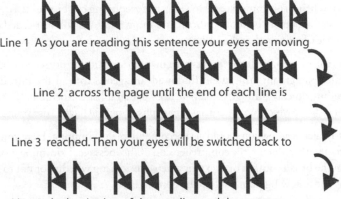

Line 1 As you are reading this sentence your eyes are moving

Line 2 across the page until the end of each line is

Line 3 reached. Then your eyes will be switched back to

Line 4 the beginning of the next line and the process....

In fact, your eyes move more than this, although you might be only barely aware of it. The eyes of a slow reader will fix on each word in a sentence in turn, before jumping to fix on the next word. Reading a sentence involves a series of fix-jump-fix-jump eye actions. To accelerate your reading, you should attempt to use fewer fixations (the technical term for the process). This demands fixing on every other word, or every third word or better still, only the significant words. By so doing, you spend less time reading the sentence, yet your understanding is just as good.

Another way that your eyes move is to flick hither and thither across the page. This not only wastes time, but also spoils your concentration. Although this movement seems involuntary, you can curb it by following the course of written text with a pen or ruler.

Subvocalisation (mental pronunciation) slows reading. The longer the word, the longer you need to pronounce it, and the greater the time of the fixation. Whilst it can be helpful to subvocalise unfamiliar words, or when reading text to be learnt by rote, subvocalisation is not helpful when speed reading for understanding. By making a conscious effort to read faster, you can avoid subvocalisation.

Different words in a sentence perform different tasks. Only a proportion of the words carry the underlying meaning of the sentence. The other words provide the structure and give less important information. For speed reading you only need to fix on the words which carry the meaning. Consider the following sentence:

Playing squash is my favourite sporting activity on a Saturday.

Six words carry the meaning: 'Playing squash...favourite sporting activity...Saturday'. The other four words: 'is my...on a' are likely to be implicit from the context. Sometimes a sentence will have few or no words that carry meaning germane to the text, in which case you can skim the sentence without fixations. Words that carry meaning are termed 'key words' and are usually nouns and verbs. An understanding of English grammar helps the eyes to find the key words in a sentence.

Other factors also influence your reading ability – mental and physical factors. Some people like to read their study notes in bed, prior to falling asleep. Bed, though, is not the best place for studying. Your mind and body tend to relax in bed and concentration wanes. Your comprehension of what is read will be weak, and you will find that you are unable to read quickly.

Your comprehension of what is read will be increased if you make notes of the content of the text. This focuses your mind on the content of the material being covered, and provides a permanent reminder and reference source of the major points raised in the text.

Effective reading, therefore, requires you to cover the text quickly, yet at a pace that enables you to comprehend what is being communicated. However, not everything can be read at a quick pace. Some parts of the text will inevitably be more difficult and more fixations will be needed. You must also understand the style of writing that the author is using.

Some authors will summarise the key points to be made in an introductory section, before expanding upon them in later paragraphs. You might find it advantageous to read the introductory section slowly, before reading quickly through the explanatory paragraphs. Unfortunately, there are no hard and fast rules that indicate which are the crucial paragraphs – you will have to use your own judgement.

In addition to quick reading you should also become adept at skimming. Here you miss out many words in the text, greatly reducing the comprehension of the message. Skimming is of use when you are trying to gain the broad content of a text, or when considering whether or not to read an article. When skimming the following points should be observed:

- Read all of the first paragraph of the text/article at normal speed. It frequently contains an overview.
- Also read the second paragraph as this might contain further insight into the content of the text/article.
- Read the last paragraph of the text/article as this frequently contains a summary or the main conclusions arrived at.
- Now decide whether the text/article is worth reading in full. If it is, run your eyes down the centre of each page at a fast pace picking out the key words on either side.
- By adopting the above approaches to reading you will find that you are able to cover more material in the study time available.

4.3   Taking Notes

In addition to developing reading skills, you must also be competent at taking notes. Taking notes when reading or listening is a very positive way of ensuring that you receive and understand the content of the message. The action of selecting and writing down the key points and ideas of the tutor or author concentrates the mind. Notes are also very useful for review and revision purposes giving you a synopsis of the area under consideration. However, you have to take care to ensure that note-taking does not get in the way of learning.

A problem that might arise is that you simply copy the material that is presented to you word for word from the printed page, or from the tutor, into your filing system. This, no doubt, will give the impression that you are working hard, but are you learning? The process of copying is a mere mechanical action. Your hands and eyes may be working, but your brain is not. It is the activity of selection and discrimination that forces you to think, and hence to learn.

(i)   Note-taking Methods

People take notes in different ways. These can range from the neat, well laid out page after page, to the odd word underlined or written in the margin. The form of notes you take will depend on your own learning style and what you are trying to achieve. You could take such voluminous notes that when you come to re-read them it is hardly quicker than re-reading the original material. Alternatively, a few words or ideas noted many weeks earlier may give you insufficient depth to be of any real value.

The purpose of taking notes is to use them as a memory jogger at a later date. To be successful at this, the notes that you make should be linked to your existing knowledge and understanding. Thus, when you make notes, they should be linked into other areas that are familiar to you. To do this, you should not simply copy words directly from the text or the tutor, but should add in your own words, phrases and comments so that the notes are personalised to your own understanding of the topic under consideration.

Another approach to adopt is that of making 'rough notes' of a text or an exposition given by a tutor, when reading or hearing it, and then immediately afterwards transposing the notes into a form that is more meaningful. You should now devise your own headings and sub-headings and re-write your 'rough notes'.

Different material will require a different approach. The more complex the material being considered, the more detailed your notes should be. At other times, with other topics, you will find that the material is easily understood allowing you to make simpler and shorter notes. From our discussion so far, we can identify a number of guidelines:

- Notes should not simply be direct copies of other material; they need to be written in a manner meaningful to you and in your own words.
- Do not make notes about everything – be discriminating and selective. Pick out the key concepts, principles and facts.
- Add in connected knowledge or examples from existing knowledge and understanding – this helps with the memorising of the new material.
- Adjust the depth of the notes to the level and complexity of the material being considered.

Apart from making written notes you can adopt other methods such as using diagrams or flow charts:

The Note Diagram

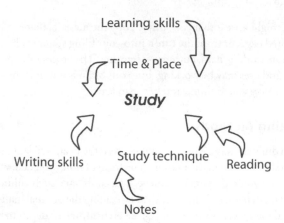

Note diagrams organise information and show connections between topics. They begin with the main subject in the centre of the page with sub-topics branching out from it. Key words only are included in the diagram to relate the ideas and branches together. Note diagrams have a number of advantages over conventional written notes:

- The notes provide a complete overview of the topic under consideration, using one sheet of paper. You are thus able to see the connections and relationships between topics.
- As only key words are used, there will be space for you to include additional, brief, explanatory notes at a later stage, should the need arise.
- During revision the chart can be used as a test of memory, seeing if you can add flesh to the bones of the diagram.
- The diagram can be used to link concepts together, thus assisting your comprehension of the topic under consideration.

When taking notes from the spoken word, you should bear additional guidelines in mind:

- Concentrate carefully on the spoken word but don't write down everything. Ignore all distractions such as others talking, or thoughts of other activities. Look at the communicator when she is talking.
- Structure the notes according to the stages of the presentation – identify the 'introduction,' the 'development of the argument,' and the conclusion, and give headings to each of these in the notes.
- Listen for signals from the communicator which indicate the important points e.g. the stressing of certain words, the repetition of phrases – note these down.
- Within each of the sections of the presentation indicate sub-headings and number them. Then write down the key words or phrases that apply to each sub-heading. Don't write down unnecessary words – in review sessions they will be a waste of study time.
- Write legibly and allow plenty of space – this enables additional points to be noted if the speaker backtracks and elaborates further.
- Write on loose-leaf paper that can be filed in a binder for safe keeping.
- After making the notes read through them to make sure that they make sense. Highlight the key points by using a highlight marker, or by underlining.

■　If any references have to be read and noted, read them immediately after the presentation, and combine any notes that are made with those taken from the presentation. However, clearly indicate the source of any additional material that is referred to in the notes, as the source might have to be referred to again at a later date.

Being a skilled note-taker is an important ES that is not only useful when learning, but will also be called into action when you attend meetings, negotiate with other people, or interview an applicant for a post.

4.4　Writing Skills

In addition to being competent at note-taking, you must also develop effective writing skills. You must be able to express your own ideas and demonstrate that you have learnt and understood the material you have been studying. In some instances you will have to give an oral presentation, while in others you will have to produce a written document. Both of these areas will be discussed in more detail in subsequent chapters. The purpose of this section is to suggest a few points that you should remember when producing any form of written communication.

1.　Prepare the Ideas

It is a rare individual who can, without preparatory thought, write a balanced and well structured document. If you are producing written work, it will be made up of a number of different ideas and points. These will be floating around in your mind. So, before starting writing, jot down the main points to be covered in the order in which they are to be made. You could use a note diagram to indicate the structure of the message and highlight the key points to be made. As the structure is being planned you should be thinking of how the points will be made and of the phraseology to be used. These should be jotted down as well.

You should then read through the points that you have noted and arrange them into a logical sequence. Any points that now do not seem relevant should be discarded. Finally, you should produce a plan of the actual format of the document. This will be the framework that you will use for the written communication.

2.　　Choosing an Appropriate Style and Structure

Now that you have developed a framework you can start writing. You have to make a decision, though, about the style of writing to use (style refers to the phraseology and structure). If a particular format has been requested, then you should adhere to it. Reports are formally structured with headings and sub-headings, and use straight-forward non-emotive language. (Report writing style is considered in a subsequent chapter.) Essays, though, necessitate a different style. Essays can use all manner of writing conventions in order to entertain the reader.

(i)　　Referencing the Text

When writing reports, essays or other written documents it is frequently necessary to refer to the works of other writers, whether it be to present their ideas, or to support the views that are put forward. Whenever you have to refer to the works of others, either directly by quotation, or indirectly by referring to someone else's ideas, then you must acknowledge them.

This is important for a number of reasons. Firstly, it is crucial that the original author is given credit for her ideas. If credit is not given then you could be accused of plagiarism – borrowing somebody else's ideas and works. If you do plagiarise when writing an assignment it is likely that you will be penalised by your tutor, possibly receiving no marks at all for your assignment. In addition, everything that an individual writes down is protected by copyright – even a simple hand written note is protected by copyright. However, if you make reference to the source of such copyright material in the body of the text, and a full bibliography is provided, then the copyright material can be used to a certain extent. Indeed, by providing a bibliography the reader of the written document can further investigate the topic under consideration. A final reason for referencing the text is that it adds academic credibility to your document. The credibility of your document will be enhanced if you show that you have read widely around the subject under consideration. You will provide evidence of this by a bibliography.

There are two main methods that can be used for referencing a text the 'Harvard Style' and the 'Numeric Style'. Chapter Four will explain in detail how you can reference your text using the Harvard Style. Read Chapter Four carefully as referencing is a very important ES that you do need to develop when writing assignments.

(ii)   Editing and Revising the Written Document

There is an enormous temptation on completing a piece of written work to put it down and not read it again before it is handed over to the interested recipient. You should resist this on every occasion, no matter how insignificant the document.

When you have finished the written document you should put it aside for twenty four hours and then re-read it when your mind is fresh. You should try and identify and correct all errors of grammar or fact. You should always adopt a conscientious and ruthless approach to the editing process. The reader will gain an impression of you from the document, and it is important to create a favourable impression. Indeed, it might be that you have to re-write whole sections of the document before you submit it.

As with all ES, your writing skills will improve with practice over time. If you think you have a limited vocabulary then you could increase your word usage by keeping a glossary of words and phrases that will add variety to your writing style. If your grammar is weak then read the finished document aloud as it is often easier to recognise grammatical errors when you hear them.

5.   Completing Assignments

An important method of receiving feedback on how successful your learning has been is by the completion of assignments, and then reflecting on the grades you receive from your tutor for the work that you complete. To attain high grades you need to work hard at your assignments, following all the instructions your tutors provide, and researching and presenting your work effectively. A number of guidelines can be provided to help you when undertaking assignments:

- Understand clearly the instructions that you have been set for the assignment, and clarify with your tutor any aspects of which you are unsure. If marking criteria have been provided read these carefully to understand what you have to do in order to achieve a high mark.
- Be fully aware of the time constraints under which you are working; know the deadline for the submission of the assignment, and plan your work and social activities so that you will be able to meet the deadline.
- Write a plan of how you wish to complete the assignment. Identify the main themes, or topics, you will include in the assignment, indicate where material you might need can be obtained.

- Collect material at the outset that might be difficult to obtain, then concentrate on material that is more readily to hand. Start your bibliography of the reference material that you are using.
- When you have collated all the research material you need for the assignment, produce a first draft of your assignment, ideally by word-processing it, read it through carefully, then modify it as you feel appropriate. Remember to reference fully the text of your assignments as you produce it.
- Leave your assignment now for at least 24 hours and concentrate on another activity.
- After 24 hours remind yourself of the instructions you have been given for the assignment, then read the work you have produced, and make sure that your assignment does actually answer the task that has been set, amending your assignment accordingly.
- When you are satisfied with your assignment, make sure that it is presented according to all the conventions that are accepted for the type of assignment you are completing, and hand it to your tutor on, or before the deadline that has been set for its submission.

When your tutor marks your assignment she will be making constructive comments that will help you to reflect on the strengths and weaknesses of your work. Read your tutor's comments carefully, and try and understand why she has made them. This is a most valuable part of learning as it will help you to improve your work in future assignments. If your tutor makes comments about your assignment that you do not understand, then ask for a personal tutorial session so that she can explain fully the reasons why such comments were made.

6. Time Management

Managing your time effectively is very important if you are to achieve all that you wish to achieve in the time available. Time is an irreplaceable resource – if you waste it you cannot recover it. You therefore need to be a good time manager. Being a good time manager involves understanding 'Where time goes?' and how time can be 'planned and saved'. In the sections below we will discuss some of these fundamental aspects of good time management.

6.1 Where Time Goes

The time available to you can be divided into time devoted to useful work, and time spent on unnecessary activities. We will look at each of these in turn.

(i) Useful Work

The majority of your time should be spent undertaking useful activities, for example if you are at college or university you will have to attend classes, complete assignments, and take part in group work. When working as an employee of an organisation your day will comprise undertaking tasks set by your employer.

Irrespective of whether you are at college, university, or in employment, you need to understand fully which components of your daily activities are in fact essential and hence useful. Most of your time, therefore, should be focused on these activities, and diverted away from the 'unnecessary activities'.

(ii)   Unnecessary Activities

We all find ourselves being distracted from the useful work we have to do. Being distracted means that you waste time – time that cannot be replaced. A number of factors result in you being distracted and wasting time.

(iii)   Lack of Focus

When you are unsure what it is that you are trying to achieve, you will find that your mind wanders, and you are unable to focus on the task in hand. Much time can be wasted if you are unsure of the objectives to be attained for the task in hand. If you find yourself in this position clarify promptly the objectives for the task and focus your energies on achieving these objectives.

(iv)   Failure to Share the Workload

In some instances, whether it be completing an assignment on a group basis at college or university, or being a member of a team at work, you will have to share the workload with your peers. If you fail to do this, to delegate work to your fellow team members, then you will find that you have too much work to complete. This will result in you wasting time at the expense of your peers who will not be working as hard.

(v)   Poor Planning

If you do not plan your daily, weekly, and monthly work you will find that you will waste time. By not knowing what work you have to complete today, this week, and this month, it will be difficult for you to achieve the objectives, and deadlines, that might have been set. Thus, you do need to plan your working hours so that your are aware of what has to be achieved, and can be achieved, in the time available.

(vi)   Interruptions

Interruptions are a major, and unnecessary, waste of time. Your friends and business associates might not appreciate that you are concentrating on your work and might disturb you for a social chat. Telephone callers when they have finished discussing their business might try to prolong the telephone conversation by talking about unimportant issues. Interruptions, no matter what kind, reduce the amount of time you can devote to completing successfully the task in hand, and have, therefore, to be controlled effectively.

(vii)   Being Tired

After working for a long period of time, without a break, you will become tired. When you are tired you will find it hard to concentrate on your work. When this occurs you might start daydreaming or worse still fall asleep at your desk. Clearly, being tired results in time being lost, and you need to plan your working day so that you have regular, short breaks, that help you to maintain your concentration on the work in hand.

(viii) Poor Anticipation

The final factor that can lead to you wasting time is that of poor anticipation, not identifying problems that might arise which could prevent you from attaining your objectives. When undertaking work unexpected problems might mean you do not complete the work expected by the deadline that has been set. You need, therefore, to try and anticipate all the problems that could develop, and produce contingency plans for coping with such problems.

Thus, the first aspect of being an effective time manager is understanding clearly 'where your time goes?' Once you have identified what constitutes your useful work and wasted time you can then move on to think about mechanisms that will help you to plan and save you time.

6.2   Planning your Time

The starting place for planning, and controlling, how you use your time is with the setting of priorities – deciding how much time should be allocated to all the tasks you have to complete, and then considering in which order you undertake the work.

(i)   Setting Priorities

When thinking about managing your time effectively you should start by taking a long term perspective – what do you have to achieve over the next three months, what targets or deadlines have to be met. Then, you should start working backwards from this date and determine what you need to have completed successfully after two months, and then after one month, in order that the three month deadline will be achieved.

Once you have set your own targets and priorities for each of the next three months, you can then think about planning your time on a weekly and daily basis. What do you have to complete at the end of week one in order to complete successfully the work in month one. By so doing, you are starting to allocate time to particular tasks. How many days are you going to spend researching your assignment? Then how long will you take to word-process the first draft?

Thinking about your working days, weeks, and months in this way helps you to decide the order in which your main tasks should be completed. This type of thinking also helps you to determine the urgency of completing successfully particular tasks. Which jobs, for example, need to be undertaken immediately, which tasks can be completed next week?

When you have determined the priority of undertaking your work, you can then move on to planning the tasks that have to be completed.

(ii)   Planning your Work

When planning your work on a daily basis you should start by understanding what has to be achieved each day. Clearly, only a few tasks can be completed successfully in the time available, and you need to allocate time to these tasks. Then you should determine the order in which you complete the tasks.

Some tasks will require you to concentrate more heavily on the work involved than other tasks. Thus, you should plan to undertake tasks that require concentration at times of the day when you will be most alert.

In addition, you should also try and reduce potential interruptions so that you can devote all your energies to the task in hand.

Other tasks that you will have to complete might be rather unpleasant, or ones that you do not enjoy undertaking. It will be easy for you to put-off completing these tasks, but this will mean you will never tackle them. Thus, you should plan to complete unpleasant or unenjoyable activities, at the outset, rather than defer them to other times. When you have started to tackle these unpleasant tasks, do not be distracted from completing them, keep on working until you have finished.

If you are working on a long job during the day, break the job into distinct components, and plan to have breaks, or changes of activity, after completing each component. In this way your concentration will be enhanced, and you will complete the job more effectively. Likewise, do not move on to a new component of the job until the preceding component has been completed. If you do, you will waste time as you will at some stage have to return to the incompleted tasks, and you may have lost the focus of what you were trying to achieve.

Thus, in planning your working day you need to decide what has to be achieved, and when should the various tasks be completed – the order of your work. Stick to your plan for the day, try not to be distracted, control your working time.

(iii)   Diaries

One aspect of controlling your time is organising each week and every day. Diaries are useful tools for planning your work in the short term, and there are many different formats for diaries.

A very detailed diary will have one page for each day divided into individual time slots, for example, the hours of the day. Against each of the time slots you can then write down the work you will be doing. This format for the diary is useful in that it enables you to plan each day quite precisely. This is important if you have a varied workload, where you undertake a range of different tasks. You are able to see quickly, if for example, you can attend a meeting at 3.00pm, or if 4.30pm is more convenient.

Other diaries, might have seven days on one page, and no individual time slots. This type of diary is helpful for providing an overview of the work you need to be completing on a weekly basis.

Diaries, therefore, are valuable tools for helping you to fit your work into the time available. Once you have planned how you will use your time, you can start work. But don't forget that time is precious, and even when you have planned your time quite carefully, you will be faced with distractions and interruptions. So, how can you save time when you are actually working?

(iv)   Saving Time

There are a number of ways in which you can manage your time to make the most effective use of it:

Handling Interruptions: Interruptions to your work will seriously affect your ability to meet the deadlines that have been set for the successful completion of the work. One way of reducing interruptions is to avoid them. Be assertive, politely inform the person who is disturbing you that you are busy and cannot speak with her. Use your diary to make an appointment to see her at a later date and time. Alternatively, you could work in a location where you will not be interrupted (but make sure that you do tell a friend where you are in case you have to be contacted in an emergency). If you are working in a team, it might be that another member of the team is better able to deal with the interruption – delegate responsibility to respond to the interruption to a fellow team member.

If you are unable to avoid the interruption, then it might be possible to minimise their effect. If you are working on a specific activity, do not stop immediately to handle the interruption, but continue working until you have come to a natural break in the activity, and then respond to the interruption.   If you can predict when interruptions are likely to occur, plan to do less demanding activities during these periods so that you can easily break off from your work to handle the interruptions. In addition to knowing how to handle interruptions, you also need to be skilful in the art of delegation.

Delegation: Delegation is vital when working in a team as it helps you to share the responsibility with the other team members for completing the work. When you delegate work, you save yourself time.

Delegation is asking fellow team members to complete certain tasks of the work. Clearly, the work to be delegated should be capable of being handled by your fellow team members, and they should have the confidence, and authority, to carry out all the responsibilities involved.

Obviously, you need to identify those aspects of your work that can be delegated to others, and then you need to communicate clearly the instructions for the work. As the work progresses, do however, review the progress that is being made so that additional guidance and support can be provided if the work is falling behind schedule.

Be Decisive: A considerable amount of time can be wasted through indecision. To save time, you need to be prepared to take decisions and put them into action, be precise in your dealings with others setting times and dates for meetings, having clear agendas, and being specific about the duration of meetings. You also need to communicate with others clearly and effectively, do not prolong unnecessary discussions.

Through being decisive you are able to devote the time saved to other important issues and decisions.

In this section, the importance of time management has been outlined. You will invariably find that there are more demands on your time than you can cope with. You, therefore, need to develop effective time management skills. Managing your time effectively involves identifying the priorities of your work, and then planning your workload so that you can meet the objectives and deadlines that have been set.

The objective of this chapter has been to introduce you to learning and study skills. As much of the emphasis of ES training lies with them, it will be important for you to be able to manage your own self-development. Learning and study skills lie at the heart of this process. In planning a self-development programme, it will be vital to accept that ES are not learnt overnight. Thus, you should pace the programme so that you do not try and learn too many new behaviours too quickly. You should set yourself realistic targets for skills improvement and then develop a timetable that will allow these targets to be met. The learning methods discussed in this chapter will enable you to learn on your own, but do not forget that you can gain much valuable learning from sharing experiences with others.

After reading this chapter please complete the following learning activities:

Learning Activities

1. In your own words explain how you learn:
    *   To do something.
    *   To memorise something.
    *   To understand something.
    *   A skill.

2.   Write down your own definition of the term 'study skills'.

3.   Identify the study skills that you can use at the moment, and identify the study skills you need to develop further. Devise a self-development programme that will enable you to improve your study skills.

4.   Buy a diary and use it to plan your activities on a weekly and monthly basis.

Chapter Three
Communication Skills

After reading this chapter you will be able to:

1. Understand the different elements of speech.

2. Communicate competently in a variety of different situations.

3. Identify the constituent components of body language.

4. Understand how to use your body language more effectively when communicating with other people and Interpret more effectively the body language of other people when they are communicating with you.

It is extremely important for you to be able to converse with others and to present ideas and opinions verbally. Everyday you will be communicating informally with other people in general conversation and sometimes you will be required to communicate in a way which is much more formal, for instance when you have to give a planned and prepared presentation. This chapter will examine the first of these, informal communication, and in Chapter Seven we will look at the skills you should use for a more formal presentation. In this chapter we consider the elements of speech which you can employ, how you can use your voice to communicate more effectively and how you can initiate, maintain and end conversations in a variety of situations. We shall also look at the use of some special verbal communication skills you should use in challenging social interactions.

1.   Speech

You use speech to communicate ideas and opinions as well as your emotions and inner most feelings. You communicate each of these by using a variety of elements of speech that you can control and use to good effect. Such elements include:

- The tone of voice.
- The emphasis used in speech.
- The content of speech.
- The use of figurative language.
- The use of humour in speech.
- The speed of speech you use.
- The pronunciation used.
- The pitch of your voice.
- The use of inferred speech.

We shall now consider the importance of each of these and the way you can use them to improve your verbal communication.

1.1   The Tone of Voice

When you speak to other people, it is important to maintain their interest and attention. The tone of voice you use, whether it is spontaneous or planned, can help or hinder this. Your tone of voice also signals emotions and feelings, such as anger or joy for example, and supports the content of what you are saying. Often it is the tone of voice that you use which actually signals the true meaning of your message. Consider the following question:

'What are you doing?'

If you were to pose this question in a harsh tone of voice then you will sound as though you are telling someone off. It is an admonishing statement, almost one of rebuke. Whereas if you speak with a soft tone of voice it becomes a caring question. Try saying the question out loud using different tones of voice and attempt to imply different meanings to it.

When you are in conversation you may need to consider carefully the tone of voice you use not only to add clearer meaning to the words themselves, but also to add variety to the speech and so help your listener maintain attention and interest. If you stick to a monotone voice you will soon cause your listener to lose concentration and so make your communication much less effective.

1.2   The Emphasis used in Speech

By putting greater stress on certain words in a sentence you can alter the meaning of the sentence:

'**What** are you doing?'

'What **are** you doing?'

'What are **you** doing?'

'What are you **doing**?'

Try asking this question out loud and each time put the emphasis on the word which has been set in bold type. In the first of these questions you focus the attention of the listener on the action that is being undertaken. The second implies an element of disbelief on your part as to what is being done. In the third question you emphasise the person that is doing it, implying that he or she is somehow at fault or in error. In the final example you again question the action which is going on. Now try each of the questions again continuing to emphasise the word in bold type but attempt to vary the tone of your voice to imply concern, anger, amazement or any number of different feelings.

Similarly by saying a particular word in a certain way, such as by stressing particular consonants or vowels, or emphasising particular syllables, you can give a different meaning to the message.

People who are skilled communicators often use emphasis in speech to considerable effect not only to help the listener to understand the message but also to indicate hidden meanings which otherwise might not have been apparent. Politicians and lawyers are adept at this and often it is only when a speech is heard rather than read that you understand its true meaning.

1.3   The Content of Speech

The actual words you use are clearly crucial if you wish to achieve effective communication. You should always try to use words which are appropriate to the 'reading age' of the listener. The words used in national newspapers are good examples of this. The Sun uses vocabulary which assumes that its readers need not have a 'reading age' greater than ten years old. In other words, the average ten year old child should have such a vocabulary and be able to read the paper. Obviously much of the vocabulary of the Guardian would be beyond the grasp of the average ten year old. It is important to bear in mind similar considerations when you are in conversation. You must assess your listener and make a suitable choice of words. Your listener should be able to understand fully the meaning of the words that you use. A common criticism of poor teachers is that they use vocabulary that is above the heads of their students. The use of jargon and technical language are prime examples of this and you should only use such terms if your listener is familiar with them or they are fully explained when they are used. It is a fallacy to think that you are being clever by using words that your listener is not familiar with. Your choice of words should be such that they clearly paint a picture in your listener's mind of your intended message and leave no room for ambiguity or confusion.

1.4   The Use of Figurative Language

At all times you should try to make the content of your message interesting to listen to, so you avoid boring your listeners. You can achieve this in a number of different ways including the use of figurative language. By figurative language, we mean the use of such things as metaphors, similes and hyperboles. We shall try and explain each of these terms using examples.

A **metaphor** is used to infer a resemblance between things or situations that are not really associated, for example if you were to describe a ferocious man as a 'tiger'.

A **simile** is a figurative comparison that uses terms such as 'like' or 'as'. You could describe an ill-tempered colleague as a bear with a sore head.

Hyperbole is the use of intended over-exaggeration. You may describe a person as being 'so fit he could swim the English Channel with both hands tied behind his back'. Obviously nobody is capable of such a feat yet by using such an expression you convey clearly the message that the person you are talking about is certainly in a good physical condition.

By using each of these you will make your conversation more interesting but do take care to ensure that there is no doubt in your listener's mind that the over-exaggeration, for example, is intended. Another important advantage you may gain by using figurative speech is that if you use it creatively, the message may well be remembered for a longer period of time.

It is extremely important, however, to make certain that your listeners are not offended by any of the associations that you might refer to in metaphors, similes or hyperboles. The figurative language you use should not dominate your speaking to the extent that the intended content of your message is diluted and lost. In today's society you must recognise that you should not make remarks which can be taken as being racist or sexist. Not only are such remarks offensive, they can often result in your listener disregarding the rest of what is being said or regarding it as having little value. People who make racist or sexist comments now tend to be held in poor regard by the rest of society.

1.5   The Use of Humour in Speech

People who are funny or humorous often maintain their listener's attention and interest to a much greater degree. But you must recognise that for many people trying to be funny is very difficult. You may not be naturally funny. It is very easy to lose your credibility and be regarded as a bore if your attempts at humour are not funny and do not amuse the listener. Jokes and funny stories need to be well told. You will no doubt know someone who persists in telling jokes and yet always manages to forget the punch line.

Many people can be extremely funny without telling jokes or stories. We often describe them as being witty. Again there are great dangers in trying to be witty if your listeners do not appreciate your humour or your attempts at wit fall flat. A witty remark about your friend's dress can easily be misinterpreted as an insult. The key to being witty is to judge the tone of the conversation and the relationship you have with your listeners. You must think quickly and respond to their remarks. In normal conversation you will not be able to rehearse witty comments but if you keep your mind alert, opportunities to bring a smile to your listener's face will often arise.

In Chapter Seven we will look at the way different forms of humour can be planned in advance and rehearsed if you have to give a formal presentation.

1.6   The Speed of Speech you Use

You can help to maintain the attention of a listener by the use of different speeds of speech. If you listen to skilful communicators you will notice that they often increase the speed of their speech to create anticipation with their audience, building up momentum before an important point, and then allowing a few seconds of silence to enable the message to sink in and the listener to reflect upon it.

If you pause while you are talking you may indicate a sense of deliberateness and thought. Using pauses can further help you to emphasise important elements, and allow you to gather your thoughts for the next stage of the communication. You must ensure, though, that you do not simply fill the silent pauses with distracting verbal mannerisms such as 'umms' and 'aahhs'. These will simply irritate your listener and detract from what you are trying to say.

1.7   Pronunciation

It is important to try and pronounce the words you use correctly. If you constantly mispronounce words it will damage your credibility especially when your listener expects you to be fully conversant with the topic under consideration. Mispronunciations will also quickly distract your listeners from what you are saying and will reduce their attention.

It is often difficult to know how to pronounce words when you have only read them. If this is the case and you are unsure of the correct pronunciation of a particular word you can always refer to a dictionary. However, even then it is not always easy to end up with the correct pronunciation. The best way to learn how to pronounce new words is to listen, particularly to the radio and television. Newsreaders and presenters generally get most pronunciations right.

1.8   The Pitch of Your Voice

The pitch of your voice is a combination of the tone that you use and the loudness of the sound that you make. You can create considerable emphasis on what you are saying by raising and lowering the pitch. Skilful communicators vary the pitch of their voices considerably, but in a conversational way as opposed to a theatrical manner. There is a need to be careful, for if you put too much variation in the pitch of your voice, this can be a further distraction for your listener.

What you require in your speech is a comfortable variation of harsh and soft tones, and of loudness and softness. Speaking loudly is not the sole key to gaining the attention of your listener. What you need to have is a voice that is pleasing to listen to. This can be developed by using different tones, varying speeds of speech, and a range of pitches. This can be developed through practice.

1.9   The Use of Inferred Speech

Another element of speech you can use to communicate your feelings and attitudes is that of 'inferred speech'. Here, the actual meaning of the words you use is not as important as their implied meaning. For example a manager might say to his deputy, 'I see you're working flexi-hours again John.' This is not simply a matter of fact but a statement from the manager to his deputy that he has noticed a different pattern to the deputy's working day. The deputy is made aware that his manager has noticed this change and depending upon the way in which the message is communicated will be able to determine whether the manager approves or disapproves of it.

In other circumstances you may wish to use inferred speech to signify friendliness to others. Travellers on the same train can show friendliness by engaging in apparently pointless conversations, such as talking about the weather. The state of the weather is not as important as the travellers instigating a conversation. By talking about the weather the travellers are saying to each other, 'Yes, I am interested in talking with you.' You will find this element of speech useful for relationship building and it frequently precedes more pertinent topics of conversation.

While inferred speech is important you should always be careful not to over use it and if possible to avoid the repeated use of distracting speech mannerisms such as: 'That's right', 'OK' 'I mean', 'You know', or 'Well then.' You will find that if you repeatedly use such terms in speech it does become irritating to your listeners and might even lead them to mimic your speech mannerisms. If a person constantly uses distracting speech mannerisms such as this it is often a sign of nervousness and lack of confidence. You should try to identify such mannerism in your own speech and if they are present concentrate on avoiding them when you are in conversation.

We hope that you can recognise from what has been said in the previous sections that there are various ways in which you can make what you are trying to say more interesting to listen to, and more easily remembered. While talking comes naturally you must realise that you are not only transmitting a message but also signalling your attitudes and feelings. Indeed, by varying your speech you can radically change your listener's interpretation of what is being said. Therefore the varied use of speech is a skill that you need to master for informal conversations as well as formal presentations.

2.   Different Types of Verbal Communication

As well as practising to improve the effectiveness of your speech, it is also important that you recognise that there are different types of verbal communication, each of which requires a differing approach in your communication style.

2.1   Conversations

The most common form of communication which you will take part in is a conversation. It is something you will do everyday of your life. However, to be a successful conversationalist you require certain skills and we will now consider some of these.

(i)   Listening Skills

Listening is an important element in any successful conversation. The word conversation implies communication between people and if you do not listen to what the other person is saying then the communication process will break down. Therefore you need to pay attention to what is being said and try to follow the conversation. If there are a group of people taking part in a conversation, there is always a chance that your mind will drift and you will lose track of what is being said. If you do not want other people to do the same thing there are a number of approaches you can adopt to encourage people to listen to what you are trying to say. You can ask them questions, or seek their views and opinions on what you are saying.

If people are listening they tend to show this both in their verbal and non-verbal behaviour. They will nod their heads, lean forward or perhaps say 'Yes', 'I see', or 'That's true', or 'I disagree with that.' Conversely, if your listeners do not look at you but at some other object, or stare out of the window, or yawn, (or worst of all fall asleep!) then they are giving quite explicit signs that they are not listening.

You can learn to be a good listener. Here are a few simple guidelines:

- Always 'listen' with your eyes as well as your ears. By looking at the speaker you hear not only the words which are being spoken but will also be able to recognise the non-verbal signs which the speaker is giving. Often such non-verbal signs reinforce the verbal message and help you to understand the true meaning that the speaker is trying to give.
- Ask questions. If anything is unclear you should ask for it to be clarified, or if you disagree with what is being said then politely make the point.

If you are doing the talking you will find that your listeners will soon lose their concentration if:

- They think they have heard what you are saying before. Many old people begin to lose their short term memory and repeat the same stories again and again and it is important that you do not start such a habit. Therefore think about what you are saying. Do not repeat yourself if you can help it.
- The subject matter is too technical. Listening to a complex topic can be difficult and the listener might 'switch off'. You have to realise this and make your message easier to understand and support what you are saying with appropriate body language.

(ii)   Talking

Conversations obviously rely upon talking and while some people are more talkative than others, it is important that if the conversation is to be a success everyone must join in. A good conversationalist does not allow the conversation to be dominated by one or two individuals, so try and bring those who are more reluctant to talk into the conversation.

If you are shy you may need to develop conversational skills through practice with people who feel more confident in a conversational setting but who are not too dominating.

(iii)   Gaining Conversational Practice

Starting Conversations: Conversations can often start with factual information being exchanged, or general statements being made, for example, 'Sales have increased by twenty per cent over the last six months.' This sort of information can then be followed by statements giving details of how this was achieved. You may find that a conversation then moves on to discussions and expressions of feelings, attitudes and opinions about what is being described, thus, 'I think much of this success has been due to the ES training programme our sales staff has been through.' You can of course get other people to join in the conversation by asking them a question. This may be helped by using open questions rather than closed ones, 'What do you think the increase in sales could be attributed to?' demands more than simply a 'yes' or 'no' response. Try to avoid closed questions such as, 'Do you think that the increase in sales could be the result of our ES training programme?'

Indeed, you should recognise that asking questions is another common method of opening conversations as is making comments about the environment or the situation, greeting others, or exchanging personal details and comments:

Questions:	'Why do you think there has been a fall in the quality of our supplier's product?'
	'Why have sales exceeded the budgeted figure this year?'
Comments:	'The productivity of the workforce has never been better'.
	'Absenteeism is always high after a public holiday'.
Greetings:	'Hello, how are you? Tell me what your research findings are'.
Exchanging details:	'Good morning. My name is Blake, Peter Blake from Sacks & Co. May I ask you a few simple questions?'

Maintaining the Conversation: Once you have opened a conversation you need to keep it going. You will find that most of the conversations you have normally develop through a sequence of questions, answers, comments and opinions. You might discuss the topic under consideration in detail, or pass over it lightly. Try and keep the conversation open so that the other people involved feel that they can contribute. People are also less likely to contribute if they feel their opinions are going to be ignored or rejected. You should try to keep the conversation going by linking the various topics under consideration and by widening the scope of the conversation, 'Talking about ES training for sales people, I must admit that I went on an ES course once and I feel it benefited my social life as well as my job'. Hopefully other people in the conversation will respond by keeping the conversation going. This statement could be followed by an open question from one of the listeners, 'That's interesting, how do you think ES training has helped your social life?'

Good conversational practice usually allows everyone to take turns in talking and listening and you must let the other person say their piece without too many interruptions.

Concluding a Conversation: At some stage the conversation will have run its course and you will need to conclude it in a reasonable way. Some conversations come to a natural end when nobody has anything else to add to the topic under consideration. Alternatively you may find it necessary to wind up the conversation in a suitable way. Normally people start to give out certain types of signal to show that they are ready to conclude the conversation. Note such signals as the person who is sitting forward in his chair, ready to stand up, or the one who repeatedly checks the time.

When the conversation is drawing to a close it is often the time to arrange to meet again: 'So I'll see you again at the same time, in the same place, next week'. Just as you develop your own style of opening a conversation, so you develop your own style of closing one. Some people tend to be too abrupt, giving the impression that they cannot wait for the conversation to end. Others do not seem able to break away, which can be equally annoying if you have something else to do but do not want to be thought rude by breaking off too soon. Try and conclude on a positive note and in a friendly manner. If you fail to do so then establishing future conversations might be more difficult.

Telephone Conversations: Much of what we have said above applies to telephone conversations, whether they are for business or social reasons. A particular difficulty with a telephone conversation is that you are unable to read the body language of the person with whom you are talking. In particular, by not being able to see the gestures and facial expressions of the other party, you lose a certain amount of insight into what the other person is trying to convey.

Telephone conversations also make it more difficult to use humour, as frequently it is your facial expressions that suggest that you are being humorous. You need to develop a good telephone technique if you are to use it well.

If you are making a call try and think through in advance what you want to say so that you will not be ambiguous in the message you are trying to give. It is often useful to make a few notes to which you can refer while making the call. If it is a business call keep it short and to the point. Pay attention to the tone and pitch of your voice. You should speak more slowly than when you communicate face-to-face. This allows both you and the person you are speaking with to make any notes that may be necessary, and helps the other person to understand the message the first time without it having to be repeated.

If you are answering a call try not to let it ring for a long time before answering it. Be polite and give a pleasant greeting to the caller. Each caller should be made to feel that he or she is important and that the call is welcomed. For example, 'Edwards & Co Accountants. Good morning. How can I help you', or 'Thank you for calling Edwards & Co Accountants. How can I help you.' Establish the caller's name and position as soon as possible, 'Who should I say wishes to speak to our Tax Accountant?' At all stages keep the caller informed of the progress of his or her call, 'I'm sorry, but Mrs Evans, our Tax Accountant, is in a meeting at the moment. Can I take your number and ask her to call you back?'

If you take a message for someone else make sure that it is passed on as soon as possible so that the necessary action can be taken. Again when you are concluding the call, be polite, 'Thank you for calling Mrs Edwards. I will make sure that Mrs. Evans returns your call as soon as she is free.' If you do not have a polite telephone manner, the caller will gain an unfavourable impression of you and your organisation. It is a good idea to keep a supply of message paper by the phone, and a pen that works, so that you can take legible notes.

2.2   Meetings

Meetings take many different forms, ranging from company annual general meetings to meetings of the local parent teacher's association committee. Meetings can be classified as being formal meetings, committee meetings, or command meetings.

Formal meetings and committee meetings have the common objective of arriving at a group decision on the topic under consideration. These meetings are controlled by the chairperson (the chair) who has to follow certain procedures for the conduct of the meeting. Command meetings are used to communicate information and tend to be called by group leaders. While the views of the group may be consulted, the group leader has the responsibility for taking any decisions, and is free to determine the procedures adopted at the meeting. At formal and committee meetings there is joint responsibility for any decisions that are taken, frequently requiring a majority vote before the motion (the proposal) is accepted. Once the decision has been taken, irrespective of the type of meeting, all parties must accept it.

(i)   Organising Meetings

You should organise all meetings in a similar manner:

- Notice should be given to all people (in this chapter we will refer to them as delegates) expected to attend the meeting well in advance, allowing them to keep the day and time free from other commitments.
- The agenda for the meeting (the topics to be covered in a pre-determined order) should be circulated to all delegates to enable them to gather their thoughts on the topics to be discussed, and to prepare any papers or handouts. Examples of a notice for a meeting and an agenda are given in Chapter Four where we also discuss the preparation of minutes.
- Any papers or handouts that are to be referred to in the meeting should be circulated in advance to allow all delegates to become familiar with them, saving time during the meeting.

You should follow any constitutional procedures regarding the organisation of the meeting. For example, some meetings require a certain period of notice to be given for those attending, and articles of association and the Companies Act prescribe certain formalities.

(ii)   Running the Meeting

To ensure that the meeting is conducted in a formal manner you need to follow certain guidelines:

- A chairperson must be appointed to control the meeting and steer the discussion through the points on the agenda.
- A secretary needs to record the points that are discussed and agreed in the minutes of the meeting. The minutes should be a true record of the discussion that takes place. After the meeting copies of the minutes should be forwarded to all those attending, being their permanent record of it. (Minutes are considered in Chapter Four.)

All delegates should follow the procedures of the meeting that specify their participation and should contribute in an orderly and courteous manner.

(iii)   Communicating at Meetings

If you are participating at a meeting you will need to use the full range of your oral communication skills. You need to bear a number of considerations in mind:

- The purpose of many meetings is to reach a decision. Therefore, all delegates to the meeting should have an equal opportunity to contribute to the discussion. If one or two delegates are dominating the meeting then they should be restrained by the chairperson.
- Discussions can become heated. To reach rational and logical decisions, however, it is important that delegates should remain calm and refrain from using emotive language.
- If differing views are expressed, adopt a flexible approach to reach agreement.

- You must listen carefully. The meeting could involve detailed debate and to keep track of the debate you will have to listen carefully to what is being said. Making notes of the discussion will be useful for this.
- You should prepare for the meeting. If you need to undertake background research, do it prior to the day of the meeting. If there are papers produced for the meeting make sure you have considered them in advance rather than trying to skim through them while the meeting is in progress.
- Speak only when you have a valid point to make. Time will be constrained, so spurious comments will reduce the effectiveness of the meeting.
- If at the conclusion of formal and committee meetings no consensus of opinion is reached, a vote should be taken (according to the constitution of the meeting) so that a decision can be reached.

(iv) Chairing a Meeting

If you are asked to chair a formal or committee meeting, you have a special role to play in that typically you must adopt an impartial stance, unless the delegates are equally divided as to the decision to be taken, in which case you will normally have the casting vote. Much of the success of the meeting will lie with your management of it. To ensure the success of the meeting, you should observe the following points:

- Always speak clearly and concisely so that all of those at the meeting can hear you. Use some of the oral communication skills mentioned earlier in this chapter.
- Set clear objectives for the meeting which should be reinforced with the delegates in the opening introduction that you give as chairperson.
- Strictly follow the agenda with no digression from the topics under consideration. If the discussion that takes place is too superficial you should, as chairperson stimulate a more in-depth discussion or guide the meeting back to the topic under consideration.
- Control the meeting. Restrain the more vociferous people at the meeting and encourage the less communicative to participate.
- Try not to dominate the discussion. Your role as chairperson is to steer the discussion through the topics on the agenda.
- Listen carefully to the points being discussed, noting down the key arguments, summarising them and agreeing them with the delegates.
- You should be courteous at all times. Thank delegates for their contributions, and try to ensure that they remain courteous in their discussion.
- Carefully manage the time to allow all the points on the agenda to be covered. Indeed, you should give careful thought to the number of points on the agenda to prevent too many being listed for the discussion time available.
- When the items on the agenda have been fully discussed you should conclude the meeting by arriving at a decision that meets the objective that was initially set. If the delegates are unanimous in their decision then there will be no need for a vote. If there is disagreement, however, you will need to take a vote, and if the vote is evenly divided between those for and against the motion, you, as the chairperson, will have the casting vote.
- At the conclusion of the meeting, you should set a date for the next one, and thank the delegates for their attendance and contributions.
- A true record of the meeting should be noted in the minutes, which should be agreed by the delegates at the beginning of the next meeting.

Command meetings tend to be less formal than those considered above and frequently do not involve the taking of minutes. To be successful, however, many of the guidelines listed here do need to be observed, especially those relating to the chairperson's management of the meeting and the delegates' contributions.

(v)   Key People

Meetings are about people. Although the items under discussion may be about issues of finance, equipment or policy, the meetings themselves are run by and involve people. Essentially, running or contributing to a meeting involves interpersonal skills and this is where the key roles involved in managing meetings come in.

Chair: The chair is the single most important role. The term derives from the fact that all comments in a meeting should be addressed via the chairperson to ensure that order is maintained.

The chair is responsible for, maintaining order; maintaining momentum; ensuring that the agenda is adhered to; ensuring fair play; motivating the participants; time-keeping and summarising key points at appropriate times.

The chair must therefore: have authority; be fair; be firm; be approachable; understand the procedures and rules; be able to create a positive atmosphere and be tactful.

Essentially these are all social skills in addition to the work-specific skills necessary to allow the individual to hold this role.

Secretary: The secretary's role is lower profile but no less important. It is the role of the secretary to ensure that everything is done to allow the meeting to proceed efficiently.

The secretary is responsible for: drawing up and distributing the documentation prior to the meeting (the notice and agenda); disseminating any documentation or correspondence needed during the meeting; briefing the chair prior to (and if necessary during) the meeting and keeping a record of the discussion (the minutes) and distributing these later.

The secretary will consequently need to be: organised; efficient; a competent 'wordsmith'; unobtrusive and supportive of both the chair and the aims of the meeting.

Treasurer: It may also be essential, if the committee controls funds, to have a treasurer.

The treasurer is responsible for: collecting, recording and banking monies; recording all payments; making payments; presenting financial reports and advising on all financial matters and ensuring the organisation is able to meet its financial commitments.

Consequently, the treasurer needs to be: financially astute; organised and honest.

However, it should be emphasised that the role of treasurer is only required where finance is present.

2.3   Communicating Information

You will frequently use speech to give information to others, information that may be factual, technical or personal. You need to give special thought to this if the information is important. Do not try to give too much information verbally as you might 'overload' the listener. To be successful at communicating information you should identify the main points of the message and then concentrate on making sure that the listener fully understands these. This can be achieved in a number of ways.

Repeat data or technical points to help the listener to appreciate what is being said. Emphasise the data by slowing the speed of your delivery. Allow for pauses after important points have been made and stress these by deepening the pitch of your voice. This will help the listener to assimilate the message. If the information you wish to get over is complex, it may be better to present it in a written form as well or to use some form of visual display such as graphs, tables, and pie charts. You can verbally draw the listener's attention to the key points of the information and to highlight their implications: 'Twenty five per cent of our sales come from the Northern Region. This table provides further detail. What this means is that …'

If you do use tables, graphs or charts to communicate information, give your listener time to read them before making the next point.

If you have a position of authority you will probably have to give instructions to others. Instructions are often central to the operation of a group. Problems will arise though, if the instructions you give are not communicated clearly. Obviously, you need to bear in mind all the previous points about verbal communication but you should take special note of the following:

- Use language that will be understood by the listener to prevent any confusion arising.
- The instructions you give must be extremely explicit, leaving no room for misinterpretation if you use ambiguous terms.
- Make sure that the person to whom you are giving instructions has fully understood them by asking him or her to repeat them.

Apart from considering the content of the instruction, you should also consider how it is to be given. You will create good team relations and respect if you give instructions in a courteous and polite manner. If you become irritable and aggressive when giving instructions you will not encourage loyalty, and also make it more likely that the instruction will be misinterpreted. Indeed, to prevent the possibility of such a misinterpretation, try to reinforce a verbal instruction in writing.

2.4   Assertive Skills

Assertiveness is the art of clear and direct communication. Being assertive enables you to:

- Express your personal feelings to others.
- Be direct and ask for what you want.
- Say 'No' clearly and firmly without causing offence when you do not want to follow a certain course of action.
- Take responsibility when necessary.
- Say what you mean clearly and confidently.
- Stand up for your rights.

Being able to express your feelings and to stand up for your rights are important verbal skills in that they help you to establish relationships with other people.

Some people are naturally assertive and do not think twice about expressing their feelings or views. Others, however, tend to be non-assertive and more reticent, and find it difficult to say 'no', or refuse unreasonable requests. If you are a non-assertive individual you must realise that being assertive does not involve aggression, but simply firmness.

There are many situations when it is appropriate to be assertive, for example when making a request, refusing a request, coping with refusal or standing up for your rights. We shall now consider a number of such situations.

(i)   Making a Request

Some people find it difficult to make a request of others, whether it be a formal request such as a demand for information, or an informal request such as asking a colleague to have lunch.

When you make a request of others it is important to be direct and positive and make sure that your message is as clear as possible. You can achieve this by maintaining strong eye contact with the other person, smiling, speaking in a pleasant tone of voice, and not being aggressive. If you are nervous about making the request, then it will help if you practise before actually asking the other person. This should improve your confidence, and will reduce the likelihood that you will 'dry-up' and be unable to make the request coherently and concisely.

One way of making the request is to turn it into a question; 'Could you get me this report, please?' This would mean that the other person would have to say 'no' if they wanted to refuse your request which is more difficult to do than to say 'yes'. If you ask the question in a polite and pleasant tone of voice, the other person will find it even more difficult to refuse your request. It is easier to refuse requests that are posed rudely, aggressively or impolitely.

(ii)   Refusing a Request

Sometimes it is necessary to say 'no' to a request from someone else, but before doing so, decide whether or not the request is reasonable. If you think that the request is out of order and you cannot accept it, then adopt a firm polite manner. You could say something like this, 'I'm sorry, but the report is in another section of the building and I can't get hold of it.' If the other person is persistent then you will have to justify your refusal, 'The Managing Director has it at the moment and I can't get it until she has finished with it.'

(iii)   Coping with Refusal

When you make a request that is refused you need to make a swift recovery and hide your disappointment. You might make a face-saving statement such as; 'Oh, well, not to worry, I'll read it when she's finished with it.' If the person who has refused your request is not in a position to do so, because, for example, they do not have the necessary authority, then adopt a firm approach and repeat the request, perhaps in a different form:

Can you word process this letter for me please? Its urgent!

I can't do it right away as I have other work to do.

I appreciate that, but the letter must be printed this morning.

Well, come back at lunch time and it might have been done.

I'm afraid that's not good enough, I'll leave it with you and telephone at 11 o'clock to see whether its been done.

Very well then, I will see what I can do.

Thank you.

In such situations it is important not to take 'no' for the answer, but to show your determination and maintain the pressure on the other person until the request is accepted. It might be that you have to alter your tone of voice if the request is not accepted, but at no stage should you lose your temper, for this will probably increase the other person's determination not to give in.

(iv)   Standing up for your Rights

People who are timid often find it difficult to say 'no' even to unreasonable requests from others. If you are asked to do something which is in breach of normal practice you must stand up for your rights to prevent yourself being put upon.

In this situation it is important to assess the circumstances quickly and to confront the other person immediately. Do not apologise but reply in a firm, polite and steady voice. For example, consider the following exchange:

> *John, I've put you down for some overtime on Saturday. I want you to start at 9.00am.*

> It's not my policy to work overtime. Why don't you ask someone else to work on Saturday.

If the other person still persists, then repeat the objection, but in a firmer manner:

> *Be reasonable, John, everyone has to take their turn at working overtime.*

> According to my contract of employment, working overtime is purely a voluntary matter. It is not something I want to do. You will have to find someone else.

(v)   Showing Appreciation

Just as it is important to be able to stand up for your rights so too is it important to be able to show your appreciation of others when the occasion calls for it. Paying compliments is one way of showing your appreciation. It helps to encourage loyalty from others. Showing appreciation of a job well done will develop the other person's self-confidence and help to develop personal relationships.

All too often managers fail to complement their staff for work that is well done. A few simple words of gratitude in such circumstances will encourage good work in the future. Individuals are motivated by knowing they have completed a task that is appreciated by their superiors. When people feel that the quality of their work is not appreciated, they are discouraged from maintaining standards. Tell other people that you appreciate what they have done as this will encourage them to act in a similar way in the future; 'Thanks a lot. Typing that letter so quickly has really helped me.'

(vi)   Making Apologies

Everybody makes mistakes and there will be times when you need to apologise. It ought to be possible to apologise without losing face. There is no need to be over-apologetic, just a simple: 'I am sorry that this happened, or I am sorry that you feel this way about it.'

Indeed, if the other person is particularly irate then an apology, no matter how simple, may defuse the situation.

When you apologise, don't use an aggressive tone of voice as this might show that you are not sincere in your apology. Once the other person has accepted your apology it is important to take steps to remedy the situation and to try to ensure the same problem does not arise again.

2.5 Meeting People for the First Time

For some people, meeting others for the first time is a daunting prospect. Notice how some people blush, avoid eye contact, or stammer or mumble their words when they first meet you.

If you find it difficult to meet people for the first time then you might adopt a few simple pointers. The first step is to 'break the ice':

- Shake hands, smile and be friendly 'Hello, my name is ..., how do you do?' Try not to seem aggressive.
- Keep eye contact but do not stare as this may be interpreted as aggression.
- Look at the others when they are speaking as this shows you are interested in what is being said. Do not look out of the window or stare at the floor. Always show that you are trying to follow the conversation.
- Try to keep the conversation going in a friendly way. Follow the guidelines suggested above.
- Hide your nervousness as it can be distracting to the other person. Control your body language.

When your meeting with the other person is drawing to a close, finish the conversation on a positive note; always part with a few friendly words such as 'It has been nice meeting you', then shake hands and end with a smile.

2.6 Developing Friendships

If you want to develop friendships with other people you must not be too self-centred. It is important to recognise when your friends are having problems and to offer help.

You might feel ill at ease about offering such help and it is important to recognise that some people are reluctant to accept help. For example when a friend suffers a bereavement it is all too easy to avoid her for a few days, and not say anything about her loss. Should a friend be made redundant, it is tempting to stop meeting her in the pub. If a friend is experiencing emotional problems, for instance as a result of the breakdown of a long-term relationship, she may be irritable, making her company difficult to enjoy. Although your friend might appear to be rejecting you, she does still need your support.

Good friends do not ignore each other in times of difficulty, they help each other. You need to be assertive, to engage in free and direct communication, but in a sensitive way that respects the feelings of the other person.

The first step in the process of supporting a friend is to identify that she is facing a difficulty. Some people do not like to talk about their problems and 'bottle them up'. Signs to look out for are:

- Changes in temperament. A humorous person may lose her sense of humour. A calm person may become angry. A quiet person may become even quieter. In fact whenever the person behaves differently to her normal behaviour this could be a sign that she is facing some difficulty.
- Change in habits. People facing problems often adopt different routines – a punctual person might forget meetings; a careful worker might become sloppy.
- Change in appearance and grooming. People facing difficulties often allow their appearance to become slovenly and unkempt.

The above characteristics are just some of the signals that will show that a friend is experiencing a difficulty. People respond to such pressure in their own way. Only by knowing someone well, and recognising when she changes mood or behaves in an abnormal way, will you recognise that she has a problem. You will easily recognise dramatic changes in behaviour. Sometimes, however, a difficulty builds up over time (for example a problem at work) and it is not always easy to recognise the symptoms.

When you establish that a friend has a difficulty, try to help in the following ways:

- Imagine how your friend is feeling. You will need to find out what lies at the root of the problem. It is likely that your friend is emotionally distressed and so you need to be sensitive in the questions you ask. Begin with questions such as 'What ...?', 'How...?', 'Who ...?', 'Where ...?' Avoid questions beginning with 'Why ...?' at first as these require your friend to give an explanation and initially this might cause further upset. It is best to try and establish the facts of the difficulty at first, rather than to try and justify it.
- Try not to express value judgements about what your friend says. Do not be overly critical about what she has done, or is finding difficulty with. The last thing your friend wants is you to compound the difficulty by telling her off.
- Do not rush at this stage. If your friend starts to cry, then encourage it. It is a form of emotional release, helping to reduce pent-up tension.
- Avoid saying too much at this stage. Allow your friend plenty of time to gather her thoughts. Do not be tempted to speak during these silences. Let your friend lead the conversation.

When you have a clear idea of what the difficulty is, try to understand how your friend must be affected by it. Try to imagine how your friend is feeling – angry, sad, shocked, annoyed, frustrated, let-down, lonely, etc. Imagining how a friend is feeling and seeing the difficulty from her point of view is known as empathy.

The next step is to show sympathy. Sympathy means showing compassion, appreciating your friend's difficulty and offering words of comfort. It is important for your friend to realise that she does have emotional support and that she is not alone at this time of stress. You might offer support with phrases such as; 'Yes, I understand how you feel, you must be very angry/upset/frustrated...'

You can also show support through your non-verbal behaviour such as holding your friend's hand or giving her a hug. Try not to dismiss the difficulty as unimportant even if you feel that the difficulty is only a minor problem. It is obviously distressing your friend. Phrases such as; 'Come on, pull yourself together, you ought to grow up', are not going to reassure your friend. Be as sympathetic as you can and perhaps follow these suggestions:

- Address the difficulty head-on, for example if your friend has suffered a bereavement, do not ignore the issue, say something like 'I am so sorry that your mother has died. I know you will miss her. She was a lovely lady.'
- Choose your words carefully so that you do not cause further stress, try not to 'put your foot in it.' For example if a friend has just been made redundant do not say 'You'll never find another job at your age.' Instead be positive and say 'With your skills and experience it won't be long before you are back in work.'

Talking about the difficulty and offering sympathy often helps to alleviate stress. When your friend is calmer try to provide additional support. It might be that simply staying with her is all that is required. Alternatively, you might have to do something else to help, such as informing other people of the difficulty – relatives in the case of bereavement, or the college or employer if your friend is unable to attend. Try and do this with the minimum of fuss. Your aim is to reduce any further potential sources of stress.

When helping a friend in this way it is important to decide whether additional, professional guidance is required, for example should the doctor be called, or a marriage guidance counsellor. Only when you fully understand the difficulty and appreciate how your friend feels can you make such a decision.

Everybody needs good friends. Good friends support each other at times of crisis and distress. Sometimes being a friend is not easy, it may involve you in much emotional upset. The ES discussed here will be useful for coping with such stress.

2.7   Being Persistent

A number of situations discussed in this book require you to be persistent and to persevere against obstructions and difficulties.

When sales staff try to sell a product they have to be persistent, trying to overcome the customers' objections. If you are applying for a job you will probably find that you have to make a number of applications, and attend a number of interviews before being offered a post. When you gather information you may well be faced with difficulties. For example, the information that you require may not be readily available in a published form, which means that you have to instigate your own survey. Planning the survey, implementing it, and analysing the results will all require perseverance.

In all these examples you need to be assertive. If you are not assertive and persistent, then it is unlikely you will achieve what you set out to do. People who are not persistent often lack the will-power to overcome objections and difficulties that they encounter. To illustrate some of the ES you could use in such circumstances we will consider one specific situation.

Let us examine a very common situation – 'seeing the right person'. You will face many situations that involve you in trying to find the right person in a certain situation. For example, salespeople who go out and visit business customers without appointments (known as cold-calling) frequently encounter the customer's secretary before meeting the customer. Often the salesperson requires considerable perseverance to persuade the secretary to let her see the customer. A customer (after buying a product) may discover it is faulty and wish to complain to the manager of the shop where it was purchased. The shop assistant at the counter may refuse to get the manager and try to deal with the customer directly.

Be persistent in such situations. Decide what you want from the situation and make sure that you get it. The salesperson mentioned above will want to see the potential customer. The dissatisfied customer will want to see the manager of the shop. Nevertheless you might have to accept something which is next-best as the person you want to see might genuinely not be available. Therefore, you may have to accept an alternative, for example you could make a firm appointment to see the person or arrange to telephone at a specific time.

If you are going to get to the person you want to see you will have to be assertive. Be direct and to-the-point. Give clear reasons why you must speak personally with that specific person and why no one else will do.

Place yourself in the position of the salesperson trying to get an interview with a potential customer. Your conversation with the secretary may follow a pattern such as this:

> *Good morning, my name is Julie Grant from Prospect Manufacturing, could I please see Mrs Brown, your Buying Manager?*

> Do you have an appointment?

No, I don't. I want to speak to Mrs Brown about a new product our company has produced that is currently saving firms like yours £250,000 per year. I know that you buy a similar product from Stapleton Engineering, but our product is right up-to-date and much more economical.

That may be the case but Mrs Brown does not see salespeople without an appointment.

Yes, I appreciate that and apologise for calling without an appointment. I will only take a few minutes of Mrs Brown's time to introduce myself, and then I can make an appointment to see her for a longer time on my next visit.

Mrs Brown is too busy to see you now, even for a few minutes, you really should have made an appointment.

Would it be possible for you to let Mrs Brown know that I am in reception, and wish to see her? She will probably have seen the advertisements for our product in the press and might be interested to learn how much she will save by using it?

Very well, but I can't promise anything. Take a seat.

Thank you.

In this conversation the salesperson is not prepared to accept 'no' as an answer. Every time the secretary says no she acknowledged it, and then continued to show how important it would be for the Buying Manager to see her, implying that if she did not the firm would lose money. Note that you should not give excuses for arriving without an appointment.

Throughout this type of encounter it is important to create a favourable first impression. If the secretary does not like you, for whatever reason, then it is unlikely that she will arrange a meeting with the Buying Manager. To help to create a favourable first impression, you need to speak pleasantly but firmly, not to lose your temper or become impolite. Maintain strong eye contact throughout the conversation and be friendly. Try not to appear nervous. It is important to attempt to interpret the secretary's body language. If it becomes obvious that the secretary will not budge and refuses to telephone the Buying Manager then if you continue to be persistent this will simply antagonise the secretary. In such a circumstance accept a next-best alternative, and ensure that you leave with a firm commitment either to speak to the Buying Manager in person or over the telephone.

Being persistent requires patience and tenacity. Like all the other ES discussed in this book you will develop it over time. The example considered above is one approach that you can adopt to 'see the right person'. However, to support the ES already discussed in this example, you will also have to be a positive thinker.

2.8   Being Positive

Being positive is really a frame of mind, an attitude, a way of thinking about situations. People who are positive thinkers always look on the 'bright-side'. No matter how difficult or disastrous a situation has been the positive thinker will try and identify something good that has arisen from such a situation. Positive thinking is to some extent the skill of receiving information, and identifying the good in it.

In contrast, negative thinkers always highlight the worst side of situations or events. These people tend to be critical, looking for faults, rather than good points.

To be positive involves being assertive not only with other people, but with yourself. Sometimes you will face difficult situations and it will be all to easy to complain about them. Complaining about situations in a negative way, simply to be critical without suggesting ways of overcoming the problem, is unhelpful – other people involved with the situation might also adopt a negative approach. In difficult circumstances both yourself and the others involved need to think positively and to look for good points.

When people think negatively a lot of time can be wasted moaning and feeling sorry for themselves. This just makes the matter worse. People who are negative in their approach to their jobs lose motivation towards their job. They lack enthusiasm and put the blame elsewhere, for instance on the organisation for which they work or the people they work with.

If you do face difficulties try to assess the situation and learn from it. Perhaps you could be more persistent, not accepting 'no' too soon. After any negative encounter carry out a self-evaluation process. Regard all experiences as part of a learning process. Indeed, it is from unsuccessful encounters that you learn most – a positive point in its own right.

To summarise – be positive. Adopt a frame of mind that always looks for successes rather than failures. Do not ignore difficulties but identify the cause of the problem and take steps to overcome it. Self criticism, while important, is on its own rather negative. Be constructive and try to improve what you do.

Being positive is an ES you should adopt frequently. Everybody suffers from upsets and disappointments, no matter what they are doing. You will overcome difficulties more quickly if you think positively. There will be times during the ES training programme when you will feel frustrated or disappointed with the progress you are making. At such times adopt a positive frame of mind.

2.9 Affective Skills

The term 'affective skills' is used in this context to refer to your feelings and emotions, your attitudes and values, and how these affect your interpersonal relationships. Very often the success of interpersonal relations with others is determined by how you are feeling at the time of the interaction, and your attitude towards the other party. When trying to establish successful interactions with friends or colleagues at work, bear the following in mind:

- Always treat others with respect. Even though you might be feeling down take care to respect others, for example do not reprimand subordinates in front of their peers; do not release your pent-up frustrations on others; try to control bouts of moodiness, do not be elated one minute and deflated the next, try for an even balance – working for and with moody colleagues can be difficult.
- Be sensitive to other people's feelings. Always consider the effect of the interaction on the other party – try to avoid offending people by what you say. Do not make personal attacks on others, particularly about their race or religion.
- Show concern for the well-being of others; learn to pick-up the signals that are communicated by the other person indicating their concerns. Make time to find out what it is that is causing concern, and provide sympathy and support when it is needed.
- Be polite when interacting with others, do not be rude or expect them to be servile. Treat others the way you would like to be treated.

Your affective skills will be called into use in the ES training programme. On occasions you may have to provide feedback to your peers on their ES. When doing so, you should ensure that your comments are offered in a sensitive way, so as not to hurt the feelings of the other people. A number of guidelines need to be followed when offering feedback:

- Offer feedback in a descriptive way rather than as a judgement. For instance a statement such as 'I find your tone of voice monotonous to listen to', is a descriptive statement. A judgemental statement would be 'Your tone of voice is boring to listen to'.
- Offer feedback only on ES that are controllable. This requires that you first consider why you are offering feedback. Informing a friend that she is thin cannot be helpful as little can be done about it. Many people are self-conscious about their 'natural features' and feel threatened when they are commented upon.
- Offer feedback only to help people. Receiving feedback can be painful. To minimise the pain you may cause another person, give feedback in as constructive and sensitive a manner as you are able . Think carefully about how the other person is likely to react to your feedback.

Hopefully, the guidelines set out above may assist you in adding a 'human' touch to interpersonal interactions. It is difficult to keep to them all the time but if you make a conscious effort to consider and respect the feelings and attitudes of others then your interpersonal interactions will be warmer and more rewarding as a result. People always have time for considerate human beings, but quickly show their dislike of those who treat others with little respect.

The ES discussed in this chapter are important. These skills, especially assertive and affective skills, influence how you react towards other people, and how they respond to you. One situation where your personal skills will be crucial for the success of the encounter, is in group situations – working with other people. Chapter Nine examines group work in more detail.

Verbal communication skills are important components of ES and if you master them it will allow you to exchange knowledge, ideas, feelings and the whole range of emotions effectively. By becoming competent at communicating orally you will be better placed to gain from and enjoy interpersonal relationships with others. While it is important to be able to communicate verbally it is also important you are able to use body language, as body language is, at times, more meaningful than the spoken word.

3.   Body Language

We all use body language when we communicate with others. It is unavoidable. Even when you are not speaking, you are sending messages to others by your physical appearance, your gaze, your posture, your gestures and your facial expressions. You are not always aware, however, that you are sending such messages, partly because the person you are talking to might not be skilled in interpreting the meaning of body language and does not, therefore, respond to it.

Being able to use body language to communicate, and being skilled in reading it is therefore an important part of interpersonal communication. Body language indicates your moods and feelings and those of your listener. If you can recognise such messages you will be able to modify your delivery and adjust what you are trying to say. Indeed, it is particularly important to understand body language because it can often demonstrate more about the person you are talking to than the words that are being spoken. If you understand body language you will be able to recognise whether there is any difference between the meaning of the words which a person is speaking and her unexpressed opinion of you.

To develop an understanding of body language you must have a perceptual sensitivity, in other words the ability to observe and analyse another person's behaviour. This is especially important in a number of situations such as interviewing, negotiating and selling. If you do not fully understand body language, or you misinterpret the messages that it conveys, then it is very easy to reach the wrong conclusion about what is happening and what is being said.

Body language, therefore, plays an important role in communication. It can replace words, it can emphasise what is being said, it can act as a stimulant to the conversation (for instance when a person nods her head in encouragement), and it can show whether there is any contradiction between what is being said and what is being thought. If you want to use your own body language successfully, and to read that of others, you should recognise what makes up body language.

3.1   The Constituents of Body Language

There are seven main individual elements of body language:

- ➢ Facial Expressions.
- ➢ Gaze.
- ➢ Posture.
- ➢ Gestures.
- ➢ Proximity.
- ➢ Touch.
- ➢ Appearance.

(i)   Facial Expressions

Facial expressions are the most important aspect of body language. Your face is highly visible, it is mobile and flexible, and is capable of indicating your innermost feelings to other people. For example, your face can communicate your likes and dislikes; after eating horrible tasting food all that is required is a 'squirming', frowning face to show you have disliked the meal despite the fact that you feel obliged to complement your host's cooking. In contrast, your broadly smiling face displays your joy at a rival's misfortune – even if you are expressing your deepest sympathy. Despair and frustration are evidenced by a deeply furrowed forehead a clear indication to the lecturer that your assignment tasks are causing a problem. Emotions are often displayed in facial expressions even when you would prefer to hide them, as the face can be a spontaneous communicator of messages.

Most people tend to have similar facial expressions reflecting their feelings and so provide you with good feedback in face-to-face communication. You should be careful to examine facial expressions closely. When you communicate you should try to ensure that your facial expressions reflect what you are saying and are not contradictory for this can easily reveal uncertainty in the message that you are trying to convey. If you are a skilful communicator you will use your facial expressions to good effect.

(ii)   Gaze

When you communicate face-to-face with others you will normally have eye-to-eye contact. This can signal a great deal about what is being felt by you and the person you are talking to. A strong gaze shows that you are being attentive and concentrating on what the other person is saying. If you become embarrassed you sometimes try to hide your embarrassment by breaking eye contact and looking elsewhere.

Breaking eye contact might also show that you are hiding something, or have made an error about which you are ashamed. Alternatively, a lack of eye contact may indicate that you dislike the other person and that you wish to withdraw from the conversation.

On the other hand if you do establish strong eye contact this usually indicates that there is a strong desire to communicate both on your part and that of the person you are talking to. In addition, by giving strong eye contact you can invite others to speak, by giving a prolonged stare with a slight nod of the head to act as a cue. To some extent its a cultural expectation that when people communicate with each other, they look at each other. If you tend to shift your eyes around when speaking, and never directly look the other person in the face, this tends not to inspire trust.

Gaze, therefore, is an important component of your body language. Your emotions and attitudes are portrayed via eye contact as well as other traits such as honesty. You have to maintain careful control of your eyes in dealing with other people. Just as shifty eyes need to be avoided so too should hard, piercing stares that might be a sign of aggression. What you should have is eye contact that looks at the other people to whom you are speaking, but this can be broken with the occasional blink and the occasional look away to make them feel more comfortable. When you talk to other people consider the eye contact they establish with you and the feeling it brings. Does the person make you feel at ease or uncomfortable? Can you tell whether they want to talk to you or merely feel they must?

(iii)   Posture

How you move your body, how you stand or sit and the position of your limbs all reflect your attitudes and feelings about yourself and towards others. You can display a warmth and liking for someone by leaning towards them, or by sitting with your legs slightly apart, arms unfolded. You clearly display your dislike for someone, however, by turning away, or facing them with folded arms, or tightly crossed legs. Of course such signals might also be caused by other factors, for example the person might be feeling upset and this may come across as a dislike for you despite the fact that you are not the cause of their distress. If you like another person, or are in agreement about a particular topic or subject, it is likely that your body movements and posture will have similar patterns. When interpreting a person's posture, as when interpreting all aspects of body language you must take into account other signs and signals coming from the person.

A person's status can often be reinforced by their posture. If you adopt an elevated, domineering position, you may make others feel subservient while if you have an erect posture this can indicate a sense of pride and self-discipline. If you always stand with slouched shoulders and arched back this may be interpreted as being slovenly. People often express a feeling of anger by a tense or rigid posture such as the tightening of muscles, clenching the fist, or stamping the foot. A person who walks in a slow, cowered and defensive manner could be thought of as being timid, as opposed to the confident, purposeful walk of a more self-assured person. Your impressions of others and the impression they will gain of you will be influenced by posture and gait. It is also an indication of your personal dynamism and self-confidence.

You can use posture and body movements as useful punctuation marks during an oral presentation or a conversation. By shifting the posture of your body, or moving to another part of the room, you signal that a particular point has been completed and that another is about to be made. Such a pause created by changing posture can help your listeners follow the structure and development of the oral communication. Compare the teaching styles of some of your lecturers. Do they sit on the desk at the front, pace the floor or stay in a chair behind their desk? Try and assess whether their posture and body movements reflect their personalities and the way in which they teach and you learn.

Your posture, therefore, if you use it appropriately, is a strong support to any verbal message you wish to put across and is a component of body language that you need to control and use effectively.

(iv)   Gestures

In certain circumstances you can use a gesture to replace the need for words. Indeed, it might be that your only way of communicating is by gestures, especially if you are trying to communicate with someone who does not speak English.

You can use gestures in a passive, informative sense as well as in an aggressive manner. A wave of the hand indicates that you have noted the presence of another person, whereas a heavily clenched fist beating down on a table shows that you are anxious, if not angry. Sometimes gestures are instantaneous such as stroking your own hair or scratching your face and these can demonstrate that you are uneasy or concerned about what is taking place.

It is quite often the subconscious gestures, of which you are unaware, that reveal a great deal about your innermost thoughts. Reading and interpreting these unintended gestures can provide a greater understanding of the communication that is taking place. If you are a person who continually fidgets, or who when talking always gesticulates, you could give the impression that you have a nervous disposition.

You should be aware of your own gestures, especially those that might be distracting to other people, so that you can take action to control them. Likewise, you also need to develop a repertoire of appropriate gestures so that you can use them to supplement the other verbal and body language messages that you give.

As with posture, you can use gestures to punctuate what you are saying. Gestures can emphasise and reinforce your verbal messages. It is important to master a variety of gestures, so that you do not over-use one which becomes monotonous or distracting. If you feel uncomfortable at using planned and controlled gestures there can be no substitute for rehearsal and practice. Just as it is important to rehearse and practise a presentation before you give it, so too is it important to practise gestures so that their use becomes second nature and spontaneous, rather than being forced and awkward.

(v)   Proximity

You can recognise how people feel about each other by how physically close they are to each other. You can communicate your status, your level of intimacy with another person and how much you like each other by the proximity with which you talk. If you like someone you tend to enjoy close proximity where other body language is used to demonstrate mutual fondness. People of a higher status tend to keep a more formal distance from those in subordinate roles.

Friends tend to adopt a closer presence to each other than work colleagues. Often if you are dealing with work colleagues and with people you are meeting for the first time you will maintain a physical barrier of distance between yourself and the other person until such time as you find you like each other and the physical barriers can be reduced.

What you are talking about also influences your degree of proximity with other people. If you are making a formal presentation there is normally a physical distance between you and your audience while more intimate exchanges take place at close quarters. Often you will find that only when the barriers to communication, such as physical distance are reduced, will you be able to communicate with other people more effectively.

Distance is not the only barrier to communication. If you speak from behind a desk this can sometimes be seen as being authoritarian, setting up a formal atmosphere. Whereas speaking to someone when you are sitting beside them is more informal, making the other person feel at ease. In certain circumstances you may wish to maintain a physical barrier between yourself and the person you are talking to. A manager reprimanding a subordinate can reinforce her authority by sitting behind her desk. A female secretary might feel threatened if her male manager sits close to her while dictating a letter. She might think he is trying to 'chat her up'. In such cases you may feel that a physical barrier is appropriate.

On occasions you will find it is best if no physical barriers exist. If a friend has just received some distressing news then perhaps he or she would appreciate the reassurance and comfort of being hugged. If you trust someone at work you might find it easier to communicate if there are no physical barriers between you, preferring to talk sitting next to each other on a sofa, rather than from opposite sides of a desk.

(vi)   Touch

How people touch one another is an important element of body language. The number of times you touch someone and the type of touch you use will depend on how well you know and like each other. Touch is important in building relationships with others. Touch can break through some of the psychological barriers between people, and says to others that they are liked. In addition, touches such as a pat on the back or shoulders indicates encouragement and emotional support.

Formal touches are important when you meet someone for the first time. If you give a firm, strong handshake this will indicate self-confidence, while a limp, weak handshake reveals timidity. Parting touches, once again the formal handshake, allow you to end on a positive note and say goodbye.

You must be careful when it comes to touching others, because some people might be naturally reserved and less open to such body language. While a brief handshake or pat on the back is acceptable to most people a prolonged and aggressive handshake, or over-intimate touch with a newly made acquaintance may make the other person feel uncomfortable, even threatened, and distrusting of the relationship with you.

(vii)   Appearance

Your self-image is reflected through your appearance, dress and grooming – whether you have neat well-cut hair, or straggly unkempt hair, whether the clothes that you wear are appropriate for the occasion or inappropriate. Your personal appearance often creates an initial impression that sometimes is very difficult to change. Your personal appearance is of importance when you consider body language because it is an aspect over which you have considerable control. Although very little can be done about the shape, features and size of our bodies, much can be done about what we wear.

The clothes you wear should be appropriate for the occasion. When you are dealing with others it is important that you should consider how you appear. It is important to recognise when casual clothes are acceptable and when they are not. If you only like to wear jeans, then it is probably not a good idea to apply to work in a bank. Obviously if you are going for an interview for a job you should wear clothes that are appropriate. Attractive dress can play an important part in influencing others, particularly at formal functions such as interviews. Frequently, perceived attractiveness in dress increases your impact on the listener and might give you an advantage over a less well-dressed person. Many people also feel that neat formal dress indicates a sense of self-discipline, self-respect and conformity.

As your personal appearance can be partly controlled, it constitutes an element of your body language and helps to create a favourable, or unfavourable, impression of you. So think carefully about what you wear and how you look and try to adjust your appearance to match the circumstances you are going to be in.

3.2   Interpreting Body Language

All of the elements of your body language that we have discussed in the previous section combine to present an image to other people. Equally you must recognise the signals that others are giving through their body language. This section will attempt to help you decode the messages more clearly. Under each heading we will give examples of behaviour which indicate the way people feel. Please note that no single characteristic which we quote is conclusive evidence of the way a person is thinking. However the examples we give are just some of the more common signs people show under these circumstances.

(i)   People Who are Willing to Listen

People are willing to listen to you when they:

- Rub their hands together.
- Lean forward when standing.
- Sit with their body forward.
- Rest their chin on the palm of their hands. Look directly at you, nod in agreement with what is being said.
- Interject with supportive comments such as 'Yes I see', or 'That's right.'

(ii)   People Who are Showing Friendliness

People show they want to be friendly when they:

- Smile.
- Use strong eye contact.
- Have a static body and posture.
- Stand or sit with open, unfolded arms and legs, facing you.
- Use non-threatening gestures such as handshakes, pats on the back or arms.
- Initiate and maintain conversation.
- Use humour in their speech.
- Are polite and courteous to you.

(iii)   People Who are Anxious to Interrupt

People who wish to interrupt you:

- Place their hand on your arm.
- Fidget with their ear or raise their hand.
- Look directly and intently at you.
- Shift their posture when sitting.
- Move when standing.
- Talk to their neighbour.

(iv)   People Who Feel Frustrated or Rejected

When people are feeling frustration or rejection they:

- Use aggressive, downward hand gestures.

- Pummel their hands together, or hit the table or desk top.
- Tighten their clothing.
- Raise the tone of their voice.
- Become red in the face and blush.
- Withdraw from verbal communication.

(v)   People Who Feel Threatened

When people feel threatened by you and are being defensive they:

- Tightly fold their arms, or cross their legs.
- Frown at you.
- Withdraw their eye contact.
- Become verbally aggressive – raising their tone of voice or shouting.
- Stand their ground.

(vi)   People Who Feel Superior

People who feel superior to you may:

- Lean back in their chair, or sit with their legs over the chair arm.
- Grasp both lapels to their jacket, and raise their heads.
- Use gestures that point at others, for example an index finger or pen.
- Look at the ceiling when talking.
- Make sure that their body position is above that of others such as standing when other people are sitting, or sitting in a chair that is higher off the ground.
- Ignore the comments of others.

(vii)   People Who do not Wish to Communicate

People who do not wish to communicate with you signal this by:

- Ignoring completely other people – not looking at them or responding to questions with one word answers.
- Looking down, placing their hands on their foreheads.
- Erecting barriers to communication such as placing their feet on the desk or table.
- Use frowning or scowling facial expressions.

You should take care not to over-generalise as each individual will adapt their use of body language according to cultural and social norms and their own personality and experiences.

After reading this chapter please complete the following learning activities:

Learning Activities

1. There are nine different elements of speech. Write down each element and explain briefly what each element is.

2. Think about the way you speak. Identify those elements of speech that you effectively use and identify those elements of speech you can improve further. How can you use your voice to communicate more effectively?

3. Reflect upon your conversation skills. How effective do you think you are at initiating and maintaining conversations with:

    (a) friends;

    (b) colleagues; and

    (c) people that you have just met for the first time.

    What can you do to improve your conversation skills?

4. Identify a challenging social encounter that you have experienced recently? Explain what the situation was and describe how you handled the situation. Reflect on how you communicated verbally during the encounter – what aspects of your verbal communication were you pleased with, what aspects of your verbal communication skills could you have improved? Now write down how you might have improved your verbal communication during this challenging social encounter.

5. Explain in your own words why it is important to be able to interpret the body language used by other people.

6. Identify the seven constituents of body language and explain how each constituent can be used to convey positive and negative messages.

7. Reflect on your own use of body language and identify those constituents of body language that you feel competent at using, and those constituents you would like to develop further.

8. This evening watch the news on television. Carefully read the body language used by the newsreader and interpret how her or his body language supports the verbal message that is being communicated.

Chapter Four
Written Communication Skills

After reading this chapter you will be able to:

1. Understand the importance of properly constructed sentences for effective written communication, and be able to identify the various components of a sentence.

2. Communicate using a variety of written communications including letters of enquiry, essays and academic reports.

3. Understand the importance of netiquette.

4. Explain which information communication technology skills (I.C.T.) are required in order to compose effective written communications using a computer – and find out where you may go for advice to help improve these skills.

5. Write an in-text Harvard reference.

6. Write a variety of bibliographical references including books, web pages, and journals.

7. Compile a full bibliography of Harvard references containing the correct information, in the exact order, with all references listed alphabetically.

8. Learn conventions for what to do when information is missing from source documentation, which may hinder your attempts to Harvard reference.

Apart from communicating by using the spoken word and body language you will also have to use the written word. All organisations generate considerable amounts of printed information in the form of handouts, memos, letters and reports. It is therefore important that you are able to demonstrate your written communication skills.

1.   The Conventions of Written Communication

Convention is concerned with generally accepted practice, and in the business world it plays a very important part in both verbal and written communication. Let us consider an example of a verbal convention. In many areas of employment it is still the convention for employees to use the formal methods of address when speaking to seniors – either 'Mister', 'Mrs' or 'Ms'. It might not constitute insubordination to speak of a senior using his or her Christian name, but it would certainly be unfavourably received. In the same way, the use of slang expressions in a conversation with the managing director or chief executive will not generally improve your career prospects. Convention is more significant in the written word, especially in business letters, notices and reports, that is in formal written communications. It would not, for example, present a very convincing picture of a well run organisation if the company decided to dispense with the use of punctuation in its business documents. It might also give rise to a great deal of confusion. As grammatical convention and construction is so important it is considered in more detail below.

1.1   Grammar

The most basic component of written language is the 'word'. We can talk of the words used in a language as its vocabulary. Whilst a single word can convey a meaning, in order to express complex ideas and the relationship of things to each other, we use sentences. Sentences are made by linking words together. A sentence should be complete in itself and convey a question, a statement or a command. To create a sentence the writer must follow certain rules that are referred to collectively as the rules of grammar.

The aim of grammar is to ensure that the words of a sentence are arranged so that together they convey a single meaning. If they are capable of bearing more than one meaning the sentence is ambiguous and accurate communication is lost. For example, consider the sentence, 'The sales manager told the production manager that his department was a disgrace to the company.' We do not know from this which department is 'a disgrace to the company'. A further example is the sentence, 'Applications are invited from men over twenty five years of age and women.' Can female applicants be under the age of twenty five? Slight changes in the construction of a sentence can completely alter the meaning of the sentence, so it is important to pay careful attention to the words being used. For instance, compare the sentences:

Only I wrote to the company.

I *only* wrote to the company.

I wrote *only* to the company.

I wrote to the company *only*.

By moving the word *only* through the sentence different meanings emerge. In addition a single word can be stressed by printing it in italic form in order to emphasise its meaning and, in doing so, possibly remove ambiguity as well. Using one of the examples above, 'I only wrote to the company', we do not really know whether the writer is emphasising the means by which he communicated with the company, or whether the writer is stressing the fact that he wrote but did nothing else.

1.2   The Components of a Sentence

There are eight different parts of speech that can be used to form sentences. These are:

(i)   verbs;

(ii)   nouns;
(iii)   pronouns;
(iv)   adjectives;
(v)   adverbs;
(vi)   prepositions;
(vii)   conjunctions;
(viii) interjections.

Verbs: The words in a sentence each perform different functions. Verbs are words indicating the state or the action of a subject and are sometimes referred to as 'being' or 'doing' words. The most common verbs are 'to be' and 'to have'. Verbs can be used in different tenses to signify the time at which the event they describe occurs, thus 'I talked' (past tense), 'I am talking' (present tense) and 'I shall talk' (future tense). They can be used actively and passively to convey different emphasis, for instance 'The government cuts civil servants' pay'. Here 'cuts' is used actively and as it immediately follows government it emphasises that word. This could alternatively be expressed as 'Civil servants pay is cut by the government.' This sentence now emphasises who has suffered the cut rather than those responsible for it.

Nouns: Nouns are words that name a person or place or thing. If the thing is tangible, with a shape and volume, such as a factory, an individual or a manufactured product then the noun is a concrete one. If the thing is intangible, such as a quality, a value or an attribute (for example justice or information) the noun is said to be abstract. Collective nouns are used to describe a group of things, for instance a 'firm' of accountants. It is important not to refer in the same sentence to a group as a single entity and then as a collection of individuals, thus, 'The management took their places and it then commenced its business.'

Pronouns: Pronouns are used instead of nouns to identify a person or thing already mentioned or known from the context of the sentence. There are personal pronouns (such as 'I', 'you', and 'they'), and interrogative pronouns (such as 'who', 'what', and 'which'). Interrogative pronouns are used to enquire or question.

Adjectives: Adjectives describe nouns, for example, 'the large warehouse', 'the green folder', 'the main entrance'. An error to be avoided is the use of superfluous adjectives. Examples might include 'a major disaster' or 'a noisy disturbance'. In fact the use of adjectives as a complete contrast to the nouns they are describing can be used to humorous effect – 'a quiet disturbance'. (This figure of speech is known as an oxymoron – a contradiction in terms.) Some adjectives are relied upon so extensively that it becomes difficult to know what they are really intended to mean. The adjective 'nice' is one of the most over used in our language.

Adverbs: Adverbs describe verbs, for instance 'the workforce is slowly learning the skills', or 'she often calls', or 'the shop is closed simply because of the power cut'. In these examples the adverbs are 'slowly', 'often' and 'simply'.

Prepositions, Conjunctions and Interjections: Prepositions describe directions or position (in, on, under etc.), conjunctions join words together (and, or) and interjections are exclamations (oh! and ah!).

Which of these eight parts of speech appear in a sentence obviously varies according to the message the writer is seeking to convey, and the tone and style that is being used. However, all sentences must consist of a subject and a verb. This can occur with just two words such as 'I called' or 'Richard paid'. In both cases there is a subject, the individual performing the action, and a verb, indicating the activity of the subject. Some verbs require an object as well as a subject to make proper sense. We are left wondering in the case of the caller, whom, why and how he called.

A group of words without a verb is referred to as a phrase. A phrase may make sense even though it lacks a verb, for instance, 'Mr. J. Owen – Quality Control Supervisor'.

1.3 Punctuation

The purpose of punctuation is to provide tone and expression to the written word and provide pauses to help the reader grasp what has been said before moving on to the next idea or set of ideas.

Different types of punctuation provide the writer with alternatives for achieving these purposes. Although grammatical rules certainly exist for the use of correct punctuation, probably the best guide to punctuation is the writer's own sense of what feels right. This often becomes clear when reading back over the written material. In oral rather than written communications the speaker has greater control over punctuation using gestures, expressions, tone of voice and pauses. For example, pauses can be lengthened to heighten the emphasis on what has just been said.

The Full Stop: The full stop is the single most important component of punctuation. It is used to end the sentence. It also appears in some abbreviations, for instance Mr. Smith, and R. Smith J. P. When does a sentence end? Perhaps the most helpful advice is to think about how the writing would sound if it were being spoken. Where would the breaks come? Bear in mind that people often manage to produce longer sentences when they are speaking than would look or feel right if seen in written form.

The Comma: A comma is used to make a short pause within the sentence. Short sentences are helpful to the reader. They are easy to follow. Used excessively, however, they restrict the writer's style and create an impression in the reader's mind like travelling in a jerky car. Whilst a straightforward writing style assists the reader's understanding, the longer sentence may be necessary to closely link related ideas. It is then that the comma becomes useful. It should be borne in mind that over enthusiastic use of commas may hinder the reader's understanding rather than help it.

The main uses of a comma are:

- In lists, as a means of separating items.
- To report direct speech, as for instance in the following sentence. The secretary said, 'The office has been busy all day.'
- To mark the end of a clause. 'In reply to your letter of 24th May, I have now spoken to the people concerned.'
- As a substitute for brackets. 'The clerical assistant, a man of fifty five, took early retirement.'
- To enable adverbial phrases to appear in the middle of sentences. Words like 'however' and 'nevertheless' are adverbial phrases.

The Semi-colon: Sometimes a writer needs to introduce a longer pause than a comma, but does not wish the sentence to end. To achieve this the semi-colon is used. The three situations in which it is usually employed are:

- To stress the separate identity of listed items. 'The file included: the clients name; his date of birth; his previous employment experience; and details about his state of health.'
- To emphasise a conjunction. 'We are not happy about your attitude to time-keeping; and we do not intend to alter your working hours.'
- To act as a conjunction by joining two related sentences. 'The word processor is a valuable asset; it has revolutionised our office procedures.'

The Colon: The colon can be used in a number of ways. It is used:

- To introduce a list, hence its appearance after the word 'used' above.
- As a means of dividing a general idea from the explanation. 'Personal computers are valuable tools: they are quick, cost effective, and easy to operate.
- To contrast one idea with another. 'Economic expansion creates jobs: economic decline reduces them.'

Parentheses: Parentheses or round brackets, are a method of providing additional information in the form of an aside. 'Mrs. Black (Company Secretary) spoke at the meeting.' Often brackets can be replaced by commas. Which method is the more appropriate in the last sentence? As a means of introducing a note of confidentiality, however, brackets can be most effective. 'You may recall me telling you (when we met over lunch last week) that the merger is likely to go ahead.'

Dashes: The dash is another device for introducing a pause, and creating emphasis. Dashes lose their impact if they are used too frequently. When a dash is introduced in a sentence the phrase or clause following it should end with a dash – or a full stop.

The Apostrophe: An apostrophe is used to indicate possession. Compare the following three sentences:

The council's duty is a statutory one – (One council)

The councils' duty is a statutory one – (More than one council)

A statutory duty is imposed upon councils – (All councils, but no apostrophe is needed because there is no possession by the councils. It is a simple plural).

Note, however, that a possessive pronoun (its, hers, theirs, yours) does not require an apostrophe. An apostrophe is also used where one word is a contraction of two, for example, 'don't' (do not) and 'it's' (it is). The apostrophe is used in place of the missing letter or letters and not, as is often mistakenly believed, between the two words forming the contraction. For example, how would you contract 'does not?' The correct contraction is 'doesn't' not 'does n't'. Note, also, the difference between 'its' (possessive pronoun) and 'it's' (contraction of it is). Although these contractions are used all the time in speech, it is usual to use them in writing only when reporting direct speech. For instance, in speech we might say 'what's the difference?' whereas we would write 'what is the difference?'

Quotation Marks: Single quotation marks are used to indicate directly reported speech: The supervisor said, 'The morale of my staff is high'. Single quotation marks are also used for titles, for instance 'The Economist'. However, where there is a quotation within the quote double quotation marks are used, see the following example. The supervisor said, 'The morale of my staff is high and the foreman said to me yesterday "...it's because of the recent government order".' There are two ways of reporting speech; directly, as in the example above, and indirectly. Indirectly reported speech involves describing past events. In indirect speech the statement above would read: The supervisor said the morale of his staff was high and that the foreman had told him the previous day it was due to the recent government order. Indirect speech is commonly used as a way of recording in minutes of meetings, the discussion that has taken place between the members present. It is an alternative to directly quoting them which is likely to be a tedious process and very demanding of the minute taker's skill.

Paragraphs: Just as words combine to form sentences, so sentences combine to form paragraphs. A paragraph contains a group of sentences related to the same idea or ideas. When the idea or topic changes, a new paragraph should begin. The pause between one paragraph and the next signifies the change of content. The use of paragraphs involves care; whilst a paragraph that is too long can cause the reader difficulty in coping with larger blocks of information, paragraphs that are too short are disconcerting and confusing.

A number of common points apply to all forms of written communication:

- The style of writing should be grammatically correct.
- The written document, whether typed or handwritten, should be neatly and legibly presented and in a consistent style.
- The simplest writing style is normally the most effective.
- You should carefully check and correct the written document before despatching it, ensuring correct spelling and terminology.

These points are general guidelines, but you do need to bear them in mind to ensure the quality of your written documents. You may have to produce many different forms of business communication. Being able to write such documents effectively is an ES. We will now consider a number of specific types of written communication.

2. The Written Word

2.1 Handouts

Handouts have a number of purposes, but are most commonly used in support of oral communications (you will also find information relating to this in Chapter Seven). They can remind the audience of the important points of a presentation; they can refer the audience to points that are difficult to communicate verbally, for example data or technical considerations; and they can be used as promotional tools for your organisation.

The design of the handout is crucial:

- Whenever possible the handout should be printed by a high quality printer.
- Only the key points should be communicated on the handout – there's no need to write a long essay, the reader will ignore it.
- Attention should be paid to the handout's layout to ensure that it is well-spaced, and visually pleasing, not distracting.
- Poorly produced handouts should never be used.

In addition to thinking about their design, you should also consider when to use them:

- Handouts distributed before the presentation act as a guide for the audience, structuring the flow of topics. A problem might be, though, that the listener reads the handout and then ignores the presentation.
- Handouts distributed after the presentation might not be read at all as the listener feels he knows all that he wishes to know about the topic that has been covered.

A compromise position is to distribute the handout during the presentation. To prevent this acting as a distraction for the audience, you should:

- Forewarn the audience that they will receive a handout of the key points being discussed.
- Reiterate the key points on the handout before distributing it.
- Once the handout has been distributed say nothing for a period, to enable the audience to read it. When they have read it ask if there are any questions about its content.

- Then instruct the audience to put the handout away before continuing with the presentation.

If these points are followed then you should be able to maintain the attention of all the members of the audience.

2.2   Memoranda

When someone wishes to communicate in writing with another person in the same organisation, it is usual to write a memorandum (the plural of memorandum is memoranda). This Latin word is frequently abbreviated to memo.

The memo is an essential and standard means of office communication. When an organisation has a number of sites you will find that memos are sent from one site to another through e-mail.

A memo can be used; to give instructions, make requests, advise or update people on decisions taken or to circulate information to a number of people. It should be brief, to the point and precise. Because a memo may be addressed to a large number of people – for example, all section leaders – a memo should not be used for confidential or sensitive information or where a more personal approach is needed (for instance when you want to wish someone well on their retirement).

Memos follow a fairly standard format, as we show in the next example.

Dolphin Shipping
Internal Memorandum

To: **Date:**
From: **From:**
Subject

The key features of a memo include:

- The name of the organisation.
- The word 'memorandum'.
- The headings given above.

Here is an example:

Dolphin Shipping
Internal Memorandum

To:	Despatch Clerks	**Date:** 21 July 200
From:	Warehouse Manager, Tilbury	**From:** WMT/LB
Subject:	Packaging Crates	

As you will be aware, there have been problems with the quality and delivery of packaging crates from our suppliers. From 1st August 200 , all crates will be supplied by Ocean Packaging. Between this date and September 200 , please double-check that all crates have the Ocean stamp on them before despatch. Our current supplier will collect all their stock fortnightly by the end of the year.

Even though a memo is a brief document, it is important that you use the right *tone*.

Consider the different impact made on the reader by the following three memos. They are written by a superior to an office junior appointed a month ago who has, until now, had a good attendance and punctuality record:

1. 'I'd like to have a chat with you about your recent punctuality. Would you please be good enough to arrange an appointment at your convenience through my secretary.'
2. 'See me in my office at 10.30am today to discuss your unsatisfactory punctuality record.'
3. 'I note that you have been late twice this week. Please see me at 10.30am today to discuss this.'

How would you describe the differing tone of the three?

Which one do you feel would be most appropriate?

2.3   Letter Writing

Even in these days of the widespread use of telephones, letters remain a vital form of business communication. Whilst a telephone conversation has the advantage of speed of contact and the facility for question and answer, a letter has the advantage of providing:

- A formal written record.
- The opportunity to re-read difficult sections until they are fully understood.
- A reference point for discussions or telephone conversations.
- The opportunity to attend to it at the recipient's convenience, when optimum concentration can be achieved.

Letters fall into two main categories, formal and informal. We are concerned here with formal letters, that is, letters you write as part of your job, or to business organisations or public bodies.

Types of business letter include:

- Letters of enquiry/confirmation.
- Letters of complaint.
- Letters of adjustment.
- Circular letter.

For all these types of letter, you should follow certain conventions of blocked layout.

Let us begin with an example of a letter of enquiry. The sections outside the main body of the letter are in 'blocks' and there is no internal punctuation in the blocks other than capital letters. The ease and speed of typing in such a layout means that blocked layout is most frequently used.

Ace Taxis

47 Hindmarsh Street
Clydebank
Glasgow
G2 5RP
18 August 200

Customer Service Manager
Blackstripe Software
Vincent Court
Milton Keynes
MK9 4BP

Dear Sir/Madam

Blackstripe Taxi Program

I am enquiring on behalf of my company about the taxi call-logging program you produce. Would you please send a copy of your brochure and current price list. Please indicate if you have any local dealers, or preferably, taxi company clients where we could see the system operate.

Yours faithfully

Jenny Boon

Jenny Boon
Office Manager

Note the following points:

1. *Your own address:* Always write the names of the road and town in full use your postcode. (On company headed notepaper, the address and postcode is already pre-printed.)
2. *Inside address* (so-called because it is identical with the address on the envelope): This gives the title (and, if known, the name) of the person to whom you are writing.
3. *Date:* Write the day as 18 not 18th. Write the month in full (for example, August not Aug). This approach is adopted for international correspondence, as in some countries (e.g. USA) a date written as 9.4.200 would mean 4th September not 9th April!
4. *Greeting:* Either *Dear Sir/Madam* if you are unsure of the person's sex, or, if you know the person's sex, *Dear Sir* or *Dear Madam*. If you know the individual's name, use it, in which case it should also have been in the inside address.
5. *Ending: Yours faithfully* if you have not used the person's name but only the title. *Yours sincerely* if you have used the person's name. In each case, note the only capital is the Y in Yours.
6. *Signature:* Print your name, leaving space for your signature. In this example, would you be able to tell the sex of the writer from the signature alone? Is it Jenny or Jerry?

Whichever type of letter you are writing you should:

- Use as simple and concise language as possible (even if the content is complex).
- Match your style and content to the purpose of the letter.
- Be polite, business-like and restrained (especially if it is a letter of complaint).
- Be clear and logical in your structure and paragraphing.
- Explain in the opening paragraph why you are writing.
- Conclude positively. (For example, if you are likely to meet the recipient soon end with a phrase like 'I look forward to our meeting on Friday 8 May at the NEC Exhibition' or 'I look forward to hearing from you about these suggestions.')

(i)   Specific Types of Letter

A Letter of Enquiry: As we show in the example above, make sure that you have stated all your requirements and have given sufficient information to allow a response. In the sample Blackstripe letter two requests (one for the name of the local dealer and the other for the name of any clients) are made about demonstration of the taxi program.

Letters of Complaint: Letters of complaint are always difficult to deal with. Essentially, if you can provide factual evidence and assemble your case in a structured, polite but firm manner, you will fare far better than with either a letter which is meek or one which is rude, threatening and abusive.

If you worked for a tour operator, how might you respond to the extracts from the three letters below from travellers on the same package holiday?

A. I just thought I'd let you know that we weren't overjoyed with our recent holiday with your company. It wasn't quite as nice as some of the others we've taken with you. I know that you can't help the poor weather, but you might possibly like to consider re-siting the tents on this site so that campers don't get quite so wet.
B. Call yourselves tour operators? You couldn't even organise an evening's drinking at the local brewery! The whole holiday was a complete shambles thanks to your incompetence. I demand a complete refund.
C. We have enjoyed several good holidays with your company previously. Unfortunately, on this occasion there were a number of let-downs at the Chateau de Normandie site which seriously affected the quality of our stay between 23-30 August.

These were:

1. On arrival, no camp couriers were available for half an hour to show us to our pitch.
2. The location of some of the tents meant that torrential rain caused flash-flooding, with many of the lower-sited tents being flooded out. Our own tent was not adversely affected in this way, and indeed remained waterproof. However, considerable inconvenience was caused through not being able to reach the nearest toilet block along a waterlogged path. The other block was at the far side of the site.
3. On the Wednesday the camp barbecue and entertainment, for which we had paid £13.50 a head, did not take place.
4. The swimming pool was out of commission for the entire length of our stay.

I am sure that you would wish these matters to be brought to your attention as they mark a considerable slip from your usual high standards.

Letters of Adjustment: A letter responding to a letter of complaint is called a 'letter of adjustment'. In such a letter you should fully answer the points made in the letter of complaint. Try and use a conciliatory or apologetic tone, whilst also stating your company policy in such matters. While you should try to make your customer feel valued, politely reject complaints that are obviously false or unsubstantiated.

Here is an example of a response to letter C:

Thank you for your letter of 4 September about your recent holiday at the Chateau de Normandie campsite.

We are sorry to learn that aspects of the holiday were a disappointment to you as we always value our regular customers in particular.

After thorough investigation we are now able to make the following comments.
1. It appears that you arrived at the site at lunch-time. May we draw your attention to page 4 of our information pack which indicates that arrivals should be made after 2pm, as our couriers are busy before that time checking the tents.
2. You will be aware that the weather during some of your stay was terrible and we are pleased that you were not inconvenienced in any way in your tent. This is a tribute to the fine quality of equipment we insist upon.
   We are in discussion with the campsite proprietors to arrange alternative pitches for our tents next year to avoid a recurrence of the problem. The proprietors are adamant that they have never previously experienced such problems with the weather but will be taking remedial measures for next year.
3. The inclement weather was a contributory factor to the cancellation of the barbecue and entertainment. You will recall that page 5 of our information pack states that we cannot be held responsible for any cancellation, postponement or change to any entertainment or facilities offered. (The entertainment was in fact held on the evening of the day of your departure).
4. The same clause applies also to the unforeseen closure of the swimming pool. Freak weather damaged the filtration system and, in the interests of the safety of all campers, it was decided to close the pool for repair.
   We hope that this explains some of your disappointment. Whilst we are not liable for any of the points raised, in the interests of maintaining customer satisfaction, we enclose a voucher for £250 off your next holiday with us.
   We look forward to receiving your booking.

Circular Letters: Circular letters convey information to a large number of people at the same time. There are three main uses for circular letters:

- To convey information to all customers – for example, an electricity supply company advising customers of a change in tariffs.
- To advertise and sell products and services to potential customers.
- To communicate information within an organisation when a memo would be too impersonal.

Circular letters are usually written on headed notepaper and follow a formal letter layout. The principal difference is that circular letters usually omit the recipient's name and address because the same letter is being sent to many people at once. The greeting, therefore, has to be as wide-ranging as possible. For example a motor manufacturer may start 'Dear Motorist' or a mail-order company may begin with 'Dear Agent.'

The tone of circular letters should be friendly and more informal than most business letters – they are often trying to persuade and the layout will often seem more like an advertisement, with imaginative use of space and different typefaces. Sometimes the letter will be personalised with the recipient's name or address being used several times throughout the letter.

The following example is a mailshot from a double glazing company targeting householders on a housing estate where many windows are beginning to rot.

You will note that many circular letters will not win prizes for excellent English. They often have; a racy style are ungrammatical, have a liberal peppering of exclamation marks and capital letters as well as a compulsory PS – often handwritten to create an informal impression.

DG DOUBLE GLAZING SYSTEMS

Castle House, Castle Street, Borden BN4 6HL
Tel. 0465336211

Date as postmark

Dear Householder

NO MORE DRAUGHTS!

How often have you looked at your windows as winter approaches and dreaded those icy gusts whipping through the gaps? BANISH DRAUGHTS FOREVER with DG Double Glazing! Factory-sealed units guaranteed to be draught-proof.

SAVE ENERGY! SAVE MONEY!

You don't throw £10 notes out of your windows, do you? Well, you do if they are badly-fitting, rotting old frames… like they often are in Sandyhill… But DG Double Glazing helps you save money, keeping those unwelcome fuel bills to a minimum.

MAINTENANCE FREE

Hate painting? Loathe ladders? Give yourself a well-earned rest with DG Double Glazing. Instead of scaling ladders every few years in the never-ending battle to maintain old windows, laze in the garden! Take in the beauty of our sealed uPVC or aluminium windows and be the envy of your neighbours.

TOO GOOD TO BE TRUE!

Not at all. Give us a ring on Borden 336211 for a FREE survey and quotation. You'll be pleasantly surprised at our good value prices. We can also offer low finance plans.

Peter Smith
Director, DG Double Glazing

P.S. Remember DG easy on your pocket now and saving you with every fuel bill!

2.4 References and Testimonials

A reference is a statement either produced as a letter or written on a special form that provides an account of an applicant's character, ability, qualities and interests with respect to a given vacancy. Below an example of a reference form.

Name:		Laura Jones		
Position Applied For:		Graduate Trainee Controller		

Could you please complete the following reference form by circling the response that is most relevant for the above applicant:

Teamworking

Always seeks to involve others	Works well as a team member	Makes good effort	Dislikes team working	A loner

Quality of Work

Consistently high quality	Good in most aspects	Of varying quality	Not acceptable

Flexibility

Rigid and inflexible	Not very flexible	Acceptable flexibility	Welcomes new methods

Ability to Work Under Pressure

Thrives on pressure	Works well under pressure	Accepts pressure	Positively dislikes pressure

Problem Solving

Outstanding	Generally good	Acceptable	Usually unable to solve problems

Quality of Decisions

Makes frequent errors	Mostly correct	Clear and always correct	Avoids making decisions

Performance Against Objectives

Does not meet any objectives	Does not achieve most objectives	Achieves most objectives	Achieves all objectives

Creativity/initiative

Dislikes change	Does not initiate	Welcomes new initiatives	Regularly seeks change

Leadership

An outstanding leader	Leads well on most occasions	Does lead occasionally	Not at all a leader

Persuasiveness

Rarely able to convince others	Mostly able to convince others	Always able to convince others

Persistence

Positively persists	Fully determined	Can be dissuaded	Rarely persists

Planning of Work

Superbly organised	Generally well organised	Inadequate planning

Communications   Verbal

An outstanding communicator	Communicates proficiently	Needs to improve	Does not communicate well

How would you rate the applicants overall suitability for the post?

Tick the appropriate response:

1. Outstanding: leaves little room for improvement, consistently exceeds objectives.

2. Highly Commendable: Regularly, but not always, exceeds objectives. Displays some outstanding characteristics, but not always.

3. Fully Proficient: Fully acceptable performance. Normal objectives m et and assignments properly handled.

4. Marginal: Performance does not fully meet requirements of position. Some objectives met, but not consistently.

5. Unsatisfactory: Below minimum requirements. Objectives rarely met. Needs constant supervision.

SIGNED............   POSITION..................

DATE.................

Reference forms have the advantage that the same information is obtained about each applicant, whereas with a letter of reference the writer dictates its content.

A testimonial is a letter of commendation in support of the applicant. The distinction between a reference and a testimonial is that the reference is requested by the interviewer and is sent direct from the referee to the interviewer, whereas the applicant keeps the testimonial until such time as it may be requested by an interviewer.

References are more highly rated by interviewers than testimonials, especially if they are written in an objective way and draw the attention of the interviewer to the applicant's weaknesses as well as strengths. References must be based on fact and should never be defamatory, otherwise legal action could be brought against you especially if malice is intended. Reference letters usually include the following:

- An indication of how long the referee has known the applicant and in what capacity.
- The current duties and responsibilities of the applicant.
- The applicant's skills, qualities, aptitudes, capabilities and personal characteristics.
- Major achievements of the applicant.
- Major weaknesses of the applicant.
- A statement evaluating the applicant's suitability for the vacant post.

As we mentioned previously, business letters are ambassadors for the sending organisation. Customers, and other recipients, base their impression of an organisation on its letters as much as anything. The letter reveals much about what the organisation is really like, as distinct from the image created by its advertising or other promotional campaigns. Every letter sent out, therefore, either further endorses or reduces the standing and prestige of the organisation in the eyes of the receiver. The standard of business letters must be maintained at all times.

3. Report and Essay Writing

3.1 Business Reports

A written business report is a document that provides an account of something, of work carried out, or of an investigation together with conclusions arrived at as a result of the investigation. Business reports, therefore, convey information, research findings, and put forward ideas and suggestions. Business reports can be classified in a number of different ways.

A **formal** report is detailed, is well-structured and is sub-divided. An informal business report is usually shorter, less structured and more generally used.

Routine reports are frequently used in business as a matter of internal procedure for the information processing system of the organisation. For example, monthly sales reports need to be produced detailing the sales of the products in comparison to the previous month.

Special reports are produced on an ad hoc basis. They are often 'one-offs' dealing with a non-routine matter, such as the development of a new product, or the success of a new training programme.

However, irrespective of the nature of the business report, you can adopt a common style to writing them.

(i)   The Format of a Business Report

Business reports are structured documents that contain discrete sections and sub-headings within each section. The structure will be based on the following format:

- A title page showing the title of the report, your name as the author, your host organisation, and date of publication.
- A contents page detailing all the sections of the report and their sub-sections, with page numbers.
- A summary of the main points raised in the report and the findings under the section heading 'Executive Summary'.
- An introduction containing: Terms of reference – for whom the report has been written, and the purpose of the report. Procedures adopted – how the information presented in the report has been obtained. Topics covered – a broad indication of the report's content.
- The content of the report broken down into discrete sections and subsections. Each section and subsection should have a title/heading, and be numbered. This is the place to present all your material, and contains the data you have found, and what you have deduced from the data. At some stage you will have to evaluate some aspect of the report's findings. This is the most intellectually challenging part of the report and needs to be conducted in an objective manner, for example analysing the strengths and weaknesses of the situation before arriving at a judgement.
- Conclusions indicating what the report has found, and which make reference to the report's objective(s). Normally, it is the first time that you draw together the threads of the report. Nothing new should appear here. The conclusion considers the main points raised in the report and arrives at a conclusion based on these.
- Recommendations for future action to be taken. These should provide a proposal(s) to solve the problem being investigated in the report. The recommendations should persuade the reader that action is practical and viable. Each recommendation should be listed, and discussed separately.
- Appendices detailing information that is relevant but which would detract from the coherence of the text, or is too lengthy or detailed to include in the body of the report. Each appendix should be numbered and referred to in the text of the report. The source of all data included in the report should be written after the data: the originator/writer, date of publication, title of publication and page numbers.
- Bibliography – Harvard Style references to information sources used e.g. articles, books etc. with details of the writer, date of publication, title of publication, place of publication, publisher and page numbers.

You should adopt a similar format with all reports, even informal ones, although some variation will occur depending upon the nature of the report and its purpose. However, like letters, reports need careful preparation as they can enhance your prestige if they are well researched, written and presented.

You should keep headings as simple and brief as possible. Sub-sections within each section should be numbered or lettered, and you should consider numbering each paragraph. By numbering the report in this way any paragraph can be located quickly:

1.   Main Section Heading

1.1   Section sub-heading

1.1.1   Sub-ordinate point

The following is an example of a report:

THE HADRIAN LODGE HOTEL
MARKETING FEASIBILITY STUDY

THIS REPORT HAS BEEN RESEARCHED AND WRITTEN BY:

JANICE CLARK BA (Hons.), MBA, MCIM

MARKETING CONSULTANT

Hotel Consultancy Services Ltd.
Broadstreet House
Northbay
NO76 6TY
Tel: 0567 45637
May 200

CONTENTS

1: Executive Summary

Detailed below are the main points covered in this report:

1.1 After a slow start to the decade, the hotel industry is now more buoyant in terms of revenue generated and profits earned. Indeed, investment in new hotels is a national trend that is mirrored locally.

1.2 As the hotel industry becomes more competitive, hotels have to be targeted at clearly defined market segments, offering them clear selling points. According to Mintel Market Research (2004), the prime consumer of hotel accommodation is the business person. New hotels, therefore, need to be located on sites proximate to such demand.

1.3 There is a well developed supply of hotel accommodation in the proposal's catchment area. However, these hotels are primarily suitable for the tourist market, as opposed to the business market.

1.4 The proposed development will be able to offer a number of unique selling points to the business person: large bedrooms; business services; meeting rooms; secure car park; and leisure facilities. No other local hotel is able to offer these facilities.

1.5 A number of factors will positively influence the demand for the new hotel: the local economy is now more stable; new companies are being attracted to the previously declining industrial sites; a new shopping centre is being built close by; a trunk road will be opened adjacent to the site later this year, enabling passing trade to be attracted.

1.6 The negative influences to the demand revolve around two other new hotels to be developed locally next year.

1.7 It is concluded that the strengths of the proposal outweigh the weaknesses, and that the new proposed hotel appears to be viable from a marketing perspective.

2: Introduction

2.1   Terms of Reference

2.1.1   According to instructions given by the Directors of Bay Islands Ltd. a marketing feasibility study has been conducted to investigate the viability of a new hotel to be developed at Eastsea, the Hadrian Lodge Hotel.

2.1.2   The sponsors propose to develop a 120 bedroom hotel on a 10 acre site adjacent to the A1(T). Included in the development will be restaurant facilities, a leisure complex, and a function room suitable for small conferences or private functions.

2.1.3   This report has been researched and written by Hotel Consultancy Services Ltd.

2.2   Procedures

2.2.1   Research for this report was conducted in two ways:

2.2.1.1   Reference was made to published data from reputable and reliable sources in order to provide background data on national, regional, and local trends in the hotel industry. A list of references is given in the Bibliography.

2.2.1.2   Personal interviews were held with representatives from the public and private sector who have an interest in the local hotel industry. A list of the people interviewed is given in Appendix 1.

2.3   Topics Covered

2.3.1   This report analyses the product, market, factors likely to influence demand, before evaluating the proposal and reaching a conclusion. No reference is made to financial aspects.

(ii)   Preparing the Report

Preparing a report is a skilful process involving a number of ES, such as research skills, intellectual skills, (analysis, synthesis, and evaluation skills), and writing skills.

Your starting point is to determine the report's objective for this will dictate to a great extent how you should research, write and present the report. Once you have clearly identified the information needs you can set about collating the information. When you have fully researched the topic under investigation and you have collated the information you can then apply your intellectual skills to argue your case and to arrive at your conclusions and recommendations. Just as with other forms of written communication, the report should be clearly written and presented, concise and relevant to the report's objective.

(iii)   Constructing the Report

You construct the report once you have collected and analysed the data. Layout is of great importance in formal reports, especially as they contain a considerable body of detailed material that needs to be carefully structured in a coherent, logical and non-repetitive manner. The structure of your report should follow the format outlined above so that it is readable and flows easily. You should use straightforward language and take care with grammar and sentence construction. Just because you are writing a report it does not mean that you should use a note-style of writing.

The report should be written in the third person singular. You should avoid personal terms such as 'I' or 'We', the word 'It' should be used instead:

> I decided to interview the Tourism Planning Officer… should read
>
> It was decided to interview the Tourism Planning Officer…

You should not use emotive language, and avoid using vacuous terms – terms which lack a precise meaning such as 'good', 'excellent' and 'most'. Indeed, at all times you should be striving for precision in your writing and remembering that the report needs to be concise and to the point, for example use 'Now' instead of phrases like 'At the time of writing.' 'Sales peaked in August' should be used instead of 'The highest level of sales in the year were recorded at the height of the summer season in the month of August.'

Thus, your aim when writing a report contrasts with the aim of a fiction writer. The latter can use all forms of creative writing style in order to amuse and entertain the reader. Suspense can be maintained until the final word of the novel. In contrast, when writing a report you should bring the conclusions and main findings to the front of the report so that the reader can decide as soon as possible how much, or little, he needs to read to find out what he requires.

The emphasis in report writing is on facts and interpretation of the facts in a logical, intellectual way rather than an emotional manner. You should write reports objectively to allow the reader to gain an unbiased view of the topic under consideration. Always remember that reports are for the benefit of those who read them, rather than the person who writes them.

3.2   Academic Reports

Writing academic reports is a normal part of student life, and in many professions competency developed as a student at report writing can be a desirable or essential attribute for an employee to possess. Most higher education courses require reports to be written as part of the assessment for certain modules. It is important that you develop your report writing skills as a student to help increase your grades, and for when you finish your course and embark on your career.

Like business reports, academic reports contain specific sections; these are a title page, contents page, summary (sometimes called a synopsis), aims, objectives, introduction (that includes terms of reference), a main body, conclusions, recommendations, references, and appendices. All sections begin on a new page, and each section after the contents page is numbered, with sub- sections given sub-numbers.

(i)   Getting Started

Successful report writers, plan their time efficiently when putting a report together. For many assessments the title of the report is already specified by the tutor. The first stage for you is to analyse the title of the report, break down the words, and be confident that you know exactly what the title means, and what is required of you in order to meet the title's requirements. An example of a report title is as follows:

An Examination of Possible Environmental Impacts from the Proposed Doncaster-Sheffield Airport upon the South Yorkshire Region

The first stage is to break down the title into smaller components, picking out key words or phrases; these are identified in the following table along with things to consider:

Word/Phrase	Things to Consider
Examination	By examining the subject area you are looking in detail at issues that could realistically influence elements of the report title.
Possible	The inclusion of this word indicates that the report is looking into the future at what could happen.
Environmental Impacts	What are these? You will firstly need to define this term, and then find related environmental impacts that have already occurred around similar developments elsewhere. It is the application of these to what is proposed at Doncaster-Sheffield that is key to the report. Research current environmental impacts at other similar sized existing UK regional airports. It may be worthwhile limiting your research in the case of this report to only UK regional airports as environmental laws with regard to pollution and emissions may vary from state to state.
Proposed Doncaster-Sheffield Airport	The airport has not been built, and is currently only proposed; you will need to give some background on the historical aspects of the proposal, and what is expected of the future planned airport with regard to size, capacity, and usage.
South Yorkshire Region	Begin by defining where this region is, how large an area it covers, and where in the region the proposed development will be. The use of a map would be helpful as an appendix to the report.
	This report is only looking at a specific geographic region; therefore you only need state what the possible future impacts of the development could be to this geographic region.

(ii)   Researching the Report

The ability to be able to search for information is extremely important to any academic report writer. Plan your information search, don't limit yourself to only certain materials, try to use a variety of information sources to collect relevant information for the report (see Chapter Ten), and from these sources select and arrange the information that will go into the report.

Suggested sources would include:

- Books, websites, electronic journals and paper journals related to environmental issues.
- Books, websites, electronic journals and paper journals related to airports or air transport.
- Existing environmental impact surveys that are based on current UK airports.
- Government publications and websites that may contain useful and relevant information.
- The websites of existing UK regional airports.
- The websites of environmental pressure groups.
- Related local newspaper articles from the South Yorkshire region, and the websites of South Yorkshire media including television, radio, and newspapers.

(iii)   Writing the Report

The first stage to writing your report is to actually get down on paper (or word-process) what your findings are, along with where these findings came from (your references). Then you need to logically consider in what order you are going to write your findings. As mentioned previously in this chapter, there are specific sections to a report that appear in a specific order, however when it actually comes to writing your report, you will find that you may take a more hap-hazard approach to getting your words down on paper – this is normal.

Many report writers begin by writing out their findings, before going on to state the relevance of them, and how these may influence the overall findings of the report – and why, before providing rationale that may increase the success of the subject area upon which the report is based. What these actually are, are the main body, results, conclusions and recommendations. After these have been written, the introduction, aims, and objectives may be written, before finally ending with a summary (synopsis) of the report. As long as they appear in the right order within the report there is no problem with this.

Of course, not everybody takes such a hap-hazard path to producing a report, and some writers will produce the sections of the report in the same order that they will appear in the final document – however you go about tackling your report make sure that you cover all of the relevant sections required within, and that they appear in the right order in the finished document.

Using the aforementioned proposed report title; the table below demonstrates what may appear in the final report document:

Section	Contents
Summary/Synopsis	A brief overview of the rationale for the report, its main findings, conclusions and recommendations in the report. This should normally be no more than one page long.
Introduction	This section should include an overview of the history and background to the proposal for the Doncaster-Sheffield Airport, along with rationale for writing the report - future environmental concerns. You need not go into detail on specifics in the introduction, as you will cover this more in-depth in the main body of the report. Include in the introduction any terms of reference i.e. why you are writing the report, e.g. this report is being written as partial fulfilment of the award BSc (Hons) Environmental Tourism.
Aims	This section is used to provide a statement of what the intentions of the report are. For example, this report is intended to provide an overview of what the possible future environmental impacts could be upon the South Yorkshire region of the Doncaster-Sheffield Airport.
Objectives	This section clearly states how you have gone about fulfilling the aims of the report, e.g. what research you have undertaken and why, the timescale involved, and any other steps that you may have taken in order to satisfy the aims of the report.
Main Body	The main body of a report is not actually called main body in its heading.
	This section typically consists of several sections that may contain secondary headings and sub sections. For this report it would be suggested to include sections with the following headings:
	Doncaster-Sheffield Airport
	This would identify fully the proposal for the airport, the background to it, and the specifications for the proposed development.
	The South Yorkshire Region
	This would identify where the South Yorkshire region was, and where in relation to it the proposed development would be. It would also highlight centres of population, and areas of environmental significance.
	Known Environmental Impacts
	This would define what is meant by an environmental impact before looking at known environmental impacts to regions around existing UK regional airports.
Results	The section that is in effect the results section would not be called Results in the case of this report, as there has been no element of primary research or scientific investigation within the report. A suggested title for this section would be Possible Future Impacts. This section would draw together your findings from the main body. It would apply known environmental impacts from existing regional airports to South Yorkshire, with rationale that takes into account local populations, areas of environmental significance and geography.
Conclusion	This section ties up the whole report, and shows how the objectives specified in the introduction have been attained. It should highlight the main themes raised and summaries what has been established within the report. The conclusion should not introduce any new subjects to the report but may be used by yourself to include explanative rationale based on what has already been stated.
Recommendations	This section is typically used for you to offer your expertise and advice on the most positive way forward. In the case of this report, the Recommendations may be used to offer advice that may minimise any negative environmental impacts from the proposed Doncaster-Sheffield Airport.
Bibliography	A full list written in the Harvard style of all sources quoted within the report.
Appendices	Any supporting material that does not sit comfortably within the pages of the report e.g. Maps, Charts, Graphs, Tables, lists.

Many reports will have a pre-specified word-count; ensure that your final draft is within ten per cent of that limit (above or below). Typically in a report such as this one, if the word count was 3,000 words it would be a suggestion to allocate your wording as follows:

- 1,000 words may be shared between the summary, introduction, aims and objectives.
- 1,400 words may be used for the main body.
- 600 words shared between the conclusion and recommendations.
- The bibliography and appendices are not typically included within a report's word count.

The first copy of the report that you write is known as a draft copy – please make sure that this is NOT the version that is handed in, as it will no doubt contain spelling mistakes, grammatical errors and may need formatting properly. After writing your draft copy put it away for a day or two, then go back to it and proof read it – it is very often easy to read over your own mistakes, so it can be a good idea to ask somebody else to do your proof reading.

(iv) Formatting the Report

Academic reports are typically written in a certain style. With many reports a proportion of the marks allocated for the report are for the appearance and formatting of it.

When writing an academic report ensure that you use a sensible font and font size, e.g. Arial font, size 12 for text, size 16 for sub-headings, and size 20 for main headings. Do not use Comic Sans MS (or any other obscure fonts), and do not make the writing too small to read for the tutor.

For alignment purposes, reports should either be left aligned or justified (the left aligned option is becoming the most accepted style due to different sized spaces between justified words causing problems for dyslexics).

Each section should begin on a new page, and each section title should be numbered (to the left of the title), titles are underlined, but the numbers are not underlined. Text is aligned with the title. Secondary headings and subheadings are indented and given sub numbers of the main heading, as in the following diagram.

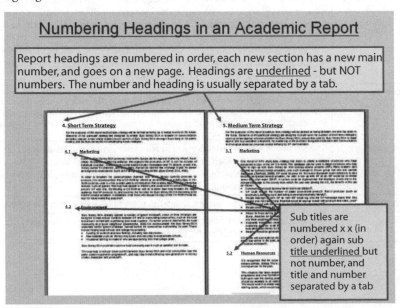

As the diagram demonstrates there are varying levels of heading, these are typically:

1.   Main Heading

1.1   Secondary Heading

1.1.1 Sub Heading

1.1.2 Sub Heading

Typically in an academic report you would not go beyond the level of sub-heading although this may be necessary in certain circumstances. If that is the case make sure that you carry on indenting each next level of sub-heading, and always make sure that the text below a sub heading is left aligned with the title – not with the number of the sub-heading.

Beneath each heading before writing your first paragraph always leave a blank line, and always leave a blank line between paragraphs this makes paragraphs stand out and gives a neat appearance.

If below a paragraph you are going to start a new sub heading, leave two spaces – and be consistent throughout your entire report with regard to spacing – see the following diagram:

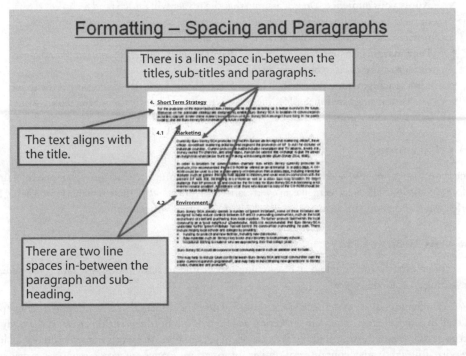

A neatly and correctly formatted report gives the impression of professionalism from the outset and can only be of benefit to the report writer.

Final tips for writing and formatting your report include the following:

- **Write in the third person:** Don't use language such as I, my, we, you, your – always write in the third person, e.g. instead of writing 'In my report I will address the following' write 'This report will address the following'.

- **Number your pages**: but not your title page.
- **Colloquialisms**:– For example, 'Our customers know what the crack is, and that we will produce the goods when we are sorted to do so' is not good English, and is a sentence constructed from colloquialisms (regional slang). The sentence should be written as follows: 'Customers of the company are aware that there are times of peak demand when immediate production of products on request is not always possible'.
- **Sales talk**: Your report is designed to be a factual and unbiased account – use non-emotional language not 'sales talk'.
- **Etc**: Suggests laziness and can be perceived that you could not be bothered to finish the sentence or are making assumptions that the reader will automatically know what you are writing about – don't use etc.
- **Numbers**: Numbers less than 11 should be written in the full worded format e.g. one, two, three – this does not apply to numbers on report headings and sub headings.
- **Referencing**: Any statements, facts, figures that you make that are NOT common knowledge need to be backed up with a full reference in the Harvard style.
- **Application of theory**: Instead of writing that something is good or bad – write *why* it is good or bad and provide justifications for the judgement you have reached. Don't just describe things in your report as this is not academic.
- **Know your audience**: Do not assume that the reader will understand technical terms, or have a prior knowledge of your subject – explain everything so that a complete novice will understand what you are writing about.
- **Page margins**: ensure that you leave sufficient space in the left margin of your page in order to allow for it to be correctly bound.
- **Line spacing**: Unless otherwise stated this is typically left to the discretion of the report writer. It is suggested that a 1½ line space is used to aid the reader of the report – but be consistent throughout.

(v)   Last Steps

Once you have proof-read and formatted your report, print it out, and read through it one final time before submission. This may seem like an overly laborious process – but there is no harm in striving for perfection – and taking pride in producing the best work that you possibly can.

3.3   Academic Essays

The rationale for the methodology of researching and writing an academic essay is almost the same as for writing an academic report.

An academic essay is a systematic or interpretive written document that is structured in paragraphs that fall in a logical order. There are no section headings or sub headings within an essay; the body of text appears beneath the title of the essay as a series of paragraphs. An essay is not structured at all like a report although it may contain very similar information. Essays are very rarely used outside of academia, but it is an academic skill to be able to write them. The style of writing within an essay is much more discussive than within a report, allowing for a smooth flow and transition between paragraphs.

Essays are usually set with a title. It is important that you fully understand the title and what is expected of your essay from that title. As with reports, breakdown and analyse the words within the title so that you are fully aware of the subject area under discussion, and what is expected of you i.e.

are you comparing, contrasting, analysing, or interpreting? (Please note that there are many more instruction words than this). Once you have been given your essay title, find a dictionary and look up the meaning of your instruction word, so that your written essay will be correct.

An essay begins with one or two summarative paragraphs that explain the main theme of the essay, the subject area being covered, and any major findings reached. Following on from this would be an introductory paragraph setting the scene, and giving some background information into the areas under discussion. After this would be a paragraph highlighting the intentions or aims of the essay, along with how the writer has gone about researching information, on which to base the essay.

The above is designed to set the scene for the main body of the essay, which follows and contains any major themes relating to the subject under discussion. The main body of the essay contains a number of paragraphs each of which may look into a different theme.

After the main body it is necessary to draw together your findings in paragraphs that contain a summary of main findings along with conclusive rationale that utilises applied theory from the main body – no new material is introduced into this part of the essay.

The final paragraphs within an essay will address any future recommendations or suggested possible future action to be taken as a result of your findings.

With regards to the word count and written language within an essay – follow the same guidelines as for academic reports.

The following diagram is designed to highlight how an essay should appear from the beginning, with some guidance on formatting:

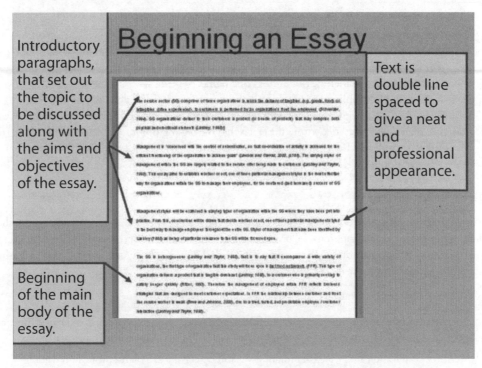

As is the case with academic reports, writing an academic essay is an investment of time and effort – however the more time you spend researching, writing, and formatting your essay, the more likely you are to achieve a high grade, and with that academic success.

4.   The Harvard System of Referencing

When writing reports, essays or other written documents it is frequently necessary to refer to the works of other writers, whether it be to present their ideas, or to support the views that are put forward. Whenever you have to refer to the works of others, either directly by quotation, or indirectly by referring to someone else's ideas, then you should acknowledge them.

This is important for a number of reasons. Firstly, it is crucial that the original author is given credit for his or her ideas. If credit is not given then you could be accused of plagiarism – borrowing somebody else's ideas and works. In addition, everything that an individual writes down is protected by copyright – even a simple hand written note is protected by copyright. However, if you make reference to the source of such copyright material in the body of the text, and a full bibliography is provided, then the copyright material can be used to a certain extent. Indeed, by providing a bibliography the reader of the written document can further investigate the topic under consideration. A final reason for referencing the text is that it adds academic credibility to your document. The credibility of your document will be enhanced if you show that you have read widely around the subject under consideration. You will provide evidence of this by a bibliography.

4.1   The Harvard System

The Harvard system of referencing was developed during the 1950s at Harvard University in the USA. It was originally used by academics within the social sciences, and has now grown in popularity and usage to be the most common method of referencing world-wide.

This system involves two key disciplines:

1.   Referencing source materials within the text of a piece of work by the insertion of the surname of the reference's author into the text whenever mention is made of his or her work, together with the (year) that the work was published. When referencing in-text there is no need to include the author's first name, or initials.
2.   The writing of a bibliography at the end of a piece of work to list alphabetically by author all work that has been referenced within the text. The difference between a bibliographical reference and a reference within the text is that the bibliographical reference is written in full to include additional information such as the title of the work, the publisher and the place of publishing.

(i)   Referencing In-Text

A useful technique for referencing in-text is known as the 3MAC method, this involves quoting the work of somebody (make a citation), followed by referencing the author of the work (make a cite), and finally making a comment upon what the author has said in your own words in order to justify the citation's inclusion in your work (make a comment):

Make a Citation + Make a Cite + Make a Comment = 3MAC

You may find this technique especially useful when you are using referencing for the first time, as it gives you a guideline as to how to use your quoted work. This is demonstrated below:

The research indicated that accountancy was still perceived 'as a bland profession whose members were all of a muchness' (Eliahoo, 1985: 50). The respondents therefore were less likely to respond to this method of research.

In the above example the citation is contained within 'apostrophes' so that it stands out as being a direct quote (Make a Citation). This is then followed by the author, year of publication and page number in brackets (Make a Cite). The page number is included, as a direct i.e. copied piece of text has been used. If the author had re-worded the text instead of copying it, the page number would not be necessary. Finally the reason for inclusion of the text is made after the cite (Make a Comment).

Where you do not use a direct quotation you are merely writing what somebody else may have said, the text could read as follows:

> A number of models have been developed to explain the role of communications, see Strong, (1925); Lavidge and Steiner, (1961); and Rogers (1962). Lavidge and Steiner, (1961), developed a 'Hierarchy-of-Effects' Model.' This model shows...

If three authors wrote a document you should use all surnames in the in-text reference. However, with more than three authors, only the first surname should be used, followed by 'et al' to signify that there were others:

Dettis et al, (2005).

In the Bibliography et al is not used, and all authors names are listed.

If no authors name is given, as is the case with some reports and publications you should cite the institution or department that wrote the report, along with the publication date. If no name or department can be found then it is acceptable to list the author as Anon e.g. (Anon, 2005) this is a last resort though.

If you make reference to more than one document written by a particular author, these will often be distinguished from each other by their different dates (years of publication). However, if the documents were published in the same year then you should use a lettering system in addition to the year:

(2004a), (2004b), (2004c)

You would decide the alphabetical order in which to place the years by looking at the titles of the pieces of work being used. The titles are sorted alphabetically in order to determine which one would be (2004a) and which ones would be (2004b) and (2004c). Below is an example of this in practice, the following three books have all been written by the same author, and published in the same year, once the titles have been placed in alphabetical order, the years can be assigned a letter. (Please note that the examples used below are fictitious and do not exist.)

Blackburn, C. (2004a) <u>Cheap student rail travel</u>. Barnsley, Dalesman Publishing.

Blackburn, C. (2004b) <u>Rail privatisation in the UK</u>. Sheffield, Kubon Books.

Blackburn, C. (2004c) <u>Trans-Pennine rail travel</u>. Barnsley, Dalesman Publishing.

What the above demonstrates is how the books would appear in a Bibliography at the end of a piece of work, if the 'Cheap student rail travel' book was used to supply information within a piece of work, it would simply be referenced within the text as (Blackburn, 2004a). What you must remember is that everything that you reference within the text of your work MUST be listed in the Bibliography at the end of your work.

The purpose of the bibliography is to list all the references that you have used. The bibliography comes at the end of the document, and provides full details of each reference in alphabetical order of author's surnames.

The term 'ibid' may be used when a reference that is referred to is identical to the immediately preceding one.

(ii)   References within the bibliography

Within the bibliography more information is given than with in-text references, to allow researchers the opportunity to accurately look up original information sources. There is a set method for writing up different types of information sources within a bibliography. This section will demonstrate some of these methods.

Books

For a book, the reference within the bibliography is written using the following information, and formatting:

- Surname of the author(s), or editors(s) followed by a comma, and a space and then the first initial of the author followed by a full stop. For example if Abbey Taylor was the author her name would be listed as Taylor, A. If no persons name is given it may be necessary to write the name of the institution responsible for writing the book – followed by a full-stop instead. If the book has been written by numerous authors but edited by one person (or more), the editor(s) name would be listed followed by the word 'Ed.' in brackets. For example if a book had been written by several authors and edited by one person called Barry Thomas, his name would be listed in the bibliography as Thomas, B. (Ed.).
  e.g. Thomas, B. (Ed.)
- A space and then the year of publication (in brackets) – this is normally found near the front cover of the book.
  e.g. Thomas, B. (Ed.) (2004)
- A space and then the title and subtitle underlined (or *italicised*) and followed by a full stop (that is not underlined or italicised). Please note that book titles are written in sentence case and not title case i.e. not all words begin with a capital letter.
  e.g. Thomas, B. (Ed.) (2004) <u>Accountancy for the health industry</u>.
- A space and then the series and individual volume number (if any) – followed by a full-stop (this information is often not applicable so will not be given in most cases).
  e.g. Thomas, B. (Ed.) (2004) <u>Accountancy for the health industry</u>. Series 2, Volume 1.
- A space and then the edition (only if not the first) – followed by a full-stop. If it is a first edition, you may omit this information.
  e.g. Thomas, B. (Ed.) (2004) <u>Accountancy for the health industry</u>. Series 2, Volume 1. 2nd Edition.
- A space and then the place of publication – followed by a comma.
  e.g. Thomas, B. (Ed.) (2004) <u>Accountancy for the health industry</u>. Series 2, Volume 1. 2nd Edition. Crewe,
- A space and then the name of the publisher – followed by a full-stop.
  e.g. Thomas, B. (2004) (Ed.) <u>Accountancy for the health industry</u>. Series 2, Volume 1. 2nd Edition. Crewe, Steam and Gresty Ltd.

In the example given, the editor is Barry Thomas, the book was published in 2004, the title of the book is 'Accountancy for the health industry', it is the first volume of the second series of the book, and is the second edition of this. It was published in Crewe by Steam and Gresty Ltd.

If a book contains a number of chapters written by different authors, and information has been used specifically from one chapter, the reference would begin with the author of the chapter, (written in the same convention as above), followed by the year of publication, and the title of the chapter, followed by the word 'in' which is then followed by the full reference for the book. In cases like this it is also useful to end the reference with the page number range of the chapter e.g.

> Otty, M. (Ed.) (2004) <u>Online banking</u>. in Foley, N. (Ed.) (2004) <u>The information society</u>. Leeds, RO Books. pp. 141-169.

Journal Articles/Newspapers

A journal is anything that may be considered as a periodical publication, such as a magazine, or a regularly produced industry publication e.g. Computer Weekly. These are often used by students, who may use the information from one specific article only, out of a publication that may contain many more articles written by numerous authors. In order to reference these articles properly the following information is required:

- Surname of the article author(s), followed by a comma, and a space and then the first initial of the author followed by a full stop. For example if Norma Jackson was the author her name would be listed as Jackson, N. If no persons name is given use Anon – followed by a full-stop instead.
  e.g. Jackson, N.
- A space and then the year of publication (in brackets) – this is normally found on the front cover or within the footer of pages.
  e.g. Jackson, N. (2003)
- A space and then the title and subtitle of the article written in sentence case, followed by a full stop.
  e.g. Jackson, N. (2003) Approaches by hotels to the use of the internet.
- A space and then the Journal title <u>underlined</u> or *italicised* written in sentence case, followed by a full-stop that is not underlined or italicised.
  e.g. Jackson, N. (2003) Approaches by hotels to the use of the internet. <u>Journal of e-marketing innovations</u>.
- A space and then the specific date of publication, followed by a comma, and volume number and/or Issue number, if that information is given, followed by a full-stop.
  e.g. Jackson, N. (2003) Approaches by hotels to the use of the internet. <u>Journal of e-marketing innovations</u>. January 2003, Vol. 5, No. 1.
- A space and then the page number(s) that contain the article within the journal, followed by a full-stop.
  e.g. Jackson, N. (2003) Approaches by hotels to the use of the internet. <u>Journal of e-marketing innovations</u>. January 2003, Vol. 5, No. 1, pp. 21 – 38.

In this example the author of the article is Norma Jackson, the article was published in 2003 in the Journal of e-marketing innovations, the title of the article is 'Approaches by hotels to the use of the internet', it was released in January 2003, and is issue number one of the fifth volume of the journal, the article appeared on pages 21 to 38. If an article appears on only one page, only one p. instead of pp. is used for the page numbers.

You may sometimes find with journals that they are produced without any date, if the information is not given it is acceptable to omit it. Sometimes the date may appear as a year, or a range of months, if that information is available then it is acceptable to use that as the date.

Web Based Resources

There is an awful lot of information contained on the world wide web, information that varies in quality, and information that often changes or disappears. In order to reference properly a web page, much more information is required about the page. This is as follows:

- Author or institution responsible for producing the page. If the page can be attributed to a person, the same convention is used for the name as with books and journals. If Simon Dennis was the author then his name would be listed as Dennis, S. Very often with web pages there may not be a persons name to refer to, so the institution responsible for writing the page would be listed as the author. For example for http://www.leedsmet.ac.uk/the_news/ there is no one person listed as being the author, so the author would be listed in the bibliography as Leeds Metropolitan University. The institution responsible for writing a page can often be found in the web address (or URL – Uniform Resource Locator) e.g. leedsmet.ac.uk gives a rather large clue that this is a Leeds Metropolitan University page. Sometimes with less obvious URLs a © may be found on the bottom of a page. Next to this you may find the name of the institution responsible. If all else fails and you really can't find the name of a person or an institution you may use Anon – however if there are no details relating to who wrote the page, is the information contained within the page legitimate? That is something for you to consider before using the information. In the example that we will use the author of the web page is Stuart Moss.
  e.g. Moss, S.

- A space and then the year of publication in brackets - as with books and journals. If you cannot find the year of publication, have a look for a last updated date on the website, or a © symbol with a date near it at the bottom of a page – sometimes detective work is required on your part in order to find the information. If there are no details relating to when the page was published, is the information contained within the site legitimate? That is something for you to consider before using the information. If there really is no year of publication or copyright anywhere on the site, and you want to use the information that it contains, the final option is to presume the year is the current year – although this is not considered to be good practice.
  e.g. Moss, S. (2003)

- A space and then the title and subtitle of the page written in sentence case <u>underlined</u> or *italicised* and followed by a full stop that is not underlined or italicised, followed by a space and then the word Internet in square brackets.
  e.g. Moss, S. (2003) <u>Welcome to Retour</u>. [Internet]

- A space and then the place of publication followed by a comma – this is not always easy to find, but in most cases can be found by tracing the origin of the page back to the main website. Sometimes you may need to look for a contact details page to find this information, but you will be able to find it most of the time. If a location cannot be found then simply write 'No location given' (without the apostrophes) followed by a comma.
  e.g. Moss, S. (2003) <u>Welcome to Retour</u>. [Internet] Leeds,

- A space and then the publisher, in the case of a private web page not owned by a company, this may be the author's name, if the page is owned by a company it will usually be the company name. The same conventions apply for finding the name of a publisher, as with finding the author of a website.
  e.g. Moss, S. (2003) <u>Welcome to Retour</u>. [Internet] Leeds, Moss, S.

- A space and then the words 'URL available from:' (without the apostrophes) followed by the full URL contained within triangular brackets.
  e.g. Moss, S. (2003) <u>Welcome to Retour</u>. [Internet] Leeds, Moss, S. URL available from: <http://www.retour.org.uk>
- A space and then the word 'Accessed' (without the apostrophes) and the date that the page was accessed inside square brackets, followed by a full-stop.
  e.g. Moss, S. (2003) <u>Welcome to Retour</u>. [Internet] Leeds, Moss, S. URL available from: <http://www.retour.org.uk> [Accessed 23rd April, 2005].

Please note that if the document being accessed on the web is not a conventional web page (HTM or HTML file), it is good practice to put the format of the document in place of the word URL, some commonly found file formats on the web include:

DOC	Microsoft Word Document
GIF	Graphics Interchange Format (graphic file - often a diagram)
JPG/JPEG	Joint Photo Experts Group (graphic file - often a photograph)
PDF	Adobe Acrobat Portable Data Format
PPS	Microsoft PowerPoint Slideshow
PPT	Microsoft PowerPoint Presentation
RTF	Rich Text Format
XLS	Microsoft Excel Spreadsheet

An example of this in practice is as follows:

Moss, S. (2003) <u>Utilising WebCT to enhance staff development and training within university halls of residence</u>. [Internet] Leeds, Moss, S. PDF document available from: <http://members.lycos.co.uk/mosscv/mossvlc.pdf> [Accessed 20th May, 2005].

CD-ROMs

Written electronic information sources are becoming much more commonplace. One media by which information may be given electronically is on a CD-ROM. In order to reference a CD-ROM within a bibliography, follow the same conventions as for a book, and at the end of the reference include the word CD-ROM in square brackets e.g.

Hind, D. (2002) <u>Transferable Personal Skills</u>. 2nd edition. Sunderland, Business Education Publishers Limited. [CD-ROM]

Electronic Journals

Electronic journals or e-journals are available via the world wide web. There are a variety of factors with electronic journals that can make them difficult to reference. Journals vary a great deal in style. Some may be an exact replica of a paper journal, produced as Adobe Acrobat PDF documents, whilst others may take on a complete new form in an electronic format, with different page numbering to the paper form of the same journal, whilst some e-journals are only available online. How you go about referencing e-journal articles is dependant on the following:

- If the e-journal is an exact replica of the paper form of the journal, with the same page numbering, it may be simpler to reference the journal as if it were the paper journal.
- If the journal article being accessed is only produced online, requires no special authorisation to access it and has no paper equivalent, it may be simpler to reference it as if it was a web page.
- The more complex e-journals are those that are produced both online and in paper format, however the page numbering and layout of the online and paper journals differs between the two. This is usually the case with journal articles that are accessed via university libraries, and that appear as HTML pages rather than Adobe Acrobat PDF documents. Where this is the case, the following conventions apply to the bibliographical reference:
- The name of the author/editor using the same convention as for books.
  e.g. McGeer, B.
- A space and then the year of publication of the article in brackets.
  e.g. McGeer, B. (2004)
- A space and then the article title written in sentence case, and followed by a full-stop.
  e.g. McGeer, B. (2004) When the top dog is of a different breed.
- A space and then the title of the e-journal written in title case, underlined or italicised and followed by a full-stop that is not underlined or italicised.
  e.g. McGeer, B. (2004) When the top dog is of a different breed. American Banker.
- A space and the word Internet in square brackets.
  e.g. McGeer, B. (2004) When the top dog is of a different breed. American Banker. [Internet]
- A space and then the exact date of publication of the journal article, followed by a comma.
  e.g. McGeer, B. (2004) When the top dog is of a different breed. American Banker. [Internet] 24th February,
- A space and then the volume number and issue number of the journal, followed by a comma.
  e.g. McGeer, B. (2004) When the top dog is of a different breed. American Banker. [Internet] 24th February, Volume 169, Issue 36.
- A space and then the page number range of the article, followed by a full-stop.
  e.g. McGeer, B. (2004) When the top dog is of a different breed. American Banker. [Internet] 24th February, Volume 169, Issue 36. pp.30-35.
- A space and the words 'Available from' (without the apostrophes) followed by a colon and the URL of the journal within triangular brackets. At this point your discretion is necessary, as to whether to copy and paste the entire contents of the URL, or to use the URL of the portal that allowed you to access the journal. An example of where this discretion is necessary is given below.
  http://web19.epnet.com/citation.asp?tb=1&_ug=dbs+buh+sid+09A995D A%2D5AD1%2D49D8%2DB35C%2DAF91279A3A09%40sessionmgr6+AC 18&_us=cst+0%3B1%3B2+dstb+ES+fh+0+hd+0+hs+%2D1+or+Date+ri+KAA ACB2B00004883+sl+0+sm+ES+ss+SO+84E3&_uso=db%5B0+%2Dbuh+hd+0+op% 5B2+%2DAnd+op%5B1+%2DAnd+op%5B0+%2D+st%5B2+%2D+st%5B1+% 2D+st%5B0+%2Dpersonal++skills+tg%5B2+%2D+tg%5B1+%2D+tg%5B0+% 2D+A040&cf=1&fn=1&rn=5

This URL is the full address that was given for one journal article, it contains a variety of parameters and access codes, that are simply not necessary or relevant to include within the reference. As the journal article was accessed via Leeds Metropolitan University's learning centre online pages, it is more sensible to use that URL instead - http://www.lmu.ac.uk/lis/lss/.

e.g. McGeer, B. (2004) When the top dog is of a different breed. <u>American Banker</u>. [Internet] 24th February, Volume 169, Issue 36. pp.30-35. Available from: <http://www.lmu.ac.uk/lis/lss>

- A space and then the exact date that the article was accessed within square brackets, followed by a full-stop.

e.g. McGeer, B. (2004) When the top dog is of a different breed. <u>American Banker</u>. [Internet] 24th February, Volume 169, Issue 36. pp.30-35. Available from: <http://www.lmu.ac.uk/lis/lss> [Accessed 28th April, 2004].

Government Reports and Publications (not Parliamentary Acts)

For many courses official government publications need to be accessed for certain assignments. In order to reference these within a bibliography, the following information is required:

- The name of the department responsible for writing the report/publication, written in title case, and followed by a full-stop.

  e.g. Department for Culture, Media and Sport – Tourism Division.

- A space and then the year that the report/publication was published in brackets.

  e.g. Department for Culture, Media and Sport – Tourism Division. (2000)

- A space and then the title of the report/publication, written in sentence case and underlined or italicised, and followed by a full-stop that is not underlined or italicised.

  e.g. Department for Culture, Media and Sport – Tourism Division. (2000) <u>Tomorrow's tourism</u>.

- A space and then the edition number of the report/publication (only if it is not the first edition). Please note that this information is not applicable in this example.

  e.g. Department for Culture, Media and Sport – Tourism Division. (2000) <u>Tomorrow's tourism</u>.

- A space and then the place of publication followed by a comma.

  e.g. Department for Culture, Media and Sport – Tourism Division. (2000) <u>Tomorrow's tourism</u>. London,

- A space and then the department responsible for producing the publication, followed by a full-stop.

  e.g. Department for Culture, Media and Sport – Tourism Division. (2000) <u>Tomorrow's tourism</u>. London, Department for Culture Media and Sport.

Parliamentary Acts

Acts of parliament may sometimes be referred to within student work. They are referenced within a bibliography by providing the following information:

- The name of the act written in title case and the year of the act underlined or italicised.

  e.g. <u>National Minimum Wage Act</u> 1998

- A space and then the chapter(s) of the act that have been referred to in brackets.
  e.g. <u>National Minimum Wage Act</u> 1998 (c. 39)
- A space and then the place of publication followed by a comma.
  e.g. <u>National Minimum Wage Act</u> 1998 (c. 39) London,
- A space and then the name of the publisher followed by a full-stop.
  e.g. <u>National Minimum Wage Act</u> 1998 (c. 39) London, HMSO.

Research Reports

Students often use research reports, as they contain valuable and original data. To reference these within a bibliography the following information is required:

- The name of the report author followed by a full-stop, (be that an individual or an organisation that wrote the report). The same convention applies here as with books.
  e.g. Mintel International Group.
- A space and then the year of publication in brackets.
  e.g. Mintel International Group. (2004)
- A space and then the report title written in sentence case, and underlined or italicised, followed by a full-stop that is not underlined or italicised.
  e.g. Mintel International Group. (2004) <u>Travel insurance</u>.
- A space and then the report number or edition (if not the first) followed by a full-stop. In this example this is not applicable.
  e.g. Mintel International Group. (2004) <u>Travel insurance</u>.
- A space and then the place of publication followed by a comma.
  e.g. Mintel International Group. (2004) <u>Travel insurance</u>. London,
- A space and then the name of the publisher followed by a full-stop.
  e.g. Mintel International Group. (2004) <u>Travel insurance</u>. London, Mintel International Group.

Dissertations/Theses

All honours degrees, masters degrees, and PhD's require the production of a thesis, frequently referred to as a dissertation. Many university libraries keep copies of the higher quality ones within their library book stock. Dissertations and theses may be used as information sources, and can prove to be very useful – as they will usually contain original research results. In order to reference a dissertation/thesis within your bibliography, the following information is required:

- The name of the author, written in the same convention as for books.
  e.g. Moss, S.
- A space and then the year of publication in brackets.
  e.g. Moss, S. (2001)
- A space and then the title of the thesis written in sentence case, this is underlined or italicised, and followed by a full-stop that is not underlined or italicised.
  e.g. Moss, S. (2001) <u>Marketing Norfolk tourist attractions online – a critical evaluation</u>.
- A space and then the level of the thesis/dissertation followed by a comma.
  e.g. Moss, S. (2001) <u>Marketing Norfolk tourist attractions online – a critical evaluation</u>. BA (Hons.) dissertation,

- A space and then the name of the awarding institution followed by a full-stop.

  e.g. Moss, S. (2001) <u>Marketing Norfolk tourist attractions online – a critical evaluation</u>. BA (Hons.) dissertation, Leeds Metropolitan University.

Television Programmes

Television can prove to be valuable in providing high quality information – especially with the onset of digital TV and entire channels dedicated to factual documentaries. As well as this, news and current affairs programmes can often give valuable and more up to date information than what is available from many printed information sources.

In order to reference a television programme, within a bibliography, the following information is required:

- The name of the programme written in title case followed by a full-stop.

  e.g. Mark Williams on the Rails.
- A space and then the year that the programme was produced in brackets.

  e.g. Mark Williams on the Rails. (2003)
- A space and then the episode title written in sentence case, this should be underlined or italicised and followed by a full-stop that is not underlined or italicised. Please note, that with some television programmes there will not be an episode title, this is often the case with news bulletins, and one-off documentaries that are not a part of a series.

  e.g. Mark Williams on the Rails. (2003) <u>Speed and power</u>.
- A space and then the place of production followed by a comma.

  e.g. Mark Williams on the Rails. (2003) <u>Speed and power</u>. Manchester,
- A space and then the channel on which the programme was broadcast followed by a comma.

  e.g. Mark Williams on the Rails. (2003) <u>Speed and power</u>. Manchester, Discovery Channel,
- A space and then the date that the programme was broadcast followed by a full-stop.

  e.g. Mark Williams on the Rails. (2003) <u>Speed and power</u>. Manchester, Discovery Channel, 28th April, 2004.

Videos/DVDs

Most university libraries now contain audio/video materials, that can be very useful sources of information. When referencing a video or DVD the following information is necessary:

- The title of the video/DVD written in title case, and followed by a full-stop, if this is a recorded video, it may be the title of a television programme.

  e.g. The Blue Planet.
- A space and then the series number of the video/DVD followed by a full-stop (if indeed it is one of a series – this is not always the case, and if it is not the case, this information may be omitted). Please note that this information is not applicable in this example.

  e.g. The Blue Planet.
- A space and then the year of publication in brackets.

  e.g. The Blue Planet. (2001)

- A space and then the title of the actual episode written in sentence case and underlined or italicised, followed by a full-stop that is not underlined or italicised (as with television programmes this information may not be applicable – if this is the case you may omit this from the reference).
  e.g. The Blue Planet. (2001) Deep trouble.
- A space and then the place that the video/DVD was published, followed by a comma (if this information is available).
  e.g. The Blue Planet. (2001) Deep trouble. London,
- A space and then the name of the publisher followed by a full-stop.
  e.g. The Blue Planet. (2001) Deep trouble. London, BBC Worldwide Ltd.
- A space and then the date that the programme was broadcast followed by a comma (only include this information if you are using a video from a library that contains a programme that has been recorded from the television). Please note that this information is not applicable in this example, as this is a purchased DVD.
  e.g. The Blue Planet. (2001) Deep trouble. London, BBC Worldwide Ltd.
- The format of the information source within square brackets. Use [video: VHS] for VHS video tapes, and [video: DVD] for DVDs.
  e.g. The Blue Planet. (2001) Deep trouble. London, BBC Worldwide Ltd. [DVD]

Conferences

Conferences and conference papers may often be published, and contain useful research information. In order to reference a conference within a bibliography the following information is required:

- The name of the conference written in title case, followed by a comma.
  e.g. Learning, Teaching and Assessment Conference,
- A space and then the number of the conference, followed by a full stop – if this is the first conference, there is no need to include this information.
  e.g. Learning, Teaching and Assessment Conference, 2nd.
- A space and then the year of the conference followed by a full-stop.
  e.g. Learning, Teaching and Assessment Conference, 2nd. 2002.
- A space and then the location of the conference followed by a comma.
  e.g. Learning, Teaching and Assessment Conference, 2nd. 2002. Leeds Metropolitan University,
- A space and then the year of publication of the conference paper being referred to in brackets.
  e.g. Learning, Teaching and Assessment Conference, 2nd. 2002. Leeds Metropolitan University, (2002)
- A space and then the title of the conference paper written in sentence case, this must be underlined or italicised, and followed by a full-stop that is not underlined or italicised.
  e.g. Learning, Teaching and Assessment Conference, 2nd. 2002. Leeds Metropolitan University, (2002) Evaluating the use of WebCT to support module delivery.
- A space and the name(s) of the author/editors of the paper, written using the same conventions as for books.
  e.g. Learning, Teaching and Assessment Conference, 2nd. 2002. Leeds Metropolitan University, (2002) Evaluating the use of WebCT to support module delivery. Hind, D. and Hayward, R.

- A space and then the place of publication followed by a comma.

  e.g. Learning, Teaching and Assessment Conference, 2nd. 2002. Leeds Metropolitan University, (2002) <u>Evaluating the use of WebCT to support module delivery</u>. Hind, D. and Hayward, R. Leeds,

- A space and the name of the publisher followed by a full-stop.

  e.g. Learning, Teaching and Assessment Conference, 2nd. 2002. Leeds Metropolitan University, (2002) <u>Evaluating the use of WebCT to support module delivery</u>. Hind, D. and Hayward, R. Leeds, Leeds Metropolitan University.

Other Sources

There are various other sources of secondary and tertiary information which can be gathered to use in your reports and essays. It is important only to use published sources of information that may easily be traced back to their source.

This section on Harvard referencing has demonstrated the technique that is necessary for the most common types of information sources that students use. Invariably some people will use other sources not listed here. If that is the case, and you do not know how to reference that particular source, make sure that you gather as much information about the source as possible, including, author(s), date of publication, titles, and what format the information source takes.

Sometimes you will have to make the best possible guess as to how to reference an information source. Where this is the case remember to be consistent throughout your bibliography, and do not reference the same types of source material in differing ways.

Consistency within a bibliography is something that cannot be stressed enough. Make sure that the correct formats are followed, and that titles are either underlined or italicised (but not both formats in the same bibliography), to give your finished bibliography a professional appearance.

4.2   Sample Work Excerpt and Bibliography

What follows now is a sample piece of writing that contains several in-text references. After the piece of writing there is a bibliography of the sources used, written in the Harvard Style.

The Internet

'The development of the internet ranks in importance alongside the invention of the railways, the car, electricity, the telephone and the TV' (*BT Plc, 1999, p.4*). The internet is a giant digital information database, that can be accessed from most new Personal Computers (PCs) purchased over the last eight years, and certainly in all new PCs purchased today, as well as a number of other devices including palmtop computers, and mobile telephones (*Clark, 1999*).

Growth in internet usage is largely limited to North America, parts of Western Europe, and Japan (*WTO, 2000*). Asia and in particular China are areas that currently have comparatively few users when compared to North America and Western Europe, however adoption and growth of the internet in Asia and China is increasing rapidly. China is predicted to have more internet users than the USA in future years (Ibid).

One component of the internet is the World Wide Web (WWW) which consists of millions of web sites, which in turn consist of web pages, that are linked to other web sites and other web pages. There are over 800 million web pages already on the internet, and 300,000 new web pages are added each week (*BT Plc, 1999*). Web pages are written using a language called Hypertext Markup Language (HTML) (*Wentk, 1999*).

People connecting to the internet are indicating in greater numbers that they are doing so in order to help themselves do what they would in the real world – this often means shopping (*McClellan, 1999*). 'Two in five users rate access to leisure and travel information as their favourite activity on the net' (*Martin, 1999, p.7*).

Bibliography

British Telecommunications Plc. (1999) The world at your fingertips – your guide to the internet. London, BT Plc.

Clark, L. (1999) Heineken is the first to bring the pub to your palmtop. Computer Weekly. 16th December 1999, p. 6.

Martin, A. (1999) The internet – cant live without I.T. Attractions Management. September 1999, p.7.

McClellan, J. (1999) The Guardian guide to shopping on the internet. London, Fourth Estate.

Wentk, R. (1999) The Which? guide to computers for small businesses. London, Which? Books.

World Tourism Organisation. (2000) Marketing tourism destinations online. Madrid, World Tourism Organisation Business Council.

As you can see in the piece of work, every in-text reference is contained within the bibliography beneath. You may also note that when providing an in-text reference you may use abbreviated terms and acronyms, however these must be written out in full in the bibliography, e.g. WTO in-text is the World Tourism Organisation in the bibliography.

Also take note that the bibliographical references appear in alphabetical order, rather than in the order that they were used in-text.

If two identical authors appeared in the bibliography, the order that their entries would go in would be determined by the year of publication (earliest first). If as was the case earlier in the chapter where the same author has more than one bibliographical entry, for the same year, the years are then allocated a letter, a, b,c, etc as:

Blackburn, C. (2004a) <u>Cheap student rail travel</u>. Barnsley, Dalesman Publishing.

Blackburn, C. (2004b) <u>Rail privatisation in the UK</u>. Sheffield, Kubon Books.

Blackburn, C. (2004c) <u>Trans-Pennine rail travel</u>. Barnsley, Dalesman Publishing.

5.   The Documents of Meetings

5.1   Notice of Meeting

In order for people to attend a meeting they have to know about it. Formal notification is called the notice. Several examples are shown below, the format depending upon personal choice and also whether the meetings are regular ones or a 'one-off'.

Nelson Mandela College   Pan-African Society

Notice of Committee Meeting

A meeting of the Committee will be held on:

Day: Date:

Time: Venue:

Please notify me by.. .. .. if you have any items you would like to include in the agenda.

Signed:

Secretary

Walton Manufacturing

Memorandum

To: All Departmental Staff

From: Department Head

Date: 11.10.200_.

Subject: Departmental meeting

The monthly departmental meeting will be held on Wednesday 22 October at 2pm. in Room GO14.

Notice of Public Meeting

Proposed By-pass, Overley

A meeting of residents to discuss the recent plans for the by-pass is to be held on:
Tuesday 7 May at 7.30 pm.
In School Hall, Overley Primary School

You are invited to attend to hear the Council's proposal and to make your views known.

Signed: D. Rees Secretary, Community Council

5.2 Agenda

For most meetings, it is essential to let participants know the content of the meeting before they arrive. It is possible to do this in a combined notice and agenda, but the agenda itself may contain items which participants want to table (discuss) once they know that a meeting will take place. In this case such requests must reach the Secretary in sufficient time (see the example above).

The agenda is essentially the menu of discussion topics for the meeting, set out in the order they will be debated.

A typical combined notice and agenda might be as follows:

The next committee meeting of the Nelson Mandela College Pan-African Society will take place on Monday 18 October 200 at 1.30 pm in the Students' Union Office.

Agenda

1. Apologies for absence.

2. Minutes of the last meeting.

3. Matters arising.

4. Arrangements for visit of delegation from Mozambique.

5. Proposal to introduce mail-order goods facility:
   That a link with Traidcraft, Newcastle-upon-Tyne, be forged to promote the purchase of mail order goods which directly benefit African producers of goods and to benefit Society funds.

   Propser: Ben Nkomo
   Seconder. Andreis de Groot

6. Any other business.

7. Date of next meeting.

Such an agenda allows participants to see clearly the topics under discussion.

However, it is common practice where a large number of participants is expected, for the Secretary to prepare a chair's agenda which enlarges upon the information available to ordinary participants. This will allow the smooth flow of information and explanations and allow the chair to seemingly 'ad lib' at ease. For example:

Federation of Textile Manufacturers North Wessex Branch
Bi-Monthly Meeting
Thursday 26 November 7.30 pm
Balcon Suite, Haldene Motel, Worthington

1.	Apologies for absence.	Andrew Fairley in hospital.
2.	Minutes of last meeting.	Already circulated.
3.	Matters arising.	Mrs Holmes to report on correspondence with national HQ.
4.	Arrangements for Christmas Dinner Dance.	All in hand for 17 Dec. at Black Lion Hotel. Coach to pick up those who have booked transport from Venn Park at 19.45.
5.	200 Programme.	Provisional programme attached.
6.	Any other business.	Jo Farmer likely to raise question of sponsorship of local bowls team again. Brought up topic last year defeated 9-3.
7.	Date of next meeting.	Thurs. Jan 14? Venue: Skilton Hall?

5.3   Minutes

From the Latin word 'minutiae' (small details), minutes provide a record of what has been said or decided in a meeting. It is normal practice to distribute the minutes of the previous meeting with the agenda for the next meeting – allowing participants to read through and check them. To distribute them at the beginning of a meeting is an inefficient use of time (and can indeed give justification to the complaint that meetings are slow.)

You will have noticed that 'Minutes of the last meeting' appears as the second heading of the sample agenda above. The minutes will be accepted as a true and accurate record of what took place only if everyone is in agreement. Advance circulation of the minutes allows people to check their own notes or memories and to raise any discrepancies. Someone may feel that their comments have been misinterpreted and want the record put straight.

There are three main ways to write minutes. These are:

(i)   Narrative minutes.
(ii)   Resolution minutes.
(iii) Action minutes.

(i)   Narrative Minutes

To narrate means to tell a story. Consequently narrative minutes relate who said what in the meeting. This will require editing skills on the part of the secretary to include only essential information and also to convert direct speech into indirect speech.

(ii)   Resolution Minutes

To resolve means to take a decision. Resolution minutes record only the decisions made, not how they were reached or who made what points in the debate. If the meeting has reached no decisions, resolution minutes would be inappropriate.

(iii)   Action Minutes

Action minutes are a combination of brief narrative minutes and a clear guide about who is to take responsibility for particular actions. Such a clear allocation of duties has its advantages but may be inappropriate if no follow-up actions are necessary.

Examples of the three types of minutes follow.

Extract from meeting of a local branch of the Society of Office Personnel:

Chair	...May I congratulate everyone on their first-class efforts to establish relationships with the Rosslyn branch. There have been a number of initiatives which are now bearing fruit. In particular, we must thank Doris Hardy for her ...um... unstinting efforts.
All	Hear, hear.
Chair	Perhaps we should issue a formal invitation to the Rosslyn branch to send a representative along to our next meeting. What do people think about that?
Various	Good idea ... Yes ... Excellent etc.
Chair	Right, that's unanimous. Jo, could you take care of that?
Secretary	Certainly.
Chair	Moving on to the next item, ... um, item 4 on the agenda. That a levy be introduced on guests to society functions of 50% above the ticket price. Denis, would you like to speak in support of your proposal?
Denis	Thank you, Mr Chairman. As you will all be aware, we are, as a society, conscious of the financial constraints under which we operate. This proposal is an attempt to increase revenue to support our current activities without being a disincentive to our guests. If we take last summer's outing, which I organised ... let me circulate a copy of the accounts for this .... (shuffle, shuffle) ..., you'll note that ....(detail omitted) Consequently, I propose that such a modest increase in prices would increase our funds substantially.
Chair	Thank you. Denis. Does anyone have any comments to make before we put it to the vote?
Zoe	Mr Chairman, as you know, I am a recent recruit to the society but I believe that this proposal is long overdue. We must be one of only a handful of societies of any sort where the members actually subsidise the guests by putting their hands into their own pockets. In today's world, we cannot survive like this. Who knows what we might be asked to help out with next?
Ricardo	No, Mr Chairman, I cannot agree. One of the main purposes of this society is to promote the cause of professional pride in office work and to attract new members. The principal way in which we can do this is to organise and host events likely to ... um ... appeal to potential members. To then say to them, 'Well of course, if you want to come, you'll have to pay half as much again' seems a very strange notion of recruitment to me. Etc, etc.
Chair	Thank you all. Let's put the proposal to the vote. (Re-reads it aloud). Those in favour – (Secretary and Chair count show of hands). Those against (count hands). Right, ladies and gentlemen, I make that seven in favour and two against. Proposal carried. We'll need to adjust the prices for the office machinery show. Carole, as you are organising the printing of programmes, can you amend the entry prices accordingly. Etc, etc.

Below follows the way in which the minutes of this extract of the meeting have been transcribed in the three different formats:

Narrative Minutes

3. The Chairman thanked all members of the committee for their efforts to establish ties with the Rosslyn branch. This was now proving productive. The committee echoed the Chairman's particular thanks to Ms D Hardy. The committee unanimously agreed to invite a representative of the Rosslyn branch to the next committee meeting and Mr Brown undertook to do this.

4. Proposal of levy. Mr Stenhouse argued that accepting the proposal would transform the branch's finances, whilst still making the price of events attractive to guests.

    Miss Howell supported the proposal, indicating that it would put the branch in line with most other organisations.

    Mr R Pasquale argued against the proposal, fearing the detrimental effect it could have on recruitment.

    The motion was passed by seven votes to two with immediate effect.

Resolution Minutes

3. It was resolved to invite a member of the Rosslyn branch to the next committee meeting.
4. It was resolved to charge a levy of 50% forthwith on guests attending social events.

Action Minutes

3. The Chairman thanked all members of the committee, particularly Ms D Hardy, for their efforts to establish ties with the Rosslyn branch. A representative from the Rosslyn branch would be invited to the next committee meeting.

4. Proposal on levy. Mr Stenhouse argued that accepting the proposal would transform the branch's finances, whilst still making the price of events attractive to guests.

    Miss E Howell supported the proposal, indicating that it would put the branch on line with other organisations.

    Mr R Pasquale argued against the proposal, fearing the detrimental effect it could have on recruitment.

    The motion was passed seven to two with immediate effect.

5. Entry prices for forthcoming exhibition to be amended.

Which type of minutes you decide upon is dependent on the nature of the meeting.

Action minutes are a useful tool for reminding people who has responsibility for what, but may not be appropriate in voluntary organisations, where participants may feel they are being coerced.

Resolution minutes are very economical, but if nothing has been decided, there may be nothing to report (in which case, one may question whether the meeting was necessary – although, of course briefing meetings may involve only the one way transfer of information.)

Narrative minutes remain the most popular. Although longer, they indicate the relative amount and effectiveness of the contributions (or lack of them) of individuals in the meeting.

Whichever style of minutes you adopt you should be consistent – whatever you do, don't mix style in the same document.

There are several other points to notice about minutes:

- In resolution minutes adopt the passive voice. *(It was resolved.)*
- Use the past tense throughout. Sometimes, for consistency, this will involve references to other events or activities in the pluperfect tense. *(Ms Green commented that it had been traditional until last year to hold a children's Christmas party.)*
- Aim for consistency, brevity and relevance yet with sufficient detail to be understood.

6. Electronic Communications

In the twenty-first century, technological advances have had an undeniable impact upon the way we communicate. It is now possible to build a relationship with a person on the other side of the world, very quickly – and without ever meeting, speaking or seeing one another.

Through what can be very impersonal mediums your written word represents you – therefore it is essential that what you write leaves a positive impression upon the person who is reading it.

6.1 Netiquette

Netiquette put simply means network etiquette, this covers a set of basic guidelines that highlight best practice when communicating online. A list of these guidelines now follows:

- DO NOT WRITE YOUR MESSAGES IN CAPITAL LETTERS as it may look like you are angry or shouting.
- Use rounded easy to read fonts such as Arial.
- Keep your communications concise and to the point.
- Be polite – behave in a virtual world in the same manner that you would in the real world, so remember 'please' and 'thank you'.
- Never swear or use bad language or derogatory terms that others may find offensive – this could have legal implications for you or the organisation of which you are a part.
- Read your messages before you send them, checking for spelling mistakes, grammatical errors and typing errors.
- If you receive any kind of electronic communication that you find offensive for any reason – DO NOT reply to it straight away – for all you know there may have been no offence meant. If this does happen it can be best to wait before composing a calm and level headed response that highlights the offence caused and questions the necessity of causing such offence. It can also be a good idea under such circumstances to speak face to face or over the telephone to the sender of the message.
- Emoticons are simple facial expressions created by a combination of strokes on a key board. Emoticons are used to punctuate a message with emotions – this helps to enforce any meanings within a message. The table below contains examples of some emoticons and their meanings – some software such as Microsoft Outlook XP will actually convert the typed emoticons into faces expressing the meaning of them.

Emoticon	Message
:)	Happy
:(	Sad
:-o	Surprised
;)	Winking
:<	Annoyed
:D	Laughing
:I	Indifference

6.2   Email

The popularity of email has been sparked by its accessibility, cost effectiveness and speed; it is now possible to send a message across the world in seconds at virtually no cost at all. Unfortunately these very positive factors have also given rise to an abundance of problems, including Spam, and viruses. Spam is junk email that is often sent for advertising purposes. Analysts currently suggest that seventy per cent of all email on the web is spam, and that this figure is rising. A virus is a program or piece of code that has a malicious payload and can infect machines that it comes into contact with, causing damage to the machine.

The two most popular types of email in the world today are web-based email and POP3. The largest providers of web based email are MSN (including Hotmail) and Yahoo! Both of these providers give users a free email account, from which they may send and receive email. POP3 email is generally managed by specialist software called an email client on a users home or work computer – e.g. Microsoft Outlook.

Both types of email system have advantages and disadvantages; however the spread of computer viruses is most common through POP3 accounts, where users inadvertently open infected messages or attachments which may infect the user's machine having any number of effects. With web based providers such as Hotmail and Yahoo! your incoming and outgoing messages are more likely to be checked online with an up to date virus checker. Therefore if you are using POP3 email, to protect yourself you must not only have anti-virus software installed you should also download and install the latest updates or 'patches' to your machine on at least a weekly basis. Never open an attachment that has been sent by somebody you do not know, or an attachment that has the extension .com, .pif, .bat. or .exe.

The above has been stated to help users of email appreciate how easily viruses are spread, and whilst this chapter is strictly on written communication, a little 'cybersense' is a must for anyone using email.

When composing your emails, and replying to other emails, the core rules of netiquette apply so that you present yourself in a positive manner.

Emails may be sent to one or many recipients. It is not good practice to forward emails that you may find humorous to many other recipients. This is the webs version of chain letters, and apart from clogging inboxes, may lead certain recipients to believe that all of your forwarded messages will be rubbish, and therefore not read them.

If you are sending an email to a person or more than one person, and the email is equally intended for all of them, their email addresses will go in the 'TO' field. If you wish somebody else to read the email, although it is not directly intended for the other person, their address would be placed in the 'CC' field of a message. CC stands for carbon copy. An example of where you may use this would be if you were emailing a colleague, and you wanted your line manager to see that you were emailing the colleague, you would include the line manager in the CC field.

Another field within some email applications is 'BCC', this stands for Blind Carbon Copy. An email address placed in a BCC field does not appear in the email received by those in the TO and CC fields. You would use this if you wanted to demonstrate to somebody that you had sent an email, but you did not want the recipient to know that the other person had seen the message. An example of where you may use this in the workplace would be to email a colleague, and include the line manager in the BCC field. The colleague would receive the email, and so would the line manager, however the colleague would be unaware that the line manager had received the email.

6.3   Web Pages

If you are creating a website as part of a student project, an assessed piece of work, or indeed for industry, there are many core rules to follow. Below are featured a summary of tips that allow for best practice in web design:

- The core rules of netiquette most definitely apply with regard to written content.
- Use contrasting colours that stand out – however do not use loud garish colours. Dark text on a pastel shaded background is a good idea, as is light text on a dark background. Try to avoid white backgrounds, as people with visual disabilities sometimes find them difficult to read against.
- Be consistent in your use of fonts and colours so as not to confuse visitors to your site.
- Try not to have more than two 'screenfulls' of information per page, so that the reader is not continually having to scroll down the screen – pages with a lot of information on can also be slow to load.
- Keep in mind that not everybody has a large monitor, so design web pages for an area that is no larger than 800 x 600 pixels.
- Write pages for scanability – many people skim read web pages, so be economical and concise with your wording.
- Make sure that hyperlinks to other pages are clearly labelled, so that the user does not have to spend time hunting for them.
- Be aware of copyright issues – copyright rules vary for materials that are produced in an electronic format.
- Keep the structure of your website simple, a site where pages are easy to navigate is more likely to keep a visitor than a site that is complex and difficult to navigate.
- Make sure that your site contains contact details such as an email address, in the case of corporate websites, telephone/fax numbers, and actual addresses of premises should also be included.
- Not everybody that uses the internet reads for themselves. Many blind and visually impaired people have found freedom online due to advances in technologies that allow for the written content of their screens to be read out loud by screen reading software. Of course this does not work on graphics and pictures, so to facilitate the screen reading process of graphics and pictures alternative text tags (ALT tags) can be added to them using most web design software, or by adding an alt tag using written html. An ALT tag is used to provide a written description of a graphic or picture that

is as good as the picture itself. An ALT tag appears when a mouse pointer is held over a graphic or picture as in the diagram below. Where the mouse pointer has been held over the middle picture, the words 'The Sugarwell Courtyard' appear – these would be read by a screen reader.

6.4   Discussion Forums/Bulletin Boards/Newsgroups

All of the above fall under the category of being online communities of practice, whereby people with a common bond may meet and communicate via the internet. There are hundreds of thousands of these types of forums available today on every subject possible. In academia these online communication portals are used to great effect and can contribute significantly to the educational process. These mediums rely solely on the written word, so it is important that netiquette guidelines are adhered to.

Participation is essential in order to benefit from an online community. If you can visualise a community as an upturned cone, those closest to the centre of the cone near the top, are regular participants that gain a lot from taking part in online discussions through increased subject knowledge (see following diagram).

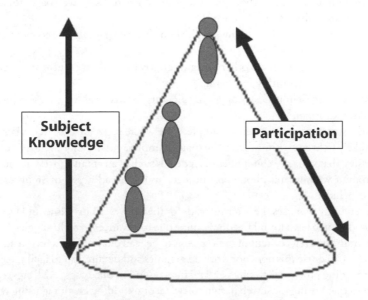

Courses that are delivered online, or courses that use a virtual learning environment (VLE) such as WebCT, or Blackboard to aid the delivery of course materials often use discussion forums for communicative purposes, as well as to stimulate discussion amongst students who may be geographically dispersed, and who may not have the opportunity to meet face to face.

Some examples of online communities are as follows:

- http://www.network54.com/Forum/193758 – Green (Environmentalist) Discussion Forum – this is an online discussion forum whereby people may make and respond to messages relating to the environment and environmental concerns in general. The common bond that the users of this board have is an interest in the environment.
- http://www.bepl.com – Business Education Publishers Ltd website, this is the website for the publishers of this book. There is a link on the front page of the site to 'Message Board' – click upon this link. This board may be used by anyone who wishes to pose a question to BEPL staff. If you wish to contact either of the authors of this book with regards to any of the contents of this book – please use this forum – don't be afraid to ask a question!
- http://pub18.bravenet.com/forum/show.php?usernum=1486811524&cpv=1 – The Apostrophe Protection Society – This is a bulletin board for people who wish to discuss the correct and incorrect use of the apostrophe in the English language, as well as other aspects of English grammar and punctuation.
- http://groups.yahoo.com/group/telescopes/ – Telescopes – this is an email newsgroup for amateur astronomers. The people who are members of this group share the common bond of having an interest in astronomy. This type of online community differs from the other two examples in that members of this group send and receive postings via email. Each posting will go to all members of the group as an email – therefore the core rules of netiquette are essential.

6.5   Instant Messengers

The use of instant messenger programs such as MSN Messenger, Yahoo! Messenger, AOL Instant Messenger and ICQ has grown rapidly over the last five years. Instant messengers can be used between people online to have a live text based conversation. Typically messages are short and emoticons are used to help enforce any meanings of messages.

Most people use instant messengers for personal reasons such as 'chatting' with friends. However these programs are becoming more increasingly used as a support tool in industry and academia. You must be aware that when using Instant Messenger programs for professional purposes, the core rules of netiquette should apply. Your online persona is representative of you as a person, and that is something you should always keep in mind.

7.   Using Images

One of the most effective ways of presenting information is through the use of visual images. It enhances and enlivens presentations and adds a degree of impact that words alone cannot achieve. Most of the information we assimilate comes through sight. In fact it is estimated that almost three quarters of all information we receive comes in this form. It is therefore a very powerful medium and you need to be able to use images to their best effect. In this section we shall examine the means by which images are used to simplify the presentation of all forms of information.

7.1   Graphical Communication

As we have seen, clear communication is not just a question of using words accurately. Sometimes, no matter how careful you are in selecting the right words in the right order, reading lists of continuous facts can be very confusing. There are just too many words. In such cases, an organisation chart can be very helpful. For a simple example:

> In the travel agency where I work are four sales girls under the management of the assistant manageress who is directly responsible to the owner/manager.

This could be represented simply by:

Organisation chart for a small company

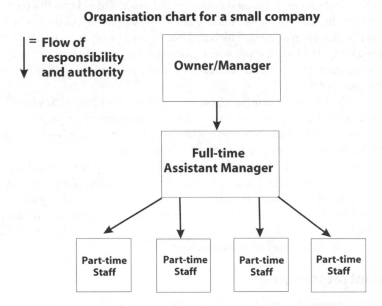

It shows clearly the status of each person. Here there are three different levels in the structure. Such a structure is called a hierarchy, and the more complex the hierarchy the easier it is to follow as a chart instead of as prose.

(i)   Diagnostic Charts

A chart can also be a more effective way of diagnosing a problem (e.g. motor, electrical, health) than chunks of prose. If one heading or section does not apply to your problem, you simply proceed to the one that does. For example, look at the two methods shown below to express when or if a married woman is entitled to a retirement pension. Read through the prose carefully, then proceed to the chart. Which do you find easier to understand?

> The earliest age at which a woman can draw a retirement pension is 60. On her own insurance she can get a pension when she reaches that age, if she has then retired from regular employment. Otherwise she has to wait until she retires or reaches age 65. At the age of 65, pensions can be paid irrespective of retirement. On her husband's insurance, however, she cannot get a pension, even though she is over 60, until he is aged 65 and retired from regular employment, or until he is 70 if he does not retire before reaching that age.

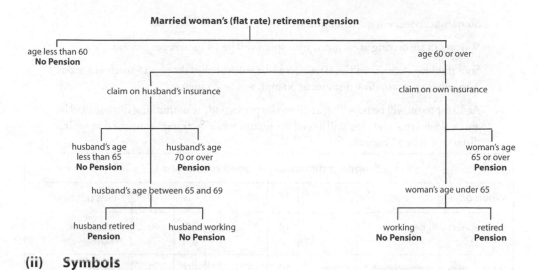

Married woman's (flat rate) retirement pension

age less than 60
No Pension

age 60 or over

claim on husband's insurance

claim on own insurance

husband's age less than 65
No Pension

husband's age 70 or over
Pension

woman's age 65 or over
Pension

husband's age between 65 and 69

woman's age under 65

husband retired
Pension

husband working
No Pension

working
No Pension

retired
Pension

(ii)   Symbols

We are all used to seeing road signs which indicate hazards, warnings, instructions or information. We know that triangular signs give a warning; circular signs give an order; and that square or oblong signs give information.

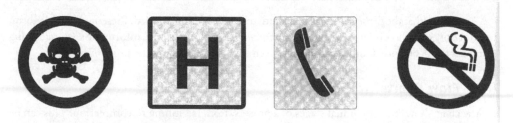

Symbols are used for two simple reasons:

- It means that there is international standardisation of signs. If you are on a holiday in France you don't have to work out what 'Défense de fumer' means if you can simply recognise one of the signs we have shown.
- The mind can absorb symbolic information far more rapidly than written information. This is crucial – when you are travelling at speed – at 60mph you are covering 30 metres per second! By the time you had tried to read 'Slippery road ahead' at 60mph you would probably have had an accident anyway!

Symbols can be used in any sphere of life where they are appropriate. They are an efficient way of communicating simple information rapidly. But symbols cannot communicate complex or lengthy information, and they must be instantly recognisable. If you have to puzzle over what a symbol might mean, it has failed in its purpose to communicate.

(iii)   Tables

Tables are a simple way of presenting information. They can be used for a variety of purposes and can present information very clearly, whilst being simple to compose.

On the following page, the same information is presented in both continuous prose and table-form:

Stopping distances in good conditions:

When you are driving at 30 mph, your speed will be 14 metres per second.

Your thinking distance will be 10 metres and it will actually take you 15 metres to brake. Altogether your stopping distance at 30 mph will be 25 metres.

At 40 mph you will be travelling at 20 metres per second. Your thinking distance will be about 25 metres and you will travel 26 metres while braking. Your total stopping distance will be 51 metres.

Stopping distances - in good conditions						
When driving at	30	40	50	60	70	miles per hour
your speed will be	14	20	25	30	40	metres per second
your thinking distance will be about	10	13	16	20	23	metres
your braking distance will be about	15	26	41	60	82	metres
your stopping distance will be about	25	39	57	80	105	metres

Notice that the prose information is both tedious and long-winded. Presented in table-form, it is not only easier to understand and to remember, but note that more information (the stopping distances at 50, 60 and 70 mph) can also be given in the same space as the prose original.

(iv)   Flow Charts

A flow chart shows the individual stages of a process, from beginning to completion. This can be useful if you want to show the sequence of actions. Here is a simple flow chart based upon how a mail-order catalogue works from the customer's point of view. Most flow charts are simply one point below another, joined by downward arrows.

More complicated flow charts include yes/no questions. These lead to alternative pathways according to whether the answer is yes or no.

Flow charts are typically used to draft instructions for computer programs.

(v)   Pie Charts

A pie chart is a form of visual presentation that breaks down a total figure into its different components. The pie chart below illustrates percentage of average household spending on a range of goods.

Such charts enable you to obtain an instant picture of the situation. They also emphasise the way in which the global amount has been divided. Thus they are a useful way to reinforce the idea of percentages spent on each of the items.

With a pie chart actual figures may be included, or percentages, or both. As with all forms of visual presentation the test is whether the method used and the information it contains is likely to aid the reader's understanding. Pie charts are valuable as ways of displaying proportions of a total. The larger the slice of the 'pie', the larger the proportion of the total. Because the pie is circular you need a protractor to divide the 360 degrees of the pie by the total number of whatever it is you are showing.

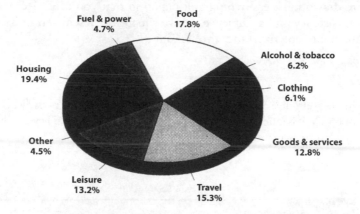

A breakdown of average household spending

(vi)   Bar Charts

Bar charts are used to compare different categories by presenting them in columns or rows of different height or length. Each category is displayed discretely and usually each column or row is of the same width. The bar chart below shows the growth of the self-employed as a percentage of the workforce over a period of time.

Bar charts need not necessarily be horizontally presented. Often a more emphatic effect can be achieved by showing them vertically, at an angle or in some other form.

These are also known as block graphs and are useful not just for showing proportions, but particularly if you wish to compare amounts. You can easily see how one 'stands' in relation to the others.

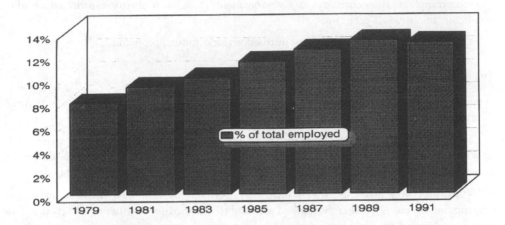

The growth of the self-employed as a % of the workforce

Bar charts are drawn most easily on graph paper, so that you can select the right scale and ensure consistency and accuracy, e.g., five squares represent ten units throughout, or five squares represent five units throughout.

(vii)   Maps

Maps are an extremely effective way to present information. We see this every day when we watch the weather forecast on TV. It is much easier to explain directions using a map. They can show the world, a continent, a country or merely directions within a town.

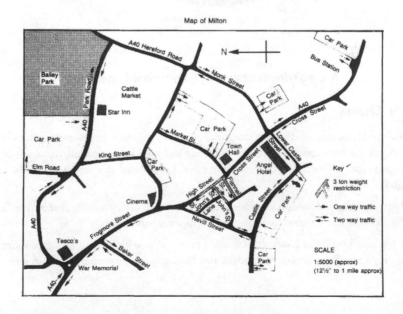

Map of Milton

8.   IT Skills for Written Communication

This section is designed to highlight the information technology skills (IT skills) that you should know in order to be able to make a variety of effective written communications. This page is not designed to teach you how to acquire these skills, however suggested internet links are provided that should be of help if you require to further develop any of your skills.

8.1   Word Processing Skills

You should be able to:

- Create a new document.
- Open a document.
- Close a document.
- Print and print preview a document.
- Save a document.
- Change the paper type and alignment (from portrait to landscape and vice versa).
- Use formatting such as changing fonts, font sizes, underlining text, **making text bold** *and italicised.*
- Use tabs and margins for correct alignment.
- Insert and write in text boxes and tables, and remove their borders to make them appear invisible, or change the lines of their borders, or individual cells.
- Create, edit and format tables.
- Copy/cut and paste text and other objects such as graphics.
- Use the spell checker to help ensure that your document does not contain spelling mistakes.
- Insert page numbers at the bottom of your pages starting at the correct page number – and centre them.
- Insert a page break.
- Insert a section break.
- Justify your text – so the right margin is aligned and paragraphs appear as neat 'blocks'.
- Double line space your text – this makes reading it by your assessor much easier.
- Perform a word count.
- For help and advice on the above using Microsoft Word visit http://www.microsoft.com/word/.

8.2   Email Skills

You should be able to:

- Compose and send emails to one person or several people.
- Use CC and BCC.
- Send and receive an attachment.
- Know when NOT to open an attachment.
- Reply to an email.
- Forward an email.
- Request a read receipt from a sent email.

For help and advice on the above using Microsoft Outlook visit http://www.microsoft.com/outlook.

8.3   Web Design Skills

You should be able to:

- Create and save a web page.
- Insert text into a web page and format it including changing fonts, font sizes, underlining text, **making text bold** *and italicised*.
- Insert a graphic into a web page.
- Add an ALT tag to a graphic.
- Insert a hyperlink into a web page.
- Change the colours of text and backgrounds on a web page.
- Create a page at a particular resolution.
- Insert tables, and make them invisible.
- Merge cells within a table.
- Use the FTP feature within your application to upload files onto a web server.

For help and advice on the above using Microsoft FrontPage visit http://www.microsoft.com/frontpage/, for help and advice on the above using Macromedia Dreamweaver visit http://www.macromedia.com/support/dreamweaver/.

8.4   Web Browsing Skills

You should be able to:

- Open a web page and browse it.
- Navigate using hyperlinks.
- Print web pages.
- Save a page.
- Copy and paste text from a web page.
- Save images from web pages.

For help and advice on the above using; Microsoft Internet Explorer visit http://www.microsoft.com/windows/ie/, for help with the above using Netscape Navigator visit http://help.netscape.com/.

8.5   Instant Messenger Skills

You should be able to:

- Download and install an instant message program (or programs) onto your computer.
- Add contacts to your list of friends within your instant message program.
- Write an instant message and send it to somebody on your list.
- Add an emoticon to a message.

For help and advice on the above using MSN Messenger go to http://messenger.msn.com/; Yahoo! Messenger go to http://messenger.yahoo.com; AOL Instant Messenger go to http://www.aim.com; and ICQ go to http://www.icq.com.

After reading this chapter please complete the following learning activities:

Learning Activities

1. Apply the techniques from within this chapter to your current or next piece of academic writing, and from doing so include the following elements within your work:

    •   In-text references from a variety of different types of information sources (books, journals, and the internet).

    •   Write up a full and proper Harvard style bibliography at the end of your work, of all in-text references within the piece – including the correct conventions for the ordering of information within references, the order of references within the bibliography, and what to do when information is missing.

2. Read the two paragraphs below, then answer the questions beneath them.

    It is true to say that people who are managed well are themselves capable of managing change and its effects more effectively. Organisational change requires the cooperation and commitment of key stakeholders including management and those persons trusted with delivering change. In order to manage this process key interpersonal and management skills are required. As a student your first introduction to this will be in the form of teamwork assignments.

    Refining these skills whilst studying will certainly go a long way in the workplace as being an effective manager of people through times of change is a very desirable attribute for an employee to possess.

    (i)   Identify which words in the above paragraph are:

    •   Component Words

    •   Verbs

    •   Nouns

    •   Adjectives

    (ii) The second paragraph contains no punctuation – add the missing punctuation marks to this paragraph.

3. Apply the techniques learned in this chapter to one of the following:

    (i)   A written letter of enquiry to an organisation that is relevant to the course that you are studying (ensure that your tutor reads this before you send it).

    (ii) A written academic report or essay for your course.

4. Have a look inside your email inbox; critically reflect upon the level of netiquette within your emails. Do they adhere to the rules of netiquette or not? Write a short reflective piece about this.

5. Assess your own ICT abilities for effective written communications – what are you good at, and which skills do you need to develop further? Visit some of the suggested online resources mentioned in the chapter for guidance.

Chapter Five
Numeracy Skills

After reading this chapter you will be able to:

1. Undertake basic arithmetic operations.
2. Present numerical data using tables.
3. Present data using graphs and pie charts.
4. Undertake basic statistical analysis of data.

It is important that you use numerical data skilfully. You will face many situations which require you to interpret data and communicate your conclusions to other people, whether it be presenting a club or society's annual accounts to its members, or showing trends in the sales of a product to management. The skill of communicating data, therefore, is an ES that you need to master.

In this chapter we assume that you are competent at basic arithmetic – the addition, subtraction, multiplication and division of whole numbers, fractions and decimals. If you feel you have a major weakness in this area you should seek to improve your arithmetic by asking for remedial help from your tutors or studying a basic school arithmetic book.

1.   Basic Arithmetic Operations

In this section we will investigate three common methods of expressing data:

- Ratios.
- Percentages.
- Index numbers.

1.1   Ratios

A ratio is a method of showing the relative size of one item in comparison to another. Ratios are frequently used to compare relative sizes, quantities, costs, or sales. Thus, a ratio shows the number of times that one quantity is contained in another quantity of the same kind.

To work out a ratio, the quantities to be expressed need to be converted into the same measure. For example, to determine the ratio of 30 days to one year, we need to express the period of one year in days (365 days). Normally, the ratio is then divided by the highest common factor. The ratio is therefore:

$$\frac{30 \text{ days}}{365 \text{ days}} = \frac{6}{73}$$

This is written as 6:73, which means the ratio of 30 days to one year is as 6 is to 73.

Another example would require you to express £0.75p as a ratio of £2.50. Once again you must find a common unit and so £2.50 is expressed in pence:

$$\frac{75}{250} = \frac{3}{10}$$

The ratio in this case is 3:10.

Ratios can be used for more than two quantities, for example when making a cake. The recipe might be 6 grammes of raisins, to 7 grammes of sugar, to 9 grammes of chocolate etc. Data expressed in this way can be used for working out simple calculations. For example, assume that a cash bonus is paid to 4 workers in the ratio of 9:11:13:15. If the total bonus is £480 then you can work out how much each worker will receive:

First add the proportions together (9+11+13+15 = 48) to give the total number of parts to the bonus. Then divide £480 by this number

$$\frac{£480}{48} = 10$$

Each part, therefore, is worth £10. Notice that this number is expressed in pounds. The cash bonus that each worker receives is calculated by multiplying his proportion by £10:

1st worker	9 x £10 =	£90
2nd worker	11 x £10 =	£110
3rd worker	13 x £10 =	£130
4th worker	15 x £10 =	£150
		£480

1.2   Percentages

Percentages are also ratios, and describe the rate of an item per hundred. If 15% of sales of the product come from the south of the country this means that for every 100 sales that are made in the country, 15 of them will be recorded in the south.

Expressing data as percentages gives a quick picture of the situation being described and is a common way of communicating data. Calculating percentages is straight-forward. The first step is to convert the data being described into a fraction. This shows it as a proportion of the total. The number to be expressed as a percentage is always divided by the base figure. Next this fraction is scaled up or down to express the fraction as a number divided by 100.

Using another sales example, assume that 1000 units of the product are sold in the country, and that 250 of these sales were made in the west. The fraction to be used to work out the percentage is:

$$\frac{250}{1000} \text{ which is then expressed as } \frac{25}{100}$$

The final stage is to convert this fraction into a percentage, by multiplying it by 100%

$$\frac{25}{100} \times 100\% = 25\%$$

Further examples are given below:

Example 1

Find 10% of £350

$$10\% = \frac{10}{100}$$

Therefore, 10% of £350 is

$$\frac{10}{100} \times £350 = £35$$

Example 2

Express 20 days as a percentage of one year

$$\frac{20}{365} = \frac{5.48}{100}$$

$$\frac{5.48}{100} \times 100\% = 5.48\%$$

This could be more simply written:

$$\frac{20}{365} \times 100\% = 5.48\%$$

1.3   Index Numbers

Using an index number is another way you can describe data, and is especially useful in showing trends. The purpose of index numbers is to show trends in a way that is easy to comprehend. This is done by comparing a set of figures with a base figure. First the base index is decided. This is commonly 100, might be 1, 10, or 100. The base value (e.g. production output in year 1) is assigned the base index (e.g. 100). To calculate subsequent indices, each data value (e.g. production output in years 2,3,4) is divided by the base data value and then multiplied by the base index. If you are making a comparison of how production output has varied over a time, then you could use index numbers to show the relative rises and falls in annual production. The annual production output of a factory was recorded:

Year	Production Output (Tins) (Data Values)
1	12000
2	14000
3	17000
4	18500

Year 1 is taken as being the base year against which all index numbers are compared. The index number is calculated in a similar way to percentages:

The year 1 index is 100 (the base)

The year 2 index is 14000 (the new production figure) divided by 12000 (the base year production figure) multiplied by 100.

$$\frac{14000}{12000} \times 100 = 117$$

The year 3 index is 17000 (the new production figure) divided by 12000 multiplied by 100.

$$\frac{17000}{12000} \times 100 = 133$$

The year 4 index is 18500 (the new production figure) divided by 12000 multiplied by 100.

$$\frac{18500}{12000} \times 100 = 158$$

Having taken 100 as the base index, it is easy to see that from year 1 to year 2 production output increased by 17%, from year 1 to year 3 by 33%, and from year 1 to year 4 by 58%. You can then draw interpretations from these index numbers, for example what accounted for such consistent growth.

There are many different types of indices, for example price indices and value indices. More sophisticated methods of calculating indices include such techniques as 'weighted indices' and 'several-item indices'. Such techniques are beyond the scope of this book and you should refer to a statistics textbook for a more detailed explanation of them.

2.   The Use of Tables

One useful way of presenting data is in the form of a table. Tables present numerical data visually. A good table shows data in a manner that highlights relationships between sets of data. At its simplest, a set of data gives values of a variable independent of any other factor. An example would be a table which shows the results of a machine which weighs all bags of flour after they have been filled to ensure that they equal or exceed the advertised weight; another would be a table to show the results of measuring the speed of cars on a motorway. Either of these examples could be presented as follows:

Weight of flour in each bag (kg)	Speed of each car on motorway (mph)
1.00	40
1.02	60
1.05	75
1.07	55
0.98	49
1.01	90
etc.	etc.

A more sophisticated version involves distinguishing classes of data items. For example, the machine weighing bags of flour might be able to distinguish between wholemeal flour, white flour and self-raising flour; a distinction between different lanes on the motorway could be made.

Weight of flour in each bag (kg)			Speed of each car on motorway (mph)		
Wholemeal	White	Self Raising	Lane 1	Lane 2	Lane 3
1.02	1.00	0.98	40	60	75
1.05	1.01	0.97	49	55	90
1.02	1.02	1.00	47	62	80
1.03	1.00	0.99	42	73	70
etc.	etc.	etc.	etc.	etc	etc.

Notice that each bag of flour has a weight, and each car a speed. The weight of flour in a bag can vary. The speed of a car on the motorway can vary. Weight and speed in these examples are termed 'variables'.

Consider a burning candle, the candle gets progressively shorter. You might have recorded the following data observing a candle.

Time of observation (Hrs: mins)	Length of candle (cm)
15.30	10.00
15.35	8.00
15.40	6.00
15.45	4.00
15.50	2.00
15.55	0.00

Most data collection and presentation concerns change of one variable in relation to change of another variable. Much data concerns change over a period of time. Most observations are recorded at intervals over a given period of time. In the example above the length of the candle was measured every five minutes. Examining the table it can be seen that as time progresses, the candle gets shorter. The length of the candle is dependent on the time. In this example, time is called the 'independent variable' and length of the candle the dependent variable.

A more sophisticated version of the table might give not only the time of the observation, but also the time from the first observation:

Time of observation (hrs: mins)	Time from the first observation	Length of candle (cm)
15.30	00	10.00
15.35	05	8.00
15.40	10	6.00
15.45	15	4.00
15.50	20	2.00
15.55	25	0.00

Processing the data in this way helps to show more clearly what relationship exists between data items. Time remains the independent variable, but now we can consider 'elapsed time', rather than 'clock time'.

Note that by using time as a variable, we could choose to take observations when we wished – we are no longer dependent on a bag of flour falling onto the weighing machine, or a car coming along the motorway. Time is a continuous quantity, as is the length of the candle, as the following table shows:

Time of observation (hrs: mins)	Elapsed time (mins)	% Elapsed time (%)	Length of Candle (cm)	% of total candle (%)
15.30	00	00	10.00	100
15.35	05	20	8.00	80
15.40	10	40	6.00	60
15.50	20	80	2.00	20
15.52	22	87	1.20	12
15.54	24	96	0.40	4
15.54.5	24.5	98	0.20	2
15.55	25	100	0.00	0

Note that, within reason, a table can include any number of columns, although there is little point in including an extra column of figures unless it helps the reader's understanding of the table.

Here are some guidelines to consider when producing material in such a way:

- Consider the purpose of presenting the data as a table as there may be better ways of presenting it.
- Include only those figures which address the purpose of the table (some tables are huge and contain columns which could be irrelevant to the immediate).
- Do not include superfluous data which does not add to the reader's understanding.

- Provide a table number and title for each table. If abbreviations are used when labelling, provide a key.
- Allow sufficient space when designing the table for all figures to be clearly written.
- At the end of the table indicate where the data, the table itself, have been obtained.

3. The Graphical Presentation of Data

Graphs, bar charts, and histograms bring to life data from tables and allow for comparisons to be made relatively quickly. When using these visual methods for presenting data a disadvantage is that some of the detail and perhaps a degree of accuracy will be lost.

Data can be presented visually in many situations, for example showing trends in costs of production or trends in market share. Your aim is to present such data clearly so that the reader can quickly identify the patterns that exist and then draw inferences or conclusions. Sometimes it is important to present the data in such a way that any inconsistencies or unusual features stand out, or alternatives to show the relationship between various sets of data. To achieve this you can use a number of different graphical presentation styles:

- Graphs.
- bar charts.
- histograms.
- trend graphs.
- pie charts.

Before addressing each of the above in turn, it is important that you recognise several distinctions between sets of data. In isolation, it might seem unimportant to distinguish between 'continuous' data and 'discrete' quantities. However, it is this distinction that helps you to determine what style of graphical representation to use. A continuous quantity is that which can (theoretically) be measured to any chosen degree of precision. Examples of continuous quantities are mass (kg), length (m), time (s) and rate of change (e.g. m/s, m/s2). Notice that each example has a unit of measure (kilograms, metres, seconds, etc.).Continuous quantities can be expressed in integers (2kg, 4m, 101s), fractions (21/72 inches), decimal fractions (27.36m) and negative numbers (–2.6m/s). Discrete quantities, by contrast, can be expressed only as integers: 3 biros, 72 eggs, 14 sheep. In trying to determine whether something is a continuous or a discrete quantity, decide whether (in context) it is like a stream of water (continuous) or like people (discrete).

Only if both aspects of a data set are continuous quantities should you plot a graph (see later). For example, plotting the speed of a sports car as it accelerates away; plotting market share through a year. Money might appear problematic because the way in which you should treat it depends on the use you intend to make of it. Petty cash expenditure per day is straight forward because days are discrete. Therefore, technically, a graph would be inappropriate. By way of contrast, a factory always has a capital value, which may vary through time, and may conceivably be measured in fractions of a penny.

If a set of data should not be presented in the form of a graph, then the alternatives include a bar chart and a histogram. These are also more appropriate ways of presenting discrete quantities because they permit the grouping of data. A simple example might be the number of students in a class earning part-time wages, grouped in bands e.g. £0.00 – £19.99; £20.00 – £39.99/week, etc. Bar charts and histograms allow such data to be presented accurately and usefully.

This shows us the second distinction to be made. The speed of a sports car through time can be plotted on a graph. If there are two sports cars, then two separate lines (curves) could be plotted on the same graph. If there are 1000 sports cars, then not only would it be impractical to plot 1000 separate (curves) on the same graph, but also our reason for testing 1000 sports cars is likely to be different from our reason for testing just one or two. For example, we may wish to find out how many can accelerate from 0-60 mph in under six seconds. The emphasis has shifted from rate of change (graph) to how many cars are in each category (bar chart histogram).

3.1   Graphs

Graphs enable you to present numerical data in a way that clearly shows the trends occurring within a given set of data. The normal way of drawing a graph is to use two axes – two straight lines drawn at right angles. One of the lines is drawn vertically, and is known as the vertical axis, or y axis, while the other is drawn horizontally and is called the horizontal or x axis. These two axes cross at the origin. The data to be presented on the graph will normally depict two sets of data, for example set A showing the months of the year and set B showing the sales of a product.

Pairs of data can be formed, for example for every A data value there will be a B value (the A data are called x-values and the B data y-values):

Months of the Year (The A data)	Sales of the product (The B data)
Month	
1	70 units
2	70 units
3	65 units
4	50 units
5	40 units
6	41 units
7	33 units
8	20 units
9	53 units
10	60 units
11	64 units
12	69 units

The ordered pairs (an x-value with its corresponding y-value) are known as co-ordinates. These co-ordinates can be plotted on a graph. Plotting a co-ordinate on a graph requires two pieces of information – the value of x (the horizontal value), and the value of y (the vertical value). The x-value is always written first. A cross is then placed on the graph paper where '1' on the x axis meets '70' on the y axis. To do this accurately, you should use squared graph paper.

The x-values are plotted on the horizontal axis, while the corresponding y-value on the vertical axis. This shows that every x-value relates to, and depends on its corresponding y-value. Graphs drawn like this help the analysis of data. For example, if you simply look at the above table it might not give a very clear picture of the sale trends of the product. When such data are plotted on a graph, however, and a line is drawn to connect the co-ordinates, you get a visual picture. It is immediately apparent that sales of the product peak during months 1-3 and 11-12. During other months sales fell with a low period during months 7 and 8.

When drawing graphs, you have to work out scales for the axes. The scale is how the axes are divided up to show the units that are being represented. Each axis should be divided up into equal sections, as on a ruler. The size of each section should be such that all the units to be represented can be included on the axis. In the table above the x-axis should have twelve equal divisions, for each month of the year. The y-axis could commence at 0 units sold and then be divided into equal sections, each representing 5 units of the product, you may have a maximum unit 80, making 8 divisions in all.

(i)   A Line Graph

A Line Graph
Showing Sales of a product over a 12 Month Period

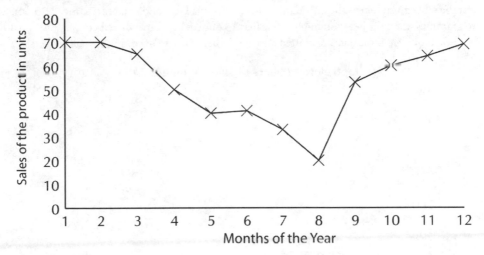

Note that the scale used for the y-axis does not have to be the same as that used for the x-axis. You should use scales so that the graph fits the area of paper you wish to cover. The axes are normally drawn with '0' as the origin. Sometimes, though, this might result in the co-ordinates all being plotted in one confined area of the graph. In such circumstances it is more appropriate to draw the axes starting at a higher value. When the axes start at values other than '0', they are referred to as false axes.

The choice of scales can greatly affect the visual impression that is given. By compressing the scale of the independent variable, trends in the data can be made to look quite dramatic, whereas expanding the scale of the independent variable can reduce the visual impact of trends in the data. You should aim to keep such distortions to a minimum as the purpose of communicating graphically is to present the data in a clearer form than could otherwise be achieved. You should continually ask yourself whether your presentation of the data gives an accurate impression.

If you have to plot negative X co-ordinates on the graph (such as -4 or –6) you should plot these to the left of the vertical axis, whereas all positive X co-ordinates (4, 6) are plotted to the right. In a similar way, negative Y co-ordinates are plotted below the X-axis.

(ii)   Interpolation and Extrapolation

Graphs are useful for plotting one variable (or value) against another variable to show trends that might be occurring. There is, however, additional information, that can be gained from graphs.

Where there is a constant relationship between two variables (one variable increases at exactly the same proportion to the other variable) then it is possible to use the graph to work out values.

For example, if the weight of a product is expressed in ounces and a particular weight has to be converted into grammes then you could use a graph to perform the conversion:

Weights					
Ounces	1		8		16
Grammes	25		200		400

If the table given here is the only data that you have available and you are to convert 13 ounces into grammes, then the best you might say is that 13 ounces lies somewhere between 200 and 400 grammes. However, if the data are plotted on a graph then you can make an accurate conversion.

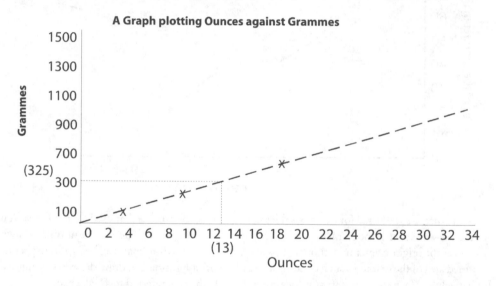

A Graph plotting Ounces against Grammes

The data will produce a straight line when you join the co-ordinates together on the graph. To convert 13 ounces into grammes, draw a vertical line up from the '13 ounces' point on the axis until it cuts the diagonal line. Then draw a horizontal line from this point to the y axis. The point (325) at which the y axis was cut, indicates the number of grammes that are equivalent to 13 ounces. The process can be reversed to convert grammes into ounces. The process of finding equivalent values from a straight line graph is known as interpolation.

Extrapolation occurs when the ounces or grammes to be converted lie outside the data presented in the table, for example converting 18 ounces into grammes. The constant relationship between the variables means that the straight line can be extended, at both ends, (see the dotted lines drawn on the graph) so that you can make further readings from the graph. The process of finding equivalent values that are beyond a given set of data is known as extrapolation.

Your interpolation and extrapolation will be accurate only if there is a constant relationship, at all values, between the variables. Should the co-ordinates not produce a straight line, when plotted and joined together but a curve, you will be unable to obtain equivalent values. Curves will still be of benefit, though, in that they show trends that are occurring with the data.

3.2   Bar Charts

Bar charts use elongated oblongs, or bars, to show quantities of a given product or item, over time. On the x axis will be plotted the days, months or years, and on the y axis the quantities of the product or item being considered. Bar charts provide a quick, clear presentation of data. In producing them it is important to ensure that the oblongs have a uniform width, and if a number of different products or items are being represented on the same bar chart, that you use colours or shading patterns to distinguish between the different products or items.

Bar charts can be drawn either horizontally or vertically. The elongated bars may be either touching or separated from one another, depending upon the amount of data to be plotted. In constructing them, you must always consider their clarity and ease of comprehension for the reader.

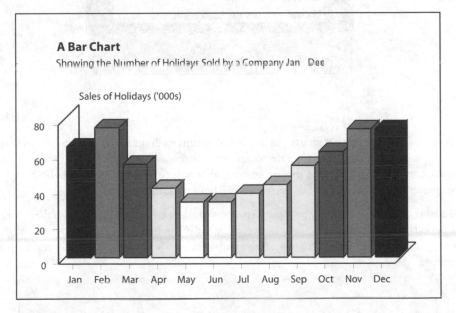

A Bar Chart
Showing the Number of Holidays Sold by a Company Jan–Dec

Sales of Holidays ('000s)

Sometimes, it may be appropriate to use a single percentage bar chart, for example when showing how a company's sales turnover is derived. The total length of this bar chart represents 100% and then divisions are made to signify the percentage contributions of different products. For example the first quarter of the bar is shaded in one colour to signify that 25% of the sales turnover comes from lawn mowers, for example. The next division is three-quarters along the bar to show that 50% of sales comes from garden tools – shaded differently – and the final quarter, 25% shows that these sales come from garden accessory equipment.

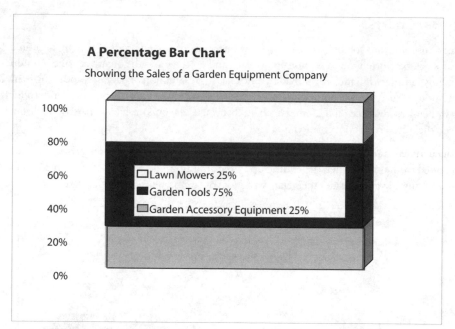

A series of percentage bar charts can be plotted against each other to show the trends that are occurring in sales over time. This gives the reader a clear picture as to whether the sales of lawn mowers as a proportion of total sales are increasing faster than sales of garden tools. Where this type of presentation is used, normally all the bar charts will be of the same length.

In other circumstances it may be appropriate to use dual, or treble, bar charts. With these, for each time period being considered, two or three sets of data are presented. For example, the data might be company sales turnover and profitability. Here, both bar charts stand side by side for the time period in question.

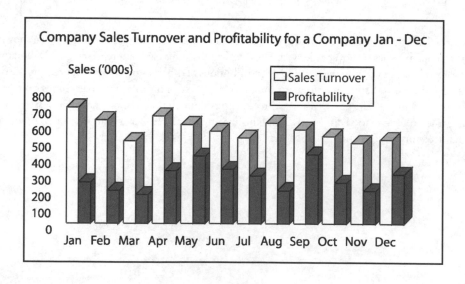

3.3   Histograms

Histograms are widely used for illustrating grouped data. Grouped data are data that have been put into classes, or bands, in order to make the information easier to handle. Typically, a population is banded into age group bands: 1-15 year olds, 16-25 year olds etc. The histogram then shows, for example, the average weekly income for each band, or average life expectancy.

A histogram differs from a bar chart (which it resembles) in that frequency is represented not by length but by area. This might seem to be a technical point. In purely practical terms it means that a histogram is best drawn onto squared paper, and that the height of a rectangle must be calculated. Each square represents one (or given number of) unit(s) in a population. For example, surveys often ask the age of the respondent. These ages are then banded in a manner appropriate to the needs of the survey. The following example illustrates this.

A survey of 1000 rail travellers was conducted in order to consider the population of passengers eligible for concessionary fares. A question in the survey asked respondents to identify to which age group they belonged:

	(years)	(years)	No of Respondents
Child	5-15	11	132
Young Person	16-24	9	333
Middle Age (a)	25-44	20	200
Middle Age (b)	45-59	15	195
Pensioner	60-80	20	<u>140</u>
			1000

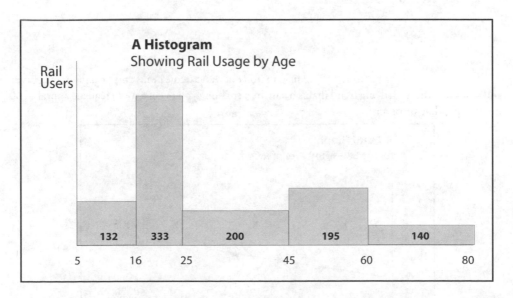

A histogram is drawn onto squared paper, with age along the x-axis. For each class, a rectangle is drawn. The width of the first rectangle is the class interval of children: 11 years. The height of the rectangle is calculated by dividing the number of respondents in that class (132) by the class interval (11 years). This gives a rectangle representing 132 children aged between 5 and 15 years. The other rectangles are drawn in a similar fashion.

The purpose of doing this would be to show rail use by age for any given age. Rather than using the precise age of each respondent (there might just happen to have been no-one aged 47 years interviewed in the survey, and therefore that age would have no bar on a bar chart), useful bands of ages are considered. Using the notion of area rather than height representing respondents means that the class interval can be variable.

3.4   Trend Graphs

Straight line graphs and bar charts might not clearly show what is the underlying trend or pattern of data. To show a trend you could use a 'moving average' graph.

Moving average graphs, as their name suggests, plot the average figure for the time period under consideration. Thus, if the graph is showing monthly fluctuations in the data, where great peaks and troughs are being recorded, it might be more meaningful if you were seeking to identify an underlying trend in the data to look at the average quarterly value rather than the monthly sales value.

Using this approach, the monthly values are added up for the quarter and then divided by three to arrive at the average. This figure is then plotted on the graph at the mid-point for the quarter in question. Once the first average figure has been calculated, the second is worked out as below:

For a quarterly moving average, where Jan, Feb, Mar, Apr, May, Jun represent months of the year, and m1, m2, m3 represent the quarterly moving averages:

$$m1 = \frac{Jan + Feb + Mar}{3}$$

$$m2 = \frac{m1 + Apr - Jan}{3}$$

$$m3 = \frac{m2 + May - Feb}{3}$$

The trend graph that is produced will help to iron out the extreme peaks and troughs in the curve, and will show the underlying trend that is occurring, enabling you to get a more realistic appraisal of the changes that are occurring.

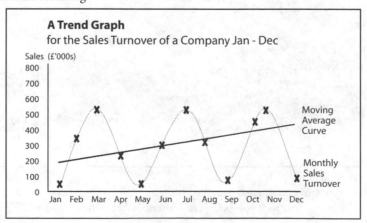

3.5   Pie charts

Pie charts are circles that are divided into proportionate segments that show how a 'complete whole' is to be divided up. From a pie chart you can very quickly establish the relative importance of the different segments. The pie chart is drawn by calculating the proportionate importance of each of the segments (for example 25% of the sales in our earlier example come from lawnmowers) and then by multiplying this figure by 3.6 (360 degrees divided by 100):

> Lawnmower sales contribute 25% of total sales, therefore on the pie chart this segment will account for:
> 25 x 3.6 = 90 degrees

> Garden tools account for 50% of total sales which is
> 50 x 3.6 = 180 degrees

> Garden accessories account for 25% of total sales, which is
> 25 x 3.6 = 90 degrees

Once you have calculated the size of each segment in degrees you can draw the circle using either computer software, or a protractor, to divide it into the appropriate segments. Give the pie chart a title and clearly label each segment. Include the percentages for each of the segments on the pie chart to give an accurate picture of the importance of each segment. You should draw the pie chart so that the size of each segment follows in a sequential pattern – the largest segment first, followed by the second largest and so on. If there are a number of segments to the pie chart it will probably be best to use colour or shading to denote each one, with a key indicating what each segment represents, otherwise too much text would be included.

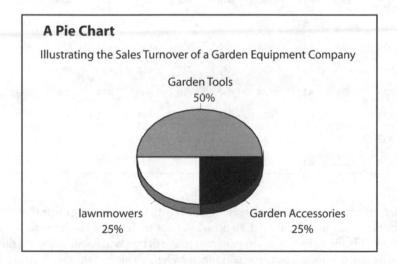

A Pie Chart

Illustrating the Sales Turnover of a Garden Equipment Company

Garden Tools
50%

lawnmowers
25%

Garden Accessories
25%

In sumary you should bear in mind a number of guidelines when presenting visual data to prevent any ambiguity in its interpretation:

- Think clearly about what you are trying to say when using a visual presentation.
- Give all visual presentations a title. The title should indicate what is being represented and leave no doubt in the reader's mind as to the nature of the data. The axes should be labelled, and clear indication given as to the scales being used, and the numerical quantities being referred to.

- All dates and time periods should be explicitly stated in the title, and on the appropriate axis.
- The source of the data should be indicated, especially if they are drawn from published material.
- Correctly drawn and presented visual material can provide a quick impression of patterns that exist in a set of data, patterns that might not be so readily apparent from tabulated figures. You must take care as a reader of such material not to be misled by techniques that might exaggerate or distort such patterns.
- Look for axes not numbered from zero. Sometimes the scales of the graph will start at numbers in excess of zero. The effect of this can be to make relatively small variations in the data seem more amplified. This technique as mentioned previously is known as the 'false zero'.

4. Statistical Analysis of Data

4.1 Frequency Distributions

The table below shows the mileages recorded by a fleet of vehicles in one week:

					Mileages Recorded by Vehicles						
482	502	466	408	486	440	470	447	413	451	410	430
469	438	452	459	455	473	423	436	412	403	493	436
471	498	450	421	482	440	442	474	407	448	444	485
505	515	500	462	460	476	472	454	451	438	457	446
453	453	508	475	418	465	450	447	477	436	464	453
415	511	430	457	490	447	433	416	419	460	428	434
420	443	456	432	425	497	459	449	439	509	483	502
424	421	413	441	458	438	444	445	435	468	430	442
455	452	479	481	468	435	462	478	463	498	494	489
495	407	462	432	424	451	426	433	474	431	471	488

A casual examination of this set of figures is unlikely to reveal anything other than the fact that most of the figures are in the 400s with an occasional one in the 500s. From a table in this form it would be very difficult to determine any patterns present in the data. For instance, are the numbers evenly distributed, or is there a certain small range which holds most of the numbers?

The statistical techniques discussed here will allow raw data such as that presented above to be summarised and presented in a form which facilitates identification of trends and allows the significance of the figures to be grasped. It should be noted, however, that as the crude data are converted into more convenient forms of representation, the fine details within them are progressively lost.

(i)   Ungrouped Frequency Distributions

A first step in the analysis of the data in the table could be to sort the figures into ascending order of magnitude and at the same time to note the number of times any figures are repeated. The next table has been produced in this manner and is termed an 'Ungrouped Frequency Distribution'. The table consists of a list of every unique mileage with its frequency of occurrence, that is, the number of times it occurred in the original table.

Ungrouped Frequency Distribution							
Mileage	**freq**	**Mileage**	**freq**	**Mileage**	**freq**	**Mileage**	**freq**
403	1	434	1	456	1	479	1
407	2	435	2	457	2	481	1
408	1	436	3	458	1	482	2
410	1	438	3	459	2	483	1
412	1	439	1	460	2	485	1
413	2	440	2	462	3	486	1
415	1	441	1	463	1	488	1
416	1	442	2	464	1	489	1
418	1	443	1	465	1	490	1
419	1	444	2	466	1	493	1
420	1	445	1	468	2	494	1
421	2	446	1	469	1	495	1
423	1	447	3	470	1	497	1
424	2	448	1	471	2	498	2
425	1	449	1	472	1	500	1
426	1	450	2	473	1	502	2
428	1	451	3	474	2	505	1
430	3	452	2	475	1	508	1
431	1	453	3	476	1	509	1
432	2	454	1	477	1	511	1
433	2	455	2	478	1	515	1

Notice that the sum of the frequencies is equal to the number of items in the original table, that is, 120.

(ii)   Grouped Frequency Distribution

Though the data have now been organised, there are still too many numbers for the mind to be able to grasp the information hidden within them. Therefore the next step is to simplify the presentation of the data further. At this stage in the production of a grouped frequency distribution, the crude data are replaced by a set of groups which split the mileages into a number of small ranges called 'classes'. The following table is an example of a grouped frequency distribution based on the ungrouped frequency distribution shown in the ungrouped frequency distribution table.

Grouped Frequency Distribution	
Mileages	**Frequency**
400 to under 420	12
420 to under 440	27
440 to under 460	34
460 to under 480	24
480 to under 500	15
500 to under 520	8
TOTAL	120

The overall range of mileages, 403 to 515, has been split into 6 classes each covering an equal sub-range of the total range of values. Notice that the class limits, that is the boundary values of the classes, do not overlap, nor are there any gaps between them; these are important characteristics of grouped frequency distributions.

The effect of grouping data in this way is to allow patterns to be detected more easily. For instance, it is now clear that most of the figures cluster in and around the '440 to under 460' class. The cost of being able to extract this piece of information is the loss of the exact details of the raw data; a grouped frequency distribution summarises the crude data. Thus any further information deduced or calculated from this grouped frequency distribution can only be approximate.

Choice of Classes: The construction of a grouped frequency distribution will always involve making decisions regarding the number and size of classes to be used. Though these choices will depend on individual circumstances to a large extent, the following guidelines should be noted:

- Class intervals should be equal where possible.
- Restrict the number of classes to between 6 and 20; too many or too few classes will obscure information.
- Classes should be chosen so that occurrences within the intervals are mainly grouped about the mid-point of the classes in order that calculations based on the distribution can be made as accurately as possible. Examination of the ungrouped frequency distribution should highlight any tendencies of figures to cluster at regular intervals over the range of values considered.
- Class intervals of 5, 10, or multiples of 10 are easier to work with than intervals of 7 or 11 (manually, that is; it is not a problem when using a computer).

(iii)   Cumulative Frequency Distribution

The next table contains an additional two columns to the data in the previous table. The entries in the column labelled 'Cumulative Frequency' have been calculated by keeping a running total of the frequencies given in the adjacent column. As expected, the final entry shows that the sum of all the frequencies is 120. The final column shows the same accumulated figures as percentages of the total number of figures.

Less Than Cumulative Frequency Distribution			
Mileages	**Frequency**	**Cumulative Frequency**	**Cumulative Percentage %**
400 to under 420	12	12	10.0
420 to under 440	27	39	32.5
440 to under 460	34	73	60.8
460 to under 480	24	97	80.8
480 to under 500	15	112	93.3
500 to under 520	8	120	100.0
TOTAL	**120**		

This new table allows further observations to be made regarding the data being examined. For example, the table now shows that 80.8% of the vehicles travelled less than 480 miles, and that 6.7% (100-93.3) of the vehicles travelled more than 500 miles; 20% (80.8-60.8) of the vehicles travelled between 440 and 480 miles.

Because the figures have been accumulated from the lowest class to the highest, this table is called a 'less than' cumulative frequency distribution. The next table shows a 'more than' cumulative frequency distribution in which the frequencies have been accumulated in reverse order:

More Than Cumulative Frequency Distribution			
Mileages	**Frequency**	**Cumulative Frequency**	**Cumulative Percentage %**
400 to under 420	12	120	100.0
420 to under 440	27	108	90.0
440 to under 460	34	81	67.5
460 to under 480	24	47	39.2
480 to under 500	15	23	19.2
500 to under 520	8	8	6.7
TOTAL	**120**		

Hence, the table shows directly that 90% of the vehicles travelled more than 420 miles and 6.7% travelled more than 500 miles. Simple calculations also allow 'less than' figures to be derived, just as 'more than' figures can be calculated from the 'less than' cumulative frequency distribution.

The data in a grouped frequency distribution can be represented diagrammatically using a histogram. Alternatively a graph could be drawn to represent the cumulative frequency distribution – this is known as an 'ogive':

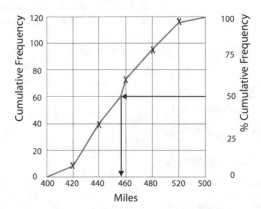

A 'Less Than' Cumulative Frequency Distribution Drawn as a 'Less Than' Ogive

Ogives start at zero on the vertical scale and end at the outside class limit of the last class on the horizontal axis. The vertical axis on the right of the diagram gives the cumulative frequency as a percentage, so that either scale may be used.

An ogive curve provides a useful and efficient method of determining 'percentiles'. Percentiles are points in the distribution below which a given percentage of the total lies. A percentile divides a set of observations into 2 groups. For example, using a 'less than' ogive, 25% of the mileages are below the 25 percentile (that is below 434 miles approximately), and 75% are above the 25th percentile. Certain percentiles are known as 'quartiles':

- The 25th percentile is the first quartile.
- The 50th percentile is the second quartile (also known as the median).
- The 75th percentile is the third quartile.

Percentiles are a very useful way of expressing such statistics as:

5% of the population of the UK own half of the individual wealth.

4.2   Measures of Location

Measures of location or measures of central value are ways of expressing averages. The most common types of averages are:

(i)   The Arithmetic Mean (or just 'the mean').
(ii)   The Median.
(iii) The Mode.

Each one of these measures attempts to represent a collection of figures with a single number. The following discussion summarises the methods by which each is calculated and its significance. Reference will be made to the data in the ungrouped frequency distribution shown in the following table:

Children in Saville Street

House Number

1 2 3 4 5 6 7 8 9 10 11 12 13 14 15 16 17 18 19

Number of Children

1 0 6 0 3 0 1 0 1 1 5 2 2 2 0 3 4 2 0

The following notation will be used:

$$\sum = \text{sum of}$$

$$\overline{x} = \text{mean value}$$

$$x_i = \text{single value}$$

$$n = \text{number of values}$$

$$f = \text{frequency}$$

(i)   The Arithmetic Mean

Calculation of the mean:

(a)   **Ungrouped data:**

(i) add together all the values

(ii) divide by the number of values.

The mathematical notation for the calculation is:

$$\overline{x} = \frac{\sum x_i}{n} \quad i = 1,.....,n$$

Using the values in the above table this gives:

$$x = \frac{33}{19} = 1.74 \text{ approx}$$

(b)   **Grouped frequency distribution:**

(i) identify classes and respective mid-point values

(ii) multiply each class mid point by the frequency

(iii) add these values together

(iv) divide this sum by the sum of the frequencies.

The mathematical notation for the calculation is:

$$\overline{x} = \frac{\sum(f \times \text{Class mid-point})}{\sum f}$$

Using the values in the Grouped Frequency Distribution this gives:

$$\bar{X} = \frac{12 \times 410 + 27 \times 430 + 34 \times 450 + 24 \times 470 + 15 \times 490 + 8 \times 510}{120}$$

$$\bar{X} = 454.5$$

The arithmetic mean indicates what value each item would have if the total of all values were shared out equally. The mean is the most suitable measure to discover the result that would follow on from an equal distribution of something (consumption of beer per head, for instance).

(ii)   The Median

Calculation of the median:

(a)   **Ungrouped data:**

(i) arrange the data into ascending order of magnitude;

(ii) locate the middle term in the series – this is the median. If there is an even number of numbers and there is no middle term then the nearest to the mid-point on either side will do.

Were you to arrange the data in ascending order of numbers of children, you would see that the median term in the Saville Street example is the 10th one and the value of the median is therefore, 1. In the mileages example, the middle term is the 60th and the median value is 452 miles.

(b)   **Grouped frequency distribution:**

(i) produce the equivalent ogive;

(ii) read off the value of the 2nd quartile – this gives the median value.

The median is merely the value of the middle term when the data are arranged into ascending order of magnitude. Consequently there will be as many terms above it as below it.

(iii)   The Mode

The mode is usually derived from an ungrouped frequency distribution by determining the value that occurs most frequently. In Saville Street, the value occurring most frequently is 0 children. In the table showing the ungrouped frequency distribution there are several modes: each mileage that occurs three times is a mode of the distribution of mileage.

As the mode is the value that occurs most frequently, it represents the typical item. It is this form of average that is implied by such expressions as 'the average person' or 'the average holiday'.

4.3   Dispersion

Quoting an average value, such as the mean, is an attempt to describe a distribution figure by a single representative number. Such averages, however, suffer from the disadvantage that they give no indication of the spread, or dispersion of the figures represented. For example, the following two sets of numbers have identical means but the range of values is much greater in the first case than the second:

10   20   30   mean value = 20

18   20   22   mean value = 20

The next figure further illustrates how two distributions with the same mean value can have different distributions:

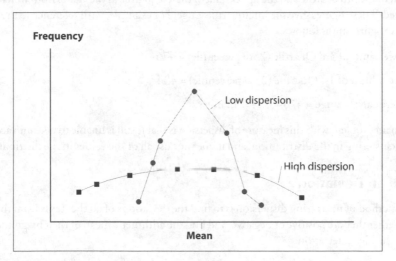

It is desirable to be able to describe the dispersion of data in a distribution with just a single figure. Four such measures will be described. They are the range; the interquartile range; the mean deviation; and the standard deviation.

(i)   Range

The range is merely the difference between the highest and lowest values:

Range = highest value – lowest value

The range of the distribution of mileages given in the ungrouped frequency distribution table is given by:

Range = 515 – 403 = 112 miles

Unfortunately the range, like the mean is influenced by extreme values. If the majority of the figures in the distribution cluster around a certain value, but there are a small number having extreme values, then the range does not provide a very accurate measure of the dispersion of the majority of the distribution. For example if in the ungrouped frequency distribution table one of the mileages had been 112 miles, then the range would be:

Range = 515 –112 = 403 miles

More than three times the previous figure, even though only one figure has changed.

(ii)   Interquartile Range

The disadvantage with the range as a measure of dispersion, as identified above, can be overcome to some degree by ignoring the extreme high and low values so that the measure of dispersion is representative of the majority of the distribution. One method of doing this is to use the values at the lower limit of the 3rd quartile and the upper limit of the 1st quartile as the values from which the range is calculated. These figures give the interquartile range. For example, with reference to the 'less than' ogive, these figures are as follows:

Lower limit of 3rd Quartile (75th percentile) = 476

Upper limit of 1st Quartile (25th percentile) = 434

Interquartile range = 476 – 434 = 42 miles.

The main problem with this measure of dispersion is that it still is unable to take into account any degree of clustering in the distribution, and it does not use all of the values in the distribution.

(iii)   Mean Deviation

Another method of measuring dispersion is to find the deviations of all the items from the average, ignore whether they are positive or negative, and find the arithmetic mean of their magnitude. This is known as the mean deviation.

As an example, suppose it is necessary to find the mean deviation of the following set of numbers:

27   33   36   37   39   39   40   44   50   55

(i) Sum of numbers = 400

Mean value = $\frac{400}{10}$ = 40

(ii) Deviation from mean:

–13 –7 –4 –3 –1 –1   0   4   10   15

(iii) Sum of deviations (ignoring sign) = 58

(iv) Mean deviation = $\frac{58}{10}$ = 5.8

The mean deviation of the numbers is 5.8

(iv)   Standard Deviation

The Greek letter s is universally adopted to represent standard deviation. The formula for standard deviation is as follows:

Standard deviation

$$(\sigma) = \sqrt{\frac{\sum (x - \bar{x})^2}{n}}$$

or where the figures come from an ungrouped frequency distribution:

$$\sigma = \sqrt{\frac{\sum f(x - \bar{x})^2}{\sum f}}$$

Setting out the calculation in the form of a table, and using the figures above for the mean deviation calculation, the calculation may be performed as follows:

x	$(x-\bar{x})$	$(x-\bar{x}^2)$
27	−13	169
33	−7	49
36	−4	16
37	−3	9
39	−1	1
39	1	1
40	0	0
44	4	16
50	10	100
55	15	225

$$\sum x_i = 400 \qquad \sum(x - \bar{x})^2 = 586$$

$$\text{Standard deviation } \sigma = \sqrt{\frac{\sum(x - \bar{x})^2}{n}} = \sqrt{\frac{586}{10}} = 7.655$$

Note that by squaring the difference between the mean and a value, the minus signs disappear.

To summarise, the steps involved in calculating the standard deviation of a distribution are as follows:

(i)   Calculate the arithmetic mean.
(ii) Subtract the mean from each value.
(iii) Square each value in (ii).
(iv) Sum the values in (iii).
(v)   Divide by the number of numbers.
(vi) Take the square root of the result of (v).

Where the standard deviation is to be calculated from an ungrouped frequency distribution, in step (ii) the result would be multiplied by the frequency of the value, and in step (v) the sum of the frequencies would be used as the divisor.

Reference is frequently made to the variance of a distribution. This is the square of the standard deviation. In the example immediately above, the variance of the distribution is given by:

Variance = (standard deviation)^2 = 58.6

and conversely, the standard deviation is the square root of the variance.

(v)   A Comparison of Measures of Dispersion

Of the measures of dispersion in this section, the standard deviation is the most important, but also the most difficult to comprehend. Basically, the standard deviation provides a measure of the likelihood of any random value from the distribution being close to the arithmetic mean of the distribution. The greater the measure of deviation, the less likely it is that any value chosen at random will be close to the mean value.

Its importance lies chiefly in the considerable use made of it in analytical statistics, and a familiarity with it is crucial to making progress in more advanced statistical techniques.

The range is easy to calculate but is sensitive to untypical values. The range takes into account only two figures, those at either extreme, and gives no indication of the clustering of data. It is neither a reliable nor an accurate measure of dispersion.

The mean distribution has the advantage of using all of the figures in the distribution and is a measure of how far, on average, the values in the distribution are dispersed from the mean value. Its chief disadvantage is that it is not particularly well suited to algebraic treatment.

If the distribution of values is fairly symmetrical about the mean, bell-shaped, and the number of items is large, that is, it is more or less what is known as 'normal distribution' as shown in the next figure, then the following relations are approximately true:

Quartile deviation = $\frac{2}{3}$ of the standard deviation, and

Mean deviation   = $\frac{4}{5}$ of the standard deviation

Thus in approximately normal distributions (which are of great importance in analytical statistics), the quartile and mean deviations may be used to approximate the standard deviation.

Frequency

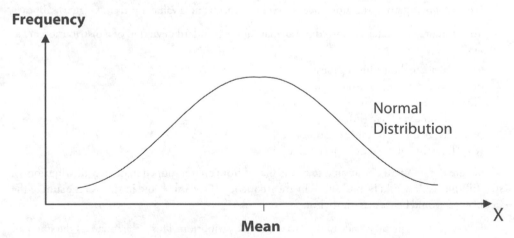

Normal Distribution

Mean   X

After having read this chapter it is hoped that you are now more aware of the value of communicating numerically. Communicating quantitative data is an ES that is important in business and commerce where it is necessary to be able use statistics and to understand the implications of statistical analysis.

After reading this chapter please complete the following learning activities:

Learning Activities

1. In your own words say when you would use 'ratios', 'percentages' and 'index numbers' to express data.

2. Write down the guidelines/conventions you should follow when using a table to present numerical data.

3. Distinguish between a 'bar chart' and a 'histogram' – when would you use a 'histogram' instead of a 'bar chart'?

4. Define the following statistical terms:
   (a) A frequency distribution.
   (b) Mean.
   (c) Median.
   (d) Mode.
   (e) Standard deviation.

Chapter Six
Career Management Skills

After reading this chapter you will be able to:

1. Write a curriculum vitae.

2. Understand how to complete an application form for a job.

3. Prepare yourself for a job interview.

4. Create a positive impression of yourself in a job interview.

In the previous chapters we have looked at a range of communication skills which you should develop. One of the purposes of doing this is so that you become aware of the various elements of these ES and can apply them in a number of different situations. One aspect of your personal development that requires highly developed ES is seeking employment. In this chapter we shall concentrate on a number of skills that will assist you when seeking employment, for example how you can write an effective application form and curriculum vitae, and how to handle the job interview. We shall also provide you with the guidelines to interview someone else. Whilst the chapter concentrates on job interviews, many of the personal skills discussed here are transferable to other types of interview.

1. Making an Application

We all from time to time have to make some form of application, whether it be for a new job, a training course, to join a club or society, or to enter college or university. Making an application requires careful thought because a second chance is unlikely if the application does not result in your being invited for interview. Applications are made in one of two ways: using a standard application form, or by sending a curriculum vitae.

1.1   Application Forms

Your task in completing an application form is to convince the recruiter that you are the ideal candidate for the vacancy. This is an important point. Once you have recognised this, you will ensure that the application form is completed to the highest possible standard, and to the best of your ability.

Recruiters receive many applications for every post and are constantly looking for reasons (valid or otherwise) to reject applications, especially in the initial screening process, known as the pre-selection. Your first objective, therefore, is to overcome this hurdle in order to be called for interview. Half-hearted applications are generally easy to detect and weed out. As a rule, therefore, only those applications into which you are prepared to invest time and commitment are worth pursuing. There is usually only one opportunity to apply for a particular job. A successful applicant will have assessed the main requirements of the post and tailored the application to reflect these requirements.

(i)   What the Recruiter is Looking For

Most recruiters draw up a list of criteria that they use for evaluating each application. A frequently used approach is to develop a profile of the likely, successful candidate, based around six broad criteria.

1.   Personality and character.
2.   Successes to-date e.g. exams, work experiences etc.
3.   Intellectual ability.
4.   Skills and competencies – including ES.
5.   Hobbies and leisure time pursuits.
6.   Personal qualities – i.e. assertiveness, self-confidence etc.

This profile has three purposes:

(a)   To draw a picture of what the recruiting organisation sees as a successful applicant so that appropriate advertisements can be placed requesting applications from individuals matching the profile.
(b)   To be used at the pre-selection stage to screen the applications.
(c)   To be used in the interview to determine whether or not the applicants match the desired profile.

Thus, before completing the application form you must 'read between the lines' of the advertised vacancy and draw a profile of the applicant that you think the recruiter is looking for. The next step is to determine whether you match the recruiter's desired profile. If you think that your profile does match that which the recruiter is looking for, then complete the application form. Should you meet most, but not all of the recruiter's criteria, however, then you should still apply as it is very unlikely that the 'ideal' candidate will exist.

(ii)   Completing the Application Form

Once you have established that your profile is suitable for the vacancy then you must set about completing the application form. In completing this task you should follow certain guidelines:

- Do not write answers on the actual application form until you have answered all questions in rough. You should give a great deal of thought to answering each question.
- Check the rough copy for grammar and spelling errors.
- Always use black ink for writing – application forms are photocopied and black ink will photocopy best.

- When completing the application form write legibly and take care not to make any mistakes as untidy applications are likely to be rejected.

You should pay great care and attention to completing the application form, not only how it is completed, but how the questions are answered. Application forms tend to be broken down into various sections reflecting the stages of the six profile criteria discussed above. Each section of the application form will provide the recruiter with further insights into the applicant's profile. A number of sections are common to most application forms:

Personal Details: This section might appear relatively straightforward to complete, but you must pay attention to ensure that you answer it completely and legibly. This will be the first part of the form that the recruiter reads so it will be vital to make a favourable first impression.

When detailing your qualifications bear in mind the nature of the vacancy. Can you use any projects that you have completed or options that you have studied at college or university to illustrate a special skill or competence that you have upon which the recruiter might look favourably?

Skills Questions: Skills are important to recruiters and you need to emphasise your competence in them. You need to take care though, to indicate that the skills that you possess will help you to do the job better, rather than be seen to be applying for the post because you want to use your skills.

Achievements: The majority of people have achieved something in their lives and it is important to show this on the application form. To complete this section you need to list all the achievements that you consider to have been important to your own personal development in your business, college, or social life.

You could mention a great variety of achievements: work experiences, examination successes, leading groups in leisure time, being a member of a successful activity, overseas travel, or sporting achievements. In mentioning your achievements, however, you should add a brief note showing what you have gained from them and any new skills you have developed as a result. The space on the application form will dictate how many achievements you can mention and the detail that you can provide for the recruiter.

Proof Questions: There will be questions on the application form asking for details of previous work experience, training and education – 'proof questions' – requesting evidence that shows you have the experience and qualifications for the vacancy.

Your answers to these questions should be factual, giving dates, the name of the organisation where the experience was gained, and the position held, with stress being placed on the successes you achieved.

Part-time jobs can impress the recruiter, especially when the special responsibilities of the job are highlighted, or the skills that you developed are mentioned.

If you have had a certain job or activity which was very interesting or especially relevant to the application, then you should elaborate further to explain its relevance. For example:

EASTERN TOURS LTD., NORTHSEA, 2004 to date

Tour operator's overseas manager in Bangkok, Thailand

This post has been of great benefit as it involves working in a foreign country ensuring that the tour clients gain satisfaction from their holiday. All client and company difficulties that are encountered have to be overcome. This often involves great use of tact, initiative and interpersonal skills.

The Crucial Question: There often tends to be an open-ended question(s) on application forms to which much importance is attached by the recruiter. Answers to these questions are frequently decisive:

Why have you applied for this post?

Why do you think you will succeed if you are appointed?

Explain how your background will assist you if you are offered a post with this organisation?

Successful managers are able leaders, effective problem solvers and competent decision takers. Can you provide any evidence that shows you possess these qualities?

To answer these questions competently you will have to have a clear understanding of:

(a)   what the post applied for entails;
(b)   the skills and competencies you can offer that match the recruiter's requirements;
(c)   why you wish to be successful in obtaining the post.

Before answering this type of question, it is important to know as much as possible about all these three areas. You should also ask yourself why this question is being asked, what is its purpose, and what will it tell the recruiter about me.

When answering such a question, you need to show how your qualities and experience fit the needs of the organisation. If you concentrate on your needs and wants and what you expect from the position, then your application will probably be unsuccessful. You should whet the recruiter's appetite when reading the response to this question, and include points that you can elaborate on in the interview.

Needless to say, you should give much thought, attention and creativity to answering these 'crucial' questions, the answers to which often hold the key that will open the door to the interview.

Referees: You need to select your referees with care. They should be people who know you well and hold respected positions in the community. You have to obtain their consent before they are mentioned as referees. It will be useful if the referee knows why you are seeking the position and what qualities and strengths you have which make you a suitable candidate.

Concluding Comments: Before you finally commit the rough draft to the application form you should ask yourself a few final questions:

▪   Have you answered all the questions on the application form?
▪   Have you left any time periods in your career unexplained?
▪   Do the answers you give address the questions asked?
▪   Has your tone in answering the questions been positive?

- Is the style of your presentation appropriate?
- Will the recruiter gain a favourable impression of you as a result of reading the application form?

And before you post the form to the recruiter:

- Are any additional items to be included with the application form e.g. examination certificates, photograph etc?

If you bear in mind all of the above points then your chance of being invited for interview will be much improved. Some organisations, though, will not ask you for an application form, but will wish to see your curriculum vitae (CV).

1.2   The Curriculum Vitae

The initials CV stand for curriculum vitae, meaning 'the course of your life'. Your CV is another means of communicating with the recruiter, and as with application forms you need to give attention to its design and submission. Normally you should not use a CV where the recruiter issues an application form. Use a CV when, for example, the advertised vacancy says; 'send full details to...' or simply asks for a CV. If you are making a speculative application, a CV with a covering letter is essential.

(i)   The Purpose of the CV

The purpose of your CV is to summarise your personal details and experience. Whereas application forms are structured with questions and spaces for replies, you can design your CV as you think fit. Your CV should include information relevant to the recruiter. Thus, each CV that you produce has to be tailored for the specific requirements of each position for which you are applying. A standard, 'mass-produced' CV is not the most effective means of presenting yourself for a specific job.

(ii)   The Style of your CV

An important point about the style of your CV is that it should be easy to read and concise, using brief clear statements. Your CV will have a stronger impact if actual facts or figures are included, such as grades achieved in examinations, and successes that you have enjoyed at work, for example increasing sales turnover by 100% in 12 months! There is normally no need, however, for sentences to be used as a note-format will suffice.

You should use certain key verbs, such as:

accomplished	contributed	produced	developed
established	implemented	initiated	mediated
motivated	negotiated	arranged	convinced
devised	sustained	tested	wrote

There is no single best way of designing and writing your CV. You need to think about the recruiting organisation and what type of applicant they wish to attract. For example, when applying for posts that demand creativity, you should use a creative approach in designing your CV, for example writing it as if it were a press release that gives your details. Alternatively, you could provide an additional 'fact file' that includes further details and examples of your creative work. You will need to give this approach careful consideration and pay attention to detail. If you are sending a fact file it must encourage the selector to read it rather than discard it in the waste paper bin.

(iii)   The Content of the CV

As we have indicated above, the content and style of your CV will depend upon the position you are applying for. A CV to impress an advertising agency will be of a different style and content to that intended to impress an accountant.

Your CV has to provide the recruiter with a picture of your accomplishments and experiences, as well as your potential capabilities. When you write your CV, however, while you must use facts, adopt a style that allows the recruiter to make favourable assumptions about you.

Once you have decided on the style and content of your CV you need to follow a number of guidelines.

You should produce an initial first draft and check the following points:

- The length of your CV should not normally be more than two A4 sides: the CV is a summary, not a report. The recruiter will receive many CVs and needs to be able to read through them quickly, gaining an initial first impression of your suitability.
- The various sections of the CV should be well spaced with ample margins. A tightly packed CV will be difficult to read and digest.
- The style of writing should be 'snappy' using verbs that suggest dynamism. Sentences, if used, should be short and to the point. Just include facts.
- The tone of the CV should be positive and optimistic creating a strong and favourable image.

You should then get another person to read through your CV to confirm its appropriateness, and to make sure it creates the intended impact. The next stage is to:

- Have the CV printed on high quality paper.
- Post the CV with a covering letter.
- Keep a copy of the CV and read it before the interview.

As with application forms, the immediate objective of using a CV is to obtain an interview. The golden rule for achieving this is to relate your skills and accomplishments to the recruiter's needs. To support the CV and to motivate the recruiter to read it you will also have to write a covering letter. The following show examples of a typical covering letter and a CV:

Flat G
College Halls of Residence
Wall Street
Southwall
SO6 5RF

30 November 200..

Ms W J Wilkes
Personnel Director
Gamble UK LTD.
33 Western Road
Westcliffe
WE24 9UH

Dear Ms Wilkes

Marketing Assistant, Post MA24

I read with interest the above career vacancy that was advertised in 'Marketing', 29 November, and would like to be considered for the post. Please find enclosed my Curriculum Vitae.

As you will see from my CV, I am in my final year at university reading for a Business Studies degree, specialising in the Marketing Option. The work placements that are integral parts of the degree have enabled me to gain valuable experience of two important activities of the Marketing Department - advertising and selling. The successes I achieved on placement, plus my studies at university, have given me a clear understanding of Marketing and its relevance to business. These experiences have also shown me the importance of marketing people developing effective transferable personal skills.

The positions of responsibility I have had at school and university have further developed these skills. I work well with others, am capable of leading others and taking decisions. Being treasurer of the Nomadic Society has shown me the importance of administrative skills and communication skills.

Your company appeals to me because it is involved with marketing fast-moving-consumer-goods. The work experiences I have already enjoyed have been in this sector, and will enable me to make an effective and rapid contribution as a Marketing Assistant to the Detergent's Product Manager, using my planning and analytical skills.

Yours sincerely

Anne Williams

Anne Williams

ANNE WILLIAMS
14 Woolcot Terrace, Northsea, NE45 9TH
Tel: 0909 76783
e-mail: a.williams@fastmail.com

PROFILE

Highly motivated, self confident team player. Capable of undertaking complex assignments to tight deadlines. Outgoing personality who thrives on challenges. Experienced in all elements of the 'Marketing Mix'.

EDUCATION and QUALIFICATIONS

2001-date   Southwall University

BA (Hons) Business Studies Sandwich Degree. Marketing Management Option. Final year project: "The Effectiveness of Advertising Expenditure for Tour Operators".

1994-2001   Trinity School, Northsea.

2001   A Levels: Geography (A), Economics (B), General Studies (C).

1999   GCSEs: English Literature (A), History (A), Mathematics (A), English Language (B), History (B), Geography (C), French (C), Physics (C), Chemistry (C).

POSITIONS OF RESPONSIBILITY

University: Treasurer of the Nomadics Walking Society - collecting expedition funds, maintaining accounts, presenting the accounts to the AGM.

School: Netball Captain – arranging fixtures, planning a tour.

WORK EXPERIENCE

Summer 2003 Procterlever Household Division – work placement, sales rep, servicing existing accounts and prospecting for new ones. Increased sales in the territory by 30% in 3 months.

Summer 2002 NBC Advertising Agency, London – work responsibility for 5 accounts, liaising with the client and buying media space.

OTHER SKILLS/INTEREST

Full driving licence, overseas expeditions, jazz music, Shakespeare.

REFEREES

Mrs A Evans, Director, NBC, Civic Street, London, SE1 6YP.

Dr J Smith, School of Marketing, Southwall University, SO2 4PL.

(iv)   Covering Letters

A covering letter must always accompany a CV. Sometimes it is also wise to include one when sending an application form, especially when you have had limited previous correspondence with the organisation to which you are applying.

The purpose of the covering letter is to introduce you to the recruiter and to encourage the recruiter to read your attached CV or application form. You must give thought and attention to writing the covering letter. It is a vital component of the selection process.

Covering letters should be brief, not exceeding one A4 side of high quality paper. If your handwriting is neat then it is good to write the covering letter by hand, supported by a word processed CV. If your handwriting is poor then you should word process the covering letter.

You should always follow standard letter writing conventions as we discussed in Chapter Four. However, you need to bear a number of additional guidelines in mind:

- Always write a rough draft first.
- State explicitly the post for which you are applying and any reference numbers quoted in the advertisement.
- Indicate where you saw the vacancy advertised, or how you heard the details about it, or why you are making a speculative application.
- Stress the factors relevant to the application such as your previous work experience, skills, knowledge, interests, aptitudes etc.
- Include relevant information not given in your CV, such as your motivation for applying.
- Inform the recruiter of convenient interview dates and any dates when you will be unavailable for interview.

As we discussed at the beginning of this chapter, making applications is important. Normally, you will have only one opportunity to be called for interview. If your application form is poorly completed, if your CV is ill-conceived and your covering letter unstimulating, then it is unlikely that you will be called for interview. If you pay careful attention to succeeding at the pre-selection stage, however, you could well be rewarded by being offered an interview.

2.   Succeeding at the Interview

You will need to master interview skills because interviews are the most common means of selecting employees. The personal skills you develop here will also have relevance in different types of interview situation such as appraisal interviews, market research survey interviewing, and indeed even for being interviewed for a radio or television programme. In the section that follows, however, we continue the theme of applying for a career vacancy and consider a number of steps that have to be followed for the interview to be successful.

2.1   Preparing for the Interview

To walk ill-prepared into an interview is foolish. You have to carry out research beforehand into a number of areas:

- The recruiter's business – what is the nature of the organisation, its markets and products, who are the consumers and competitors, what position does the recruiting organisation hold in the market place? This information can be found from company reports, press articles, and informal discussions with other employees of the firm.

- The responsibilities involved in the job, what will be expected of you, where will you fit into the organisation? It is very helpful to have had a discussion with the person for whom you will directly be working prior to the interview. By contacting this person before the interview you will be showing that you are keen to be selected for the vacancy.

You need to collect as much background material as possible. You will also have to review:

- Why you have applied for the post, your motivations and ambitions, where the post fits into the logic of your career development.
- Why you will find the job interesting.
- The skills you will be able to offer the employer.
- Your relevant previous achievements.
- How you meet the job specification and selection criteria for the post.

The clothes that you are to wear for the interview will require preparation. Do they need dry cleaning, should you wear a new pair of shoes? What about your hair style, what will be appropriate for the interview? Do you have to conform to certain standards of appearance and dress or would a more individualistic style be appropriate? Appearance and grooming are important because they help to create that vital first impression that the interviewer will gain of you.

Whenever possible, visit in advance the place where the interview will be held. This will give you an idea of how long it will take you to travel there on the day of the interview. Allow sufficient time for the journey so that unforeseen problems and delays (e.g. rush-hour traffic) do not make you late for the interview.

It is helpful to know what type of questions are likely to be asked in the interview. Not only will this help you to prepare, it will also boost your confidence because you are unlikely to be taken by surprise. A list of typical and general questions is given below. Questions specific to the vacancy can be worked out by looking carefully at the job specification and the selection criteria. Interview panels use these to frame the questions for each candidate. For each question, work out your best answer using the guidelines below. Rehearse the interview the evening before, a friend acting as interviewer asking the questions. You should also prepare several questions to ask at the interview.

2.2   The Interview

You should plan to arrive before the interview is scheduled to start. This will allow you time to gather your thoughts and calm your nerves. Be polite and courteous to everyone you meet – they may be future colleagues.

When you are invited into the interview room you should enter with a purposeful and confident walk, erect posture, and with a smile. You should greet the interviewer, or the chairperson if it is a panel interview, with; 'Good morning/afternoon Mr/Mrs/Miss...pleased to meet you. My name is...', accompanied by a firm handshake, pleasant facial expression, and strong eye contact. When you are asked to sit down, adopt an erect posture, with your hands folded in your lap, making sure that you maintain eye contact with the interviewer.

The interviewer will then take control, probably by outlining how the interview is to be organised. Then the questioning will commence. The questions you are asked should relate to the job specification and selection criteria for the post. If your research and preparation have been thorough then a number of the questions will come as no surprise, questions like:

Why are you applying to this organisation?

Why did you choose that particular course to study at university?

What other organisations have you applied to?

Where do you see yourself in five years time?

What do you know about....(a technical point)....?

How would you define....(a technical term)....?

What skills or qualities do you possess that make you a suitable candidate?

What do you know about our business?

Who do you see as our main competitors?

What would you say are the main difficulties facing us?

What has been your greatest achievement?

What are your weaknesses?

How do your friends perceive you?

When answering questions you need to remember a number of points:

- Always look at the interviewer and other members of the panel.
- Use effective verbal and non-verbal communication skills – don't fidget, avoid distracting mannerisms, control facial expressions, use appropriate gestures, try to hide your nervousness by controlling your voice and speaking with varied tones and pitch, and different speeds of speech. Use pauses in speech to stress important points.
- Always be positive and optimistic when you are replying to questions, look for opportunities to highlight your achievements, turn unsuccessful elements in your career todate into successes.
- Never be derogatory, cynical, facetious, or sarcastic. Rather, use humour to show the warmth of your character and personality.
- Be honest, don't invent answers. If you cannot answer a question say so – this will earn more respect from the interviewer than a garbled invention.
- Answer the question that is posed, not the one that you wish had been asked. Recognise those questions requiring brief answers and those intended to produce a more in-depth response. Don't use one word answers, always elaborate.
- If you do not understand a question, ask for it to be repeated.
- Try and give practical examples of what you have achieved in your career to-date to support the answers that you give.

One purpose of the interview is to allow you to communicate with the interviewer using your well-developed verbal and non-verbal communication skills. In addition, the interviewer will be seeking to establish your intellectual skills and so a problem may be set, or specific situations put before you to solve:

Sales of our product have been declining, what would you do?

How would you motivate other people who are working with you?

The quality of the products produced fluctuates greatly, how can this be overcome?

These problems are not posed to test your in-depth knowledge of the given situation, but to establish whether you can think logically and solve problems in a structured way.

When the interviewer's questioning has finished you will be given the opportunity to ask questions. Valid questions that you could ask are those relating to:

- The job, the organisation, its employees, products and processes.
- Future career prospects.
- Additional staff development and training which you might receive.

You should ask only three or four questions at most, after which the interviewer will conclude the session by thanking you for attending and informing you of the next stage in the selection process. You should always use a concluding handshake to end the interview on a positive note, accompanied by pleasing facial expressions – remember to smile even if you think the interview has not gone terribly well.

You should thank the interviewer for giving you the opportunity to discuss your application in more detail, and should then walk out of the room in a confident and purposeful manner.

Your hard work does not end here as there are follow-up tasks to complete.

2.3   After the Interview

You should regard each interview as a valuable learning opportunity. To learn from each one and to develop your repertoire of ES you need to analyse each interview carefully.

Make notes as soon after the interview as possible on the questions that were asked and the responses that you gave. This will be useful to you if you are offered a second interview, and will help you to think of more effective ways of answering such questions. Following this you should critically evaluate the ES that you used, writing down your perceived strengths and weaknesses. Spend time on analysing where your weaknesses were shown and think about how you might improve them.

The first interview will probably be used by the recruiter as a means of drawing up a short list of candidates for the second (final) interview – your last hurdle before they offer you the job.

(i)   The Second Interview

The first interview will have been a screening process, rejecting applicants thought to be incompatible with the organisation's needs. The second interview will establish from the short list of applicants which one has the skills, qualities, experience and potential to succeed in the vacant post.

In preparing for the second interview you should follow similar steps as you did for the first. The main difference between the two interviews will be the way they are organised. Second interviews are frequently spread over a two day period and include a variety of activities held at an assessment centre. The assessment centre might be a special room or suite of rooms in the employers own premises, or the employer might hire rooms in a hotel.

The Night Before: Second interviews for more senior posts frequently start the night before when the candidates are invited to dine with senior managers from the recruiting organisation. Recently recruited employees may also be present. It will probably be stated that the evening session is to be informal, but the senior managers and other employees will be observing your social behaviour that may be fed back to the interviewers (if they are not present). Thus, you will need to display ES of a high standard to ensure that another favourable first impression is created:

- You will have to display the appropriate etiquette as the hosts will be observing how you cope with such situations, and evaluating the image you will portray when you work for the organisation.
- You should be careful about your verbal and non-verbal behaviour so that the observers develop a favourable impression.
- You should prepare intelligent work-related questions and topics for conversation beforehand as this will show an interest in the organisation and its work.
- Alcohol should not be consumed.

During the evening it may be possible to steer the conversation around to the proceedings of the next day. You should do this sensitively in order to find out a bit more about how the day will be organised and the skills and competencies that the interviewers will be looking for. Typically, though, the recruiters will be keen to see the full range of ES as discussed in this book being displayed by the successful candidate(s).

The Next Day: The format of the interview day will vary according to the interviewing practice of the recruiting organisation, and as we have already stated you should, if possible, try and find the likely format beforehand.

The organisation could provide a variety of activities for the candidates:

- Interviews by different people, with different numbers of people on each panel, each with a different objective.
- Written and scientific tests to determine the mental agility of the candidates, their aptitudes, and suitability for the work in question.
- Psychometric tests to help understand the personality of each candidate.
- 'In-tray' exercises, a type of situational analysis, where certain tasks or problems relevant to the vacancy have to be completed in a certain period of time.
- Group exercises where a problem has to be solved by the candidates working as a team. This identifies those with leadership skills, those who can work effectively with others as well as each individual's intellectual skills.
- Case studies which are completed individually, to establish the knowledge and understanding of the candidates, and their ability to analyse, synthesise, and evaluate a problem, before taking a decision.
- Formal presentations which may be spontaneous, for example having to speak for three minutes on a particular unknown topic or on a topic chosen by you. These entail using a broad range of ES.
- Group discussions to determine the ability of the candidates to develop persuasive arguments and to defend their views when questioned by others.

The ES we have discussed previously, and those which we will discuss in the remainder of this book, will be of use to you in second interviews where a variety of activities are performed by the candidates. Clearly, you must obtain as much information beforehand about the type of tests you are likely to encounter and you should endeavour to practise the skills involved. For example, if part of the second interview is contributing to a group discussion note that the assessors will be looking for you to:

- Contribute fully to the discussion, helping the group meet the objective that has been set for the discussion (to show your team player skills).
- Think quickly and logically – be prepared to express your views, bouncing your ideas off the views expressed by the other participants, and elaborating on the views of the other candidates (to demonstrate your critical thinking skills).

- Focus your views and the views expressed by the other candidates on the task set – don't digress away from the topic. If the discussion does digress steer it back to the topic under consideration (this will highlight your organisational capability).
- Involve the other candidates in the discussion – if a fellow participant is not contributing to the discussion ask them a question so that they also take part (this will demonstrate your team leader skills).

Remember in any group task you participate in not to:

- Be too dominant at the expense of others – be aware of how you are contributing to the group.
- Dismiss rudely the views of other candidates – be assertive but polite at all times.
- Ridicule the views expressed by other people.
- Swear or make derisory or derogatory comments about other people.

Your objective throughout the group exercise should be to make a very positive impression of yourself and to leave the assessors in no doubt that you are the best candidate for the job.

Some second interviews will require you to make a short presentation either on a topic of your choice, or one set by the assessors. If you have a free choice of presentation topic choose an interesting or slightly different topic that highlights a pertinent element of your character, your leadership skills for example. Irrespective of the topic of your presentation ensure that it is well structured and organised – the interviewers will be looking for this, see Chapter Seven.

If role-playing exercises are used you should firmly slip into the role to be adopted, but be careful not to over-exaggerate your behaviour. If the role-playing involves performing a situational task, such as completing work in the 'in-tray' then you need to prioritise the work in the 'in-tray' so that you complete the more pressing tasks first. Should you be asked to solve problems, then you need to identify the underlying causes of the problem before you take action to overcome them. Be ready to justify the decisions that you reach.

Situational tasks are favoured by some interviewers because they enable a number of traits and skills to be identified, such as the candidates' abilities to solve problems and take decisions, as well as their ability to maintain relationships with others, or to show sensitivity to the feelings of others. When attending a second interview, you should try to anticipate a number of different situations that might be put before you, and think about possible ways of handling these situations.

Some second interviews will require you to complete a psychometric test to help identify your attitudes, beliefs and self-motivation. The psychometric test is a lengthy series of statements that you have to read carefully before giving your rating to each one – how much do you agree or disagree with each statement, sometimes registering your response on a 1-5 scale. Psychometric tests may take up to 45 minutes to complete depending on the number of statements you have to respond to. Do not become anxious if you have to complete a psychometric test as there are no right or wrong answers to each statement. Read each statement carefully and give the answer, or rating, that reflects your personal opinion. Do not try and give the response that you think the assessor is looking for as this will be counter productive as you will not actually know the preferred personality profile for the post. When analysed, the psychometric test will provide further information about your personality and whether you will 'fit' into the organisation and the team you will be joining.

To gain practice of undertaking ability and personality tests visit the following website: www.selfasses.faststream.gov.uk – this is the UK government's site for civil service practice tests.

You may need to consider some additional points:

- A second interview will be more related to the work involved with the post than was the first interview. Therefore you might need to do some further research.
- Interviewers for a technical post will be more interested in technical knowledge and competence than was the case with the first interview – you must emphasise such competencies if you have them.
- You need to keep a positive frame of mind at all times. You should try to project the appropriate image that the recruiter is looking for.
- The person for whom you will be working will probably be a major influence on the decision made at the second interview.
- Recruiters will be looking for evidence that you will be committed to the employing organisation and will be able to follow a structured career path.

If you remember all of these points, as well as the previous ones made in this chapter, then you will be well placed to succeed at the second interview.

3.   Interviewer Skills

Hopefully the person who is interviewing you has well developed ES which will make you feel at ease and allow you to communicate to the best of your ability.

You may, at some later time, be called upon to carry out interviews as an interviewer. In this section we will examine some of the skills you will need to have if you are to conduct a successful interview.

The importance of the interviewer managing the interview efficiently cannot be overstated as the face-to-face interview is still the most commonly used method of selecting new recruits. If you adopt an inappropriate style as an interviewer then it could result in your organisation employing a candidate who is not the best suited for the post in question. In addition, each applicant should have an equal opportunity of being selected for the job, so it is essential to treat each applicant in a consistent manner.

Candidates attending for interview will naturally be nervous and anxious, some will be highly stressed. As the interview is to some extent a 'false' situation, in that all the participants will be playing specific roles which may not be a true reflection of their typical behaviour, it will be important for you as the interviewer to organise the interview process carefully so that an accurate assessment can be made of each candidate.

A number of potential problems might arise if you are inexperienced as an interviewer:

- You may not have established a clear profile of the likely candidate prior to the interviews, making it difficult to assess the suitability of each candidate.
- You might not have framed the structure of the interview, and the questions to be asked, on the job specification and the selection criteria.
- You might dominate the interview to the extent that the candidate has hardly any opportunity to speak.
- You might assess only the candidates' interpersonal skills, or you might be distracted by the physical appearance of the candidates, ignoring their other qualities.
- Although you might have produced a list of questions to ask, you might not have evaluated what an appropriate response is, reducing the value of such questions.

If you avoid these pitfalls an interview can be an effective way of collecting information about each candidate, enabling you to make a suitable choice. However, a key factor will be whether or not you understand the data you need to collect from each candidate.

One way of deciding the type of information to collect is to identify the skills, competencies, and characteristics of those employees currently undertaking roles similar to that for which the applicants have applied. By studying people who are already successful at carrying out the work you can draw up a profile of the likely candidate. Once you have done this you can devise questions that you can ask all candidates. Their answers should show whether or not they are suitable for the post. For this to work, though, you must ask each question in the same way to all candidates, and you must listen to each response to see which candidate appears to be the most suitable.

Interviews are primarily used for obtaining information. If you wish to gain insight into how well the candidate is likely to perform in the post, then situational analysis should be used. This should give a systematic assessment of a candidate's suitability to undertake certain job responsibilities, rather than you having to rely on assumptions based on the candidate's previous employment experience.

In a situation interview you present the candidates with either real or hypothetical problems that they might encounter were they to be appointed. The candidate's task is to decide how to respond to each problem. This method of interviewing is useful if the candidate has no previous experience of the type of work involved with the vacancy. You can then probe the candidates on their responses, to provide further insight as to their suitability.

It is important that you listen carefully to a candidate's responses. Make notes or record the interview. You will have to develop the skill of probing the candidates through the subtle use of open-ended questions beginning with 'What..?', 'How..?', 'Which..?' and 'When?' Posing questions in this way invites candidates to talk about an issue, enabling them to reply at an intellectual level. This will indicate to you the candidates' knowledge and understanding of the issue. If you probe further you can discover the candidates' ability to develop logical arguments or uncover their motivations, perceptions, beliefs and attitudes.

Use 'Why ...?' questions in moderation only as these can feel quite threatening to candidates, requiring them to justify what they believe about a particular issue.

Situational interviewing helps to reduce the subjectivity that often creeps into the interview process and allows you to adopt a more objective stance from which you can evaluate each candidate against work related criteria.

Irrespective of the type of interview that you use to select the successful candidate, however, you should follow certain guidelines to help candidates relax and contribute to the best of their ability:

- You should select carefully the physical environment where the interview takes place to ensure that:

  - the temperature is not too hot or cold;
  - there will be no distractions such as telephones ringing, or third parties entering the room;
  - the layout of the chairs will allow the candidate to communicate freely, there are no physical barriers that might impede the interview such as tables or equipment.

- You should be well briefed on the candidates and have studied their application forms or CV's in detail.

The interview needs to be planned and structured. There should be an introduction, the questioning period (for both the interviewer and interviewee), and a conclusion. In the introduction you should explain to the candidate how the interview is to be conducted, you should introduce the members of the panel, and help to relax the candidate. The questioning period should include a variety of different types of question, most of which will have been pre-planned and designed to elicit information that will show whether the candidate matches the job specification and selection criteria. You should then allow time for the candidates to ask questions before concluding the interview by informing them of the next stage in the process.

- The questions you ask should be clearly phrased so that they are unambiguous and easily understood, and designed to draw out the qualities of the candidate. If a candidate struggles to answer a question, allow time for thought before probing more deeply.
- Ask questions in a warm, friendly tone of voice. If the answer that is given is incorrect do not admonish the candidate. Acknowledge correct answers by nodding your head, smiling, and giving positive verbal support.
- At no time during the interview should you be patronising or condescending.
- You can apply pressure to the candidate by carefully listening to the answers that are given, and asking for clarification of points that were not clearly explained. If you adopt an assertive, rather than an aggressive manner this will show how the candidate responds to such pressure.
- Do not dominate the interview. The candidate should be given the opportunity of speaking for at least 60% of the time. If a panel interview is to be held, the same rule applies. A chairperson should manage the interview inviting colleagues to ask questions. Ideally, one person's sole role should be to observe the proceedings paying particular attention to the candidate's non-verbal behaviour noting whether it supports or contradicts what he is saying.
- When the interview has concluded you need to complete an assessment form to indicate how well the candidate performed against the criteria which you had established as being important.

If you follow the above procedures you will adopt a professional approach for the interview which should allow you to identify the most suitable candidate for the vacancy. Interviewers who have had no previous experience need to be trained in the skills required. Indeed, before being faced with a real interview, you should use role-playing situations to practise and to receive feedback on the ES being employed by both the interviewer and the interviewee.

In this chapter we have considered employability skills, and highlighted ways in which you can improve the success of the selection process either as an interviewee or interviewer. Another skill area that draws upon a broad range of ES is that of making a formal presentation. We shall discuss this topic in Chapter Seven.

After reading this chapter please complete the following learning activities:

Learning Activities

1. Design, write and word process your own CV. Then ask your tutor, or a colleague at work, to read it to ensure that it represents your skills, qualifications, interests, and personality in a very positive way.

2. Select a job vacancy that is advertised in the press. Obtain a job application form from the employer. Read through the various sections, draft your responses to the different sections and questions, and then complete the application form. Ask your tutor, or a colleague at work to read your completed application form and to provide you with feedback on the impression you have created of yourself through the application form.

3. Using the same job vacancy as in (2) above read through the job specification and the selection criteria and write down the questions that you think the interview panel might ask to the short listed applicants. Then write down the answers you would offer to the questions posed. Review your answers to ensure that they do present you in the best possible way to the interview panel.

4. Reflect on your chosen job vacancy and consider what other factors will be important to the interview panel when selecting the ideal candidate for the job.

Chapter Seven
Presentation Skills

After reading this chapter you will be able to:

1. Recognise the fundamentals of what makes an effective presentation.
2. Understand the usefulness of visual aids within presentations.
3. Learn best practice techniques for technology based presentations.
4. Realise the importance of properly planning your presentations.

At some stage in your career it is more than likely that you will have to make an oral presentation. It may be a highly formal event, perhaps speaking at a conference, but most commonly it will be of a less formal kind, for instance delivering a presentation as part of an assignment or giving a presentation in a work based setting. Some people, such as teachers and lecturers, spend much of their time presenting information to others and enjoy doing it. Other people, though, do it infrequently and find it a nerve racking experience.

No matter in what situation you have to make a presentation, or the frequency with which you do it, or the size of the audience you face, you can apply similar principles to make your presentation more effective. In this chapter we will examine some of the principles which can improve your presentation technique.

1. Preparing the Presentation

You must prepare all presentations. Very few speakers can make a successful presentation without preparation. Your starting point is to establish why you are making the presentation, and then to set yourself clear objectives that you must achieve in delivering it.

1.1   Setting Objectives

You should begin by considering the needs of the audience – what will the audience be expecting to hear and what do they wish to gain from hearing the presentation? These are the objectives of your audience, to whom we shall return shortly.

Your objectives are equally important. You might want the audience to accept and agree with your views or to change their behaviour in some way as a result of hearing you speak. You may simply want to give information in an instructional or explanatory way. The objective of an instructional presentation might be to increase the knowledge of your audience, which you can subsequently test by asking questions, or by requiring the audience to perform what they have learnt. If you are giving an explanatory presentation you may be trying to improve the understanding of your audience.

Once you have clearly established the purpose of the presentation and set your objectives, the next stage in the preparation process is to consider the nature of the audience.

1.2   The Nature of the Audience

We have already identified that it is important to consider the size and structure of the audience during this preparation stage. The skills you will use when making a presentation to an audience of one will be virtually identical to those you will require when making a presentation to an audience of one hundred. With a smaller audience, however, there is more scope for including the listener(s) directly in the presentation and it requires a different presentation style.

Similarly, when you know all the members of the audience personally you can adopt a more informal style. In contrast, if the members of your audience are drawn from quite varied backgrounds with different expectations of the presentation, you will have to try and meet as many of their differing needs as possible.

It is vital, therefore, to know who the audience is, what their role is, and what they are expecting to learn. Linked to this is the need to be aware of what the audience already knows about the topic under consideration. Are they experts or novices? This will clearly determine how you pitch the content of the presentation.

1.3   Content Preparation

Next you must pay careful attention to preparing the content of the presentation. Decide on the specific topic to be covered in the presentation taking into account the objectives of the presentation, the previous knowledge of the audience, and what it is they are to learn. Pay careful attention to the content of the presentation. Try and make sure that what you say, is interesting, to the point, can be clearly understood, is appropriate for the nature of your audience, can be feasibly presented in the time you have available, and will achieve what you set out to achieve.

You should not overload the audience with information, as you can make only a certain number of points in the time available. If the presentation is very short, not lasting more than a few minutes, then make only one or two points. If your presentation is longer then obviously you have more scope to expand on what you have to say. Be careful with presentations which are too long, however, as the audience is likely to lose concentration and remember little of what is said.

If you are trying to make a number of points you must follow a logical sequence, so that each point builds upon the previous one. The presentation needs to be broken down into manageable stages and you must give it a structure. To help with this draw up a presentation plan.

2. The Structure of the Presentation

A plan will help you to structure the presentation into three distinct stages each of which needs to be allocated a specific time. The stages are:

- The Introduction.
- Developing your argument.
- The Conclusion of your presentation.

2.1 The Introduction

In the introduction you should:

- Welcome your audience.
- Identify yourself and the topic on which you will speak.
- Explain the purpose of the presentation (its objectives).
- If the presentation is one of a series, then re-cap on the previous ones.
- Outline what you are going to say and how you will say it.
- Explain what will be expected of the audience in terms of their participation.
- Tell the audience whether they should ask questions during, or after, the presentation.

In preparing the introduction you should aim to whet the appetite of the audience and to stimulate their interest. To do this successfully requires a little imagination. Many presentations begin with the speaker saying: 'Good morning, the purpose of my talk today is to….' While this is business-like, direct, honest, and down-to-earth, a more interesting introduction might be one that tempts the audience: 'In the next ten minutes I am going to tell you how the profitability of your company can be increased by 50 per cent.' Or a startling statement such as: 'If you do not adopt the proposals I am about to make, you may well find that our competitors will outstrip us in the next five years!'

Another means of introducing the presentation might be by way of quoting statistics, or research findings: 'Did you know that only thirty per cent of British companies are geared towards marketing their products successfully? In the next thirty minutes I am going to show you how your company can adopt a more positive approach to marketing and improve its efficiency and profitability.'

You could begin your presentation with a straight quotation: 'I wish to introduce my talk by referring you to a quotation from Peter Drucker, one of America's leading business academics and business consultants: "The further away your job is from manual work, the larger the organisation of which you are an employee, the more important it will be that you know how to convey your thoughts in writing and speaking." Ladies and gentlemen, the purpose of my presentation is to help you improve your communication skills.'

You may use a rhetorical question to gain the audience's interest and attention: 'Are you dissatisfied with your communication skills? Do you find the audience falls asleep when you talk? Do you want to be more persuasive? If your answer to each of these questions has been 'yes' then listen closely for the next 45 minutes…'

Finally, involving the audience in some way during the introduction might help to gain their attention, either by asking a general question, or one specific to an individual. Alternatively, you could use a handout with a series of questions that the audience must complete. You can then use their answers to focus attention in a specific direction. In using this approach you must take care not to embarrass any member of the audience or to create an air of tension that might deter audience participation.

Clearly, you need an imaginative and creative introduction to gain the attention of the audience and stimulate their interest. Try to avoid apologetic introductions: such as, 'I will only take fifteen minutes of your time...', or ones using clichés: such as, 'Unaccustomed as I am to public speaking...'

If you are going to speak to the same audience on a number of occasions then try to vary the style of introduction on each occasion. Avoid gimmicky introductions, and ones that are blatantly patronising or condescending. Never speak down to your audience.

2.2   Developing your Argument

During this part of the presentation you should specifically state your key ideas in a logical sequence. To convince the audience that your ideas are valid, however, requires you to do more than simply state them. You must support what you say. This is achieved in a number of ways. These are:

(i)   Establishing your credibility with your audience.
(ii) Providing supporting rationale.
(iii) The pattern of the presentation.
(iv) Answering questions.

(i)   Establishing your Credibility with your Audience

The audience must trust you if they are to accept what you are saying. You establish this credibility in a combination of ways:

- Demonstrating that you have knowledge and understanding of the topic.
- Referring to learned sources of relevant information.
- Showing sincerity and integrity, and recognising the views of others.
- Appearing to look composed and confident during the presentation.
- Using your verbal and non-verbal communication skills effectively.

You will enhance your credibility by being thoroughly prepared and by delivering what you are saying with enthusiasm, belief, and commitment. Indeed, these qualities are contagious and if you show that you are enthusiastic the audience will be more likely to share this enthusiasm.

(ii) Providing Supporting Rationale

To convince the audience that your views are correct you should provide supporting rationale in a number of ways:

- Make reference to similar situations – analogies. This helps the audience to understand the point that is being made as they can relate the new knowledge to a familiar, similar situation.
- Draw examples from personal experiences. By including a personal story or two you not only demonstrate the truth and relevance of your major point, but you also add interest to the presentation, which might help your audience to remember what you have been saying.
- Refer to research findings and empirical data. Material produced by other people can substantiate what you are saying and help to make your views more credible.
- Include interesting quotations from a respected authority.
- Ask the audience to support what you are saying. If members of the audience can support what is being said from their own experiences then this will add credibility to the points you are making.

In addition to the above points, pay attention to the structure of your presentation.

(iii)   The Pattern of the Presentation

You can use various patterns for presenting your message:

The Main Idea First: Using this method you propose your main recommendation first and then provide supporting rationale. If your time is restricted then this is a feasible approach. It is business-like and logical.

This pattern will be unsuccessful, however, if your audience does not know the details surrounding the issue under consideration or if you do not expect them to agree immediately with the recommendation that you are proposing.

The Build-up Pattern: In this style of presentation you set the scene surrounding the issue, giving background information and details before arriving at a proposal. You would then introduce supporting rationale.

This is a feasible approach to adopt to persuade an audience which knows little about the topic under consideration, or which might be sceptical towards your proposals. You will need more time for this approach, however, and you will need to think how the various arguments can best be developed.

The Choice Pattern: A variation of the build-up pattern that is useful if you are making a presentation on a problem-solving issue, is to detail the criteria which identify the most appropriate outcome, before proposing alternative solutions and evaluating them against the criteria. In this way you inform the audience of the alternative solutions that you have considered and they will understand why you have rejected them.

This approach is fine if you have time available to develop all the arguments. Part of its success, however, will depend upon the audience agreeing with your evaluation of the alternatives.

The Informative Pattern: The patterns we have discussed above are useful if you are trying to persuade the audience of something. Other considerations are necessary if your presentation aims to provide information for the audience.

When you present information it is important to structure your delivery so that the audience is able to assimilate it. You can adopt various approaches to achieve this. Firstly, you can deliver the information in chronological order. This is appropriate if the presentation is an updating session informing the audience of developments since the last session.

You could use a variation of such an approach if you are informing the audience of how to perform a certain task. In this case you can break down the task into steps and discuss each step separately until you have built up the overall picture. Use this approach when it is important for the audience to understand the development of a concept.

Another useful pattern is the cause-effect approach. With this pattern of delivery you discuss the cause of something before analysing its effects.

A final pattern can be employed when a complex topic is being discussed. To reach the complex issue it is best if you start the content of the presentation at a relatively easy level before building up to the more difficult issues. It will be important to make sure, however, that the audience grasps each point before moving onto the next level of complexity.

With any of the patterns of presentation we have discussed you must carefully organise the key ideas in your presentation. Draw up a flow chart which lists the topics to be covered in order of precedence. Question the logic of the order to confirm that the audience will be able to follow the development of your argument.

Pay particular attention to the way you develop the argument, and to the links within the presentation that add to its flow and assist your audience in remembering what has been said.

Linking Techniques: Linking techniques are a valuable device as they add further structure to the presentation, and allow the audience to see how the argument has developed so far, and where it is heading.

Before making a new point, preview it. Stress the topic headings you are using and repeat them to act as 'sub-headings'. Summarise important points to ensure the audience has grasped the message. For example:

> So, to summarise this point it can be seen that… The next stage in the argument is to consider the effect of transferable personal skills training on the motivation of the sales force. The area that I will now draw your attention to is the role of transferable personal skills training. The role of transferable personal skills training is multi-dimensional…

You can reinforce these markers in the presentation with handouts, direct aids, or projected aids. The purpose of using them is to make the structure of the presentation explicit. Think also about how you use your voice. Slow and speed up the pace of your delivery, stressing certain words, repeating key phrases.

The success of your presentation, therefore, will in part be dependent on the content, and whether or not you present and substantiate the key ideas clearly and with due conviction and the use that you make of linking techniques to guide the listener through the presentation. You might provide an outline of the topics to be discussed in the presentation for the audience, either on a handout, by a direct aid, or a projected aid.

(iv)   Answering Questions

While you must give thought and attention to the introduction and development of your arguments, you must also consider how to answer questions.

At some stage during the presentation you may be asked questions by the audience. The questions might require you to clarify a point, or they might be extending the content of your presentation into a different area. No matter what the questions are, however, they should be treated in a similar way:

- You should welcome questions from the audience: not only do they show that the audience is interested and listening to what you are saying, but questions give you an opportunity to engage with what is of direct concern to the audience.
- Repeat the question, or rephrase it, so that all members of the audience can hear it. You will frequently find that those who ask questions speak in soft tones of voice.
- Try to answer each question that is posed directly. Do not ignore the question and answer some other that you would have preferred. This will substantially reduce your credibility with the audience.
- Give short answers if possible so that you can answer more than just one or two in the time available.
- If you cannot answer the question, say so directly. Your audience will soon realise if you are giving a less than truthful answer. You could try to elicit the correct answer from other members of the audience, who might have the necessary experience or information.

- If you cannot answer a question or get other members of the audience to answer it, tell the person asking the question that you will find out the answer after the presentation and will provide it at the next session or forward it. Always obtain the information and make sure that the person who asked the question receives it, or recommend a particular source of information from which the answer might be obtained.
- Never ridicule a member of the audience for asking a question. Welcome audience participation as it adds further interest and stimulation to your presentation. If you make the audience feel foolish because of the nature of the questions they ask, then they will stop participating.
- If you get one questioner who is particularly persistent to the extent that she is dominating the questioning session, assert yourself and politely refuse to answer any more of this individual's questions, by offering to answer further of her questions after the presentation.
- As the questioning period is coming to an end, indicate this to the audience by saying something like 'I'm sorry but there is only time for three more questions.'

2.3   The Conclusion of your Presentation

The final part of your presentation is the conclusion. This will have a number of purposes:

- To answer any final questions that the audience might have.
- To summarise the main points discussed.
- To emphasise the key arguments.
- To commit the audience to a change in behaviour or a programme of action that they can follow.
- To introduce the next step/course of action/presentation.

Do not introduce new material in the conclusion, but reiterate the key points of your presentation. Draw the audience's attention to the objectives that you initially set and try to measure whether they have been met. To do this, put questions to the audience. For example, 'Now that you have heard my presentation, what does employability skills training mean to you? How will it help you in your future careers?' If you have prepared and delivered the presentation well such a conclusion should bring it to a successful close. All that remains to be done is to thank the audience for their attendance, attention, interest and participation.

3.   Bringing the Presentation to Life

In addition to preparing the structure of your presentation you should also pay attention to bringing it to life, personalising it, and making it enjoyable to listen to. This will help to maintain the attention and interest of the audience.

Particularly where the presentation is formal it will be important to consider ways of livening it up, making the content interesting to listen to, and preventing boredom setting in with the audience. You can use a number of techniques for this purpose.

The first point to remember is that the audience is made up of individuals. Therefore, you should seek to acknowledge their existence. If you know their names, then use them during the presentation. Make eye contact with all members of the audience, not just to select individuals. Show that the message directly applies to the audience, rather than speaking in abstract terms. Think about using the techniques we discussed in Chapter Three under the heading of figurative language. Use metaphors, hyperboles and similes to add a touch of humour to the presentation, but be careful not to overwork them. When using humour, your role is not to be a stand-up comedian, but a witty speaker. Do not offend the audience and do not let the humour detract from the objectives of the presentation.

3.1   Visual Aids

To add a further dimension to your presentation you could incorporate carefully designed visual aids. Visual aids offer you a number of benefits:

- They add structure to the presentation.
- They act as an aide-memoire/notes for you during the presentation.
- They act as 'memory joggers' for the audience, helping them to remember what you have said.
- They can help to clarify difficult concepts.
- They are a good way to communicate data/statistics/technical details.

They stimulate the interest of the audience and help to hold their attention, especially if they are creative e.g. cartoons.

By being skilful in their design, creative in their production and implementing them as integral parts of the presentation, further interest can be created for the audience, helping to bring the presentation to life.

(i)   Direct Aids

Direct aids can be directly written on, such as dry-boards and flip-charts. These can be used for a variety of purposes:

- Displaying data in tabular form/graphs/pie charts so they can be more easily understood.
- Displaying key words or phrases that help to structure the presentation.
- Summarising points.
- Illustrating how calculations are carried out.
- Displaying pre-printed posters/leaflets/cartoons/photographs.
- Noting down points raised by the audience, or building up a concept step by step, thus helping the audience to follow the development of the argument or presentation.

If possible prepare most of the visual aids in advance of the presentation and build them into the presentation plan. In using direct aids refer to the following checklist:

- Keep the visual simple: use only key words.
- Use co-ordinated colours to add to its appeal.
- Only use visuals that are neatly produced and are legibly written.
- Do not overload the visual with too much information, write only a few lines on each flip-chart.
- Write in large letters so that all the members of the audience will be able to read the message.
- Always direct the audiences' attention to the visual when referring to it – use a pointer.
- Make sure the visual aid can be seen by everyone, do not stand in front of it, but beside it.
- Only display the visual aid when referring to it.
- Speak to the audience, not to the visual aid – it is only an aid.

In addition to written visual aids, you can use models, prototypes or the actual physical item itself.

(ii)   Projected Aids

As technology advances, improvements are made in the means of projecting messages onto a screen, or screens. The three most commonly used methods of visual projection are overhead projectors (OHPs), 35mm slide projectors, and PowerPoint data projectors. The advantages of using these are that the visual might be more visible than direct aids in larger rooms, as they enable your written words to be magnified and projected onto a screen. In addition, they are sometimes easier to use and to refer to. Indeed, careful slide design can add a strong visual impact to your presentation.

Using an Overhead Projector: You use an OHP by writing onto an acetate slide which is then projected onto the screen. These transparencies can be hand drawn or a printed or word processed message can be copied onto the slide by some photo-copiers.

When using the OHP bear in mind the following points:

- Always face the audience, do not speak to the screen, or look at the projector.
- Stand or sit to one side of the projector, never behind it.
- Switch off the OHP between each transparency, otherwise the light and noise from it will distract the audience.
- When drawing the audience's attention to a particular aspect of the OHP slide, point to the transparency, never to the screen.
- Make sure the projection plate of the OHP is clean.
- Carry a spare bulb in case the one in the projector blows.

Overhead projectors can be used for projecting a variety of different material in addition to the single transparency:

- Overlays. Here, a series of slides are hinged onto a single mount which are laid on top of each other. At appropriate stages in the presentation new slides are overlaid in order to build up a point, concept or scenario as the presentation progresses. This is an effective way of developing a complex picture or argument in discrete stages, helping the audience to understand the message as it evolves.
- Revelation Technique. Using this, certain parts of the transparency are hidden behind masking paper. When it is appropriate to refer to a particular point it is revealed from under the masking paper.
- Movements. These can be illustrated on the OHP, for example iron filings being attracted by a magnet.

If you are going to use any of the techniques mentioned above it is important that you practise them beforehand if you are to achieve the correct effect during the presentation.

Using Slide Projectors: Using 35mm photographic slides in a presentation is another effective means of communication. Recent advances in computer graphics now permit clear images to be produced of graphs, tables, pie charts, maps, as well as conventional images, direct onto 35mm slide film.

All the points raised above for using an OHP apply to the use of slide projectors. You need to pay additional attention, though, to the projector itself, for instance ensuring that it is correctly positioned and is not too noisy.

3.2   Technology Based Presentations

Most conference and presentation venues now provide opportunities to project computer based presentations using a data projector connected to a variety of computers including laptops, PDAs, and fully networked PCs.

If there is no technical support available on site to set up the laptop and data projector ensure that you know how to do this, and allow yourself sufficient time to test the equipment, and have a 'dry run' through of your slides. If you are presenting from your own media for example floppy disc, CD-ROM, DVD, zip disc, smart card or memory stick, always ensure that you have a backup copy of all of your files on another media type. This is mainly for two reasons: in case your original media fails for any reason; or in case the venue does not have hardware suitable for your media device. It is always best to check what hardware and facilities are available in advance. However it is always wise to consider all possibilities and cover yourself in the case of any mishap.

With regards to software the most common type and the accepted industry standard is Microsoft PowerPoint. If you are using PowerPoint, consider which version of PowerPoint you are using, and which version is available at the venue. The reason for this is that if the venue is using an older version of PowerPoint some features such as animations on bullet points may not work quite as expected. This is another reason to do your homework on what facilities are available, and to get there early so that any problems can be identified before the audience arrives.

If you do find that you have created a presentation in a more modern version of PowerPoint than what is available at the venue, and it is having an adverse effect on the animations on your slides, make a backup copy at the venue. Then re-save the backup copy to be the same as the version at the venue – then redo your animations. If this fails, and for whatever reason you cannot correct any problems you are having, simply explain to your audience before you begin that you have experienced some compatibility problems between the versions of PowerPoint, and due to that, some animations may not work as you would have liked. Most audiences will be understanding of such technical difficulties.

One final point – it can be a good idea to have a final backup plan such as printed acetates of your slides that can be used on an overhead projector should the technology at the venue fail completely.

If you are going to use PowerPoint you need to be aware of some of the software's basic functions. You need to be able to:

- Create a new PowerPoint document.
- Open a PowerPoint document.
- Close a PowerPoint document.
- Print and print preview a PowerPoint document as well as printing slides, handouts and notes pages.
- Save a PowerPoint document in its existing format as well as a variety of PowerPoint versions using the Save As command.
- View a presentation in layout view, slide sorter view, and slide show view.
- Enter notes in the notes window.
- Change the order of slides in slide sorter view.
- Use formatting such as changing fonts, font sizes, underlining text, making text bold *and italicised.*
- Insert and write in text boxes and tables, and remove their borders to make them appear invisible.
- Create, edit and format tables.
- Copy/cut and paste text and other objects such as graphics.

- Use the spell checker to help ensure that your document does not contain spelling mistakes.
- Insert slide numbers at the bottom of your slides.
- Insert pictures and clip art.
- Insert animation on objects within your slides.
- Alter the alignment of your text.
- Use the slide transition feature.

For further help on using these features visit the Microsoft PowerPoint help site at http://office.microsoft.com once at the site click upon the link to PowerPoint on the left of the screen. Here you will find many resources designed to help you get the most out of this presentation software.

3.3   Preparing and Using Projected Aids

Just as direct aids have to be carefully prepared so to do projected aids. The guidelines presented here apply to both overhead transparency slides as well as PowerPoint slides:

- Keep the slides simple, write separate messages on separate slides. Write only four or five words per line, any more will be difficult to read. Allow only six lines, or fewer, on a single slide.
- Fonts - use an easy to read rounded font such as Arial in both upper and lower case letters. Avoid writing in all capitals as IT MAY LOOK LIKE YOU ARE SHOUTING. A minimum height of 6mm will be required for projection purposes. For PowerPoint presentations use a minimum font size of Arial 16.
- Graphics – use charts and graphs instead of tables; use maps, diagrams, photographs and other pictures to help enforce your message – remember a picture can paint a thousand words.
- Colours – in general stick to either dark text on a non-patterned pastel shaded background, or light text on a dark non-patterned background – but be consistent. The use of other colours within your presentation can help to subliminally enforce messages – however do not over-use colours. If you would like to make subtle use of colours the following is a guide to the type of message certain colours can give:

Colour	Message
Black	Authority, power, potency
White	Innocence, peace, innovative, fresh
Red	Striking, prominence, warning, signal
Brown	Trust, friendship, maturity
Purple	Distinction, stateliness, majesty, formality
Green	Environmental, health, expansion
Orange	Achievement, confidence, buoyancy, excitement
Yellow	Warmth, knowledge, understanding, perception
Blue	Tranquility, calm, harmony, serenity

A good rule of thumb with colours is to stick to those colours that are most fit for the purpose of the presentation. If you were making a presentation about a theme park, then colours implying fun, excitement and action would be suitable. However if you were making a presentation about a nature reserve, colours indicating, environmentality, tranquility, health and peace would be most suitable.

If you become skilled at using Powerpoint, you will quickly develop the ability to produce high quality professional presentations.

The slides below highlight some of the good and bad points about using PowerPoint for presentations.

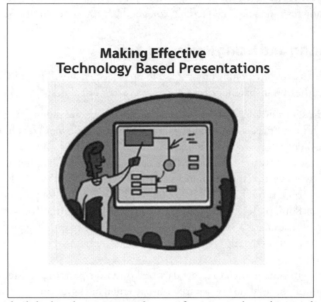

The above is a title slide that demonstrates the use of writing and graphics to clearly set out what the presentation will be about.

The following slide is designed to highlight the effective use of a title and bullet points:

An Effective Presentation Process

- Analyse the audience.

- Identify any critical issues.

- Select you presentation technique.

- Identify relevant facts, figures and statistics.

The following slide is designed to highlight how graphics and bullet points can be used together in order to help get the message across:

Use Graphics to Demonstrate Points

✳ Seating within the venue is tiered for maximum occupancy, and to allow a greater view.

✳ Foldaway seating is used to facilitate movement.

✳ Toughened plastic is used for resilience.

The following is a problem slide and is designed to demonstrate what NOT to do with Powerpoint:

Crowded Slides are Ineffective

✳ This bullet point contains far too much information, for an audience to properly read and understand whilst listening to the presenter speak, and also watching for the non-verbal gestures a presenter may use.

✳ By putting too much information on your slide you are reducing its effectiveness as a communicative tool, this slide would have been better as two slides.

If you have to cram your slide with information, build it up slowly using animation

---

Remember, when using the projected aid to:

- Make sure the screen can be seen by everyone, and speak to the audience not to the screen.
- Use slides to support what you are saying; ensure the presentation does not simply become a commentary of the slides.

- Dim the room lights when showing the slides, but do not switch them off.
- Use efficient equipment, check that it is working before making the presentation. Make sure that the projector operates quietly and does not distract the listeners.
- Memorise the order of the slides so that every time they change you know the content of the next one, reducing your need to be continually looking at the screen.
- Do not use too many slides – their over use is monotonous.

As well as using direct and projected visual aids you could also consider using videos as another means of stimulating the audience's interest. Commercial organisations such as Video Arts for example, provide well-produced training videos and DVDs that have clear objectives, are well-structured, expertly acted, and which can liven up a presentation. Videos though, should not simply be used to entertain the audience. Pose questions to the audience prior to watching the video, and return to these questions afterwards to draw out the salient points of its message.

3.4   Questioning the Audience

Questions have a role to play in most presentations as they are a form of direct audience participation. The questions you put to the audience should be open ones, and hence should commence with, 'What', 'Why', 'How' or 'Where'.

Your purpose in using questions should be to motivate the audience by challenging them, or intriguing them. After a period when you have been doing all the talking and the audience has simply been listening, use questions to get them thinking and to involve them more. Think about how you phrase questions:

- Use simple wording that can easily be understood.
- Make sure the questions are reasonable and are answerable.

Do not use trick questions or ones that will make members of the audience feel foolish.

4.   The Presentation Plan

When you have set your objectives for the presentation, and considered the characteristics of the audience, and when all the elements that constitute the content of the presentation have been carefully prepared, you are then in a position to write your presentation plan.

The plan is the king pin of the presentation, it acts as a game plan, ensuring that all the previous points discussed in this chapter will fall into place on the day of the presentation. Without an explicit and clear plan all the preparation that has been carried out will be futile. The plan ensures that the delivery of the prepared material takes place as intended in a logical and interesting format.

To produce a plan divide an A4 sheet of paper into four columns:

PRESENTATION PLAN

KEY	PRESENTER ACTIVITY	AUDIENCE ACTIVITY	RESOURCES
Introduction	Welcome the audience Outline the presentation		OHP
5 mins	Using a video Ask questions at end	Listen	
Development			
2 mins	Definition	Note taking	
2 mins	Amusing anecdote	Listen	Cartoon
5 mins	Background details	Note taking	
3 mins	Introduce the video	Listen	
15 mins	Play video	Watch and take notes	Video
5 mins	Ask 3 Open Questions	Answer Questions	
Conclusion			
5 mins	Reiterate key points	Listen	OHP
	Cover arrangements for next week	Note taking	

The Key Column: This column serves two purposes. Firstly, it is used to divide the presentation explicitly into the three distinct stages of introduction, development of the argument and conclusion, serving as 'tram-lines' to prevent you deviating from this structure.

Secondly, timings are placed in this column against distinct stages of the presentation to ensure that all the points that you need to make can be covered in the time available, and also to act as a guide for you when giving the talk. By checking the timings in this column against the lapsed time of the presentation you will know whether to speed up or slow down your delivery.

Allocating specific times to specific parts of the presentation is essential and cannot be overemphasised, for otherwise you will not know whether time is available to make all your planned points. A presentation can be ruined by running out of time before it has run its carefully thought out course. Similarly, you will appear unprofessional if you finish an hour long presentation in fifteen minutes.

Once you have prepared the content of the presentation and you have determined a structure, place timings against each section, and add them up to make sure that all the time you have available for the presentation is being used and the presentation will not overrun. The content of your presentation should be noted in the next column – 'presenter activity'.

The Presenter Activity Column: The purpose of this column is to provide the structure for your presentation. Note down each stage of the presentation and include certain key words as a memory jogger. Outline the content of your talk here not in sentence form but in the form of single words or phrases.

Do not use a pre-worded script during the presentation but develop the exact wording of your speech as the structure progresses, elaborating on the key words on the presentation plan. By so doing you will achieve a more natural delivery, which allows you to maintain stronger eye contact with the audience as you do not need to look down at a script. During the presentation place the plan on a lectern or table. Many speakers place a watch beside their notes. Otherwise ensure that a clock is within easy view. At intervals check that the timings are running to schedule and that you are delivering the content of the presentation according to the plan.

If you are familiar with the topic under discussion then a single sheet should be enough for most presentations lasting up to one hour. If the topic is unfamiliar or complex, however, then you might need additional sheets but these should be kept to an absolute minimum. The fewer sheets there are the less likely that you will lose your place.

By using a presentation plan you will not need to resort to cards with points written on them. The use of cards is frequently distracting and clearly indicates that as a presenter you are unsure of your material. If you are using PowerPoint you can use the 'notes view' when setting up your slide to write additional notes that will not appear on the slide itself.

The Audience Activity Column: It is important to plan all the ways in which the audience will be involved in the presentation – hence the audience activity column. Specify when you expect the audience to listen, when they are to write notes, and when you will ask them questions. Think how you will ask the questions. Should they be directed to named individuals or delivered as open questions for anyone to answer? Anticipate the likely responses to make sure that you are asking the right questions.

If you are giving a longer presentation change the type of audience activity at least every twenty minutes. This means that you should not speak for more than twenty minutes at any one time.

To break up the presentation use a variety of activities:

- Ask questions.
- Form small groups and hold discussions.
- Circulate handouts and ask the audience to read them.
- Play videos or audio tapes.
- Ask the audience to take notes.
- Give a demonstration.

The Resources Column: Note all the additional material that is to be used during the presentation in the resources column. Use just one or two word descriptions in this column, for example, 'definitions handout', 'cartoon OHP', or 'video'. Before the presentation check to make sure that all the necessary resources are to hand, that they will function correctly, and that they are in the right order.

The presentation plan can be used in a diagnostic sense as it will show you whether you have devoted too much or too little time to a particular aspect of the content. The presentation plan forms the key to a successful presentation as it enables you to structure your talk in a logical way. Presenters who do not structure their talks will appear to be unprofessional and less competent.

4.1   Rehearsing the Presentation

Once the presentation plan has been produced you will find it helpful to rehearse the talk in private before giving the actual presentation. Although this might feel a little strange at first, most public speakers do it, as it highlights areas which need strengthening, and through added familiarity with the material and the sound of your own voice, boosts confidence. Rehearsal will enable you to confirm all the timings and to make sure that the presentation does not overrun or finish too soon. It will also give you the opportunity to become familiar with the structure of the presentation as well as the aids and technical equipment you are going to use.

It is best to try and rehearse the presentation in the actual room to be used on the day. This allows you to become familiar with the surroundings and will highlight possible distractions that might arise during the presentation. Check all the equipment you are going to use to make sure that you know how to work it, and that it does work.

During your rehearsal, as well as concentrating on the content and structure detail of the presentation plan, you should also pay attention to the other aspects of your presentation style.

(i) Delivery Style

Your physical presence gives a message to the audience even before your presentation starts. As you walk into the room or onto the stage, or as you are being introduced, the audience will form a first impression of you. Try not to look anxious. You will establish a more favourable first impression if you look confident. If you are familiar with the room within which your presentation is to take place this will help to reduce your nervousness.

The next stage in the rehearsal process is to work through the presentation plan and actually deliver the talk to the empty room. Pay attention to the following:

- The space between you and the audience – are you too far away, creating a barrier to communication?
- The physical barriers of the room – should you stand in front of or behind the desk?
- Body language – are you using appropriate and complementary body language? Have you any distracting mannerisms? Do you move around too much ?
- Verbal communications – can people hear you clearly? Are you varying your tone of voice and are you using intonation, inflection and different speeds of speech? Is your grammar correct and have you checked your verbal mannerisms/distractions?
- Personal appearance and grooming – are you appropriately dressed?
- Are you using visual aids efficiently in the presentation?

If possible a friend should be invited to the rehearsal to provide additional feedback on points about which you might not have been aware, such as sniffs, coughs, shrugs, ear-scratching, 'er's' and 'um's'. Otherwise you could record the rehearsal and play it back and analyse it. The purpose of the rehearsal, though, is not only to practise the style of presentation but also to practise your activities and those of the audience.

(ii) Presenter and Audience Participation

The rehearsal session should also allow you to become familiar with using your presentation plan. You should work through the activities outlined on the plan to confirm that they are feasible. Test the memory-jogging words and terms to make sure that they do direct you in the right direction. If you find that your notes are too brief, then add further comments to the plan.

Practise the questions that you are going to ask the audience and consider their likely responses. What will you do if one of your open questions is not answered? What will you do if you direct a question at a specific individual and that person is unable to answer? In these situations you need to adopt a sensitive approach to prevent the audience feeling embarrassed. Rephrase the question, or give clues to the correct answer.

At no time should you reject answers out of hand, for this will discourage further contributions from your audience. Acknowledge and reward even partly correct responses to encourage further audience participation.

Make contingency plans for signs that the audience might be losing interest. Such signs include the audience reducing their eye contact with you, a person talking to her neighbour, somebody writing when they are not supposed to, people looking out of the window or even falling asleep. If you see these signals then change the audience activity.

The second purpose of the rehearsal, therefore, is for you to consider and practise the presentation. Familiarise yourself further with all the equipment you are going to use. Write on the board. Find out where all the switches and heating controls are, and even where the nearest toilets are – a member of the audience might not have planned ahead!

Rehearsing thoroughly for the presentation, knowing all the material to be used, and critically evaluating all the skills to be employed, should reduce your nervousness and apprehension. All that remains to be done is to deliver the presentation.

5.   Delivering the Presentation

This is the shortest section of this chapter for the key to a successful presentation is preparation, planning and rehearsal. If you have taken care to follow the guidelines we have already proposed then the presentation will be delivered extremely competently and professionally. There might be disturbances and distractions during the presentation, however, and you need to know how to deal with these.

5.1   Dealing with Disturbances and Distractions

You might have to face disturbances and distractions during the presentation. Somebody might arrive late, or a member of the audience may leave early. Noise could be a problem if you have aircraft passing overhead or a car alarm goes off. A member of the audience could faint. The power supply to the room might be cut off, or the bulb in the data projector cease to function. The list of possible distractions and disturbances is endless. The way to deal with each of these depends upon the circumstances. However, a number of generalisations can be made:

- Remember that you are in control of the audience and must take the lead. If you have to evacuate the room, it is your responsibility to manage this in a calm, orderly manner.
- If the distraction is only temporary, such as a member of the audience arriving or leaving, stop talking until the distraction has finished. Simply explain why you are pausing.
- No matter what the distraction or disturbance is, remain calm and collected. If you become irritated you will not be able to think as clearly.

Once you have delivered the presentation, all that remains to do is evaluate it.

5.2   Evaluating the Presentation

You improve your ES every time you use them. This improvement will be greater if you evaluate the effectiveness of your skills and learn from the process. Following a presentation you can get feedback from a variety of sources:

- You can get a formal evaluation of the presentation by asking the audience to complete a specially designed questionnaire, that focuses on the ES you used. (Ask your tutor for a copy of such a questionnaire).
- Complete a self-evaluation questionnaire yourself.
- You may get informal feedback from comments made by members of the audience.
- You could make a recording of the presentation and then analyse it.

By adopting a systematic approach to evaluating the presentation you should be able to identify your strengths as well as areas you could improve. In this way you should find that your presentation technique improves and you become more confident about making presentations.

6.   Special Types of Presentation

In the previous sections we have covered points which have a wide applicability and you should bear them in mind when making a presentation of any kind. It is essential to plan, prepare and rehearse a presentation before delivering it. There are, though, a number of situations that require you to adopt a slightly different approach.

6.1   Making a Short Presentation

In certain circumstances the time you have available for the presentation might be limited. At meetings, if there are a number of points on the agenda, each speaker, or proposer, might be given only a few minutes to make a point by the chairperson. Management teams receiving presentations from consultants pitching for a particular contract might only allow the presenters ten or fifteen minutes to present their views. Applicants being interviewed for a career vacancy might be required to make a ten minute presentation on a certain topic. In these situations you must adopt a special approach.

Obviously, time is of the essence and everything you say must count. You will not have time to deviate from the central theme of the presentation. If your presentation, for which time is short, is to be successful, bear the following points in mind:

- You must clearly understand the purpose of the presentation and set explicit objectives.
- Consider carefully the nature of the audience and what they will be expecting from the presentation.
- When competing against others then try to find out what approaches they will be adopting.
- Present the main idea first, and then justify it. Get to the heart of the issue as soon as possible. You will have little time for considering alternatives in great detail.
- Once you have made the recommendation, give the audience reasons for accepting it – therefore, stress its advantages and benefits. How will they gain? Will they enjoy improved profitability or reduced costs? To do this you must be clear about what will motivate the audience before making the presentation or by establishing this at its outset.
- You can produce a report providing greater detail that is given to the audience prior to the presentation, giving them further background information. You can then refer to data contained in the report during the presentation.
- Remember, time is short so the style of your presentation should be clear, to the point, but at the same time creative and imaginative, and based around a well structured format.

As your time available for the presentation is limited, it will be essential to ensure that the audience is not overloaded with information – you can make only two or three points effectively in a short period of time. If you are presenting data, then be creative rather than using a mundane tabular form. It will be crucial to rehearse the presentation to ensure that you can make all the points in the time available. Your delivery will need to be meticulously paced so that you do not overrun.

A further constraint you may find with a short presentation is that you might not be able to rehearse in the actual room that you will use. In these circumstances clarify beforehand what equipment will be available, how the furniture in the room will be laid out, and what the seating arrangements will be. Make sure that you have all the necessary back-up material of all visual aids to hand. For example, make photocopies of your PowerPoint slides that you want to show as a precaution in case the data projector is unavailable or not working on the day.

Making a presentation in an unfamiliar setting requires you to assess the situation as soon as you enter. Quickly appraise the physical surroundings. If there are problems with the room decide immediately how you can overcome these. Spend as little time as possible gathering your thoughts, or arranging the material you are going to use. You should have covered these details in your preparation process, thus allowing you to start the presentation as soon as possible. If you demonstrate an amateurish approach at the outset you will not create a favourable first impression, especially if the previous presentations have been highly professional.

In a short presentation you can realistically aim only for the creation of a professional and favourable image with the audience. You should show that you have grasped the nature of the situation under examination, and are able to make recommendations that are logical and feasible and of benefit to the audience. You should encourage the audience to solicit further information from you. Short presentations, therefore, require a slightly different approach to those where more time is available.

6.2   Group Briefings

Group briefings also require special consideration. They tend to be more informal than persuasive or informative presentations as you will frequently know the people present. Nevertheless, you still have to adopt a structured approach:

- Notify all people who will be attending the briefing session in advance of its time and place, and that they will be expected to attend.
- Prepare the room in which the briefing will take place. Arrange the seats in a circle or horse-shoe, and try to prevent the briefing from being interrupted, for example transfer all incoming telephone calls elsewhere, put a 'Do Not Disturb' notice on the door.
- Set objectives for the session and prepare, plan and rehearse as you would for any presentation. You will find, however, that as you become more familiar with the processes involved the need for detailed rehearsal will be reduced.
- You will find that you have more frequent and spontaneous interactions with the audience. You will need to pay attention to possible questions that might arise, and give some thought to handling them. If a question is asked that you cannot answer, admit to this and arrange to find out the answer after the briefing session.
- Keep the briefing session brief! It is likely that the audience will have other things to do.

Briefing sessions are of value in a number of situations. It is important to keep the group informed of progress that is being made and helps to reduce the likelihood of rumours developing and spreading.

The morale of the group will be improved if you give praise for work that is completed on time and to a high standard. If working relationships are changing then keep the group fully informed of new developments. You can use de-briefing sessions as follow-up exercises after an event to find out why an activity was successful or unsuccessful.

In this chapter we have discussed the ES that you require when making a presentation. Presentation skills will not be mastered, however, purely by reading this chapter. It is only by practising that you will find where your strengths and weaknesses lie. Critically appraise your own performance in giving a presentation and ask others to evaluate your performance. It is only in this way that you will be able to improve your presentational skills.

With any kind of presentation remember the six Ps – Practice, Planning and Preparation, for Perfectly Performed Presentations!

After reading this chapter please complete the following learning activities:

Learning Activities

1.   Write out a plan for a 20 minute presentation on a subject of your choice, to be delivered in a venue that you are familiar with. Consider the needs of the audience, and the timings of your presentation.

2.   Prepare a visual aid, in the form of a hand-out, to be distributed during the above presentation.

3.   Utilising best-practice techniques create between five and ten PowerPoint slides to accompany your speech within the above presentation.

4.   Rehearse your presentation in front of a friend. After your presentation write up a critical reflection of your presentation performance – what went well, and what could you have done better? Ask your friend for feedback to help you with this.

Chapter Eight
Selling and Negotiation Skills

The art of management lies in persuading other people to want to do whatever it is that one wishes them to do. An effective communicator is far more likely to succeed in this respect.

Peter Youdale, Chairman, Pirbic Group Management Consultants.

After reading this chapter you will be able to:

1. Plan and deliver a formal sales presentation.

2. Communicate effectively in a one-to-one selling situation.

3. Prepare yourself to take part in a negotiating exercise.

4. Understand the factors that lead to success when negotiating with other people.

Selling and negotiating skills are of value far beyond simply encouraging customers to buy your company's products. These personal skills are highly transferable. When being interviewed for a job, you have to 'sell' yourself to the recruiter. If you are a manager making a presentation to colleagues, you will frequently have to 'sell' your ideas before they are accepted. Negotiations take place in a wide variety of situations, from determining who will carry out certain tasks or negotiating new terms and conditions of employment.

In all situations where you have to display such skills, there are certain principles in common. The selling skills you would use when encouraging a customer to buy the product will be similar to those used when encouraging colleagues to accept a new idea. The purpose of this chapter is to make you aware of the constituent components of these selling and negotiating skills.

1.   Selling Skills

Everybody has sold something at some time in their lives, and everybody is involved in selling, whether they realise it or not. To be successful at selling you need skills beyond simple instinct (although this will, of course, help). At the heart of effective salesmanship lies the controlled use of ES.

Successful selling requires you, as the salesperson, to be well-prepared. Few salespeople are able to sell their product (no matter what it is) unless they have given prior thought and consideration to the situation which faces the customer. We shall consider two different selling situations in this chapter:

- A formal sales presentation – in which you make a presentation to a large group of buyers.
- One-to-one selling – a more informal setting in which you are selling to a single customer.

1.1   The Formal Sales Presentation

All of the skills covered in Chapter Seven apply to sales presentations. The purpose of this section is to elaborate the special considerations that you need make when giving such a presentation. In this section we shall look at the following points:

(i)   Setting objectives.
(ii)   The nature of the audience.
(iii)   Structuring the presentation.
(iv)   Delivering the presentation.
(v)   The venue.

(i)   Setting Objectives

In Chapter Seven we stated that all presentations must have an objective, a purpose. Sales presentations are no different. The purpose of a sales presentation, however, is to influence the audience in some way, and so you need to adopt a slightly different approach. Your audience will have a reason for listening. As it is a formal sales presentation, they know that you are trying to sell something. Thus, the starting point for your presentation will be to establish its purpose both from your point of view and from the audience's. Before the presentation pose yourself some of the following questions:

What is the purpose of the presentation from the audience's point of view?

What do the audience expect from the presentation?

What are the audience's objectives in attending?

What is your purpose in making the presentation?

What are your expectations from the presentation?

What are your objectives?

In answering such questions it is likely that you will come up with answers that are similar to these:

To communicate ideas.

To provide information.

To persuade the audience to buy.

Only when you have established a clear understanding of your audience, especially their readiness to buy, can you set explicit objectives for the presentation. If the audience is unfamiliar with you and your product it is likely that your presentation will concentrate on building their awareness and communicating information to them. If the audience already know your product, however, then your purpose will be to persuade and to sell.

(ii)   The Nature of your Audience

Once you have established the purpose of the sales presentation and you have set your objectives, you need to consider the nature of your audience:

- Who will comprise the audience?
- Who are the members of the audience who will make the decision to buy?
- What is the status and standing of the audience?
- What is the level of their technical ability and comprehension of jargon?
- What kind of presentation do they expect?

These factors will be crucial in helping you to structure the presentation and decide on its content. In particular, you need to identify the key decision-makers in the audience so that you can observe their reactions closely during the presentation.

If you notice that these key decision-makers are losing interest (which may be clearly indicated by their body language) then your presentation is proving ineffective, and you will have to introduce a different tactic. Prior to making the presentation, you will need to find out what will motivate the key decision-makers to buy the product. Are cost savings the deciding factor, or is it product quality? If the audience is made up of senior managers of the host organisation, who have little contact with the product being considered, how much will they know about its technical qualities, will they be lost if you give a detailed technical analysis?

You need, therefore, to undertake research into the nature of your audience before making a sales presentation. If you understand their motivations, needs, technical abilities, and status, designing your message and structuring the presentation will be straightforward.

(iii)   Structuring the Presentation

The structure of a sales presentation will be essentially the same as for the other types of presentation:

- Introduction:
  - to communicate your plan for the presentation;
  - to establish a rapport with the audience.
- Development:
  - to convey the key message of the presentation;
  - to develop the sales argument;
  - to provide supporting evidence, facts, data.
- Conclusion:
  - to reiterate the main points raised;
  - to emphasise the key selling points;
  - to encourage the audience to respond positively to your message.

The main purpose of a sales presentation is to influence the audience favourably towards the product. Frequently you will want a definite decision from the audience, it will not be sufficient to provide them with information and conclude the presentation. When you require a decision, however, you must provide the audience with sufficient information to enable them to arrive at a decision.

To decide on the type of information to provide which will allow the audience to reach a decision you will need to be aware of their motives, in other words why they will be interested in buying the product. People buy products because of the benefits they gain from using them. A major element of your sales presentation, therefore, will be to emphasise the benefits the audience will enjoy from buying the product.

Untrained sales presenters often emphasise the product's features in the presentation, describing them in some detail. While such a description of the product has a role to play, the main part of your presentation should be devoted to showing how it will benefit the audience. You should show the features of the product to be benefits of the product. For example, consider the two following statements a salesperson could make during a presentation:

The Product Description: 'Our new production line is electronically controlled by micro-chip technology…'

The Benefit Statement: '…which means that we will improve manufacturing efficiency by 15%, saving our company £200,000 per year.'

From the above you can see that two words link a descriptive phrase with a benefit statement: **'which means'**.

The main thrust of your sales presentation should be on highlighting the benefits of the product. You could provide impartial evidence, for example, by referring the audience to articles published in the press, or to testimonials from satisfied customers. You can make comparisons with competing products to show the differences that exist and why your product is superior.

To assist you in developing your sales arguments you should draw up a product features-benefits table:

PRODUCT FEATURE	PRODUCT BENEFIT
A hatchback car with 5 doors.	Easy accessibility for the family.
A 1600cc engine.	Lively performance.
A 6 speed gear box.	Economical fuel consumption.
Steel braced radial tyres.	Harder wearing and better road holding.

Such an approach helps you to get a clear idea of the main selling points of your product and the benefits it offers. You should make a similar analysis of competing products so that you can identify their unique selling points and counter them in the presentation.

When you have presented the arguments for buying your product to the audience, offer them a set of options as to what they could do next. Would they like you to expand on any part of the presentation? Do they require further information? Would they like you to make another presentation at a later date? Would they like to buy the product on the spot? You need to obtain some form of commitment from them at the conclusion of the presentation rather than letting it end with matters undecided and 'up in the air'.

Thus, although the structure of your sales presentation is the same as that discussed in Chapter Seven, your content will be such that it should influence the audience to follow a particular course of action. Your delivery of the presentation will also require competent use of ES.

(iv)   Delivering the Presentation

Establishing your credibility with the audience is crucial. Customers will not buy a product from someone they do not trust. Audiences will judge much of the value of your presentation from their perception of your status and character.

The rapport that you develop with the audience will be important in helping to establish your credibility. Rapport does not just occur, you will have to use a range of ES to build up such a rapport:

- Use effective body language:
  - smile at the audience;
  - maintain eye contact (shifty eyes suggest dishonesty);
  - control your gestures;
  - maintain a composed posture;
  - make sure your appearance and dress are appropriate.
- Vary the way you speak:
  - use strong intonation;
  - allow pauses in the speech;
  - emphasise certain words;
  - always make sure that you are audible to everyone in the audience.
- Be interesting in the way you make your presentation:
  - be humorous;
  - be clear in expression;
  - avoid jargon;
  - use simple concise language.
- Show enthusiasm:
  - look as though you believe in what you are saying
  - convince the audience that you believe it
  - put over the message energetically, not in a lack-lustre manner
  - do not look bored.
- Be relaxed and confident:
  - try not to be nervous;
  - do not fidget;
  - avoid being apologetic;
  - exude confidence in what you are saying.

(v)   The Venue

In addition to considering special aspects of delivering the sales presentation you must also think about the venue to be used.

Sales presenters pay great attention to the venue used for their presentations. The accommodation should suit the type of audience and their expectations – their number and status. In some cases you might have to hire special function suites in hotels for the occasion and provide hospitality for the delegates. The seating arrangements should be such that you can interact comfortably with all members of the audience with no barriers to communication.

The venue you use can add further credibility and prestige to your presentation and can help to ensure that the audience is influenced to act in a certain way.

You need to consider all of the points we have discussed here as well as those considered in Chapter Seven when making a sales presentation. With a sales presentation, however, you must give more thought to the audience, the structure and content of your message and the physical environment in which you will make the presentation. If you pay attention to these then you will achieve a more successful outcome.

1.2 One-to-one Selling

You should take a different approach when selling to individuals to that discussed above. When selling to groups there will be less scope for audience participation. With one-to-one selling, however, if you are skilful you will involve the customer much more in what is happening. There are a number of steps you should take in this type of selling:

(i)   Listening first.
(ii)   Explaining the product benefits.
(iii) Handling objections.
(iv)   Closing the sale.

(i)   Listening First

Before you can start to sell a product you must first establish your customer's needs. How else will you be able to decide what is the most appropriate product to give your customer satisfaction?

To establish the customer's needs you must ask questions and listen to the answers given. You should develop a repertoire of questions designed to establish the true needs of customers. This will be the starting point for the sale – posing questions and listening to the answers. As the customer gives you answers you should probe further. Below we give an example of a typical introductory conversation between a salesperson and a customer.

Good morning sir, how can I help you?

I want to buy a new lounge carpet.

Before I show you the types of carpet we stock, may I ask you a few questions? Firstly, are you looking for a hard wearing carpet or one which is less durable?

I need to buy a hard wearing carpet as we have two young children who play in the lounge with their toys.

I take it then that you will also be needing a stain-resistant carpet?

Yes, you know what small children are like spilling food and drink everywhere.

And a carpet that is washable?

Exactly.

As the questioning continues the salesperson is able to build up a picture in his mind of the product that will most closely meet the consumer's needs. Once he has arrived at that point he can then confirm the conversation:

Right, let us see where we are then. You are looking for a hard wearing carpet, that is stain-resistant, easily washable, that is not foam backed, that is patterned, comes with a guarantee, and is reasonably priced.

Yes, that's exactly what I am looking for.

We sometimes call this the 'agreement staircase' as both salesperson and customer reach an agreement as to what the customer wants. Once the 'agreement staircase' has been climbed, the salesperson is then in the position of being able to select those products that meet the criteria identified by the customer. If the customer disagrees with any of the summarised points the salesperson should clarify them before proceeding to the next stage which is explaining the product benefits.

(ii)   Explaining the Product Benefits

When you know the type of product the customer wants to buy you can decide which of the ones you stock will meet the needs of the customer. While demonstrating them and describing their features, you should be stressing the benefits the customer will derive from buying the product. We will continue the conversation about the carpet:

> *Let me show you this carpet here, Mr. Evans. It is stain-resistant to the extent that just a wipe over with a wet cloth will remove the stain. With other carpets you would have to use a carpet shampoo which is not only expensive, but leaves spot marks where it has been used.*

A features – benefits table (as explained earlier in the chapter) would be useful at this point as it will give you a clear understanding of the unique selling points of the product and how it differs from the competitors.

After you explain each benefit you should seek the customer's acceptance of it. We go back to the carpet sale example:

> *You can see the value of this stain-resistant carpet can't you Mr. Evans.*

If the customer does not accept the benefit then you should find out why this is so, and try to overcome it. Indeed, you should try and show that you welcome any objections that are put forward by the customer.

(iii)   Handling Objections

It is natural that many customers will have objections to the products they are buying. Objections are positive signs that the customer is interested in buying the product, but requires further clarification on particular points before the purchase decision is made. Thus, you should welcome objections and handle them positively.

If the customer objections relate to some of the product features then you might find it possible to re-work the various features and benefits so that they do meet the customer's requirements. Returning to the carpet showroom:

> It was really a larger patterned carpet that I was looking for.

> *Yes, I can see your point but a larger pattern would show stains and dirt more than this pattern. With growing children you will have a lot spilt on it in years to come. Indeed, these smaller patterned carpets are fully guaranteed against stains which you cannot get out.*

You can handle objections that are based on a lack of knowledge by the customer by providing the necessary additional information.

If the customer's main objection is to the price you are asking, you might ask whether the concern is about the quality of the product or simply the price. Indeed responding to objections with questions is a very effective way of dealing with them. Let us see how the carpet salesperson is able to deal with such an objection:

Unfortunately, the price of this carpet is more than I wanted to pay.

Well, Mr. Evans, are you concerned more about price than quality?

No, I do want to buy a quality carpet.

Well, it might seem more expensive now, but it will last while your children grow up.

By countering objections with a question, the answers you get may provide further insight into what the customer is thinking so allowing you to stress further benefits.

Some objections will be fundamental with the customer showing a clear disinterest in the product, and in such circumstances there is no point in trying to pursue the sale. If you have climbed the agreement staircase with the customer, however, and you handle the customer's objections competently and courteously, then the customer should be ready to buy your product. You can now close the sale.

(iv)   Closing the Sale

As a salesperson, the most important part of your role is closing the sale – it is what you are employed to do, selling the product to the customer. Identifying when the customer is ready to buy will involve you in listening to what the customer is saying and interpreting his non-verbal behaviour. Among the signals that a customer begins to give when buying a product to show that he is interested in making the purchase may be some of the following:

- The objections to the sale will cease.
- The customer will start to express strong interest in the product – 'Yes, I do like the colour', 'It will match the wallpaper', 'The guarantee will be most useful.'
- A customer may begin to give strong eye contact with complementary body movements – to nod his head, smile and adopt an open non-defensive posture. The customer might make positive actions such as keeping a firm hold on the product rather than putting it down.

You should respond to these buying signals and start to close the sale. Rather than simply asking if the customer wishes to buy the product, you could adopt one of two closing techniques. These are:

- The Assumptive Close.
- The Alternative Close.

The Assumptive Close: The assumptive close assumes that the customer is ready to buy the product, and so you, as the salesperson, need to make a statement which signifies that a sale has been made. Let us see how our carpet salesperson would do this:

Will it be OK if we come round and fit your new carpet next Thursday?

The onus is now on the customer to indicate that he does not wish to buy the carpet – it is easier to say 'yes', than it is to say 'no'.

The Alternative Close: With this approach, you offer the customer some kind of choice. Our carpet salesperson might say:

Would you like to pay for the carpet with cash, by cheque, or on credit?

The salesperson, acting on the assumption that the customer wishes to buy the product, offers a choice between alternatives. In making a choice, the customer signifies that the sale has been agreed.

When the sale has been closed the salesperson should ensure that appropriate after-sales-service is provided for the customer.

The example we have used above shows a number of skills involved in selling. At the beginning of this chapter we stated that selling skills are highly transferable. For instance if you were attending a selection interview you may try to translate your achievements into benefits that will appeal to the recruiter:

> Last summer I gained my Duke of Edinburgh Gold Award. What this means is that I am now confident when leading others. I am happy tackling new tasks and using my initiative to overcome problems.

You should draw up your own features – benefits table.

Similarly, at a selection interview, if the interviewer were to raise objections to you, use sales techniques for handling them:

> *It appears from your CV, Mr. Wilson, that you have little experience in selling.*

> That's true. What I have to offer is motivation and determination. Does your company recruit only people with a track record in sales?

Here, the interviewee acknowledges what the interviewer has said, states his/her own 'product benefits', and asks the interviewer to evaluate the interviewee's strengths in relation to the vacancy.

Selling skills can be transferred, therefore, to a variety of different situations. In the next section we shall look at negotiating skills which are equally transferable to a number of different circumstances.

2.   Negotiating Skills

You will need to use negotiating skills when you have to resolve differences. Your aim in a negotiating session is to reach an agreement that serves the best interests of both parties and encourages the development of a long-term relationship based on trust and respect.

Disagreements can arise in many diverse situations, ranging from the negotiation of the terms to build a new power station in China to resolving a domestic conflict in the home between parents and children. Each negotiation situation requires the parties to it to use ES and you will become a successful negotiator if you can master the necessary ES.

To be a successful negotiator you need to:

- Plan meticulously.
- Be controlled in the use of your interpersonal skills.
- Understand fully the nature of the conflict.
- Design strategies to overcome the conflict.
- Recognise all the outside forces likely to affect the decision making of the other parties involved.
- Set yourself targets and objectives for a successful outcome.
- Have a series of alternative outcomes planned as 'next-best-solutions'.
- Apply pressure when necessary to the others involved in the negotiation.
- Recognise and build on your own strengths, both in terms of the strength of your argument and your own strength as a negotiator.

The skills demanded of a negotiator are the same as those used by a sales person making a presentation. As a negotiator, you must listen to what others are saying and interpret their body language. You must be able to communicate persuasively using both verbal and non-verbal means. You may work in a team of negotiators so your skills in working with, and leading, others will be important. In many negotiating situations you will face pressure and stress and your ability to cope with these may well prove crucial.

Negotiations involve a complex combination of ES. The purpose of this section is to break the negotiating process down into its constituent parts so that we can examine each of these skills in more detail. We will consider three stages in this process:

1. Understanding the nature of the conflict.
2. Setting objectives and devising strategies.
3. Generating alternative solutions.

2.1   Understanding the Nature of the Conflict

Disagreements arise when people are in conflict over a particular issue. To resolve a conflict requires the joint efforts of all those involved. Before negotiations can take place, however, all of the parties involved must understand fully the nature of the conflict. To gain a better understanding of this, you should analyse the conflict from the perspective of each of the parties involved.

For instance, let us take as an example a conflict that arises between a car-hire company negotiating to buy 500 new cars from a motor manufacturer. The buyer, the car-hire company, will naturally seek the best possible package from the seller, the motor manufacturer. The car-hire company expects this because it is buying in bulk. The seller, on the other hand, will be interested in maintaining the profit margin on the sale of the cars. The starting place for understanding the true nature of the conflict is to analyse this situation from both the buyer's and the seller's perspectives. To do this you need to follow a systematic process.

(i)   **Identify the issue under negotiation:**
   ▪ the purchase of the five hundred cars.
(ii) **List all those issues which are important from the buyer's perspective:**
   ▪ the discount expected on the normal price of each car;
   ▪ the time period over which the payments for the cars can be made e.g. four instalments;
   ▪ the warranty facilities offered by the manufacturer;
   ▪ discounts off further cars that the car-hire company might purchase in the future;
   ▪ the delivery dates for the five hundred cars.

Then look at the same topic from the seller's perspective:

(iii) **List all the issues important from the motor manufacturer's perspective:**
   ▪ the minimum discount on the price of each car to maintain acceptable profit margins;
   ▪ the need to ensure prompt payment of the full cost of supplying the cars;
   ▪ the standard warranty terms to be offered to the buyer;
   ▪ the need for an early decision to purchase so that the cars can be manufactured;
   ▪ an agreement from the buyer to purchase additional cars in the near future.

When you have completed both lists, analyse each of them to identify the most important considerations for each party. You should identify the outcomes desired by each party as clearly as possible. The next step is for you to consider each desired outcome and evaluate whether or not the other party to the negotiation would be willing to accept it. This will help you to gain a clear understanding of the perspective and stance of each side and allow you to identify issues that can be resolved at the outset so that some agreement is reached before the more contentious issues are tackled.

To negotiate on behalf of one party you would need to develop arguments that counter some of the likely claims and proposals of the other party. This demands a wide understanding of the conflict, which will probably require research into developments outside your own organisation. Were you negotiating on behalf of the car-hire company you would need to be aware of new car prices being charged by other motor manufacturers, as well as the terms, conditions and warranties on offer elsewhere.

Such preparation and planning is vital. When you have a clear understanding of the nature of the conflict, you can then set your objectives and devise appropriate strategies for attaining them.

2.2   Setting Objectives and Devising Strategies

You need to set clear objectives before negotiation begins and these are frequently linked to the outcomes you wish to achieve. These objectives act as your bargaining framework around which your discussions will take place. They enable you to identify the important issues where you recognise little movement is possible on your part, as well as those areas where you feel concessions can be made. Objectives also clarify your expectations from the negotiations.

If you enter the negotiating session with high expectations you will achieve more than if you have less ambitious objectives. Those who expect a lot frequently gain more than those who do not. Thus, set your target levels high. Your targets, though, need to be flexible. The other party will be thinking in a similar way but with many objectives diametrically opposed to your own.

When your objectives have been set, you will need to devise strategies to achieve them. To be a successful negotiator you should always minimise your losses – seek to gain as much as possible from the session without making too many concessions. To achieve this anticipate the arguments that the opposition will be using during the negotiations and produce counter arguments in advance. In a similar way you need to devise arguments which support each of your claims and to prepare a number of alternative solutions.

2.3   Generating Alternative Solutions

Negotiating requires you to use creative skills to look for alternatives acceptable to both you and the other party. Neither you nor the opposition will wish to lose face as a result of the agreed outcome. Before the negotiating begins, therefore, consider as many different solutions to the conflict as possible. Rank these in order of preference, with your preferred outcome ranked in first position. This should be the outcome that most closely meets the objectives you have set. Alternative outcomes that require you to make major concessions should be ranked at the bottom of the list.

By generating alternative solutions you will enter the negotiating sessions with a positive frame of mind which is open to creating the necessary movements and concessions required to reach an agreement. A skilled negotiator, though, will tend to concede on points that are less important than the other party believes them to be, and so the negotiation concludes with them accepting a next-best-solution.

You will require a range of ES for successful negotiating. As we have already mentioned you must plan and prepare. You must be as knowledgeable as possible about the issue under discussion. During the negotiation sessions you will make use of your communication skills. We will now consider some of the more critical skills which you will have to develop. These are:

(i)   Your listening skills.
(ii)   Your use of body language.
(iii) Your verbal communication skills.

2.4   Listening Skills

Your ability to listen and to understand what the other party is saying is crucial. The process of negotiation involves considerable personal interaction. A common dilemma is that while you are listening to the other party, you are also thinking about your response and counter-arguments. To some extent this distracts your listening.

One way of trying to ensure that you do not misinterpret what the other person is saying is to confirm at regular intervals what has been said in the form of a brief summary. You might phrase it something like this, 'So what you are saying here is that you are willing to move on the price for the deal but you are not willing to budge on the delivery dates that you can give us.'

This type of recap helps prevent misconceptions from arising on either side as to what has been said, and confirms that all parties have kept track of the way the negotiation is developing. It also helps to keep your concentration more finely tuned to what the other party is saying. To ensure that this process does not dominate the negotiating session, however, you will have to be a quick thinker in order to steer the discussion onto your own arguments after making the summary.

2.5   Body Language

If you control the use of your body language during negotiation it will help you considerably. In Chapter Three we noted that a person's body language can show whether there is any discrepancy between the words spoken and their true feelings. For example, a negotiator may say that he is happy with the way the session is developing, yet has a worried look on his face. Similarly a negotiator may say that you can rely on his word, yet does not look you in the eye when saying it. Both are giving signs that what they are saying does not reflect their innermost feelings.

To be a skilful negotiator you must be a perceptive reader of body language and adept at using it to communicate to the other side. For example, consider the following actions:

Forceful, downward hand moving gestures: These should be used to emphasise important points, or to indicate that a strong stance is being adopted.

Open postures, upward facing palms of the hands combined with strong eye contact: These signify honesty.

Nods of approval coupled with smiles: Indicate that agreement is being reached.

Folded arms, crossed legs, closed postures: Indicate a defensive stance and signify that the person is putting up barriers to negotiation.

The body language that you use, therefore, must support and endorse what you are saying in the negotiation.

2.6   Verbal Communication

The only way to negotiate is to talk to the other side. When you are doing this there are certain key rules you should remember:

- Speak clearly and forcefully. This allows the other side to understand what you are saying and will indicate your strength of feeling.
- Control your speed of speech. Increase the speed to make a point and then allow pauses to let the other side assimilate it. Long pauses in the negotiating process can put pressure on the other parties to break the silence and also the deadlock.

- Do not use emotive language. Your emotions will no doubt be aroused during negotiations, but it is crucial that you do not allow these to influence the proceedings. Make an effort, therefore, to remain calm during the negotiations.
- Stick to the important issues. At times the discussion might digress from the key issues involved. If this occurs steer the discussion back to the important issues. Digressions are distractions and waste time.

In addition to the ES outlined above, you will also have to pay attention to your other personal skills. For instance, be assertive, think about how you should work with others and be critical in the way you think. These are all skills in their own right and we will discuss them in detail in other chapters. You should be aware, though, that you will have to use them all if you wish to be successful in the negotiation.

3.   The Negotiating Process

Negotiations move through distinct stages. The stages are as follows:

(i)   The first stage of the process will involve listening to the arguments put forward by the other party, assessing their underlying logic, and formulating counter arguments.

(ii) The second stage identifies areas of agreement where movement is made towards finding a solution.

(iii) The final stage is when agreement is reached.

Progression through these stages is neither smooth nor easy. You will feel frustrated, you may become emotional and, at times, you may feel that you have reached deadlock. You will have to overcome all of these if you are to reach a successful conclusion to the negotiation. Indeed, it may be that the negotiation will move forward at quite a slow pace. We shall now examine each stage of the negotiation process that you are likely to encounter.

3.1   The Early Phase

The starting point in any negotiation is to find out what the other party expects to get out of it. What are they hoping to achieve and what are their desired outcomes? You should try to get them to 'lay their cards on the table' as soon as possible and clearly identify what they want as an outcome from the negotiation. This will allow you to see how close the anticipated desired outcomes that you arrived at in your planning stage are to the actual desired outcomes of the other party.

To do this ask open questions that start with, 'How', 'Why', 'Where', 'When', and 'What'?

Put pressure on the other side by asking probing questions. But when you have to reply to one of their questions answer only the question asked. Take care not to digress from the question asked or to provide them with any further insights into what is your next-best-solution in case you have to make any compromises.

Once you have identified all the issues, if it is clear that the other side are unwilling to accept your position immediately, then you will have to think about using the strategies and counter arguments that you have already planned. Your arguments should aim to show that their desired outcomes are based on ill-founded logic. Using the example of the car-hire company negotiating for the purchase of the cars, take the part of the negotiator for the car manufacturer and assume that you are trying to counter the buyer's argument for a bigger discount:

You want a 30% discount on the purchase price. Come on, you have to recognise that this is completely unrealistic. You must know that in the motor industry a car manufacturer's profit margin on this type of vehicle is only 20%. If we were to agree to a 30% discount, we would be making a loss on the deal.

If you are to succeed using this sort of tactic then all the arguments that you put forward need to be objective and based on fact, rather than on speculation.

As the negotiations progress you should try and settle all those issues that can quite easily be resolved in this early phase and carry forward the more contentious ones to the middle phase. Returning to our negotiation on the car purchase, the car manufacturer's negotiator might say:

Before negotiating the price discount, let's first of all discuss the warranty facilities to be offered with the cars. I think that our initial talks indicated that we both have similar views on this, and hopefully we can reach an agreement on the warranty quite quickly.

3.2   The Middle Phase

The middle phase is where the hard bargaining takes place. The early phase is a testing period for both sides, and to some extent sets the terms of reference for what is to follow. Now your objective is to reach agreement on the issues where there is some diversity of opinion. The starting point is to select an issue and to identify the areas of agreement. The negotiator for the car manufacturer might say:

Well, we have now agreed the warranty terms, let's return to the price discount. You've heard our view, we cannot offer you anywhere near a 30% price discount. At best we can manage a 9% discount. How do you feel about that?

You may well have to offer concessions at this point if agreement is to be reached. If you are a weak negotiator you might offer major concessions whereas if you were a more effective one you will have a number of minor concessions to use in this give-and-take period. Effective negotiators will also explain why a counter-proposal is unacceptable before putting forward their own. Again returning to the car sale:

Unfortunately, a 9% discount is not acceptable given the size of our order. We would be looking for a discount of 12%, especially if we commit ourselves to buying more cars from you.

12% discount on the first order is still rather high. However, we could agree to it if you sign a contract to purchase a further five hundred vehicles from us.

When putting forward arguments to counter a proposal it is important not to use them all in one go, but to ration them so that you can come up with further arguments if the other party has still not conceded.

This phase of the negotiating process is normally the most involved and fraught. The session might have to be halted so that both sides can appraise the progress that has been made or modify their strategy and stance in some way.

In many circumstances for the conflict to be resolved satisfactorily, it is likely that both you and the opposite side will have to make movements to reach agreement. If neither side is prepared to make any movement you will reach a deadlock. In these situations it will be important to ask questions to find out why the opposition is not prepared to move, and for you to establish the underlying cause of the deadlock. Until you both understand this, you will not be able to propose alternatives to progress the negotiations.

A useful strategy that you can use in deadlock situations is the 'conditional bargaining' approach:

If you accept this, then we will accept...

Here your every concession has a condition attached to it. In this way you will put further pressure on the other side to move their position, showing that you are willing to make concessions.

Sometimes, though, the other party will seem resolute and unwilling to make any concessions to reach an agreement. In these situations, you will have to adopt a strategy to break the deadlock. You may have to resort to more drastic measures such as:

- Seeking the services of an impartial mediation, conciliation or adjudicating body.

If this proves unsuccessful then you could try the following:

- Threaten to use the influence of the media to highlight the unreasonableness of the opposition.
- Try to bring pressure from third parties to encourage the opposition to break their dead-lock.

An agreement will be reached only if the interests of both parties are met. Both you and the opposing team of negotiators have to accept this and must work towards reaching such a position by making movements and concessions. Indeed, either you or the opposing side might help the other by identifying those forces that are hindering the agreement process, and by suggesting solutions.

Another approach you could try is to break down the issue that is causing the dead-lock into its constituent parts, to see whether you can agree upon the various components individually, before putting them back together again. This might help to move the negotiation process forward and can be seen as a positive move by both sides.

To add further pressure the other party may start to pose threats:

If you don't give us the deal we are looking for, we will simply take our business elsewhere.

The use of threats is a sign of weakness and desperation, and your response should be to acknowledge that it is a threat and ask that it is withdrawn. If the deadlock persists then you could adopt the following procedures:

- Agree to disagree – do not waste any more time and effort. Often reaching this type of agreement will help to reduce some of the tension.
- Draft a statement that fully outlines the issue that cannot be resolved, indicating the crucial difference between both sides. Look for the solutions for overcoming these disagreements – e.g. set up a joint working party.
- Move the negotiations forward onto those points that can be agreed.

You will continue to be deadlocked in your negotiations if either side has no intention of reaching an agreement. If both sides are prepared to make concessions and to accept their next-best-solution then you should be able to reach a mutually acceptable agreement.

A tactic that is sometimes used during negotiations is to apply pressure and create stress for the other side in the hope that this might force them to make concessions. You may find that the other side try to apply pressure on you in a number of ways. Examples of these would include:

- Emotional outbursts or personal insults – these might be used to try to get you to lose your temper and hence your controlled thought processes.
- Accusations of incompetence – this tactic might be used to upset you and undermine your confidence.

- Threats to walk out or to refer the negotiations to a higher authority might be bully tactics to encourage you to reach agreement.
- The hard and soft negotiator. The other party might assign distinct roles to members of the same team, one might be willing to offer concessions which will lull you into a false sense of security, while another might be the taker who spots your weaknesses and takes immediate advantage.

When faced with such pressure you should:

- Stay calm and show the irresponsibility of such tactics by indicating that they will have no effect.
- Appeal to the better nature of the opposition to act more rationally.

Call a halt to the negotiations until such time as the opposition are prepared to retract what they have said and are willing to resume businesslike discussions.

Pressure and stress of one kind or another will be inevitable in a negotiation and can be quite unsettling if you are an inexperienced negotiator. Stress affects your emotions and thinking ability; as a negotiator, therefore, you need to practise facing up to and coping with such pressure.

From the above discussion it is clear that you will need to demonstrate a range of skills while negotiating if you are to reach a satisfactory agreement. When an agreement has been reached, you will then enter the final phase of the negotiating session.

3.3   The Concluding Phase

The agreements that you reach need to be ones that will be respected by all parties. To ensure that this will happen each finalised agreement needs to be repeated during the concluding phase and noted down in fine detail. If either party disagrees with what is being said or written down, then you need to clarify the position and make any necessary amendments. When both sides are satisfied with the agreements reached you should end the session, hopefully with you and the opposition parting on friendly terms.

The focus of this chapter has been to consider persuasive ES. To be a successful persuader you will need to develop effective verbal communication skills – read again Chapter Three to refresh your memory of these.

After reading this chapter please complete the following learning activities:

Learning Activities

1. Explain the steps you should follow when preparing and planning a formal sales presentation to a group of people.

2. Describe the four stages that you need to follow to be successful in one-to-one selling.

3. How would you prepare yourself before a negotiation exercise?

4. Identify the three stages of the negotiating process and write down the ES you will need to use at each of these stages.

Chapter Nine
Group Work Skills

After reading this chapter you will be able to:

1. Understand group dynamics and factors that may contribute to or impede the success of a group.

2. Understand the role of a group leader.

3. Learn about the four stages of group development.

4. Understand your own group working, and group leadership ability.

The ability to work effectively with other people is a demand made by everyday life. There will be many times in your life when you will have to work in a group and be responsible for completing certain tasks which will contribute to an overall whole. To establish effective working relationships in a group you will need to develop interactive skills. Such skills are highly transferable and will be useful in many situations at work or university or in your personal life.

Most organisations have some form of management hierarchy with a recognised leader. This is because it is generally accepted that groups work most efficiently with a leader. The leader's task is not simply to administer the tasks which the group will carry out but to lead the members of the group.

This chapter will try to develop your group work skills in two ways. Firstly, we shall consider how to establish good working relationships with others, and secondly how to lead others. Finally we shall consider the group dynamics which exist when you work with others.

1.   Establishing Effective Working Relationships with Others

If you wish to have good working relationships with other members of a group you will need to develop your interactive skills. This involves a number of factors including:

- Presenting yourself to others.
- Adopting an open attitude.
- Being sensitive to the feelings and needs of others.
- Allowing an equal opportunity for all to contribute.
- Being able to accept criticisms.
- Working with self-confidence.
- Working to the best of your ability.
- Acknowledging the role of the leader.

1.1   Presenting Yourself to Others

If you wish to work with others you generally have to conform to the norms of the group. Part of this involves how you present yourself to the rest of the group. For example, a new recruit in a bank who arrives for work on his first day with long straggly hair, dressed in faded denim jeans and pop star tee-shirt, may not be accepted by his carefully groomed and neatly dressed colleagues or by the bank's management. The new recruit is not conforming to the dress and appearance requirements of the job. The same individual, however, dressed in the same way would fit in perfectly at a rock concert. Personal presentation plays a part in establishing relationships with others. First impressions are crucial in interpersonal interactions and although your personality and character might be perfect for a career in banking, if your appearance and dress are non-conformist, then you will not be accepted.

1.2   Adopting an Open Attitude

In group situations it is important to be open with colleagues on all matters relating to the group's activities. All information relevant to the group's performance should be freely distributed and consultations between the group members need to take place at regular intervals to discuss what has been done and what will be done in the future.

If communication fails to take place then the group will be acting simply as a series of individuals. Information and communication are the life-blood of groups. Information should be circulated to maximise group cohesion. Some individuals withhold information to provide themselves with a power base, giving them an advantage over their colleagues. This practice leads to the alienation of some members of the group.

You need to build the exchange of information, and consultation processes, into the group's routine activities. One way of doing this in a large organisation is to circulate a 'perusal file' of memos, letters and reports to all members of the group.

1.3   Being Sensitive to the Feelings and Needs of Other People

When you work closely with other people, you may find that frustrations and tensions build up. To reduce these it is important to gain an understanding of the feelings and needs of your colleagues, for instance whether they are sensitive individuals with strongly held personal views or more easy-going and willing to accommodate views which differ from their own. Tensions can arise between group members because one person is insensitive to the feelings of another. This may become apparent when one person makes a personal remark that is offensive to another. When such tensions arise, people stop talking to each other and this can seriously damage the cohesiveness of the group.

When tensions exist, part of the group's energy will be taken up by the conflict. This energy ought to be used in meeting the objectives of the group. To reduce tensions it is important for all group members to gain a clear picture of the personalities and characteristics of their colleagues and to respect them.

1.4 Allowing an Equal Opportunity for all to Contribute

When you work with others you will find that group members feel more committed if they have contributed in some way either to planning the work or deciding how the responsibilities are to be divided. Thus, when a new task is to be undertaken each member of the group should be given the opportunity of contributing to the formulation of the plan of action. It might not be feasible to accept all the ideas that are put forward, but nevertheless the opportunity should be made available to all members of the group.

If members of the group are always simply told what to do then they may become apathetic, or feel resentful and be less committed to the group. By involving all members of the group at the outset you will get a broader range of ideas as to how to plan the work, and this in itself might lead to greater efficiency.

Conflicts might arise as to who should complete certain tasks. This is the time for negotiation. You will need to assess the suitability of each group member for the task, taking into consideration each individual's strengths and weaknesses.

1.5 Being able to Accept Criticisms

In all group situations individuals make mistakes or fail to perform as well as they might. To minimise the impact on the group of such imperfections, you must inform the individual concerned of the way in which he went wrong. Your criticisms, however, must be made in a constructive manner, referring to the task that was undertaken rather than specifically to the individual. You should spend time finding out why the error occurred, what if anything can be done to remedy the situation, and what steps could be followed to prevent it occurring in future. You need to be sensitive to the feelings of the individual concerned. If there is a point of contention between members of the group this should be freely expressed. By saying nothing and trying to ignore it greater tension and stress will be created.

When you face criticism, learn to accept that it is not personal, but a criticism of the way in which you undertook the task. It is important to remain calm whether you are giving or receiving criticism and to see this as a positive learning aspect of group work. If you have to criticise individuals try to provide them with help to change their behaviour. This might involve counselling sessions or retraining.

To help in this process of giving and receiving constructive criticisms, it is useful to hold regular appraisal sessions where the members of the group can express their feelings about the way the group is operating. By expressing feelings, including frustrations, the group will be able to dissipate tension.

1.6 Accepting Differences

We are all different. For example, as human beings we each have our own cultural backgrounds, interests, dress codes and ways of working with others. It is such differences that makes working with other people interesting, but also challenging. When working with other people we should try and prevent our own perceptions of others influencing the judgements that we make about them. In fact we should welcome diversity in society, and accept differences in other people. If we pre-judge someone because of her ethnicity, her dress, or grooming then we are doing them great injustice. The well known saying 'don't judge a book by its cover' has great relevance in interpersonal situations. Try not to judge someone by the way they look, or on the basis of their cultural or ethnic heritage. If you do, you might be creating barriers to effective group working.

1.7   Working with Self-confidence

Problems will arise if group members doubt their ability to perform as required. To prevent this arising it is important that members of the group are required to complete only tasks which they feel confident about undertaking. By negotiating with each person about what he or she will do you should be able to overcome this. If you simply delegate responsibilities within the group, then you might find that some people will fail to complete their tasks adequately.

Some tasks, however, may be unfamiliar to all members of the group. To cope with this situation it is crucial for the group to maintain a positive attitude. A healthy group welcomes challenges and encourages all members to contribute.

1.8   Working to the Best of your Ability

Group work requires all members to complete their specific tasks to the best of their ability. If you do not complete your tasks, then you will be letting down the rest of the group. To encourage everyone to complete their tasks to the best of their ability, you should agree at the outset the standards of performance for which each person is aiming. If someone performs to a higher than expected standard then they should be congratulated. Conversely, when a person fails to meet the standard set, it is important to establish the reason why.

If a member of the group refuses to co-operate, find out why. Clearly point out the consequences of their actions. If, between you, no positive solution can be found, then you will first have to warn the unco-operative person. Eventually, if they still refuse to work as part of the group they will have to be excluded.

Groups achieve their objectives only if all the members work together harmoniously for the benefit of the group. Personal ambitions should never take precedence over the group's objectives. Part of the success of the group will lie with each member's determination to succeed. Each member has to be motivated towards the success of the group. This involves all members accepting responsibility for fulfilling certain tasks to the best of their ability. Each member's responsibilities should be made clear at the outset, with each individual having the right to accept the responsibilities and hence to join the group, or to reject them and so dissociate from the group.

1.9   Acknowledging the Role of the Leader

Some types of group work require one member to work as leader. Most organisations operate in this way. The leader is responsible for over seeing the group's activities and making sure that the group's objectives will be met on time and in the desired manner. This is the traditional, hierarchical view of leadership and groups.

In the traditional model all group members have to accept the need for a leader, and consequently accept the decisions that the leader takes. If the members of the group do not accept the leader and challenge the leader's position, then some of the group's energies are being used in a negative way to destabilise the group. To prevent such a challenge the leader must establish effective working relationships with the other members of the group. In the next section we shall consider the skills you will need if you are to lead others.

2. Leading Others

The traditional, hierarchical view of leadership suggests that for the group to be successful a leader has to accept a number of responsibilities. These include:

- Setting group objectives and targets.
- Agreeing mutually acceptable objectives and targets for the individual group members.
- Negotiating responsibilities with group members.
- Consulting with group members on the progress they have made in reaching individual targets and group objectives.
- Motivating the group.
- Encouraging co-operation and communication within and outside the group.
- Coping with the human relationship problems of the group.
- Taking decisions and solving problems.
- Accepting the views, opinions and ideas of the group.
- Encouraging initiative within the group.
- Creating a harmonious atmosphere which encourages others to contribute to the best of their ability.
- Disciplining group members where necessary.

The above list is not exhaustive, but serves to indicate the wide ranging roles of a leader – facilitator, motivator, planner and negotiator, to name but four. To be a successful leader you will need well-developed ES. As a leader you will have to be a competent communicator. You will need to be assertive to persuade team members to act in the way you consider to be best for the group. You must be aware of your own interpersonal skills and use your own strengths to good effect.

Given the range of ES required by a leader, one could ask the question 'Are good leaders born, or can they be trained?' We shall now consider the following approaches to this question:

(i) The Qualities Approach.
(ii) The Situational Approach.
(iii) The Functional Approach.

2.1 The Qualities Approach

One view of leadership is known as the 'Qualities Approach'. This suggests that certain personal qualities a person may have contribute to an effective leadership style. For example some people might display initiative, courage, intelligence and humour, which when combined create a competent leader. This approach suggests that the potential for leadership varies between individuals and is determined by their particular qualities.

Such personality qualities are seen as inherent rather than developed through training and experience. Furthermore, there is little agreement as to which personal qualities are essential for leadership. The qualities approach, therefore, offers little scope for structured learning. Moreover, this view implies that leaders should be recruited rather than trained.

2.2   The Situational Approach

The 'Situational Approach' proposes that leaders come about in a specific situation. Different leaders come to the fore, depending upon the tasks involved, the organisation and the specific circumstances. This approach sees leadership not just as a series of qualities but as a relationship, in which the leader possesses knowledge appropriate to a given situation.

This approach can be criticised in that it regards leadership skills as relating purely to a specific situation. This is true to a certain extent, however there are obviously some people who are able to lead whatever the situation.

2.3   The Functional Approach

The 'Functional Approach' sees the group as having a common goal and the group members work together because as individuals they cannot complete the task alone. They must work as a cohesive team. Rules which will promote the unity and cohesiveness of the group are needed. Those who break the rules may be penalised. For the group to work together successfully, certain functions have to be performed. The term 'function' is used here in a very broad sense to include behaviour or areas of leadership responsibility, as well as a particular activity. Some important leadership functions include:

(i)   Planning

The first function of leadership is to define the group's purpose, objectives, or goals. Once this has been done a strategy must be drawn up to allow the group to attain these objectives. The next step is to convert the strategy into a detailed plan of action that can be implemented.

Objectives, strategies and plans provide a sense of direction for the group and form a basis of measuring its success. Leaders, therefore, need to be effective planners, able to distance themselves from short term issues and look to the future. They must evaluate where the group is, where it is heading, and most importantly, where it should be heading.

(ii)   Initiating

Once the planning stage is completed, the next function of the leader is to consult the group about the objectives, strategies and plans. The leader needs to discuss and explain the rationale for these with the rest of the group. Negotiations should take place as to who should perform which tasks. Guidelines need to be agreed with the group members for completing their tasks to a certain standard. Encouragement should be provided to motivate the group towards attaining its targets. Assistance and guidance should be given to group members to help them reach their individual goals.

(iii)   Controlling

When the group members begin work on their individual tasks it will be the leader's role to monitor their progress and to control their activities. The leader has to maintain the group's guidelines and norms, and discipline those who contravene them. The leader has to regulate the pace at which the work is completed to ensure that deadlines will be met and objectives achieved.

When group meetings are held the leader will take the chair and encourage all members to contribute. It is the leader's responsibility to mediate if disputes arise between group members. Part of this function involves the leader maintaining the morale of the group and encouraging good working relationships.

(iv)   Supporting

If you lead a group you must be supportive to your group members. People tend to be encouraged and motivated if they feel that their contributions are being appreciated and if they are being supported by their leader when they face criticism from others.

If group members have personal problems then, as leader of the group, it is your task to be sympathetic and help them cope with their difficulties. You should try to get to know each member of the team on a personal basis. It helps to know the ambitions, motivations, attitudes, perceptions, capabilities and interests of each group member. You can achieve this by holding individual counselling sessions with all members at regular intervals. If you demonstrate a caring attitude as leader this tends to encourage loyalty from the group.

(v)   Informing

As circumstances change or new information becomes available it will be necessary for the leader to communicate this to the rest of the group. Keeping everyone informed of developments helps to prevent the spread of ill-founded rumours that can damage group cohesiveness and morale.

Just as it is important for the leader of a group to relay news and information to the team, it is important for the group leader to receive news and information from group members. As group leader you should welcome suggestions and comments. Members of the group should feel that their views are important to their leader. This will lead to a stronger commitment to the group.

(vi)   Evaluating

Once group members are working together effectively, as leader, you will have to evaluate what is happening to make sure that everything is going according to plan. If it looks like things are not going to plan then you might have to introduce a new initiative, or consider a complete change of strategy.

Once the group has achieved an objective, you should evaluate what has been achieved in order to identify those elements of the plan which were successful and those which were not. Your findings from this evaluation will be helpful when devising future strategies.

The functional approach endorses the view that leaders are multi-talented individuals who have mastered a wide range of ES. The leadership personality is distinctive: a leader is intelligent, maintains enthusiasm and a positive attitude, and displays personal qualities such as empathy, sympathy, and humour to lead and gain the respect of the group.

Thus, group work skills are vital ES. Relationships between a leader and a group are apparent in many aspects of life. It is important to recognise, though, that simply being given a leadership position does not make you a competent leader. Nor does simply possessing knowledge. Leadership is more than the sum total of a person's so-called desirable qualities. Group members follow their leader because they are motivated to do so. A leader understands what motivates the members of the group and encourages them to be loyal through a 'human' approach.

3.   Group Dynamics

If you are going to work with other people or lead them you need some understanding of group dynamics. We have already noted that groups play an important role in organisations, and the successful attainment of group objectives will be determined partly by how well the members of the group work with each other.

The purpose of this section is to investigate different forms of groups, how groups are developed, and finally different types of groups that can be found in modern organisations.

3.1 The Nature of Groups

A group is two or more people who form some kind of relationship, whether it be because they have social interests in common, or are colleagues at work, or students at university. Forming groups is a natural process for human beings – individuals seek the companionship and friendship of other people, and because being a member of a group offers distinct advantages:

- Groups allow people to pool resources, making the group more effective as a whole than each individual acting independently. Groups frequently accomplish tasks more easily and more efficiently than individuals.
- Groups offer a sense of security. Individuals feel 'protected' when working with other people. Individuals can rely on the expertise of fellow members, and feel more secure if they can share their ideas and views with others before having to make decisions and take action.
- Groups can provide emotional support. When working with other people you can turn to other group members for help and friendship. If you are not a member of a group you might not have such support available to you.
- Groups provide a sense of identity. It is important for people to create an identity for themselves which can increase self-esteem and self-confidence. Being a member of a group in some way gives credibility to the individual. Many groups develop a sense of identity by their dress and appearance – bankers wear pin-stripe suits; soldiers wear army uniforms; punks dye their hair. Other groups might develop a sense of identity through their entry qualifications and requirements.
- When accepted by a group some people feel a sense of pride, of being of value to the other members of the group. For other people joining a particular group may be a question of status. People accept a position of responsibility in the group to gain a sense of importance. If they do something positive for the group and are praised for it, this will increase their self-confidence.

Thus, it can be seen that being a member of a group offers distinct advantages. Most people belong to one form of group or another. We can classify groups into two categories – formal groups and informal groups.

(i)   Formal Groups

Formal groups exist to accomplish specific tasks. Formal groups are usually established with stated goals and objectives. In employment, workers are frequently assigned to departments or sections. At university, students are divided into formal groups to complete assignments. In the public sector, committees are formed to take decisions.

In the world of work it is difficult to identify organisations that do not use formal groups in some way to achieve their objectives. Most employees will belong to at least one formal group and many employees will belong to a number of such groups.

(ii)   Informal Groups

Informal groups tend to be more socially orientated than formal groups. Membership is based upon a common social interest such as a hobby, or arises as a result of family ties or through friendship.

Informal groups do not have to set tasks or objectives, rather they are a means for the group members to meet and relax, and to discuss areas of common concern or interest.

Formal and informal groups can also be classified according to whether they are 'open' or 'closed'.

(iii) Open Groups

An open group is one in which membership is not tightly restricted. Frequent changes of membership may be common as new members join and existing ones leave. Open groups tend to be primarily informal, membership is voluntary, and no entry qualifications have to be obtained to gain membership.

The organisation of open groups tends to be less bureaucratic with positions of authority being granted on a voluntary basis to those who seek them. Members holding positions of authority might remain in post for only a short period of time before another member assumes the responsibility.

Thus, open groups have a certain fluidity – they are not rigid and their organisation and membership change with time. Only a limited amount of formal procedure might need to be followed. Examples of this type of group are:

- Friendship groups formed by a few friends who live near each other, go to the same university, or work for the same organisation.
- Social clubs and societies in which the main criteria for membership is an interest in the activity or hobby common to all members – photographic clubs, badminton clubs, motor sport societies, amateur dramatic societies etc.

The changing membership of open groups makes it more difficult for them to set long term objectives and strategies. They tend primarily to address immediate areas of concern and interest. However, the regular influx of new members brings new ideas and perspectives to the group.

(iv) Closed Groups

Closed groups are characterised by a greater stability in membership than open groups. Closed groups frequently have some form of constitution (governing regulations) and entry requirements for members. This form of group is more rigid in the sense that members are given positions of responsibility for which they may be accountable. Authority and status may be associated with membership and positions of responsibility.

Closed groups come in many different forms, two examples are given here:

- Professional groups – the Institute of Chartered Accountants; the British Medical Association; the Association of British Travel Agents. Each of these require members formally to join the group either by passing examinations, and (or) complying with specific entry requirements. To become a member of such groups may take a number of years, especially if a series of examinations has to be passed. Once membership has been granted the member will have to follow the 'code of conduct' that has been agreed by the professional group, otherwise membership of the group will be terminated on the grounds of misconduct.
- 'Executive groups' – this term is used to include all those groups which take a management role for their members. Included here are Boards of Directors and Management Committees. Certain responsibilities are bestowed on these groups as laid down by their constitution. Frequently, to become a member of the group the individual has to be elected to a position of responsibility, perhaps for a fixed length of

time. Members are elected because of their technical expertise, their standing in society, or for some other reason.

A benefit of the closed group is that it allows stable relationships to develop between the members and the wider community it serves or represents. Such stability enables a long term perspective to be taken by the members who can divorce themselves from day-to-day issues and think about long term objectives and strategies.

Thus, certain types of activity are better performed by each type of group. The closed group is better placed to concern itself with planning issues while open groups might be more appropriate for the management of current activities. This is not to say, however, that the role of each group is mutually exclusive. Some open groups might be quite stable (in terms of changing membership) allowing long term decisions to be taken as well as the addressing of short term issues.

4.   Developing Groups

When thinking about forming and developing groups a number of factors have to be taken into account. Some of the points covered earlier on body language are relevant here.

4.1   Physical Proximity

Members of a group will be able to interact more effectively with each other if there are no barriers to communications within the group. We noted earlier that when people are physically close to each other more intimate relationships can be developed (if all parties wish). When there is a physical distance between people or a physical barrier, then the communication process will be more difficult.

When thinking about developing a group you need to consider the setting in which the group is to operate:

- All group members should be able to communicate easily with each other. You might have to attend to the design of the office or working area. While individual members of the group will need their own work areas these should if possible be in close proximity. Members of a group who are located on different floors of a building or worse still in different buildings often have difficulty in communicating and interacting with each other.
- While the group members will need individual working areas (that they might share with colleagues), if possible there should also be an area set aside for group meetings. This should:
  - be large enough to seat all members of the group in a circle so that they can see one another, and communicate with all members of the group;
  - contain all equipment for the group meeting to take place, for example desks and chairs, audio or visual equipment, or technical equipment;
  - allow confidential discussions to take place. Some meetings will address confidential topics such as future group plans, or might involve disciplinary proceedings being taken against a group member.
- To encourage the group members to mix socially an area should be set aside for relaxation, such as a small lounge where group members can meet for coffee and

lunch. Comfortable chairs, drinks facilities, and small tables should be made available for such rooms.

- All services and equipment that will be required by group members in their activities should be located close to the work area. Secretarial support, photocopying machines and the like need to be close at hand rather than being some distance away.

If you bear in mind the above points then the physical distance between members of the group should be reduced and the cohesion of the group enhanced. Problems will arise for the group if it is located in a setting that has a rigid structure, such as a building that was built in the nineteenth century. These buildings might be divided into small rooms with small interconnecting corridors. Such a setting will cause difficulties for the group. Modern office buildings tend to be designed on an 'open-plan' basis in which the people using them can erect dividing walls and smaller partitions as they think fit. These office buildings enable the group to devise the optimal layout for its needs.

4.2   The Individual Characteristics of the Group Members

The individual personalities and characteristics of group members will influence the cohesion of the group, and the efficiency with which the group achieves its objectives. People with similar personalities and characteristics tend to work together more harmoniously than opposites.

Group members who find that they have a number of different attitudes to other group members will have difficulty in working with them. Obviously, everybody has their own attitudes, but the more attitudes held in common, the more harmonious the group will be.

In addition to attitudes, the needs and motivations of each group member should be similar in some way. People who are motivated by the desire to earn as much money as possible might find it difficult to work with people who are more interested in working for the 'job-satisfaction' derived from completing a task to a high standard. When people work with others who share similar needs and motivations they can co-ordinate their efforts and energies to ensure that all objectives are met as efficiently as possible.

Apart from individual variables such as attitudes and motivations, the temperament of each group member will influence the success of the group in working together. If the group is dominated by people who easily lose their temper and have little patience, this might have an adverse effect on more timid group members. Less forceful group members will probably feel ill-at-ease working with impatient people, and may therefore contribute less well.

Balancing the personalities and characteristics of group members is a difficult task. Groups work more effectively with a balance of different personality styles. Establishing clearly the characteristic of each member when he wishes to join the group is not always possible, especially if the group is an open, informal one in which no membership procedures, such as an interview, are held. Even if you hold interviews prospective group members might be on 'their best behaviour' and put across an image they think appropriate. It might be only when individuals start working with other group members that their true personality and character become apparent. To help prevent this situation arising you should follow the points discussed in the chapter on Career Management Skills.

4.3   The Process of Developing Groups

After considering the physical environment and physical characteristics that can help to improve group cohesiveness, you should attend to the process by which groups are developed. It is commonly suggested that groups pass through four stages of development:

(i)   Forming.
(ii) Storming.
(iii) Norming.
(iv) Performing.

(i)   Forming

The first stage that all groups pass through is that of formation. Here the group members spend time establishing the reactions of other members to themselves and to the tasks and activities to be carried out.

This is a 'testing-the-water' phase during which group members become acquainted with each other and determine what contribution they can make to the group and how they will be expected to behave. They establish the bounds of what is acceptable, and what is unacceptable, by initiating conversations with other members of the group. This is an important stage of the group development process because it helps to set the standards of behaviour to which the group conforms.

When passing through the formation stage each of the group's members tries to create favourable images of themselves:

- Creating a favourable first impression is important. You need to pay particular attention to dress and appearance. Group members who wear clothes that are inappropriate might be treated with suspicion by the other members.
- You need to communicate with the other members of the group. Initiate conversations, ask open questions, and be friendly.
- Listen to what other members of the group are saying. You create a good impression by showing genuine interest and attention.
- It is important to be assertive in this formation stage, for if you do not you may find that decisions are taken with which you disagree. There may not be an opportunity to reverse such decisions at a later stage. Thus, you should assert your influence on the decision making process from the outset.

(ii)   Storming

The second stage of the group development process is known as 'storming'. After the group has been formed conflicts arise within the group as members argue and disagree as to how power and status will be divided between the group members. Some individuals might want a leader to be appointed with certain responsibilities and authority. Others might seek a more democratic approach, in which decisions are taken by committee as opposed to being taken by one individual. Other group members might feel that a combination of both approaches would be advisable.

At this stage of the process you should use your higher order ES:

- You will need your negotiation skills to help resolve conflicts that arise. Obviously the group will not be able to achieve its objectives until it is reasonably harmonious. The ES we discussed in Chapter Eight will be called into use here.
- You will have to use your thinking skills to solve problems that arise and to make decisions. You will need to employ your critical thinking skills when negotiating with others to highlight false assumptions that might have been made, or to offer alternative logical solutions.
- You will have to communicate effectively and be assertive, presenting your views firmly, but not aggressively, to the group.

(iii)   Norming

Once the initial conflicts have been resolved, a sense of cohesiveness is likely to develop within the group. This is the third stage of the group development process and is called 'norming'. The group now establishes itself in line with the criteria determined in the storming phase. The positions of responsibility agreed in that stage are now adopted, and any procedures that need to be established are implemented. The group is now preparing itself to undertake its tasks and activities.

(iv)   Performing

The final stage of the group development process is that of 'performing'. The 'norming' stage resulted in group establishment of the norms to which, all group members should adhere. Each group member should now be working for the good of the group, rather than for his own benefit, and undertake all responsibilities that are required of them. Conflict between members should have been reduced, if not overcome completely. The group, and its members, can now concentrate on attaining its objectives.

For this final stage in the process to be successful you will need to employ a wide range of FS. The group work skills discussed in this chapter will naturally be of importance, as well as the communication skills discussed in Chapter Three.

The process described above is a model. Models simplify reality so that the complex issues and inter-relationships in the real world can be more easily understood. Not all groups will pass through the four stages sequentially. Some stages might be missed out entirely, while additional ones might be added. In formal groups where there might be less scope for debating and negotiating the 'norms' of the group, 'storming' may be ignored completely. Once the group is operational and performing its activities, the stages in the model might be followed through again. For example, when a new leader is appointed the status quo that was arrived at previously might be disturbed. The new leader might wish to alter how the group operates and so temporarily returns to 'storming' or 'norming'.

Understanding how groups develop is important when working with others. Groups are not static entities comprising inanimate objects. They are dynamic, made up of human beings. Each of the group members influences the group by bringing their own personality and characteristics to the group development process.

4.4   Influences on Group Performance

Once a group has been established and is operating, a number of factors will influence how successfully it operates:

(i)   The Influence of Other Group Members

If the group members work together cohesively and harmoniously, communicate openly, share problems and difficulties, then the group should be more effective in achieving its goals. Group members who tend to work independently may not contribute efficiently to the efforts of the group as a whole. We have already noted that one of the advantages of group work is that the group members can pool their resources. If members do not do this, then one of the benefits of operating as a group will be lost.

(ii)   Group Size

The number of people in the group will influence how effectively it operates. There is no specific optimum group size. This depends upon the group's objectives and the skills of those in the group. If the group is performing a relatively straightforward routine task, such as a group of accountants conducting an annual audit for a long standing client, then it might be that a small group will be the optimum size. If a major task is being tackled that requires specific technical skills from different people, for example developing a totally new design of aeroplane, the group will necessarily be larger. Of course as the group grows in size the contribution of each member to the task as a proportion of the whole might be diminished. Each member may contribute only a small part of the work required to achieve the overall objective.

Another important aspect to consider is that the administration and organisation of the group will become more complex as more members join the group. It is likely that more leaders will have to be appointed to monitor and control the work of sub-groups. With increased size some flexibility in decision making and action might be lost. Larger groups can be compared with ocean going tankers – once under way it is difficult to change direction and takes a long time to come to a halt.

Smaller groups, for instance those with fewer than twenty members, are easier to administer, permitting the use of less rigid systems of administration. Decisions can be implemented more quickly and there is more flexibility both in day-to-day operation and in longer term strategy. It is more feasible to have decisions taken by a committee of all the members if the group is smaller and in this way all group members will be able to influence the decisions that are taken. A further benefit of working in smaller groups is that it is easier for the members to identify colleagues who are not working as efficiently as they should be. Such people can be informed that their contributions to the group's objectives are not what they could be, and that improvements are needed. Thus, the productivity of each group member could be higher than for people working in larger groups.

(iii)   The Skills of the Group

The performance of the group depends upon the skills of its members. We mentioned above that group members will be able to work more harmoniously together if they have similar personalities and characteristics such as common attitudes, motivations, needs and temperaments. This is true. However, if the group members all have similar skills as well as similar personalities and characteristics, this may be counter productive.

Groups which comprise members all of whom have similar skills will probably be unable to look at the task facing the group from different perspectives. They will all see the task in the same way, adopting a 'blinkered approach'. Earlier we noted that one of the benefits of working in groups is that the resources of each group member can be pooled and drawn upon by others. Should all group members have similar skills (a resource), then there might be little to be gained from working as a group. Therefore when a group is established care should be taken to ensure that the membership comprises people who possess a range of skills and experiences. In this way the group should be more creative and innovative. This is not to say that as many different skills and experiences as possible should be included in the group. If the group becomes too large then it may well be more difficult to administer. In addition, the larger the group becomes, the more likely it will be that group members do not share common personalities and characteristics and this may hamper the effectiveness of the group.

(iv)   Delegating Responsibilities

Another influence on the performance of the group is whether or not the group members have clearly defined responsibilities. Each member of the group should have a specific role to play which will help the group to attain its objectives.

The responsibilities of each group member can be negotiated between the members, delegated by the leader, or arrived at by using a combination of both of these methods. Whichever method is used, it will be important for all members to know what is expected of them. To make sure that there are no misconceptions, the role of each group member should be written down and circulated within the group. It may also be possible at this stage to specify the standard of performance required from each group member.

If group members do not have clearly defined roles and responsibilities, then difficulties might arise. Group members might contribute to the group as they think fit and this may be counter-productive in that the group becomes unco-ordinated. The group members are all working in different directions. Another difficulty is that an overlap of responsibilities could occur. Here, two (or more) members of the group might perform the same task which leads to a duplication of effort.

Clearly, there must be effective communication within the group to keep the group members informed of their responsibilities. Each person's responsibilities should be specified:

- In writing: The responsibilities of each group member should be clearly stated in writing.
- Verbally: Responsibilities should also be verbally explained to each group member to ensure that they are understood.
- Regularly: Regular meetings should be held to review the work of each individual and make sure that they are performing satisfactorily and that they are not encountering difficulties. If problems are identified then action can be taken to overcome them.

It is important to follow these communication guidelines. Groups sometimes fail simply because the group members do not know what it is they are trying to achieve. Group members may operate in isolation from each other and have no clear idea of their roles within the group. All new members to the group should have explained to them not only their own roles, but also the responsibilities of their colleagues.

If these guidelines are ignored you might find that role conflict develops. Role conflict refers to the situation where different people have different perceptions of what each individual group member should be doing. This arises because the communication within the group is inadequate and there is ambiguity about the responsibilities of each individual.

(v)   Status

Status can be defined as the individual's standing in the group. It may also refer to people's social standing and how they are socially placed against the other group members. Status can be signified in the following ways:

- Job title – manager, supervisor, clerk etc.
- Salary – the monthly earnings of the individual.
- Tangible rewards – the type of car that the person is given by the organisation, the size and location of a person's office (is it on the top floor, for example?).
- Tangible awards – receiving a prize as the 'top salesperson of the month' such as a free holiday.
- Authority – what the individuals can do as part of their responsibilities and their right to use power.

Status symbols are designed to differentiate between the members of the group. In certain circumstances the performance of the group could be influenced by the presence of such status symbols. Some people find that they are motivated to work more effectively if, as a result of their efforts, they gain status, either through an increase in salary, promotion, a reward or an award, or increased authority. Some group members also appreciate the stability that status can offer the group. Some individuals like to feel that there is someone in authority, in a higher position, who receives a higher salary, and takes the major decisions. This makes those group members feel more secure, especially if they are individuals who lack self-confidence.

Status symbols also help to create an identity for individual group members. Individuals in positions of authority frequently like their status to be displayed to others by tangible signs such as more prestigious offices, cars and job titles. This helps to satisfy their need for self-esteem and self-gratification.

Thus, status can influence the group's performance. Clearly defined status symbols that are acknowledged as being appropriate by all group members may increase motivation. This is particularly true if all group members gain status as a result of the group's success.

However, a status symbol for one group might be inappropriate for another. Some people will be motivated to work harder if they are promised an increase in salary. Other people might be motivated to work harder by being offered a change in job title. Before introducing such status symbols to the group it is important to recognise the factors that motivate each group member, and the reward and award system built around these.

(vi)   Group Regulations

Group regulations are the guidelines or rules of the group used to ensure that group members behave consistently when working together. Group regulations are either formally written and circulated among the group, or informally agreed verbally.

Group regulations help members to conform to certain patterns of behaviour. This is important if a consistent image is to be portrayed to the wider environment. The Association of British Travel Agents (ABTA) has its own Code of Conduct that all ABTA members (travel agents and tour operators) must follow. The Code of Conduct covers all areas of a travel agent or tour operator's business activities and inter-relationships with customers. ABTA members contravening the Code of Conduct can be expelled from the Association.

When a group operates without regulations, especially a large group, its members can lack a sense of purpose or direction, and feel uncertain about how to behave in particular situations. Guidelines help to reduce uncertainty.

If regulations are to be accepted by group members, however, they should not be imposed on the group, but should be negotiated by as many group members as possible. People find it difficult to commit themselves to regulations imposed on them without negotiation by other people. It is easier to accept regulations, and therefore to conform to them, when the regulations have been agreed by those group members who are expected to respect them. It is important that all regulations help the activities of the group, rather than restrict the group's productivity or output. For this reason, rules and regulations should be regularly reviewed.

(vii)   The Group's Cohesiveness

Cohesiveness is the ability of the group to work together harmoniously and effectively. For the group to be cohesive the group members must want to work together and they must be attracted to the group. When the group is cohesive, a number of benefits arise:

- Each individual's personal satisfaction gained from working in the group is improved. When all group members work together harmoniously, free from conflict and tension, it is more enjoyable and less stressful.
- The performance of the group is improved. Communication within the group is more effective.
- Commitment to the group is increased. Individual group members will feel more loyal to the group when it is cohesive and will have a greater commitment to contribute to the best of their ability.

Given the advantages outlined above, how can the group ensure that it is cohesive? The answer lies in adopting the points we raised earlier in this section. For group members to work together harmoniously:

- They should have similar personalities and characteristics.
- The group size should not be so large that problems of administration arise.
- The skills of each individual should be complementary to the skills of other group members.
- The responsibilities of each individual should be explicit and unambiguous.
- Rewards and awards should be used to motivate the group members.
- Regulations should be accepted by all.

5.   Different Types of Groups

We have considered already the different forms of group, for example whether they are informal or formal, closed or open. The next section of this chapter considers the different types of groups to be found in organisations.

5.1   Committees

A committee is a group of people who meet to further a shared concern, with a view to steering action by themselves or by other people. Committees may operate over a period of time or until a problem has been solved. They are found in many different types of organisation in the public and private, and voluntary sectors. Below we give a few examples:

- In universities, committees are formed to discuss and evaluate the progress of courses. Teaching staff and students will be represented on the committee.
- In business organisations, committees are formed to manage day-to-day activities (such as the spending of a particular budget) and to develop long-term strategies.
- In local government, committees enable councillors to determine policies, for instance on the Housing Committee.

Committees generally meet at regular intervals to discuss their business. They are managed in a formal sense, with a Chairperson and a Secretary. Minutes are recorded and agendas produced. The more formal the committee, the greater the likelihood that members are elected to it. Elections follow procedures laid down in the committee's constitution.

Should the area of interest to the committee require further research, investigation, or action, a sub-committee could be formed. This comprises fewer members than the main committee and has certain set objectives. For example a committee formed in a university to look after the Outdoor Activities Programme, might set up a smaller committee to raise funds so that the programme can be implemented.

Committees are primarily vehicles for discussion and decision making. When a decision has been made, the committee may ask an individual or group of individuals to carry out the specified task. Committees and sub-committees are disbanded when they have met their objectives.

5.2   Project Groups

A project group is normally established to handle a specific problem. In this way it is similar to a sub-committee. A project group differs from a sub-committee in that it does not have to be related to another committee. The project group could be an entity in its own right.

Project groups have many different uses. In business a project group might be established to investigate organisations that could be suitable for take-over. In a university a project group could be set up to plan an overseas field trip. In a local authority a project group could be used to monitor the success of changing the road system in the town centre, drawing members from a number of different departments, for example the Highways Department, the Department of Environment and the Housing Department.

One of the benefits of a project group is that, if it includes members from different departments, it may be able to cut across the normal structure of the organisation. Such groups often improve communication and co-operation throughout the organisation. The project group will be dissolved when it has completed its task.

5.3   Executive or Command Groups

Executive or command groups are usually composed of managers and their staff who are elected or appointed to serve on the group because of their technical expertise. Such groups have wide responsibilities and tasks which may include:

- Planning future developments for the organisation.
- Organising the implementation of plans.
- Motivating other group members.
- Co-ordinating the different groupings within the organisation.

It is likely that each executive or command group will have its own specialism, for example the New Product Development Group, or the Production Planning Group.

Within an organisation there might be a number of these groups, each with a different purpose. To ensure against duplication of roles, however, effective communication between groups is necessary. Good communications between the groups will also prevent each group from operating in isolation, so that they are all co-ordinating their efforts.

Administration of a group will usually be handled by the manager responsible for the group's performance, for instance, the New Product Development Manager, or the Production Manager. The manager of such a group will normally have authority to implement decisions taken by the group.

5.4   Quality Circles

Quality circles originated in the early 1960s in Japan and are a popular way of encouraging group work. Quality circles generally consist of 8 – 10 workers engaged in associated work. They meet as a committee on a frequent and regular basis, usually once a week, to discuss problems or concerns associated with their work. The purpose of the meeting is to discover solutions to these problems or concerns, which are then implemented after managerial approval.

Quality circles have specific features:

- Membership of the quality circle is voluntary and open to all workers in the section.
- One purpose of the quality circle is to solve work-related problems. To help the members do this, training may have to be provided in problem-solving (see Chapter Eleven).
- Once a potential solution to a given problem has been identified, management must be informed (requiring presentation skills as discussed in Chapter Seven).
- When approval is given to implement the solution the members implement it and monitor how successful the solution has been.

The use of quality circles is growing because this approach to group work offers five distinct benefits:

(i)   Social Benefits

Workers make friends when they are working in a group. Workers can share problems which in itself helps to reduce anxiety and stress. By offering solutions to problems, workers feel that they have more influence and control over their working activities.

(ii)   Technical Benefits

Workers have a good knowledge and understanding of the processes involved in their work. They are well placed, therefore, to be able to propose solutions to problems that arise. Quality circles enable such solutions to be proposed and implemented.

(iii)   Managerial Benefits

Quality circles are popular with workers as they allow workers to take more of an active role in the operational side of their work. This leads to increased motivation at work, improved quality of work, and a source of suggestions for improving the way in which the work is completed. These benefits free the managers to concentrate on other elements of their work.

(iv)   Operational Benefits

Workers are more willing to accept changes in their methods of working if they have recommended such changes themselves. There is less uneasiness than when changes are imposed by those in authority without discussions or negotiations with the work force.

(v)   Financial Benefits

Quality circles in effect act as a consultant for the organisation. No additional direct payments are made to quality circles, however, as the group members are volunteers. Compare this to the costs the organisation would incur if a firm of external consultants were to be employed.

For the quality circle approach to be successful, all concerned must be committed. Senior managers must endorse the quality circles and implement any feasible solutions that are proposed. Middle managers have to allow time during the working day for the quality circles to meet, and need to provide a room that is conducive to a group discussion.

It might be the middle manager's role to see that a senior member of the quality circle is trained in group management skills. The individuals forming the quality circle must be aware of how to organise and run meetings.

Group members in a quality circle must be confident that they will not suffer through contributing to it, especially when their proposals appear to criticise the organisation. Instead, the group should be rewarded for any suggestions that are implemented, for example by cash bonuses or a special gift.

Quality circles offer benefits to organisations that use them, but there are also some cautionary aspects that need to be borne in mind:

- Quality circles should not be seen as a solution to all the problems faced by the organisation. The problems best tackled by such groups are problems related to the immediate working methods and surroundings of the group members.
- Workers who do not volunteer to participate in the quality circle might be unwilling to accept proposals made by the quality circle, especially if such proposals lead to an increase in the pace of the work, or to cut backs in the labour force.
- Some people may volunteer for the quality circle simply to receive time-off from their normal working activities. Their value to the group is questionable. Other volunteers might see the quality circle as a vehicle for venting their frustrations, rather than as a means of solving problems.

If the organisation using quality circles is aware of these potential difficulties, however, then steps can be taken to reduce the likelihood of them arising.

Group work skills are important. When working with other friends or colleagues, much thought must be given to knowing and understanding their personalities, interests and skills.

5.5   The Team Player/Team Leader Matrix

How much of a team player or team leader are you? By taking the following test, and then following the instructions that follow, you will gain some idea of your own team working and team leadership abilities.

In order to complete the test you must record how much you agree or disagree with the statements that are listed to the left, do this by placing a X in the box that most fits with how much you agree or disagree with the statements. Make sure that you read the statements carefully as some are phrased positively and some negatively. If you do not want to write in this book, it may be a good idea to write the question numbers and your answers on a separate piece of paper or to photocopy these pages.

	Statements	Strongly Agree	Agree	Neither Agree or Disagree	Disagree	Strongly Disagree
1	I usually prefer to work alone.					
2	Team working means utilising a variety of skills in order to achieve something.					
3	I am not afraid to speak my mind.					
4	I prefer to be told what to do.					
5	Group work means that I dont have to do as much.					
6	Cohesion between group members is important.					
7	I am able to empathise with those around me.					
8	I do not like to be seen as being outspoken.					
9	I tend not to make decisions when working in groups.					
10	Working in groups and teams is an every day part of life.					
11	I am able to prioritise and organise my workload to great effect.					
12	I would rather go with the flow than look for new ways to do things.					
13	I usually end up doing everything when working in groups.					
14	I believe that I am an effective communicator when working with others.					
15	I consider myself to be a good negotiator.					
16	I try to avoid conflict.					
17	If you are working in a group there is little need for communication.					
18	I understand the importance of listening as much as speaking.					
19	I am not afraid of making unpopular decisions.					
20	I tend to sit quietly in meetings.					
21	Group working is more hassle than what it is worth.					
22	Working in a team gives me a sense of belonging.					
23	I am willing to chair meetings.					
24	I easily get frustrated with other people.					
25	Group working means losing your sense of identity.					
26	I always try my utmost not to let others down when working in a group.					
27	I believe in keeping those around me informed of progress.					
28	If I give an instruction, I dont need to explain why.					
29	I will only carry out tasks that I want to do.					
30	I am willing to help others who are struggling to cope.					
31	I am willing to appraise others be that positive or negative.					
32	I am not naturally confident.					
33	Its not my problem if someone else in the team hasnt done their work.					
34	I really enjoy taking part in group tasks.					
35	I would consider myself a natural leader.					
36	I often struggle to motivate those around me.					
37	I find it difficult to motivate myself when working with others.					
38	It is important to participate in meetings when working in groups.					
39	I am aware of the symptoms of stress and make steps to reduce it.					
40	I often get depressed when under pressure.					

Once you have placed a X in each box it is time to score your responses – use the grid below to record your score against each statement number, so that you may produce a list numbered 1 to 40 with the appropriate score alongside each number.

	Statements	Strongly Agree	Agree	Neither Agree or Disagree	Disagree	Strongly Disagree
1	I usually prefer to work alone.	-2	-1	0	1	2
2	Team working means utilising a variety of skills in order to achieve something.	2	1	0	-1	-2
3	I am not afraid to speak my mind.	2	1	0	-1	-2
4	I prefer to be told what to do.	-2	-1	0	1	2
5	Group work means that I dont have to do as much.	-2	-1	0	1	2
6	Cohesion between group members is important.	2	1	0	-1	-2
7	I am able to empathise with those around me.	2	1	0	-1	-2
8	I do not like to be seen as being outspoken.	-2	-1	0	1	2
9	I tend not to make decisions when working in groups.	-2	-1	0	1	2
10	Working in groups and teams is an every day part of life.	2	1	0	-1	-2
11	I am able to prioritise and organise my workload to great effect.	2	1	0	-1	-2
12	I would rather go with the flow than look for new ways to do things.	-2	-1	0	1	2
13	I usually end up doing everything when working in groups.	-2	-1	0	1	2
14	I believe that I am an effective communicator when working with others.	2	1	0	-1	-2
15	I consider myself to be a good negotiator.	2	1	0	-1	-2
16	I try to avoid conflict.	-2	-1	0	1	2
17	If you are working in a group there is little need for communication.	-2	-1	0	1	2
18	I understand the importance of listening as much as speaking.	2	1	0	-1	-2
19	I am not afraid of making unpopular decisions.	2	1	0	-1	-2
20	I tend to sit quietly in meetings.	-2	-1	0	1	2
21	Group working is more hassle than what it is worth.	-2	-1	0	1	2
22	Working in a team gives me a sense of belonging.	2	1	0	-1	-2
23	I am willing to chair meetings.	2	1	0	-1	-2
24	I easily get frustrated with other people.	-2	-1	0	1	2
25	Group working means losing your sense of identity.	-2	-1	0	1	2
26	I always try my utmost not to let others down when working in a group.	2	1	0	-1	-2
27	I believe in keeping those around me informed of progress.	2	1	0	-1	-2
28	If I give an instruction, I dont need to explain why.	-2	-1	0	1	2
29	I will only carry out tasks that I want to do.	-2	-1	0	1	2
30	I am willing to help others who are struggling to cope.	2	1	0	-1	-2
31	I am willing to appraise others be that positive or negative.	2	1	0	-1	-2
32	I am not naturally confident.	-2	-1	0	1	2
33	Its not my problem if someone else in the team hasnt done their work.	-2	-1	0	1	2
34	I really enjoy taking part in group tasks.	2	1	0	-1	-2
35	I would consider myself a natural leader.	2	1	0	-1	-2
36	I often struggle to motivate those around me.	-2	-1	0	1	2
37	I find it difficult to motivate myself when working with others.	-2	-1	0	1	2
38	It is important to participate in meetings when working in groups.	2	1	0	-1	-2
39	I am aware of the symptoms of stress and make steps to reduce it.	2	1	0	-1	-2
40	I often get depressed when under pressure.	-2	-1	0	1	2

The next step is to work out your team player score, this is a score that may range between minus forty and forty. The question numbers listed below will allow you to calculate your team player score, simply add up the numbers that are equivalent to your responses.

1,2,5,6,9,10,13,14,17,18,21,22,25,26,29,30,33,34,37,38

Finally you need to work out how strong a team leader you may make. This is also a score that may range between minus forty and forty. The question numbers listed below will allow you to calculate your team leader score, simply add up the numbers that are equivalent to your responses.

3,4,7,8,11,12,15,16,19,20,23,24,27,28,31,32,35,36,39,40

In order for a better visualisation of your combined team player/leader role, it is a good idea to plot your two scores within the matrix below.

Plot your team player score on the horizontal scale, and plot your team leader score on the vertical scale.

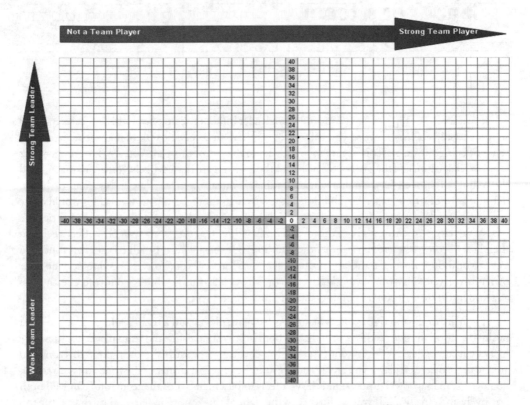

So how did you do in your results? The following diagram gives an indication as to the various team player/leader attributes (or not) that the differing zones on the matrix represent.

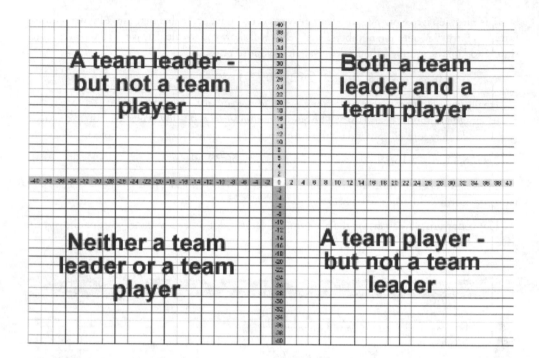

If you are in the top left zone, you are a team leader but not a team player, this indicates that you have leadership abilities; however you will most likely have an autocratic style of management, as your sense of being a team player is negative. The closer to the top of this zone you are the stronger your sense of leadership, and the further to the left of the grid you are the less likely you are to understand the feelings of those in the team that you are leading. If you are in the top left of this zone you have a definite sense of strong leadership abilities, but few feelings for those in your team. This would make you a dictatorial manager – these people often rule by fear. In modern serviced focused industries this type of manager, experiences a high turnover of staff within their teams, and can be ineffective due to their lack of compassion to those under their authority. If you are near the left edge of this zone, you need to be more empathetic and understanding of those around you. You also need to develop your own team player skills – you obviously have some positive leadership attributes – but your effectiveness as a leader will suffer if you do not understand those around you.

If you are in the top right zone, you are both a team player and a team leader, this is the most positive zone on the grid, as this zone indicates both positive leadership and team player abilities. The higher you are in this zone, the stronger type of leader you are, the further to the right in this zone you are the more of a team player you are. If you are near the top right corner of the zone you are a strong democratic manager who understands how it feels to be a member of the team, and can lead both positively and effectively. If you are further to the right of this zone than left, and further to the top of this zone than the bottom of it your skills and abilities would serve modern day industries well. The main danger with being in this zone is complacency, your well honed skills will still need working on from time to time, otherwise your abilities may lessen.

If you are in the bottom left zone, you are neither a team leader or a team player, this is the zone that you do not want to be in – and demonstrates that you are better working alone than with other people. Few positions these days can offer you that opportunity so you desperately and quickly need to go about improving both your team player and team leader abilities. The further you are to the bottom left of this zone the more desperate your situation is, and the more urgent it is that you seek training opportunities to improve your skills.

If you are in the bottom right zone, you are not a team leader, however you are a team player. You have positively demonstrated your ability to work in a team situation, however you do not feel as though you are able to lead a team of individuals. This could be because you have not yet developed leadership skills, or it could simply be a matter of confidence. The further you are towards the bottom of this zone, the weaker your leadership skills are. Ideally you should be placed further to the right of this zone than the left, indicating stronger team player abilities, and further towards the top of the zone than the bottom, indicating that you have abilities that can be developed in order to make you into a leader. People in this zone are recognised team players, and will often find suitable jobs that can use good team player abilities. It is with time, experience and confidence that the people in this zone best develop their managerial skills.

If you are very close to the centre of the matrix in any of the zones (within the 10 or – 10 diameter) you have indicated some contradictory answers. This may mean that you have not understood what has been asked of you within the questions, or it could mean that you have not concentrated on your answers. It could possibly mean that you are a contradictory person – who can often find it difficult to fit into a team situation. If you are in this zone, retake the test at another time, if the answers remain the same, try another type of test, such as the Belbin personality test – which is also very useful for indicating how you fit into a team situation.

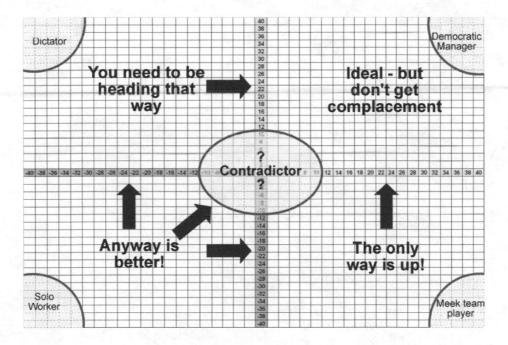

After reading this chapter please complete the following learning activities:

Learning Activities

1. Apply what you have read in this chapter about group dynamics to a group working situation that you have been involved with, in the past. Write a short reflective piece describing the group dynamics, and about how effectively the group worked together.

2. Consider a time when you have been a group leader, or when you have been in a group that has had a leader. Write a short piece that critically appraises either your (or the other persons) role as group leader. Were you/they an effective group leader or not? Have you learned anything from this, which may improve your own group leadership performance in future?

3. The next time that you are required to work in a group, consider the four stages of group formation. Write a reflective piece about the purpose of the group, and the occurrences within the group that indicated each of the four stages of group formation.

4. Complete the team player/team leader questionnaire and matrix from this chapter – what has this told you about yourself? Write a short reflective piece.

Chapter Ten
Information Gathering Skills

After reading this chapter you will be able to:

1. Learn about different sources of information that may be useful to you.

2. Understand advanced searching techniques using the internet.

3. Explain the difference between primary and secondary sources of information.

4. Design a questionnaire.

Many different situations which you will face require the gathering of information. Prior to attending for an interview you have to research the organisation to which you are applying for background information in order to show the interviewer that you are knowledgeable about the organisation and its operations. In negotiation sessions you have to research the background issues that will affect the discussions you are involved in. If you are a salesperson selling a product to a customer you must be knowledgeable about competing products, and how they differ from your own. As a consultant undertaking a project for a client you would be frequently involved in some form of research – finding information in order to support your conclusions.

Information gathering skills, therefore, are personal skills that are highly transferable to different situations. You need to be aware of different types of information gathering, and the steps involved in the research process.

1. The Nature of Information Gathering

Information gathering can be thought of as being the systematic collection and recording of data (data is used here in a wide sense, and refers to any type of information). Information gathering is not an end in itself, however, as the data must be analysed and evaluated. When you have completed this stage you can use the data for problem solving and decision making. This chapter is primarily concerned with the data collection process. Other skills which are mentioned are covered elsewhere in this book.

Before considering information gathering techniques, we should first try to identify situations in which the collection of data will be useful.

1.1   The Role of Information

The primary objective of gathering information is to answer questions. These questions will be diverse, and will depend on the situation with which you are faced. But by answering questions, you will be better placed to understand an issue, to make a decision or to solve a problem.

The collection of information, its analysis and its evaluation will help to reduce the uncertainty and inherent risk in decision making and problem solving. Very few people can make decisions or solve problems without a store of knowledge to draw upon. A lack of appropriate information can be responsible for you making an incorrect decision which in turn causes grave difficulty for you and your organisation.

While the overall objective of gathering information is to answer questions, we can identify a number of other situations in which information gathering would be useful:

- General background data can be collated that helps you to put into perspective a situation you are faced with. For example, you can follow trends in the market place, study competitor activity, identify new opportunities or highlight threats.
- When you are planning a course of action information is useful to help you to decide which course of action you should implement. Consider the possible outcomes from your decisions by posing questions which begin with 'what if ...?'
- When you have taken the decision and implemented the plan, information can be collected to help you to evaluate the success of the decision. Did you reach the expected outcome by following a particular course of action?

From our discussion here it is apparent that three types of information can be collected – firstly, general information about the situation under consideration; secondly, information that is useful in forecasting likely occurrences in the future; and thirdly, information that can be used to evaluate the success of having followed a particular course action.

Information that is gathered can be quite specific, relating to one discrete area, for example the effect of spending an extra 10% on advertising as opposed to spending that cash on sales promotions. Or the information can be of a general nature – the different types of political systems that can be found in the world today.

In all organisations, information gathering should be part of a continuous process, and be conducted in a systematic manner. As we have already seen, you should gather information when you are faced with a situation for which you do not know the answer. Rather than making an irrational decision with little information, you should gather data that sheds light on the situation and which allows you to arrive at a rational and informed decision.

1.2   The Characteristics of Information

As part of the process of understanding information gathering, it is clearly appropriate to consider the characteristics of information itself:

- Information covers all forms of knowledge from hard facts such as a set of monthly sales data to abstract ideas, for example the product life cycle concept that is considered in marketing courses.
- Information is exchangeable – many different exchange techniques can be used ranging from high technology communications systems that use satellites to transmit messages from one part of the world to another, to the simple use of speech.
- The medium in which information is expressed is closely related to its content, its purpose and its intended audience. For example, the evening news bulletin on television uses speech, graphics and visual images to inform the viewer.
- Information may be transmitted erratically and in an unplanned way, such as a person's response to an unexpected telephone call, or it can be communicated in accordance with an overall plan or structure, such as the information system operating within an organisation.

Different types of information are available to you, ranging from the personal types such as anecdotal information received in conversations, to the more formal types of information obtained by rigorous survey techniques. Determining your information requirements when faced with a given task or problem is a personal skill, and in a broader sense is part of a research process.

2.   Information Retrieval

Imagine that you are in your workplace one day when suddenly your boss calls out: 'Find out the time of the next train to London – I've got to get there as soon as possible.'

What alternatives are open to you to find this information? Before going any further, jot down on a sheet of paper as many ways as you can think of for obtaining this information.

The possibilities you have listed might include:

- refer to rail timetable in office;
- ask if anyone has been to London recently and can remember the times;
- go to railway station and ask;
- phone railway station;
- check website;
- ask a travel agent;
- use teletext;
- go to local reference library.

How many of these would suit your situation? Some of them are obvious, like phoning the station or referring to an up-to-date timetable. Others are of dubious reliability and efficiency, such as asking someone at work who visited their cousin in London last weekend if they can remember the times. However, an important facet of information retrieval is realising that there can be a number of valid routes to discovering the same information. If one route is blocked (e.g. the company phone is out of order), you can try another route. Using a travel agent located a few doors away would be an efficient route, or using the Internet to see if there was any news of rail delays would be helpful. A quality highly-prized by employers is using your initiative and knowing what the various options open are.

Let us now consider some of the main methods of information retrieval with which you should be familiar.

2.1 Files

Businesses use different filing systems for storing information. Filing is usually done either alphabetically (most common), chronologically or numerically. When filing is done alphabetically by clients' names, all the information in each file would be stored chronologically within that file. As you are more likely to need to refer to recent correspondence, the most recent would be at the front of the file and you would progress through the file to find earlier correspondence.

With alphabetically arranged information, it is essential that you know your alphabet of course. But it is also important to recognise that you might find *St. John's Ambulance* and *Saint David's Shopping Centre*. You would also need to check precise spellings, such as *Davies* or *Davis*, *MacMillan* or *McMillan*, *Thompson* or *Thomson*.

2.2 Microfiche

Fiche is French for 'slip of paper, form or index-card'. Microfiche is a means of storing data on microfilm that can then be read by a magnifying machine called a microfiche reader. The fiche is a postcard-size sheet of celluloid containing printed information too small for the naked eye to read. This use of microfilm does not have the excitement or glamour attached to James Bond's use of the medium, but it does mean a tremendous saving in space. For example, in libraries, Whitaker's list of *British Books in Print* occupies a single A4 ring binder as opposed to volumes of weighty hardback information. Microfiche also has the facility for updating rapidly-changing information in a quick and cost-effective manner.

Although some uses of microfiche are being replaced by computer-stored data, microfiche is still very common. Organisations like hospitals may store information from patient files to payroll details on microfiche.

2.3 CD-ROM/DVD

You will be familiar with CDs – compact discs, DVDs – Digital Versatile Discs. In the music business CDs have taken over from compact cassettes and records as the most popular medium for storing pre-recorded music, in the movie and video business DVDs have taken over from VHS video tapes as the most popular medium for storing pre-recorded films.

The information is stored electronically and read by a special beam of light known as a laser. The consequent quality of reproduction, lack of distortion and alleged indestructibility of this medium are all attractive.

CDs have other applications, particularly for use in computer-based information systems where enormous amounts of data can be stored and easily accessed. Such a system is known as read-only memory (ROM). Home computers are now available with DVD/CD-ROM facilities – whether to store the *Encyclopaedia Britannica, The Complete Works of Shakespeare* or other information. Apart from the availability of the information in the way it might be presented on the page of a book, CD-ROM also allows easy cross-referencing. For example, it would be possible to find out how many times and where Shakespeare refers to business. Apart from having a hobby basis, such facilities might be of use to scholars, and have other serious applications. One such practical use might be the CD-ROM version of the reference source mentioned above *Whitaker's Books in Print,* known as *Bookbank.* This allows you to access not only information about this book (title, authors, publisher etc.) but would also allow you access to:

- the titles of all books written by the individual authors (irrespective of publisher);
- a complete list of titles published by the company;
- using a keyword in the title (e.g. communication) the titles of all books with that word in the title;
- a printout of any information you need.

This is obviously a more sophisticated system than microfiche as it allows you to rearrange the data and gain print-outs as you wish. Indeed, DVD/CD-ROM may be considered the basis of an individualised hand-held 'electronic book'.

Many home computers may come with DVDR or CDRW/CDR facilities – DVDR is a DVD onto which large amounts of data may be written (including computer files, video, audio, movies, graphics), CDRW/CDR is a CD that may have data recorded onto it in the same way, although a CDRW/CDR holds much less data than a DVDR. A DVDR may hold several Gigabytes of data, where as a CDRW/CDR only hold a maximum of 700 Megabytes. Both of these formats now dwarf the 'almost defunct' floppy disc that can only hold 1.44 Megabytes.

2.4   Internet Searching

The internet is the world's single largest source of information. Billions of web pages contribute to making millions of websites, which contain an almost infinite amount of data and information. Being able to perform an effective information search using the World Wide Web (WWW) is now an essential skill to possess.

The question first of all is – how does one search for information using the WWW? The main mediums by which to do this are:

(i)   Search Engines.
(ii)   Web Directories.
(iii) Subject Gateways.
(iv)   Online Databases.
(v)   Bulletin Boards/Discussion Forums.

(i)   Search Engines

A search engine is a website that is the user interface for a collection of programs, which search the WWW and catalogue individual web pages. The user interface allows you to type a word or words into a box on the screen, and then click upon a 'search' or 'go' button. This will activate the search engine into seeking out the web pages that it has catalogued that contain the words that you are searching for. There are thousands of search engines on the WWW, most of which are run as commercial enterprises, some examples of search engines include:

Search Engine	Uniform Resource Locator (URL)
37	http://www.37.com
Alta Vista	http://www.altavista.com
AOL	http://www.aol.com OR http://www.aol.co.uk
Ask Jeeves	http://www.ask.co.uk
BBC	http://www.bbc.co.uk
Dogpile	http://www.dogpile.com
Excite	http://www.excite.com
Go	http://www.go.com
Google	http://www.google.com OR http://www.google.co.uk
Hot Bot	http://www.hotbot.com
Info	http://www.info.com
Lycos	http://www.lycos.com OR http://www.lycos.co.uk
Metacrawler	http://www.metacrawler.com
MSN	http://www.msn.com OR http://www.msn.co.uk
Search	http://www.search.com
Wanadoo	http://www.wanadoo.co.uk
Yahoo!	http://www.yahoo.com OR http://www.yahoo.co.uk

Some search engines are Meta search engines, which mean that they also search the catalogues of other search engines, this is the case with Dogpile and 37, and some search engines are based on portal pages (an Internet Service Provider's first or main page) as is the case with Wanadoo and AOL.

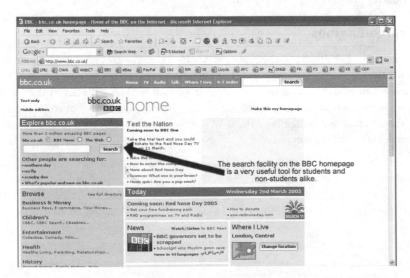

The search facility on the BBC homepage is a very useful tool for students and non-students alike.

The majority of English language search engines are based in North America, which often means that the results are from an American perspective. However some search engines also have a British version that may be searched from, that will allow for a greater penetration of British results to searches – as is the case with Google, Yahoo, AOL, MSN and Lycos. The BBC search engine is on the BBC home page, and is British based, it allows users to search either BBC archives, the WWW or both, and is a useful (and by students underused) search engine for searching British based information sources.

Search engines work in different ways depending on how pages are catalogued in the first place. Some search engines work on a paid submission basis, whereby an organisation or an individual may pay for the privilege of having their website listed, and the more they pay, the higher the website becomes in the rankings of the search engine. Other search engines may determine how pages should be ranked, by assessing which pages are clicked upon from the search engine, after a search has been performed. Others may simply place page rankings in order of how many times the word(s) being searched for appears on a web page.

Performing an information search with a search engine, is an example of a horizontal information search – this can be likened to fishing with a net – the net is thrown into the water and then hauled in. It may contain some fish, but it may also contain rubbish that has been thrown into the water, and even items that are dangerous. Exactly the same can be said of the internet, and searching using search engines. There is no guarantee, that the information you will retrieve when searching with search engines is what you are looking for – and indeed some information that may be retrieved could be dangerous, in that it may contain sales rubbish, explicit words or pornographic images. This is largely a down-side of using search engines, and it does take time and experience to be able to recognise the 'prize catches' in what can seem like a 'sea of rubbish'.

The above image is a screen grab of the results from a Google search for the 'history of shoes'. The returned results displayed on the screen contain a mixture of useful information and 'sales junk'. The first result returned for 'Shoes Galore' is a commercial website that is designed to sell shoes. The two results beneath that are both related to a museum that has a collection of boots and shoes, and could both be valid to somebody researching the history of shoes, as is the fourth returned result which is linked to an American university's website. The results to the right of the screen are purely commercial 'paid for' advertisements that are best ignored by researchers.

Searching for information using a search engine involves more than just typing in a word and clicking upon 'search', and then choosing the first few pages that the search engine recommends. You first of all need to decide upon a search strategy, this includes the following:

- Being aware of the topic that you may wish to research.

- Are there time constraints on the topic – e.g. are you researching a specific event that happened at a certain time, or is this not the case?
- What key words or phrases may be associated with the topic that you wish to research – write down a list of these grouping them by relevance. As many search engines are American, consider the spelling of the words you are searching for e.g. realise in English is realize in American English. Also consider synonyms of the words you are searching for. If you haven't got a thesaurus handy, try typing a word in Microsoft Word, and then clicking on it with the right mouse button, this will produce a sub menu – one of the, words within the sub-menu is 'Synonyms'. Click upon this and Word will produce a list of synonyms of the word that you are searching for.
- Does your search term have a geographic limitation? Is it something that is based in one country, for example the English Lake District, or is it something that can happen anywhere in the world e.g. pollution.
- Don't be afraid to cross over into other subject areas that your topic may be involved in. For instance a student studying tourism management may end up using marketing, law, finance, business, and environmental resources that share commonality with aspects of the tourism industry.

Once you have planned your search, the quality of the items that are found ought to be considered. The following should be taken into account:

- How specific are the pages that you have found to the topic – are they very relevant, or only partially relevant. Partially relevant sources can still be useful, but the most relevant sources may be more worthwhile concentrating on in the short-term.
- How credible is the information? It is very easy for ANYONE to put a page on the internet about a subject of their choice – is the source of the information on the page a credible one, or not? This is something that you must decide for yourself. Check the URL (web address) does it give the impression of an official organisation or an individual? Does the page look 'home-made' – and does information found on other pages agree with the information on this page? Be sure that the information is credible before using it – this also includes bias – especially in the case of commercial organisations that may have a vested interest in the information on the page, or may be trying to sell a product using the information on the page. A neutral perspective is usually more credible and therefore better to use.
- Is the web page up to date? Check for a last updated date – or cross reference the information from the page with that on other sites.

By far the major success story of all of the world's search engines is Google. It is reputed to have catalogued more web pages than any other search engine. In March 2005, this figure stood at almost 8,058,0445,000 web pages – and is continually increasing. Google has been so successful as it is easy to use, and has a very effective 'spider' which is the name given to a program that scours the internet collecting details from (and cataloguing) web pages. Google also searches the Open Directory – which is the largest human edited directory on the WWW, and is something that will be focussed upon further into this chapter, the culmination of these factors (amongst other things), means that the quality of items found from a Google search is better than with some other search engines.

Due to the high number of search engines, and due to the fact that Google is recognised by many as a leader in the search engine market, this section will focus upon internet searching using the Google search engine only. Please note that many of the techniques used with Google, will work with other search engines – but some will not.

Searching with Google: The first recommended step would be to go to www.google.co.uk instead of the American .com version. If you go to www.google.com and you are within the UK you will most likely be re-directed to www.google.go.uk.

Decide if the search term you are looking for applies to the UK or globally – if it applies to the UK only, click upon the option beneath the search box that says 'pages from the UK' – if you do not, the entire web will be searched, as would have been the case with the .com version of Google.

With Google there is no case sensitivity so you do not need to worry about capitalisation of letters within words. Google will also ignore certain words such as 'and', 'the' so you can omit these from your searches.

A useful word that you can include in your searches is 'or' this will allow you to search for more than one term, and the results displayed will show pages that contain one of the words you have searched for or the other one, as well as pages that contain both words. For example it is possible to search for 'coal or fossils'. The results show a variety of pages that mention coal, a variety that mention fossils, and a variety that mention both words. If you just wanted to search for pages that contained both 'coal' and 'fossils' then in the search box you only need type 'coal fossils' and the search will produce pages that contain both words. How words are ordered also makes little difference, a search for 'fossils coal' would produce the same results as 'coal fossils'.

You will note that with most words and phrases searched for, that, Google returns thousands of results – far too many. In fact it has become a virtual sport to enter two words to search for with Google that only yield one result – this is known as 'Googlewhacking'. Try it for yourself, but you will find that it is not easy. Visit http://www.googlewhack.com for further information on this pastime.

The point of this is that search engines often return far more results than you will ever have the time or motivation to read. The key is learning to sift through the results, and skim read the findings before going to a selection of pages that seem useful. A handy tip is to open the pages which seem the most useful in a new window, by right clicking on the link to the page and choosing the option 'Open in New Window'. This then keeps your search results page open also, and helps to prevent you from losing it amongst many other open pages.

You can refine your search in Google by doing an advanced search, which will ultimately lead to you receiving fewer results to your searches, which in theory should make the relevance and quality of your findings greater and the process of sifting through them more manageable. To the right of the Google search box is a link that reads 'advanced search'. Clicking upon this will allow you to add the following filters or criteria to your search results:

- Limit the number of your results.
- Search for pages that contain exact matches to phrases.
- Search for pages that contain at least one word, from a number of words being searched for.
- Search for pages that do not contain a certain word.
- It also allows you to set a number of the above criteria, so for example it would be possible to do a search for 'coal' and 'fossils' but not display pages that also contain the word 'limestone'. This technique could prove useful to a student searching for academic information by reducing the number of sales and advertising pages that are listed in a Google search by choosing not to display pages that contain the word 'sale' or 'price'.
- Search for specific types of file only, for example Adobe Acrobat PDF files, or Microsoft PowerPoint PPT files (there is also the reverse option, not to display files of a certain type).

- Search for pages that were published over a certain time period.
- Search for pages that contain the word(s) that you are looking for in a specific part of the page, for instance in the title of the page, in the URL, or in the body of the text on the page.
- Look for certain words within websites that begin with a particular URL (there is also the reverse option, not to look in certain websites).

Another useful tool within the Google search engine is the ability to search specifically for graphical images – in order to do this click the word 'Images' above the search box. The results are returned as thumbnails (small graphics) that may be clicked upon to display the full sized image.

Search engines are enormously powerful tools, which can be extremely useful in finding information quickly. It would be true to state that in this modern era, students tend to make great use of search engines when undertaking research – however, it is the effectiveness of their use that will ultimately impact upon the quality of findings, and the time spent using them in order to gather the information that is required. There is no substitute for a well planned search strategy, combined the effective use of your chosen search engine – which often means taking into account advanced searching options.

(ii)   Web Directories

A web directory is a more structured and organised collection of web pages, than a search engine. In a web directory web pages are filed under a specific topic, which is in turn filed with a larger topic, which is in turn filed within a larger topic and so on. An example of this could be 'Rattle Snakes', which may be a web directory category within a larger category called 'snakes', within a larger category called 'reptiles', within a larger category called 'animals', within a larger category called 'Nature'.

In this example the largest (or top-level) category is 'Nature' and this would have many sub categories, each of which may contain links to web pages – the following diagram demonstrates how this structure may appear within a web directory.

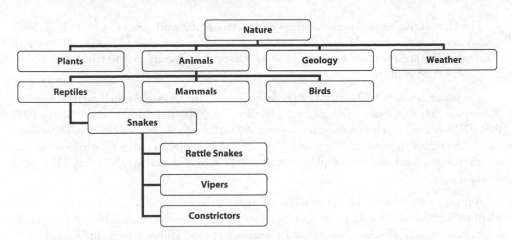

In this simplified diagram of how a web directory may be organised the top level category out of a number of top level categories, other top level categories may include 'Reference', 'Regional' and 'Business' – amongst many others, which would all contain hundreds if not thousands of sub categories. Within the 'Nature' category are four sub categories, each of those sub categories would have further sub categories. The diagram only demonstrates some of the sub categories, to show how the Rattle Snakes category could fit into a web directory. This is designed to give you a more structured and orderly perception of web directories than search engines.

When searching with a search engine, the analogy was used of fishing with a net to perform a horizontal information search (casting your search wide and pulling in many items, which may not always be the ones that you wanted). Searching using a web directory can be likened to fly fishing, whereby a certain type of fish is what you are looking for, and the likelihood of catching another kind is rare. This type of search is called a vertical information search and involves going through the various categories to find the category which is most likely to contain the websites that you are looking for. This certainly takes more time and thought than using search engines, but ultimately the greater relevance of your findings can make the effort seem most worthwhile.

There are a number of directories on the internet; the table below features some of them.

Directory	URL
BBC Directory	http://www.bbc.co.uk/directory/
Google Directory	http://directory.google.com
Looksmart Directory	http://search.looksmart.com/
The Open Directory Project	http://dmoz.org
Yahoo Directory	http://dir.yahoo.com

An advantage that some directories have over search engines, is that the pages and websites listed within them, have been put there by a person rather than a 'web-spider' (automated program). Therefore it is much more difficult to fool web directories into storing 'junk' website details (predominantly sales related) in inappropriate categories. For example, within the Open Directory Project (ODP) it is possible to find a category on 'snakes' that does not contain any websites that are selling snakes, or snake related products – these types of websites have their own categories.

The ODP is the largest human-edited web directory in the world today; it is run by a global 'community' of volunteer enthusiasts who edit the listings within their chosen category. This helps to ensure a certain quality control over the sites that are listed, as editors try to maintain and keep 'tidy' their own section of the web.

The contents of the ODP are used by a number of other directories and search engines including Netscape Search, AOL Search, Google, Lycos, HotBot, DirectHit, and many others. In March 2005 the ODP contained over four million sites, within 590,000 categories, maintained by 67,220 editors – and these figures are continually growing. This resource is certainly worth getting to know how to use; the paragraph below is an example of how a vertical information search within the ODP may be carried out.

A person who is interested in looking at websites on the subject of accommodation at Leeds Metropolitan University, would start with the major category of reference, and then on through the following categories: education; colleges and universities; Europe; United Kingdom; England; Leeds Metropolitan University; housing (see following diagram).

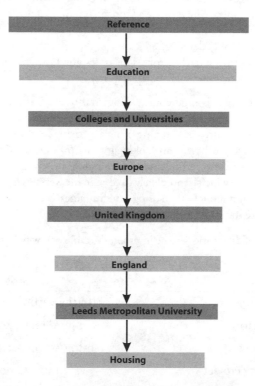

Once in the Housing category the pages that are listed are all relevant to accommodation at that particular university. This is a more organised and structured way of searching, that ultimately provides a greater concentration of high quality results, than by merely typing a term within a search engine. This type of vertical information search is sometimes referred to as a 'funnel' approach to information searching, by starting with a very broad term, and then narrowing it down, stage after stage.

In the previous diagram, the number of pages per category diminishes the further down into the funnel you search (as further levels of sub categories are reached) this is demonstrated by the width of the bar on each category name. In March 2005, the reference category (including all sub-categories within) contains a total of 66,300 websites; this figure reduces at each sub category level, until at the very bottom of the funnel, the housing category contained only eight websites.

The following diagram shows the homepage for the ODP, and the top-level categories of this directory, that are all linked from this page.

(iii) Subject Gateways

Subject Gateways are websites that allow the user to search high quality academic resources that are designed to support learning in a specific subject area. Subject gateways may be searched in the same way as search engines (and sometimes as with web directories), and often yield high quality and relevant results. Some examples of subject gateways are listed within the following table.

Subject Gateway	URL	Subject Area
Argus Clearing House	http://www.clearinghouse.net	Arts & Humanities Business & Employment Communication Computers & Information Technology Education Engineering Environment Government & Law Health & Medicine Places & Peoples Recreation Science & Mathematics Social Sciences & Social Issues
Biz/ed	http://www.bized.ac.uk	Business and Economics
Business Net	http://www.bnet.co.uk	Business and Management
eLSC	http://www.elsc.org.uk	Social Care
English Server	http://eserver.org	English Literature Humanities The Arts
Resource Discovery Network	http://www.rdn.ac.uk	Arts Engineering Maths Computers Geography The Environment Health Medical Science Hospitality Leisure Sport Tourism Humanities Physical Science Social Science Business and Law
USNAL	http://www.nal.usda.gov	Agriculture

When searched, subject gateways often provide links to articles based upon the subject area, of that particular subject gateway. For example the RDN subject gateway covers a variety of different subjects, including the arts, science, hospitality, and technology. This site could be used by a student wishing to further their knowledge of mobile phones for a report based on that subject. By searching for 'mobile phones' from RDN, the user is directed to a number of useful online resources. These resources give valid and relevant information about this subject area. Each suggested resource is listed along with a detailed critique of what the site has to offer, and most of the resources provide an unbiased account of the subject.

If a student decided to use only search engines, and did the same search from Google, the results would include many websites that were biased, and many that have a vested interest in mobile phones, or were indeed the websites of mobile phone manufacturers. A Google search on this subject would also reveal many websites that were intended to market and sell mobile phones and mobile phone products.

(iv)   Online Databases

A database is an organised collection of related information. The web contains many databases that are specific to a certain subject, and can be used as a search tool to gain further information upon that subject. The results of searches with online databases are usually highly relevant, and can almost always be guaranteed as being credible. Subject gateways do not contain such marketing and sales related 'junk'. Some examples of online databases are as follows:

Name of Database	URL	Subject Area
Census 1901	http://www.census.pro.gov.uk	General UK census information for that year, including a name searching facility.
Census 2001	http://www.statistics.gov.uk/census2001	General UK census information for that year including socio demographic data.
Encyclopedia	http://www.encyclopedia.com/	General reference online encyclopedia.
Hansard House of Commons	http://www.parliament.the-stationery-office.co.uk/pa/cm/cmhansrd.htm	House of Commons daily debates.
Hansard House of Lords	http://www.parliament.the-stationery-office.co.uk/pa/ld/ldhansrd.htm	House of Lords debates.
HealthPromis	http://healthpromis.hda-online.org.uk/	Health.
Internet Movie Database	http://www.imdb.com	Films, Movies, Show Business.
National Electronic Library for Health	http://www.nelh.nhs.uk	Health.
National Electronic Library for Mental Health	http://www.nelmh.org	Mental Health.
Public Health Electronic Library	http://www.phel.gov.uk/	Health.
PubMed	http://www.ncbi.nlm.nih.gov/entrez/query.fcgi	Health and Medicine.
Researchers Guide Online	http://www.bufvc.ac.uk/databases/rgo.html	Film, TV, Radio .
Soccerbase	http://www.soccerbase.com	Football including clubs and transfer news.
Webopedia	http://www.webopedia.com	Networking, Technology and the Internet.

(v)   Bulletin Boards/Discussion Forums

Bulletin boards and discussion forums can provide useful information on a variety of subjects. There are thousands of bulletin boards and discussion forums on the internet. To find one on a subject of your choice you may need to search using either a search engine or a web directory.

The main issue to be aware of, with regards to using information from bulletin boards or discussion forums, is the quality and accuracy of the information posted. It is very easy to post a question within a bulletin board or discussion forum, and anyone who reads your question may post an answer. However, how can you be sure of the validity and accuracy of this response? The answer is that you cannot – unless you independently verify the information from another source, such as a book, journal or website. Very often a response may be verified with a simple web search using the information gained from the bulletin board or discussion forum.

Possibly the most useful way to use a bulletin board or discussion forum is to ask for recommended sources of information on your chosen subject, and see what is suggested by the users of the board – rather than directly asking a subject specific question of the other board users.

2.5   Using a Reference Library

A library, even if restricted to traditional print materials, is still a fund of information and it pays to know how to access material quickly and efficiently.

Most libraries, throughout the world use one of two systems – both developed in America. By far the most common is the Dewey Decimal System, invented by a librarian, Melvil Dewey in 1876. Also becoming more common, particularly in institutions of higher education, is the more sophisticated American Library of Congress system. We will concentrate here on the Dewey system which is still likely to serve your needs fully.

Dewey broke down all areas of human knowledge into ten broad categories, giving each category a code:

000	general books	600	technology
100	philosophy	700	the arts
200	religion	800	literature
300	social sciences	900	geography, history
400	language	B	biography
500	science		autobiography

Each category of knowledge is given a hundred numbers, and is further sub-divided, as you can see in the table on the following page.

Further sub-division can take place, so that you can identify specific subjects and also to allow for the introduction of new subjects.

If you are using this book in a college or university, you could look to see if there are copies in the library. You can check by either author or title. Either way you should come up with the same reference code! Incidentally, this is the section of books in a library that you will need most frequently for your course, so it's worth getting to know your way around this part of the library.

(i)   How to find a book

FICTION is arranged on the shelves in alphabetical order under the names of the authors, and all novels by the same author will be found in one place.

BIOGRAPHY is arranged in one alphabet of the Names of Persons written about.

ALL OTHER WORKS are arranged in numerical order according to the Dewey Decimal Classification which separates all books into ten main classes: as shown.

Dewey Decimal Classification

Showing Arrangement of Books on the Shelves

000	**GENERAL WORKS**	340	Law	670	Manufacturers
010	Bibliography	350	Public Administration	680	Manufacturers (continued)
020	Library Science	360	Social Welfare	690	Building Construction
030	General Cyclopaedias	370	Education	700	**ARTS AND RECREATIONS**
040	General Collections	380	Commerce	710	Landscape architecture
050	General Periodicals	390	Customs	720	Architecture
060	General Societies Museums	400	**LINGUISTICS**	730	Sculpture
070	Journalism	410	Comparative	740	Drawing Decoration Art
080	Collected Works	420	English Language	750	Painting
090	Book Rarities	430	German Germanic	760	Engraving
100	**PHILOSOPHY**	440	French Provencal	770	Photography
110	Metaphysics	450	Italian Rumanian	780	Music
120	Metaphysical Theories	460	Spanish Portuguese	790	Recreation
130	Fields pf Psychology	470	Latin Other Italic	800	**LITERATURE**
150	Psychology	480	Greek Hellenic Group	810	American
160	Logic	490	Other Languages	820	English
170	Ethics	500	**PURE SECIENCE**	830	German Germanic
180	Ancient Philosophy	510	Mathematics	840	French Provencal
190	Modern Philosophy	520	Astronomy	850	Italian Rumanian
200	**RELIGION**	530	Physics	860	Spanish Portuguese
210	Natural Theology	540	Chemistry	870	Latin Other Italic
220	Bible	550	Geology	880	Greek Hellenic Group
230	Doctrinal Theology	560	Palaeontology	890	Other Languages
240	Devotional Theology	570	Biology	900	**HISTORY**
250	Pastoral Theology	580	Botany	910	Geography
260	Ecclesiastical Theology	590	Zoology	920	Biography
270	Christian Church History	600	**APPLIED SCIENCE**	930	Ancient World History
280	Christian Churches & Sects	610	Medical Sciences	940	Europe
290	Non-Christian Religions	620	Engineering	950	Asia
300	**SOCIAL SCIENCES**	630	Agriculture	960	Africa
310	Statistics	640	Domestic Economy	970	N. America
320	Political Science	650	Commerce	980	S. America
330	Economics	660	Chemical Technology	990	Oceania and Polar Regions

(ii) Using a Book

Once you have located a book it is essential to check whether it is going to assist you effectively in your studies. There are three key ways in which you can check this:

▪ *How suitable is the information?* Who is the target audience for the book? Is it above or below your own level? By looking at the information on the back cover you will get a clear idea of who the book is most suited to. Always check through this in a library or bookshop where there may be several different books dealing with the same topic in different ways and at different levels.

- *In what style is the information presented?* By leafing through a book, you'll get an idea of the style and format and whether it is suited to your own learning needs and style. If you like books with plentiful illustrations, diagrams, summaries or self-check questions you can see how many of these are present.

  If you find a particular author's style easy to get on with, you might look for further publications from the same author, or for other books from the same publisher in a series which you have found particularly stimulating, helpful or easy to follow.

- *How up to date is the information?* Inevitably there is a time-lag between the writing of a book and its publication. Even so, in-formation as up-to-date and topical as possible is vital, particularly in areas such as law or computing. The inside front page of a book can tell you a lot about how useful the book might prove. Following is a printed copy of the inside information from a companion book to this one, from the same publisher. Take a look at it and the annotated notes now.

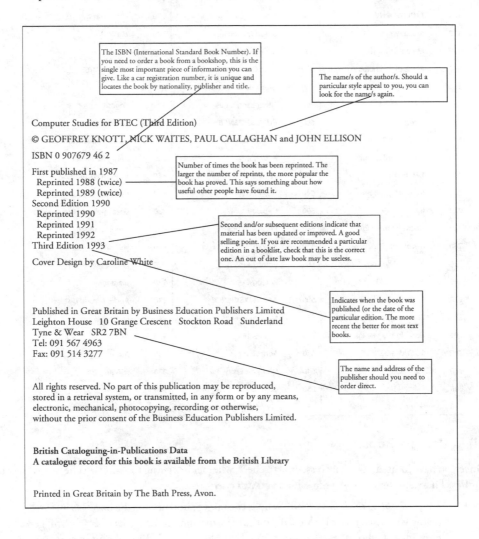

The ISBN (International Standard Book Number). If you need to order a book from a bookshop, this is the single most important piece of information you can give. Like a car registration number, it is unique and locates the book by nationality, publisher and title.

The name/s of the author/s. Should a particular style appeal to you, you can look for the name/s again.

Computer Studies for BTEC (Third Edition)

© GEOFFREY KNOTT, NICK WAITES, PAUL CALLAGHAN and JOHN ELLISON

ISBN 0 907679 46 2

First published in 1987
  Reprinted 1988 (twice)
  Reprinted 1989 (twice)
Second Edition 1990
  Reprinted 1990
  Reprinted 1991
  Reprinted 1992
Third Edition 1993

Cover Design by Caroline White

Number of times the book has been reprinted. The larger the number of reprints, the more popular the book has proved. This says something about how useful other people have found it.

Second and/or subsequent editions indicate that material has been updated or improved. A good selling point. If you are recommended a particular edition in a booklist, check that this is the correct one. An out of date law book may be useless.

Published in Great Britain by Business Education Publishers Limited
Leighton House   10 Grange Crescent   Stockton Road   Sunderland
Tyne & Wear   SR2 7BN
Tel: 091 567 4963
Fax: 091 514 3277

Indicates when the book was published (or the date of the particular edition. The more recent the better for most text books.

The name and address of the publisher should you need to order direct.

All rights reserved. No part of this publication may be reproduced, stored in a retrieval system, or transmitted, in any form or by any means, electronic, mechanical, photocopying, recording or otherwise, without the prior consent of the Business Education Publishers Limited.

British Cataloguing-in-Publications Data
A catalogue record for this book is available from the British Library

Printed in Great Britain by The Bath Press, Avon.

3. The Information Gathering Process

The quality of information available to you can vary from an uninformed opinion to thoroughly researched facts. The aim of the information gathering process is to provide you with the most accurate and reliable data possible within the limits imposed by time, cost, and your research ability. If you are a skilful information gatherer you will be able to use the most sophisticated techniques and methods available to you within these limits. You should always strive to collect the most reliable and accurate information within the constraints we have just noted. If you collect unreliable or inaccurate data then you are likely to make faulty judgements and decisions.

To ensure that you collect accurate and reliable information you need to adopt a systematic and orderly approach. If you use a systematic approach then whatever may be your particular reason for collecting the data, your approach to collecting them will be uniform and hence highly transferable.

Your research process should:

- Define the research problem and set research objectives.
- Determine the information required to solve the problem.
- Determine the sources of information to fulfil the research objectives.
- Gather the relevant data from primary and/or secondary sources.
- Analyse, interpret, and present the findings.

Your task is to execute each of these stages with objectivity and accuracy. The stages are the same for all situations you will face. Let us now consider each stage in more detail.

3.1 Defining the Problem and Establishing Objectives

The first stage in the information gathering process is to define clearly the problem that needs information to solve it, and then to set specific research objectives. This is quite a difficult stage in the information gathering process as you might not be fully aware of the nature of the problem, or may not have clearly defined it, and so collect the wrong type of information. You can waste much time and effort, as well as cost, if you have defined the problem inappropriately.

Put yourself in the position of Lord Teasdale who opens his Historic House in the summer months to tourists. In recent years the number of tourists visiting each year has been declining. This decline in visitors has resulted in your sales revenue falling, and hence the profitability of your business. You are unsure of the reason why visitor numbers have been decreasing. Thus, the problem that needs investigating is the factors which are responsible for the reduced numbers of visitors at Teasdale House.

Once you have defined the problem the next step is to set research objectives. The purpose of setting objectives is to give a focus for the research to ensure that all your energies and activities are relevant to the problem that you have identified. By stating explicit research objectives, you can take measures to gauge whether they have been met. As with all objectives, research objectives can be either quantitative or qualitative, or a combination of both. In Lord Teasdale's case you might set the following objectives:

- To determine which factors have had greatest effect on causing visitor numbers to the house to decrease.
- To produce a profile of the existing visitors to the house – (so that strategies can be devised to encourage more of these consumers to visit the house in the future).
- To establish the existing visitors' satisfaction with their visit (in order to determine whether any modifications or improvements have to be made to the house to attract more visitors).

The objectives that are set should enable you to proceed towards a solution of the problem.

The next stage is to identify the types of information that you will require to help solve the problem and attain the objectives.

3.2   Determine Types of Information Required

You can use a number of different approaches to help determine the type of information you need to gather. You should ask yourself a number of questions to help you to gain a clear idea of your information needs. You will require creative and divergent thinking here. Your aim should be to produce as long a list as possible of different questions. In Lord Teasdale's case your questions might include the following:

- Who are the competitors and what selling points do they offer visitors, that Teasdale House does not?
- What are the visitors' views with regard to the house opening hours?
- Is the house open on sufficient days per week?
- Are the entrance fees too high?
- Are the staff friendly to the visitors?
- Are the rooms open to the public interesting?
- Is the food on sale appealing to visitors?
- Are the souvenirs on sale tempting to visitors?
- Is the advertising that is undertaken effective?
- Do tourists enjoy visiting historic houses, or will some other attraction be more appealing?
- What trends are occurring in tourism and leisure?
- Can any new features be added to Teasdale House that will make it more attractive to visitors?

It is useful at this stage for other people to review the questions to see if they can add a new perspective. As a result some additional questions might be forthcoming, for example:

- Do tourists only visit when the weather is wet?
- Does the house only interest a certain type of person?
- Can the sign at the entrance to the house be seen easily by passing motorists?

By asking other people to consider the problem, you get further objectivity, and additional causes of the problem may be identified.

As well as simply posing questions, a brain storming session is sometimes of value. Brain storming involves a group of people considering the issue together. The purpose of the session is to suggest as many different causes for the decline in visitors as possible. Each person listens carefully to what the others are suggesting and tries to think of additional causes. All the suggestions are accepted without any discussion as to their validity. The aim is to produce as many different causes as possible.

When a lengthy list of questions and possible causes of the problem have been produced, the next step is to think about the types of information that will have to be gathered in order to answer the question and to shed further light on the problem.

Your intellectual skills will be called into use here, with you having to decide the information requirements based upon your evaluation of the situation. As Lord Teasdale you might conclude that you have a number of different information needs:

- Information concerning competing tourist attractions, both local ones and national ones – to indicate trends that are occurring in the tourism industry.
- Information describing who your current visitors are, why they visit the house, what they enjoy about their visit and what they dislike.
- Information showing how your visitors heard about the house and what motivates them to visit.

When all the different types of information that you require have been listed, you can then decide the sources you should refer to in order to collect the appropriate data.

3.3 Determine the Sources of Information

Your starting place is to determine what information is readily available to you either internally within your organisation, or externally in some other published form. Information collated in this way is known as secondary data, since it is obtained from secondary research, that is research carried out by others for another purpose. If no information has been collated and published internally or externally, you will have to devise ways of collecting the necessary information yourself. This is known as primary research.

3.4 Gathering the Data

The diversity of secondary data available to you may be considerable. Your main constraint will be that you are unaware of all the possible sources of secondary data available. The starting place for the search process should be with data that are already collected and published by your own organisation:

- Most organisations collate data referring to their level of activity i.e. sales achieved, number of units sold. This information, when compared with that of competing firms or industry trends will show whether the organisation is performing at the same level, or better or worse than its competitors.
- Data referring to costs. All organisations keep accounts detailing the costs involved with their operations. If you analyse these they may indicate if a particular cost centre has over spent its budget, thus having a negative effect on profitability.
- Geographic data. The organisation may well collate information on the source of its business by region. If certain regions are increasing their contribution to the organisation's business, and others are declining, then this is a trend that you need to explain.
- Customer feedback. Many organisations use customer satisfaction questionnaires to find out whether their clients are satisfied with the products or services provided for them. If the number of customer complaints has increased then this might provide further insights into the problem.
- In addition to the above there might be a variety of other information that has already been collated, for instance market research surveys which have been conducted and have findings which are still valid. Special reports might have been purchased from other organisations, or produced by consultants.

You should undertake an extensive trawl of possible sources of information that might be available internally. Indeed, the organisation might maintain its own library or data index, which you should investigate thoroughly before you consider external sources.

If the information that you require has not been collated by your organisation then your next step should be to consider external sources of published data. There are many sources of published data, the most widespread of which are libraries and the world wide web. Different types of library are designed to meet different needs. All towns have a general public library primarily containing fiction sections but also holding non-fiction reference books. Universities and colleges have academic libraries housing journals, reports, professional magazines, as well as academic texts. The sections in these libraries will be classified according to subject.

Specialist libraries also exist. These tend to be located in the larger cities such as London, Leeds, Edinburgh and Manchester. Examples include the Westminster Central Reference Library, the City Business Library in London, and the British Library at Boston Spa near Leeds. Government departments collate material that can be accessed by members of the public. For example the Department of Trade and Industry in London has a library containing information that will be of use to British exporters wanting information about overseas markets.

Irrespective of the type of library that is used, a diverse range of information will be available:

- **Government Statistics**: Some libraries have extensive sections devoted to collating data published by the government. Indeed, the government is one of the largest research organisations in the UK and it makes available much of this information to the public. All the government departments publish reports and statistics, and you should become familiar with what is available. Two major government research bodies are the Government Statistics Office and the Office of Population Censuses. The former collates data on all businesses incorporated in the UK, while the latter conducts the Census of Population every ten years.

- **Special Reports**: Various private sector organisations specialise in collecting information and publishing it in report form. Libraries will stock a selection of these. Examples include the Mintel organisation that publishes monthly market research reports investigating different products or services. The Jordan Reports analyse the financial performance of organisations. Euromonitor Reports adopt a similar approach.

- **Consumer Publications**: The 'Which' publications investigate a variety of different products and services each month, informing the reader about potential faults or problems that might arise. Specialist interest magazines cover every hobby or interest that might be of concern to the researcher. They provide up to date information on new products and developments, and assess existing ones.

- **Professional Publications**: Each Professional body will have its own publication, for example the British Medical Association journal, 'The Lancet'. These document recent developments in the sphere of interest of the members, for example new drugs that have been developed and launched onto the market.

- **Reference Journals**: These are academic journals such as the 'Cambridge Law Journal', which allow authors to consider theoretical issues relating to their subject, or to present research findings. Each article includes a list of references to enable the reader to investigate further the topic being considered.

- **Directories**: Large reference directories contain factual information. The Kompass Register lists companies situated in the different regions and counties of the UK. Publications such as this give you an idea of potential competitors, or a list of possible suppliers for the product.

- **Extel**: Extel collates information from company reports and publishes it. These data are useful for discovering financial trends that are occurring within an industry, or for finding out how competing firms are prospering.

- **Dictionaries, Glossaries and Encyclopaedias**: These do not simply cover the meaning of and pronunciations of words, but also provide technical and factual information or data.
- **Audio & Visual Data**: In addition to books, magazines, and journals, libraries also contain video tapes and audio tapes. These will be of an educational nature and might contain the information you are looking for. The Teletext and information services contain up-to-date information. Most libraries will have television sets able to receive Teletext data.

It is clear from the above that libraries contain a great wealth of secondary data. Your task will be to become fully familiar with your local library, to know what information sources are available, and just as importantly how to find them. Each library will have its own referencing system – normally an on-line system. You should fully understand how the referencing and index system works so that information can be obtained quickly, without wasting time. If the source of information is not available at the local library then it can be obtained under the Inter-Library Loan System.

The Inter-Library Loan System requires you to provide your local librarian with full details of the text or article you wish to see: the author, publication title, article title (if applicable), the publisher, date of publication, page numbers (if applicable) and ISBN number if known. These details are then sent to the British Library Document Supply Centre which is able to obtain copies of all texts and journal articles published in the UK.

If you are unsure what texts or journal articles have been published on a subject and cannot find any suitable references or texts using the local library's index system, then two further sources of information are available – the Abstracts, and the On-Line Search System. Abstracts are published reference sources that provide synopses of all articles published in a given time period, on a particular subject. For example, the Anbar Abstract lists journal articles published on the subject of 'marketing', giving brief details of the content of each article, along with the author's name, the journal where it was published, and the publication date.

The On-Line Search System involves you typing key words into a personal computer linked to a journal and subject data base. Details of any articles that are found which contain the key words are then displayed. For example, Lord Teasdale might wish to see if any articles have been published on the subject of the 'Marketing of a Historic House'. Thus, the librarian would key in the words 'Historic House' into the personal computer, and the details of all articles on this subject held in the data base would be printed out.

As well as visiting the local library to discover what information is available, you should be aware of the following further information sources:

- Local authorities. Local councils are involved in collecting data on the local environment and have information that might be of interest to you.
- Public bodies. A number of different public bodies exist. National and Regional Tourist Boards operate in the UK and collate tourism statistics. The Civil Aviation Authority publishes data on air-traffic into and out of the UK.
- Professional associations. Organisations such as trade unions and professional associations like ABTA (the Association of British Travel Agents) collect information that is pertinent to their members and sometimes publish special reports.
- Banks. Domestic banks, in particular the National Westminster, HSBC, Barclays, and Lloyds TSB, publish reports and special journals that are available to members of the public.

- Commercial research organisations. Private sector research agencies conduct research and publish the results, selling their findings to interested parties. These publications, though, tend to be expensive. The British Market Research Bureau (BMRB) conducts an annual survey of 24,000 respondents in the UK, known as the Target Group Index (TGI). The survey involves respondents completing a seventy page questionnaire that details their purchasing habits of some 4,500 brands, as well as their media buying habits. Information produced by the TGI will inform an organisation who their customers are, and which media methods should be used to communicate with them.

- Internet Access. Most libraries now contain computers that can be used to search the internet, in order to make use of the vast amount of information that is stored and available online.

The above list is not exhaustive, as the sources of information available to you are continually changing. Apart from being aware of these 'formal' sources of information there are also 'informal' ones that you can refer to. The 'Yellow Pages' can be used to analyse the number of companies competing in a given area. Local newspapers are a valuable source of up-to-date information on local environmental trends, such as new roads being built, new employers locating in the vicinity, or details of competitor activity. National newspapers and magazines, as well as television and radio programmes are useful sources of up-to-date information. Leaflets and brochures from competitors can be analysed to see how their products differ from yours. Indeed, you can attend exhibitions and conferences to meet competitors and to see their products.

Thus, there are many potential sources of secondary data that you can use to obtain the information you require. The internet has considerably increased the volume of data that is published. However, when undertaking a literature search do not just confine your search to on line sources. Remember that there is a wealth of information in hard copy forms, and it is frequently easier to confirm the validity and reliability of such data, than information gained from the world wide web. Indeed, tutors at university are frequently sceptical about the value and accuracy of data down loaded from internet sources.

Before you use **secondary data** to solve your problem you must evaluate its validity and reliability. This requires you to screen the data; to do so you should ask yourself the following questions:

- Who collected the data? Have they been collected by a reputable organisation? Would there be any reason for them to deliberately misrepresent the facts? (e.g. to present a product in a favourable manner).

- For what purpose were the data collected? Was it for a similar purpose to your needs? If not are the data still valid?

- How were the data collected? Was the sample size (if a questionnaire survey was conducted) large enough to enable generalisations to be made?

- Are the data internally consistent and logical in the light of known data sources or other factors?

You should look very carefully at the source of the data and not use it if you are in doubt as to its accuracy. Some organisations when obtaining data do not adopt reliable methods of data collection, and publish findings that are too optimistic. However, much valuable information can be obtained from secondary sources and all researchers should start their information gathering by referring to data that have already been published. Not only is it less expensive than primary research, but it is also less time consuming.

If the information that is required has not been published then you will have to undertake primary research. Lord Teasdale will be able to obtain some of his information requirements from published sources, for example about trends in the tourism industry, but will need to instigate primary research to determine the attitudes, perceptions and motivations of the visitors to the house.

When there are no adequate sources of secondary data, you must collect **primary data** – undertake your own research in order to obtain the information you need. There are three approaches to collecting primary data:

(i)   By Observation.
(ii) By Experimentation.
(iii) By Questionnaire.

(i)   By Observation

A relatively simple way of collecting primary data is by observing a given situation and noting down what is happening. Data collected in this way will help to describe what is happening. For example, if you were Lord Teasdale you might observe visitors when they are touring the house, recording how they react to the different rooms, or recording how long they spend in each room before moving on to the next. To give an idea of the level of demand achieved at different times of the day you might ask the cashier to record how many visitors enter the house at the different times it is open, and on the various days that it is open.

When you carry out observations yourself it is vital that you concentrate fully on the situation being observed and do not lose concentration, or undertake any other activities. If you lose concentration, especially if you have to note down every single occurrence, then you will make inaccurate observations and the research data obtained become biased. If other people are acting as your observers, specially designed observation record forms need to be used that explain what is to be observed, how it is to be observed, and the way in which the record form is to be completed.

You must ensure that you do not distract the person being observed. If this person feels that he or she is being watched then he or she might not act in a normal way, which again will cause inaccurate recordings to be made. Thus, you need to be discrete when observing the actions of others. To overcome problems created by human observation you can use a variety of mechanical aids, such as tape recorders and video-cameras.

In other situations it can be appropriate to ask respondents to keep a record in a diary of all the times, on what occasions, and for what purposes a particular activity was undertaken. For example, the users of a product might be asked to keep a diary. In this the respondent will be asked to record all the occasions that the product was used, the time it was used, the circumstances of its use, and how satisfactorily it performed.

It is generally believed that data obtained from observations is more objective than that derived from questioning techniques, as purely factual information is being recorded. In addition, the data collected has not been influenced by questioning, nor by the respondents' ability to answer. Care has to be taken, though, to ensure that any measuring or recording equipment that is used is reliable and accurate. Attention has also to be paid to the particular respondents used to ensure that they are representative of the population at large.

Some inferences might be made from the results of the observational study, but your main purpose in using such a technique is to become better acquainted with what is happening in the situation under observation. Data collected by this method should be used to confirm data gained from the other two approaches.

(ii)   By Experimentation

A more sophisticated approach than simple observation is that of experimentation. Here you propose a hypothesis which is then tested in a controlled way, before you draw conclusions.

If conditions permit you could conduct a rigorously designed and implemented laboratory experiment. This type of experiment will allow you to control the experimentation process in order to prevent error or bias creeping into the research. Special equipment may be needed for this, as well as a specially controlled environment. For example, when new cars are designed they are tested in a wind-tunnel to determine their aerodynamic qualities; models of new ships to be built are tested in special water tanks to establish their sea-worthiness before the actual ship is built. With these 'lab experiments' the findings of the research will be unambiguous. However, a problem that sometimes arises is that the experiment is not a true simulation of what occurs in reality, and the results of the experiment may not be totally transferable to the real setting.

An alternative is to conduct experiments 'in the field'. Here the experiment takes place in circumstances as close as possible to reality. A difficulty that will arise will be that of controlling a number of external influences that might affect the recorded results. However, if you identify possible sources of error and bias and endeavour to minimise their effect, then the results which you produce should be valid.

Experiments can be used in many different situations. Using Teasdale House as an example, Lord Teasdale might experiment by opening the house for more hours in the day, and for more days in the week, in order to see what effect this has on the demand by visitors. Another approach would be to see whether the visitors are price conscious. Thus, on certain days of the week the entrance fees might be reduced, and the effect on the demand measured. The advertising that is used to inform tourists of the house could be modified to see whether this attracts more visitors. Observations are made to evaluate the results of the experiments.

To record the data obtained from experiments special forms need to be devised that can be used in the analysis process. Experiments like those discussed here can provide you with much valuable information.

(iii)   By Questionnaire

A questionnaire is a prepared document used to obtain information from respondents by asking questions. Questionnaires can serve a variety of purposes.

Market researchers use them to obtain information about consumer needs, attitudes, beliefs, perceptions and motivations towards a company or its products, advertising, or pricing strategy, and so on. Organisations in the public sector use them to find out whether their 'consumers' or clients are satisfied with the services provided for them. Employers use questionnaires to investigate the motivations of their employees. Students use questionnaires to discover information to assist with their project work.

The benefits provided by using questionnaires for obtaining information are that they:

- Allow you to ask questions the answer to which will meet your information needs.
- Enable information to be collected in a standard form, which ensures the information obtained from one respondent can be analysed in conjunction with that obtained from others.
- Provide a way of obtaining the information relatively quickly, and if the questionnaire is correctly designed permit data collection and analysis to be achieved efficiently.

- Allow for a large number of people to be questioned, all in the same way, thus improving the validity of the data that are collected.

The questionnaire approach offers considerable flexibility. The questionnaire can be completed by an interviewer or by the respondent. Interviews can be conducted at the respondent's home, in the street, at work, in social situations, over the telephone, or the questionnaire can be mailed to the respondent.

Personal Interviews: You should use personal interviews where the questionnaire is quite long, or complex. It is best to train interviewers to conduct the interviews, otherwise error and bias will undoubtedly creep into the research process. This type of questioning allows props, samples, or other aids to be shown to the respondent. A successful interviewer will be able to sustain the respondent's interest throughout the interview.

With this type of interviewing you will probably have little direct control over the interviewers. To confirm that the interviews were conducted in a professional way you should make sure the name, address, and telephone number of each respondent is obtained. From this list you could later contact ten per cent of the respondents to ask them whether they were interviewed and if they felt satisfied with the approach adopted by the interviewer.

By Telephone: With telephone interviews you are unable to use any visual aids when talking to the respondent. Thus you have to ask straightforward questions. However, an advantage of the telephone survey is that certain types of respondent can be more easily reached than by the personal interview, for example business people at work in different parts of the country.

This method of obtaining information is rapid, and it enables the interviewers to work safely at unsociable hours. You have direct control over the interviewers (if they are working from the research office) and thus you are able to monitor the way in which the questions are being asked and recorded.

Both personal interviewing and telephone interviewing require you to brief the interviewers fully as to the purpose of the survey and the ways in which the questions on the questionnaire are to be asked. Each question should be discussed in turn, with you drawing the interviewers' attention to the wording and any special props or aids that are to be used. The method of completing the questionnaire also needs to be addressed.

By Post: Personal interviewing and telephone interviewing do tend to be expensive. In addition to the costs of producing the questionnaire, you have to recruit, train and employ a team of interviewers. Postal questionnaires, however, are not so costly, as a team of interviewers is not required – the questionnaires are mailed direct to the respondent.

Postal questionnaires, though, tend to suffer from low response rates. To overcome this problem you will have to draft a polite introductory letter informing the respondent of the purpose of the survey, and giving a deadline for the return of the completed questionnaire. In addition it is useful to offer the respondent an incentive to encourage him or her to complete and return the questionnaire. Such an incentive might be free entry into a prize draw – the respondent whose name is drawn out receives a free gift.

Another limitation of the postal questionnaire is that the respondent can read all the questions before answering them. If he or she decides that the questions being asked are too confidential, too complex, or too 'uninteresting' then they might discard the questionnaire.

From the discussion here, it is evident that the way in which the questionnaire is to be used will to some extent determine its design. If the survey is to be conducted using trained interviewers then more complex questions can be included in the questionnaire. However, if a postal survey is to be used you will have to take care to ensure that all questions can be easily understood by the respondent.

No matter which method of implementing the survey is chosen, adopt a systematic approach to its design.

By Email: A faster and more economical way of distributing questionnaires is to send them via email - either within the written body of the email, or as an attachment. Please be aware that some email addresses will block attachments for security reasons, so it is better to include your questions within the body of the email, so that the recipient can press reply to answer the questions before sending it back.

The problem with sending email based questionnaires is a low response rate – mainly due to the amount of junk email (spam) that people receive. It can therefore be a good idea to contact the recipients in advance (by mediums other than email) to ask if they would mind completing the questionnaire, so that when it arrives they have some idea of what it is, and are therefore more likely to complete and submit it.

Please be aware that sending out masses of unsolicited emails to unknown recipients that have not agreed to receive them – may be in breach of the law if you are doing this for commercial purposes.

Web Based Questionnaires: Another way of gathering data is to collect information from a web based survey. These are actually web pages that contain forms with interactive areas allowing respondents to click upon check boxes, and to write answers in text boxes before submitting the survey which can be sent to the person who set the survey up as an email.

The main problems with this type of survey are that there is little control over who can access it, and there can be difficulties in directing people to complete the survey.

A simple way to 'point' people towards the survey is to use an email with the URL of the survey in the body of the email – please be aware that what is stated above under 'By email' also applies to this type of scenario.

A simple way to create these surveys is to use specific survey building software such as Snap 8 – which can be found at http://www.snapsurveys.com.

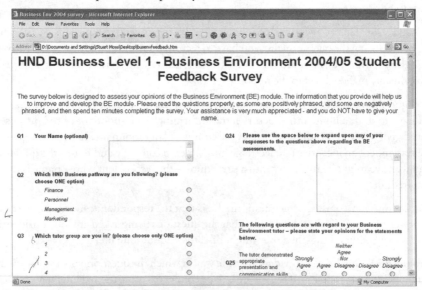

3.5 Questions to be Asked

The questions to be included in the questionnaire will be determined by the research objectives, and the way in which the questions are asked will be influenced by the method you are using to undertake the survey. A number of general guidelines, though, need to be borne in mind when actually writing the questions:

- You should only ask questions that the respondent will be able to answer. Hypothetical questions should be avoided. Questions that concern an occurrence too long ago should not be used – the respondent's memory might not be reliable, and they may give an incorrect answer.

- The use of words on the questionnaire is critical. Use words and phrases that are unambiguous and familiar to the respondent. For example, 'dinner' has a number of different interpretations – an alternative would be to use 'evening meal'.

- Vacuous words/terms should be avoided. 'Generally', 'usually', or 'normally' are imprecise terms with various meanings. You should replace them with quantitative statements e.g. 'at least once a week', 'at least once a month' etc.

- Questions should only address a single issue. For example, questions like: Do you take annual holidays to Spain? should be broken down into two discrete stages, firstly find out if the respondent takes an annual holiday, and then secondly find out if they go to Spain.

- The wording of the questions should avoid all unnecessary words – keep them simple and to the point. Make sure that the respondent will be able to express an answer in words. If the respondent finds it difficult to respond he or she might simply end the interview.

- If you are providing additional information for the respondent, or the respondent is required to make a choice from a set of answers, then provide this information on a 'show card' that the respondent can read. Show cards can act as 'memory joggers' for the respondent.

- Ensure that the questions asked do not test the respondent's intellect. For example, asking the respondents whether they know a particular fact will probably result in all of them answering in the affirmative. This is because the respondents will not wish to appear ignorant or foolish to the interviewer.

- Give careful thought to the wording of questions concerning a respondent's behaviour. Respondents might answer in a way that shows they conform to what they believe is the norm, rather than answering in a way that suggests that their behaviour is somehow abnormal.

- Avoid leading questions. Such questions encourage the respondent to answer the question in a certain way because of the way the question is asked. For example if you were to ask someone 'You believe in God, don't you?', this indicates that you expect the answer to be yes.

It is evident that designing the wording of the questions to be asked is an intellectually challenging task. If you give insufficient attention to this part of the research process then you will possibly face a great number of potential sources of error and bias, which could invalidate the survey. You should prepare draft questions before polishing them into a final form for inclusion in the questionnaire. In addition to thinking about the wording of the questions, pay attention to the type of questions that are used.

You can include a number of different types of question on the questionnaire:

(i)   Closed Questions.
(ii)   Open Questions.
(iii) Direct Questions.
(iv)   Indirect Questions.
(v)   Attitude Questions.

(i)   Closed Questions

Here a question is asked, and then a number of possible answers are provided for the respondent. The respondent selects the answer which is appropriate to him or her:

How have you travelled to Teasdale House? Tick the mode of transport that is applicable:

By car ☐

mini-bus ☐

coach ☐

motor bike ☐

public transport ☐

walk ☐

other means ☐

please specify: _____

_____

You should always include an 'other' response category because not all possible responses might have been included in the list of possible answers. Sometimes the respondent can indicate that more than one answer is applicable. These are called multiple-choice questions:

Why have you visited Teasdale House? Tick the relevant answer(s) – (you may tick more than one):

(a)   I enjoy visiting historic houses.   ☐

(b)   The weather was bad and I could not enjoy outdoor activities. ☐

(c)   I have visited Teasdale before and wished to return.   ☐

(d)   Other reason, please specify: _____

_____

(ii)   Open Questions

With these, respondents are free to answer the question as they wish, in their own words. The interviewer has to write down the exact words that are used:

What new features would you like to see introduced at Teasdale House?

Sometimes analysing the answers to open-questions is quite time consuming as you can get many different responses. Therefore, take this into account when deciding the number of open questions to be included in the questionnaire.

(iii)　Direct Questions

These seek to obtain direct information from the respondent about behaviour, attitudes, beliefs, motivations or perceptions:

> What have you most enjoyed about your visit to Teasdale House?

These questions are useful in that they help you to gain an understanding of how respondents behave, and why they do so.

(iv)　Indirect Questions

If the topic under consideration is sensitive, so that the respondents might feel embarrassed by giving their own answer, you can use indirect questions:

> What do you think people least enjoy about their visit to Teasdale House?

Posing the question in this way might be less threatening to the respondent and so you might get a more honest answer.

(v)　Attitude Questions

It is frequently important for you to understand the respondents' attitudes towards a given situation, and also to be able to quantify the number of respondents holding a given attitude. To do this you can follow two approaches. Firstly, you could provide a battery of attitude statements and then ask respondents to say how much they agree or disagree with each one, using what is referred to as a 'Likert Scale':

> Listed below are five statements. Read each statement carefully and then indicate by a tick, whether you strongly agree, agree, neither agree or disagree, disagree, or strongly disagree with it:

Statement	Strongly agree	Agree	Neither agree or disagree	Disagree	Strongly disagree
1 My visit to Teasdale House has been good value for money.					
2 The opening hours from 1.00pm to 4.00pm are adequate.					
3 The staff on duty have been friendly.					
4 The souvenirs on sale are varied.					
5 The rooms I have seen are interesting.					

The four categories of agreement detailed above, you could include an additional one – 'neither agree nor disagree' – to ensure that all possible answers have been catered for. When analysing this type of question it will be possible for you to say how many people agree or disagree with each statement. An alternative is to ask the respondent to rank the various attitude statements, so that the most important one is ranked first and the least important, last.

To see how strongly an attitude is held by the respondent, a 'semantic differential scale' can be used. This is the second approach that can be used for determining the respondents' attitudes.

With semantic differential scales double-ended terms are put to the respondents who are asked to indicate where their attitude lies on the scale between the terms:

Place a tick on the following scales to indicate what your attitude towards Teasdale House as a venue for a family day out has been:

Very interesting + + + + + + Uninteresting
Excellent value for money + + + + + + Poor value for money
Educational + + + + + + Not educational

To assist with the analysis of this type of question, you could use a nominal scale between the two semantic differentials, and respondents are asked to circle the value that indicates where their attitude lies:

Very interesting   1   2   3   4   5   6   Uninteresting

3.6   Designing the Questionnaire

Questionnaires can be either:

(i)   Structured.
(ii)   Unstructured.

(i)   Structured Questionnaires

Here, the questions are asked in a pre-determined order, and a pre-determined manner. The interviewer must not alter or explain questions, or deviate from the order. Many of the questions used will be closed questions.

When designing a structured questionnaire a number of points have to be borne in mind:

- Confirm the objective of the research. Ensure that both its purpose and the information required are clearly understood.
- List the topics that need to be covered in the questionnaire. Then sequence the topics so that their order is logical and will come across coherently to the respondent without causing confusion.
- Include an introduction to the questionnaire that explains its purpose, what the findings will be used for, and who is undertaking the research.
- Start the questionnaire with easy, non-threatening questions and topics. Explore the respondent's present behaviour, rather than ask for future actions or attitudes.

- Place threatening, embarrassing, or personal topics towards the end of the questionnaire. These are best asked when the respondent trusts the interviewer i.e. details about the respondent's age, occupation, name, income etc.
- Use a variety of different types of question. Too many of one particular type will not motivate or interest the respondent.
- Check and double-check the questionnaire for questions that will lead to error and bias invalidating the findings e.g. leading questions, ambiguous questions, questions that might be seen as a test of the respondent's intellect etc.

We have already noted that planning a questionnaire is an intellectually challenging task. It is likely that you will need a number of attempts to achieve an appropriate design. To test out your design, conduct a test survey (pilot survey) which not only provides you with feedback on the success of the design, but also the wording of the questions.

In addition to thinking about the design and wording of the questionnaire, pay attention to its layout:

- Each questionnaire should have an identification code/number. This helps to locate individual questionnaires when they have been completed and stored.
- Each question should, wherever possible, be pre-coded for computer analysis.
- Provide instructions informing the respondent or the interviewer how to answer the questions, for example should answers be ticked or circled.
- Provide sufficient space so that all questions can be answered legibly. Give some thought to the space allowed for the answering of open-questions.

Designing questionnaires is an ES, and like all skills your ability to design effective questionnaires improves with practice. The true test of a questionnaire will be whether it collects the information that is required in order to solve the problem. Shown on the following page is the first page of Lord Teasdale's Visitor Questionnaire.

Teasdale House Visitor Questionnaire

Introduction

(Interviewer to read out)

Good morning/afternoon. Have you enjoyed your visit of Teasdale House?

Lord Teasdale is concerned to make sure that visitors have been satisfied with their visit to his home and w ould be extremely grateful if you could spare ten minutes to answer a few questions about your visit. Analysing the views of visitors to the house, enables us to make modifications to the facilities available to visitors and increase the enjoyment of future visitors.

Can you spare me ten minutes of your time to answer a few short questions? (If the response is yes ask the questions. If no thank the visitor for visiting the house, and wish him or her a safe journey home).

	Column Code
Questionnaire Number	1
	2
	3
Interviewer reference	4
Date of Interview	5
	6

1.   Your Journey

    (a)   How have you travelled to Teasdale House?   7
        Please tick the appropriate mode of transport:

        By Car   ____

        Mini-bus   ____

        Coach   ____

        Motor bike   ____

        Public transport   ____

        On foot   ____

        Other means   ____

        Please specify: _____

    (b)   Have you travelled from your home, or from
        holiday accommodation? Please tick the
        appropriate answer:
        From home   ____   8
        From holiday accommodation ____

        If you are on holiday what is the name of the
        campsite, hostel, guest house or hotel at which you
        are staying? Write your answer in the space below:

        9

        10

(ii)   Unstructured Questionnaires

This form of questionnaire uses a number of open-ended questions, and allows the interviewer to modify the order of the questions, depending on how the interview is developing. This approach allows for 'in-depth' interviews to be held with the respondent. When one answer is given the interviewer can ask supplementary questions to probe further and elicit more detailed information. Structured interviews do not always permit this, but allow for many more respondents to be questioned in the time available.

In addition to thinking about the questionnaire's design, you must also consider the sample of respondents to interview.

3.7   Sampling

There are many different ways of choosing respondents to be included in a survey. We shall examine the main ones:

(i)   Probability Sampling (or Random sampling).
(ii)   Purposive Sampling.
(iii)   Stratified Sampling.
(iv)   Proportionate Sampling.
(v)   Quota Sampling.

(i)   Probability Sampling (or Random Sampling)

In this type of sample each member of the population has the same known chance of being selected for the survey. You need to have a list of all members of the target population, for example all the members of a club or society. The sample is then drawn from the list in a random way – each name is given a number and respondents are then selected using random number tables.

(ii)   Purposive Sampling

The selection of respondents is based purely on human judgement. You select whichever respondents best fit the sample you are investigating. If you are researching the satisfaction gained by families with children under fifteen years of age to their visit to Teasdale House, it is only these visitor groups who are included in your sample.

(iii)   Stratified Sampling

In this type of sample the population in question is divided into groups with similar characteristics (known as strata) whose relative size is known, for example age groups, or socio-economic groups. Each strata used must be separate and self-contained. A random sample is then taken of each strata.

(iv)   Proportionate Sampling

The strata sampling approach is used, but instead of a random number of respondents being chosen from each strata, a fixed proportion of respondents is drawn e.g. ten per cent of the population from each strata will be interviewed.

(v)   Quota Sampling

Here, strata are identified, for example different age groups, and the interviewer is given a number of respondents to interview who fall into each of the different strata. For example, the interviewer might have to interview fifty people aged 25–44 years, and forty people aged 45–64 years. The number of people to be interviewed in each strata will be proportionate to the relative size of the strata to the population as a whole.

Probability, or random, sampling is the approach that is most commonly used. This is because random sampling offers two distinct advantages to the researcher:

- Random drawing of respondents from the population allows statistical relationships to be established between the sample and the population from which it was drawn.
- When respondents are drawn randomly there is less chance that the sample will be affected by the researcher's judgement.

Irrespective of the sampling method used, the objective is to draw respondents from the population in such a way that the sample chosen provides a good representation of the population being surveyed. If you achieve this, and the sample you interview is large enough, then you can make generalisations about that population based on the results of the survey.

There is no definitive answer to the question – 'how large should the sample be?' This depends on the population being surveyed and the resources available to the researcher. What is important is that the sample is large enough to pick up variations in the behaviour and attitudes of the respondents, and that these variations apply to the total population. Some surveys of the national population of the UK might interview five thousand respondents, while surveys in one region might interview one thousand people. When surveys are conducted of specialised populations that have a total population size of one hundred, for example, then a sample size of fifty would be sufficient for you to draw generalisations from the survey.

Not only is it important to consider the size of the sample, it is also important to consider where the interviews will be conducted (if the survey is based on personal interviewing)? Again no definitive answer can be provided for this question. What you should ensure is that the interviews do not all take place at the same location. This in itself could lead to error and bias. Try to include a number of different locations for the interviews to take place, locations that will enable a broad section of the population to be included in the survey.

When the sample of respondents has been selected you can then contemplate how to manage the interviewing process.

3.8   The Research Interview

You should apply the ES discussed in Chapter Six on interviewing when conducting interviews to obtain information. In addition, you have to bear further considerations in mind:

- Respondents frequently resent being interviewed and often erect barriers to the interviewer. To overcome these barriers you need to appear non-threatening and sensitive. You can achieve this by:

  - dressing smartly and appearing well-groomed;
  - smiling;
  - explaining the purpose of the survey and its rationale;
  - stressing the confidentiality of the information that is given;
  - sympathising with respondents who say they are pushed for time,

while still being assertive, 'it will only take ten minutes of your time';
- speaking in a soft, yet audible tone of voice;
- speaking slowly and deliberately, pronouncing each word carefully so that its meaning can be clearly understood;
- controlling the body language signals that you give – try not to show your reaction to the respondent's answers, for example don't raise your eyebrows to unexpected answers;
- being polite and courteous at all times.

- Always carry some form of identification to indicate that you are a bona-fide interviewer undertaking a legitimate survey.
- If you are holding interviews on private property, for example in a shopping centre, obtain the permission of the owners or management before starting to interview.
- If you are interviewing outdoors, use interview points that will not be affected by bad weather.
- Try to avoid outdoor interview sites that are too noisy.
- During the interview ask all the questions on the questionnaire. Try not to deviate from the structure of the questionnaire.
- Ask all the questions in the same way to each respondent. Do not give signs of encouragement to the respondents to answer the questions in a particular way, for example by nodding or shaking your head.
- Never suggest answers for the respondent. If the respondent cannot answer a question then note this on the questionnaire.
- Be familiar with all the questions on the questionnaire, practise using any aids, show cards, or other items before starting to interview respondents. You will lose credibility if you appear to be disorganised.
- Complete each questionnaire neatly and legibly. Untidy and difficult to read questionnaires might lead to errors occurring at the data analysis stage.
- Remain calm at all times during the interview. Do not become ruffled by the attitude, or any of the responses given by the respondent.
- When all the questions have been asked, thank the respondent for taking part in the survey.
- Be aware of your own health and safety – select interview locations where your personal safety will not be compromised. Inform a friend or family member where and when you will be conducting the interviews.
- Always adopt an ethical approach when conducting primary research.

If you follow the above guidelines then the likelihood of error and bias creeping into the information gathering process will be reduced.

When all the questionnaires have been completed, the final stage in the research process is to analyse the results of the survey and to draw conclusions.

4.   Analysing the Data

You need to translate the data produced from the survey into a form that is meaningful. You should use the data handling and presentation skills discussed in Chapter Five.

When drawing inferences and conclusions from the data, you will use your thinking skills, especially the critical thinking skills as discussed in Chapter Eleven. This part of the research process will call for great objectivity to ensure that you make no false assumptions, or ignore findings produced from the survey, especially if they contradict your personal view.

Returning to the questionnaire implemented by Lord Teasdale, it might be that the following findings are produced by analysing the questionnaires:

The Age Structure of Visitors to Teasdale House	
Age Groups	**Percentage of Visitors %**
0 15 years	19
16 24 years	5
25 34 years	11
35 44 years	20
45 54 years	15
55 64 years	18
65 years plus	12
	Total 100%

From this table it can be seen that the 16–24 year age group is the least likely to visit Teasdale House. An explanation could be that people within this age group are not as interested in history, and/or have other leisure activities that are more adventurous and active than visiting a historic house. There is a strong incidence of children visiting the house. Given the house's rural location it is likely that these children are visiting on a family outing. A visit to a historical house is probably seen as an educational occasion by the family.

Turning to the socio-economic group of the respondent to the questionnaire, the following data were produced from the survey:

The Respondent's Socio-economic Group	
Socio-economic Group	**Percentage of Respondents %**
A	5
B	38
C1	27
C2	2
D	0
E	20
	Total 100%

When a socio-economic group is used for classifying a population, the respondent is classified according to the occupation of the head of the household, in which he or she lives. Six broad socio-economic group classifications are identified:

Socio-economic Group	Occupation of the Head of Household
A	Higher managerial, administrative or professional.
B	Intermediate managerial, administsrative, or professional.
C1	Supervisory or clerical, and junior managerial, administrative or professional.
C2	Skilled manual workers.
D	Semi and unskilled manual workers.
E	State pensioner or widows, casual or lowest grade workers.

The data displayed above indicate that the visitors to the house are primarily from the B and C1 socio-economic groups. Indeed, virtually no visitors are drawn from the C2 or D groups. The high incidence of visitors in group E reflects the house's appeal to retired individuals, who probably appreciate the nostalgic side of a visit to such a tourist attraction.

When the responses to the attitude statements were analysed it was found that:

96% of respondents felt their visit represented good value for money.
33% of respondents felt the opening hours/days were inadequate.
100% of respondents felt the staff on duty were friendly.
42% of respondents felt the souvenirs being sold were of insufficient variety.
100% of respondents felt the rooms on view were interesting.
69% of respondents had no complaints about their visit to Teasdale House.

The findings from these attitude statements are now providing useful information about the satisfaction visitors gain from their visit. The fact that ninety six per cent of respondents felt their visit to be good value for money might be seen as implying that the prices charged could be increased, especially as visitors found the rooms on view interesting and the staff friendly.

Clearly no major changes need to be made to Teasdale House to make it more attractive to visitors. It could be concluded that a reason why visitor numbers have not been increasing is that very few tourists know about it. Now that Lord Teasdale is developing a profile of his existing visitors it will be possible for him to devise communication strategies that will reach more of these people.

The above discussion has been an example of how you can gain information from a questionnaire survey. By having such information available you are in a much better position to evaluate alternatives and make sensible and well reasoned decisions.

Information gathering skills are highly transferable. At some stage in your career you will inevitably need information to help you with your work. The skills discussed in this chapter will ensure that the information you collect will be valid and reliable.

After reading this chapter undertake the following learning activities:

Learning Activities

1. From what you have read in this chapter, consider the different types and sources of information that are available to you on your course of study, make a list using the table below, the first line is given as an example.

Information Source	Specific Titles	Useful For
Mintel Online	Mintel Reports (various titles of note)	Marketing, UK consumer behaviour, UK shopping trends.

Continue on a separate sheet if necessary.

2. Using search engines, web directories, and subject gateways, perform information searches on the following subjects: your local council; interest rates in UK banks; trends in house-buying habits in the UK; Great Yarmouth Pleasure Beach; train times and fares between where you live and a UK city; Winston Churchill; obesity amongst children; politics in central Africa; AIDS; citrus fruits; Australian Rugby League; statistical data on male impotence; racism in Western Europe. After you have performed these searches, write up an appraisal of which internet search tools were the most effective at producing quality information sources for each subject (not marketing or advertising sources, but quality information sources that may be useful to somebody researching this topic for academic purposes). Discuss what you have learned from undertaking this exercise by writing a reflective piece on what you have done, and what the outcome has been.

3. Using the techniques described in this chapter, construct a small questionnaire of approximately ten questions that could be a relevant and useful information gathering tool for the subject that you are studying.

Chapter Eleven
Thinking Skills

After reading this chapter you will be able to:

1. Understand how to think creatively.
2. Develop critical thinking skills.
3. Explain the process to follow when solving problems.
4. Be systematic when taking decisions.

To be successful in your career you need to be competent in the use of your ES. Yet these skills by themselves will not be sufficient to take you to the higher levels of management. You also require the abilities to think creatively and critically, to solve problems and to take decisions. If you work in a rapidly changing environment, you cannot depend on routine behaviour or tradition when making decisions, you must be capable of intelligent and independent thought. Perhaps these skills are the key to how far up the managerial ladder you will progress.

But what are thinking skills? A dictionary definition would include the following:

> …to summarise; to believe; to consider; to esteem; to reason; to form judgement; to imagine.

Clearly, thinking involves a series of high level intellectual skills. In fact a hierarchy of intellectual skills can be identified.

1. The Hierarchy of Intellectual Skills

There is a hierarchy of intellectual skills that you need to be aware of when considering the thinking process. Each of these levels plays a part in critical thinking. These are:

- Gaining Knowledge.
- Understanding.
- Applying Knowledge and Understanding.
- Analysing.
- Synthesising.
- Evaluating.

We shall now consider what each of these involves.

1.1   Gaining Knowledge

The lowest level intellectual skill is that of knowing something, by remembering, or recalling, facts, ideas, or phenomena. Nevertheless acquiring knowledge underpins critical thinking as it is the reference source from which facts or ideas are drawn to start the reasoning process. The knowledge you acquire helps to provide you with a picture of the situation being considered.

Knowledge helps to answer questions such as, 'Who?', 'What?', 'Where?', 'When?' When individuals have a store of knowledge they are able to recall facts, make observations or arrive at definitions: 'What does marketing mean?', 'Who is Tony Blair?'

Some individuals have a hunger for knowledge, and assume that the greater their store of knowledge the better equipped they are to make the optimum decision. The key, though, is to ensure that the knowledge that you gain is relevant to your needs. You must therefore, always be discriminating in the knowledge you seek. Indeed, with the wealth of knowledge available to managers it is now, more than ever, important for them to have skills to interpret knowledge rather than simply to retain it.

1.2   Understanding

The second level of the hierarchy of your intellectual skills involves understanding facts, ideas or concepts. By understanding these you can transfer such knowledge to new, unfamiliar situations. Understanding is part of the critical thinking process and enables you to, describe, compare, contrast, and explain.

For example, when you have understood facts, ideas, or concepts you will be able to, explain in your own words the problems faced by the economy as a result of inflation, or, compare the duties of a cost accountant with those of a tax accountant.

A good test of your understanding is the ability to explain to other people the situation or concept being considered.

1.3   Applying Knowledge and Understanding

The application of facts or ideas to predict consequences or to solve problems is the next level in your intellectual hierarchy. This process involves first of all understanding the fact (or idea), then restructuring it or reorganising it, so that you can use it to draw meaningful conclusions about the new situation.

The key verbs here are: apply, solve, classify, select, employ, use.

For example when you are able to apply facts or ideas you can answer questions such as, 'What is the latitude of London?' or, 'If you wanted to telephone New York at 10.00 am local time, what time would it be in London?', and to undertake tasks such as, 'classify these customers according to their contributions to our profitability.'

1.4   Analysing

Analysis involves breaking down a given situation into its constituent parts. This intellectual skill is of value to you as a critical thinker because it allows you to separate and to categorise data. When you have done this you can probe behind the surface and look for unseen or abstract principles that give you a greater understanding of the problem you are considering. If you are skilled at analysing material you will be able to answer 'Why?' questions, for example, 'Why do you think increasing advertising expenditure leads to an increase in sales?'

You will then be able to draw inferences, identify motives, or causes, and be skilled at finding evidence to support generalisations. Once you have completed the analysis you should be able to undertake synthesis.

1.5   Synthesising

This is the penultimate intellectual skill in the hierarchy and is the one that draws together individual components after they have been analysed. Synthesis involves recreating the whole once it has been dissected, and learning from this process. When you have completed the synthesis you will be able to plan, predict, propose, or develop. The questions that you will be able to answer will be ones similar to, 'What action could our organisation take to improve the loyalty of our work force?', or, 'What do you predict would happen if we were to increase the size of our work force by 20%?' In addition you will be able to, write a report detailing company progress over the last 20 years. When you have mastered this skill of synthesis you will be capable of original thought.

1.6   Evaluating

When the whole has been created again you can then evaluate the situation, judging it in order to reach an opinion, or conclusion. To be evaluative you must look at all the evidence surrounding a given situation and consider the arguments supporting it, as well as those against it, to look at 'both sides of the coin'.

If you can evaluate a situation you will be able to, judge, decide, and appraise.

You will be able to give opinions on issues, determine the validity of ideas, or judge the merit of a solution to a problem. You will need evaluation skills to answer questions such as, 'Do you think it is true that increased advertising expenditure leads to increased sales of the product?', 'Should our work force be given a 10% pay rise?' and, 'Which product would you drop from our product portfolio?'

Being able to arrive at a reasoned and objective judgement on a particular issue is considered to be the highest level of intellectual skill that you can develop. To reach a judgement involves all the skills listed above. You must have knowledge that you understand and can apply to the situation under consideration. You must be able to break the situation down and consider each element independently, before putting the whole back together again. The final evaluation will involve looking at all the evidence in favour, and all the evidence against, before arriving at the judgement.

The intellectual skills discussed here help to constitute your thinking process. Referring back to the definition of thinking we gave at the beginning of this chapter it is clear that in order to summarise, believe, consider, or reason you must be able to use all the skills discussed in the hierarchy.

Critical thinking skills, though, warrant further analysis.

2.   Critical Thinking Skills

Critical thinking could be thought of as independent thought where you use all the intellectual skills in the hierarchy in order to arrive at your own judgement of a situation or issue. Another term to use instead of critical thinking might be reflective thinking, implying that you divorce yourself from your immediate surroundings, take a step backwards, and then judge the issue in an objective and rational manner. We can divide critical thinking into a number of steps:

- Interpreting Data.
- Applying Facts and Principles.
- Logical Reasoning.

2.1   Interpreting Data

To be a critical thinker you must be able to interpret data of various sorts and to generalise from them. The term 'data' is used here in a broad context to include statistics, the written word, diagrams, formulae, and even cartoons. As a critical thinker you should be able to digest the data and derive meaning from them. The process of interpretation will involve singling out important facts or ideas, relating them to each other, and deriving generalisations from them.

Interpretation in its lowest form might simply involve reading points off a graph or looking for trends. At a higher degree of complexity, interpretation will consist of inferring causes or consequences from a situation. Let us use an example to illustrate this:

Cinema Admissions 1998 2004		
Year	Millions	Index
1998	60	100
1999	64	107
2000	54	90
2001	71	118
2002	73	121
2003	75	125
2004	78	130

From the table it can be seen that cinema admissions have risen by 18 million since 1998, although a fall in attendances was experienced in 2000. A critical thinker might deduce that this could have been a result of a steep rise in admission prices in 2000 and the wider availability of videos and DVDs for home viewing. The critical thinker might continue by reflecting that since 2000, however, cinemas have been refurbished and a stream of higher quality films been released, which could account for the increase in cinema admissions.

Evaluating the dependability of data and recognising their limits is also involved in critical thinking. Certain data are rendered academically unsound, or ideological, because of the way in which they are written:

- Ambiguous terms or statements make data unsound. If the meaning of the sentence, phrase, or word appears to have more than one interpretation, then the quality of the data should be questioned.

- Vacuous terms, terms which are hollow and lacking in content make data academically unsound. For example, 'good', 'bad', 'many', 'few', or 'heavy', are vacuous as each individual could interpret the term differently.
- Inconsistent statements – ones which contain contradictory terms or arguments, should not be accepted.
- Selective use of evidence makes data ideological e.g. if consideration is given only to one side of the argument, where there are reasons for and against a view, or not all relevant considerations are made, then the data will be unsound.
- Inaccurate account of evidence. If evidence is used to support an argument, and the evidence is inaccurately reported or inaccurately used then the validity of the data will be questionable.
- Over-generalisations make arguments invalid. Here a person argues a case by showing that all situations will follow a similar pattern, but uses an unrepresentative sample, or a sample whose size is not large enough, in order to make the generalisation.
- Appeals to consensus, where the person arguing a case makes a suggestion which she thinks will be accepted by the majority, but which in fact is not, means the soundness of the data can be questioned. Even if there is consensus about some view it does not make that view correct. Only when independent authorities or individuals can provide evidence supporting such data should it be accepted – this indicates the importance of fully referencing reports and other types of communication to show the source of data that has been used to compile the report.
- Appeals to authority – just because an expert supports a view does not mean that it is correct. Like appeals to consensus, appeals to authorities are only valid when the expert has evidence to support her view; however, different experts might have different views and the real test of their validity will be the way in which the research was conducted.
- Appeals to self-evidence – when an individual supplies the data herself, great care should be taken to evaluate the reliability of the data collection method, and the interpretation of the data.
- Appeals to common sense – when data indicate that the conclusions drawn are based on common sense, care needs to be taken as common sense to one individual might not be common sense to another.
- Emotive language – when data use certain words such as 'lively', 'challenging' or 'interesting', the writer is being complementary, or commendatory, towards the issue or course of action. The use of such a writing style makes the data unsound.

If you identify the above points in data it makes them academically unsound, and their validity and value can be questioned. Indeed, when you produce your own data you need to ensure that your writing does not include any of the above.

When interpreting data, if you are a critical thinker, you will be able to identify the relevant facts and ideas in each and draw appropriate inferences.

2.2 Applying Facts and Principles

Applying facts, principles and academic concepts in order to solve problems, or to predict, or to explain new phenomena are other aspects of critical thinking. This process involves you first understanding the relevant fact, principle or concept then understanding the problem, and finally seeing the relationship between the two.

Some facts, principles and concepts are highly transferable, whereas others are not. For example, the law of gravity applies in the United Kingdom, the United States of America, and the United Arab Emirates. Other generalisations are less universal, for example generalisations that account for the causes of inflation. If you are a critical thinker, you will be able to distinguish between hypotheses and universally dependable principles.

As a critical thinker, you will also be able to determine when a value judgement is being made. A value judgement is what an individual believes and feels about an issue without having any empirical evidence to support that view – an opinion. Value judgements may interfere with an individual's clarity of thought and result in her reasoning being subjective, biased or irrational.

Part of the critical thinking process is to be able to apply facts, principles and concepts logically without reference to or at least acknowledging value judgements.

2.3   Logical Reasoning

Being able to reason logically and critically are the final component parts of critical thinking. To be able to reason logically and critically sometimes requires you to identify faulty assumptions that others propose and formulating adequate ones yourself. In this situation logical reasoning is not accepting assumptions, or evidence, at face value, but analysing their underlying rationale.

As a critical thinker, you will judge where facts end and opinions begin, and you will be able to recognise conclusions based on faulty logic or reasoning. For example, when listening to a discussion on the causes of inflation, you should be able to determine what is taken for granted in the discussion, whether all relevant facts and arguments have been considered, and how relevant they are to the conclusions drawn. Thus, you, as a critical thinker are using your knowledge, understanding, application, analysis, synthesis, and evaluation skills in order to judge the arguments of others. You will be looking for ideological statements using the points raised above – for example, identifying emotionally charged words, or vacuous terms.

The use of 'what if...' and 'if then...' statements will form part of your portfolio of reasoning skills as a critical thinker. It has to be stated, though, that being able to evaluate critically other people's arguments does not necessarily improve your own reasoning. You must practise this in a variety of contexts.

Critical thinking skills, like the other ES discussed in this book are not developed overnight. Whereas it is relatively straightforward to demonstrate most of the other ES in action it is less easy to demonstrate critical thinking skills as they are to some extent intangible. Developing these high order intellectual skills will also be determined by your capacity for abstract thought, as without this ability you will find it difficult to evaluate the assumptions and arguments of others.

Your ability to judge critically the arguments of others (in other words to be a critical thinker) will determine your ability to reach the upper levels of management. Senior managers have to be able to evaluate the arguments of others and decide whether they are logical and feasible. Without this skill as a senior manager you will not be fulfilling all the functions of your role.

Another type of thinking skill you need to be aware of is that of creative thinking.

3.   Creative Thinking Skills

Creative thinking is quite different to critical thinking. Critical thinking requires a structured process to be followed in order to arrive at a judgement. Creative thinking in contrast requires you to be less structured and more informal and relaxed where you are uninhibited in your thinking. The aim of creative thinking is to suggest as many ideas as you can, where totally new perspectives on the situation are forthcoming. A number of differences can be identified between critical thinking and creative thinking:

- In critical thinking you might be looking for one outcome, or to reach a single judgement. In creative thinking you welcome more than one outcome and encourage a variety of possible outcomes.
- In critical thinking logical and realistic answers are sought, but in creative thinking you welcome a diverse range of outcomes some of which might be very innovative.
- In creative thinking the intention is to produce a wide range of possible answers or solutions, so less evaluation occurs at an early stage to reject what might seem illogical options.
- In creative thinking the opportunity should be taken to think widely and laterally without any pre-determined constraints. Critical thinking will take into account constraints (such as the availability of resources) when considering options.
- When undertaking creative thinking everyone involved should feel free to make as many suggestions to solve the problem as they wish, no matter how trivial or illogical their solution might be. In critical thinking this will be seen as inappropriate.

Clearly, there are significant differences between critical thinking and creative thinking. For creative thinking to be effective everybody involved in the process must feel confident about expressing their ideas without being criticised by the other members of the team. All solutions, options and ideas should be welcomed, no matter how different or creative they appear. Stifling the creative thinking process might result in sub-optimal solutions being suggested. The members of the team involved in creative thinking should be prepared to accept what might first appear to be risky options. They need to be prepared to go beyond the 'norm' and accept the unconventional. The following guidelines will encourage a free flow of creative ideas:

- start the creative thinking process with a blank flip chart paper;
- write down the first idea that is generated by the creative thinking team;
- then write down on the same paper the next idea that is 'sparked' by the first;
- as the session continues, try and group ideas on the flip chart paper until a picture starts to emerge of the different ideas/options that are being generated.

There are other intellectual skills that you need to master, namely those of being able to solve problems, and to take decisions. We shall now break these down into their constituent elements and examine them.

4. Problem Solving Skills

One of the main aspects of life is solving problems of one degree of complexity or another. Your success as a manager can partly be gauged by how effective you are at producing feasible solutions to difficult situations.

Problems can be regarded as open-ended in that a number of potential solutions will probably be apparent. The key is to select the solution that is the most feasible. When solving problems, however, it is frequently the case that not all the information that is required to reach the best solution is available, and you have to reach a solution on imperfect knowledge of the situation.

You can follow a series of steps when solving problems that should lead you to identify the most feasible solution to the problem.

We can simplify this model into the main eight steps that are:

- Defining the problem.
- Formulating the problem.
- Planning the research.
- Experimenting.
- Collating the data.
- Selecting a preferred solution.
- Implementing the solution.
- Evaluating the solution.

We shall now look at each of these in turn.

The Problem Solving Process

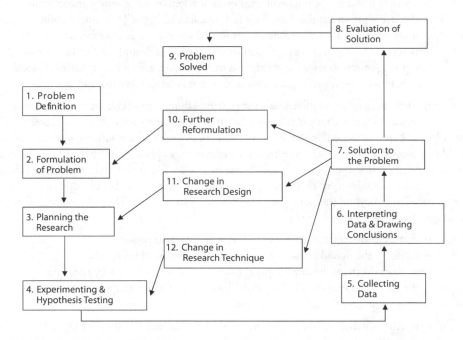

4.1   Defining the Problem

The first stage in being able to solve a problem is to be able to define it. The important thing is to identify the difficulty clearly, defining precisely its characteristics. You must collect relevant information about the problem and consider it from various perspectives. You need to clarify all the background issues and identify its scale and constraints, as well as the opportunities posed by it. If you have identified a number of problems, they may need to be ranked in order of importance and in the priority in which you will try to solve them.

To illustrate the problem solving process we will use the problem of a travel agent who wishes to open a new travel agency. The travel agent currently has five shops but wishes to expand her business. The problem facing the travel agent is where to site the new shop.

4.2 Formulating the Problem

Once you have defined the problem it then needs to be formulated, or broken down further, into a form that allows you to investigate it. Using the example of the travel agent, she has formulated her problem and has decided that she wishes to open another shop aimed at the mass market consumer, the consumer who visits the Mediterranean for an annual two week holiday, rather than opening an outlet that specialises in business travel.

4.3 Planning the Research

It will be at this stage in the problem solving process that you will suggest hypotheses for the problem's solution. Brainstorming techniques could be used here to produce a wide range of possible hypotheses. Brainstorming is a process where a group of people concerned with the problem sit down together in order to produce as many potential solutions as possible. The purpose of the brainstorming session is to produce a long list of solutions, not to evaluate them. One person suggests a solution that is written down. This suggestion might spark off another idea with someone else – this solution is again written down. For the session to be successful, no comments at all should be made about the solutions that are proposed, nor individuals ridiculed for making a particular suggestion. If comments were to be made then the participants in the session might feel reticent about contributing further, denying the group solutions that might be feasible and appropriate. You should seek creative and imaginative solutions, especially for problems that you have not encountered before. This is known as divergent thinking. If you are a divergent thinker you consider as many aspects as possible and try to choose the best solution from these alternatives.

For example, consider the travel agent's problem. The divergent thinker might consider a wide range of possible towns to site the new agency, and within those towns believe that there are several viable locations. She might think about locating in Birmingham, Manchester, or Glasgow, and possible sites might be in shopping centres, in high streets, or in residential suburbs.

An alternative type of thinker is known as the convergent thinker. This is a person who converges straight away on an answer. This approach can be used to solve problems for which there is a known or generally accepted answer. So, in the example of the travel agent the convergent thinker assumes that the best location is in the new shopping centre that has just been built on the outskirts of the town where she currently operates. Her decision is based on the fact that the shopping centre will attract large numbers of the type of customer in whom she is interested. It is close to her existing operations enabling control to be maintained over the day-to-day running of the agency, and that there will be no other travel agency in the shopping centre.

The thinking process adopted, therefore, is to some extent dependent on the problem. With some problems there are no alternative solutions – just one. Many managerial problems, however, will involve more than one solution and you will probably have to use divergent thinking in your approach. Where there is no one right solution it is important not to arrive at an answer too quickly – you must spend time on hypothesis testing.

4.4 Experimenting

When you have formulated hypotheses (or possible alternative courses of action) the next step is to devise experiments that will show whether, or not, the hypothesis holds true. Experiments in the world of science can be carefully designed, implemented and controlled, and clear results obtained. In the world of business and commerce, however, experiments might sometimes be influenced by external uncontrollable factors that affect the results. Alternatively, the research methods you use for collecting the data might be prone to error and bias, restricting the validity and reliability of the data collected. Market research questionnaire surveys fall into this category and need to be rigorously designed, implemented and monitored.

4.5   Collating the Data

The experimentation stage of your problem solving process will produce data that need to be recorded and translated into meaningful forms for analysis, such as tables, graphs, pie charts and histograms. You should follow the conventions discussed in Chapter Five to ensure that you make correct representations of the data.

Once you have represented the data in this way you can then interpret them, looking for trends that have occurred and identifying relationships that allow you to draw conclusions. Your critical thinking skills will be called into use here, and you must ensure that an objective and rational view is taken of the findings from the research.

4.6   Selecting a Preferred Solution

The next stage in the problem solving process requires you to use the highest order intellectual skill in the hierarchy – evaluation. When all your hypotheses have been tested, when you have analysed and synthesised your findings you should now evaluate them in order to select a preferred solution.

In this stage you evaluate the results of the experiments, looking at the conclusions drawn from each of the hypotheses that was tested and arrive at a judgement as to which solution to the problem, or which hypothesis, should be accepted. You should devise criteria that you can use to judge each possible solution. You need to evaluate each solution to see how close it comes to meeting your preferred criteria. You have to adopt a balanced view that considers the strengths of each solution as well as its weaknesses. Reject those solutions or hypotheses that do not meet your criteria. When you have completed this process you will then have either one or two solutions that do meet the criteria.

Referring again to the travel agent, if a number of possible locations for the new retail agency have been identified then each one should be evaluated against a number of criteria, for example:

Criteria for Evaluating the Site of a New Retail Travel Agency				
Criteria	Optimal Site characteristics	Site 1	Site 2	Site 3
1. Proximity to bus stops.	100 metres			
2. Proximity to car parks.	200 metres			
3. Average pedestrian flow.	50 per minute			
4. Number of competitors close by.	fewer than 3			
5. Demographic profile of the catchment area.	C1 & C2 socio-economic groups			
6. Cost of rent and rates.	£400 per month			
7. Size of the unit, sq metres.	1000 sq metres			

If after the evaluation stage, however, you reject all the hypotheses or potential solutions you have three further options:

1. You can return to the problem formulation stage and consider whether the problem was initially defined correctly. If it was not then you should reformulate the problem.
2. Failing (a). above, you should examine the investigation stage of the research process – were appropriate hypotheses formulated or do new ones need to be proposed?
3. The final area to consider is that of the implementation of the experiment Did error or bias creep into the research process causing incorrect results to be obtained?

By evaluating these stages in the problem solving process you will gain insight as to why you have not found a solution to the problem and you may gain ideas for modifying your research.

4.7   Implementing the Solution

Now that you have identified a solution to the problem you need to implement it. You will need to have the necessary resources required for implementation such as finance, personnel, computer or production facilities, and a plan drawn up (a Gantt chart – see Chapter Twelve) allocating responsibilities to those involved in the implementation process. As well as considering resources, your plan will also provide a time scale that prioritises the actions to be taken and allocates responsibilities to all those concerned in the implementation process. This enables the close co-ordination of all activities and provides you with a logical pattern for sequencing the implementation stages.

In the implementation stage you should consider contingency plans to provide alternative courses of action if problems arise while implementing the original plan.

4.8   Evaluating the Solution

The final stage in the problem solving process requires you to carry out an evaluation once your plan has been implemented. The purpose of this is to determine how successfully the problem has been overcome. You will have to collate information that can be used to judge the results achieved from the implementation process. Actual outcomes are compared with expected outcomes, and if the former do not equal the latter, or under perform, then the problem solving process has not been fully completed, and you might have to follow the cycle again. If the actual outcome is the same as the expected outcome, or surpasses it, then you have solved the problem.

The travel agent before opening her new shop will have set a target sales turnover figure that she would expect to achieve, for example a sales turnover of £500,000 in the first six months of operation. If this figure is attained, then she will have chosen a feasible site for the new agency and her problem solving process will have been successful.

Problems can be regarded as obstacles. These obstacles can be overcome by following a logical methodology that takes you step by step towards the solution. If any of the steps are missed out then it is likely that you will come up with an incorrect solution. Each problem that you face, however, will be different and will involve different factors. You must not become complacent and treat all problems alike, but must use your critical thinking skills to ensure that the most feasible solution to the problem is found and successfully implemented.

5.   Decision Making Skills

Problem solving and decision making are closely linked. The problem solving process normally precedes decision making. Problem solving will generate a number of solutions to the problem but decision making is where the final choice is made – one of those solutions has to be chosen for implementation. A key element of decision making is that of balancing risk. You must try to be aware of all the risks that may arise when a particular decision is taken, and take only those decisions for which the risk is acceptable.

There are overlaps between problem solving and decision making skills in terms of the methodologies you will use to solve problems and those to arrive at optimal decisions, but there are also differences. The steps in the decision making process are as follows:

- Specifying Aims.
- Reviewing the Factors.
- Determining the Possible Courses Open.
- Making the Decision.
- Implementing the Decision.

5.1   Specifying Aims

Your first stage in the decision making process is to ensure that the aim of your decision is clearly understood – what is the task under consideration? What is the purpose of the decision? What is to be achieved? What is the expected outcome likely to be?

Synthesis is important here to pull together the various strands of the situation and to look beyond its constituent parts. You need to take a broad perspective, thinking laterally and divergently.

5.2   Reviewing the Factors

Having confirmed the aim or purpose of the decision, you then need to consider the factors surrounding the decision. These should be analysed, synthesised and evaluated. You should list all the factors which are important in the decision, and you should determine the impact on the decision of each one, giving weightings to indicate their relative importance. This process should highlight the critical factor(s), the one upon which the success of the decision really hinges.

Returning to the example of the travel agent, the most critical factor she has determined for the success of the new agency might be the pedestrian flow on the pavement outside, followed by the proximity of bus stops and then car parks. These factors are given higher weightings than the size of the shop or the rent and rates, when arriving at a decision regarding the most feasible site.

You then need to establish the combined impact of all the factors to create a clear picture of the situation. This is a critical step in the decision making process and you should carry it out with great accuracy.

5.3   Determining the Possible Courses Open

Having considered all the relevant factors you may be able to recognise a number of courses of action that may be feasible. These need to be listed. Indeed, you need to keep an open and creative mind at this stage to produce a broad range of possibilities, before narrowing them down. At this stage in the decision making process you should be concerned simply to produce as long a list as possible of potential actions, without attempting to evaluate them.

5.4 Making the Decision

When you have proposed a broad range of possible courses of action each one then has to be analysed, synthesised and evaluated against the critical factors identified above. You must take as wide a view as possible of each alternative, considering its advantages against its disadvantages. In addition, you have also to bear in mind what risks are associated with each possible course of action particularly if it were not to be successful when implemented. You must decide what is an acceptable level of risk and that should be an important factor in the evaluation process.

Your most important intellectual activity at this point is critical thinking – questioning all the assumptions you have made, evaluating the arguments of others, appraising the data to make sure they are academically sound and not ideological. You should record your thoughts as suggested on the following:

Option 1	
Reasons for:	Reasons against:

You should produce such a framework for each option you are considering – it will really focus your mind on the key factors that will have to be taken into account when reaching your decision.

You will then be in a position to either reject or retain possible options. You should reach a decision when only one option remains, after all the other possibilities have been shown to be less feasible or impractical.

This should be a logical decision if you have followed all the steps mentioned above.

5.5 Implementing the Decision

To complete the decision making process you need to implement the decision. When the consequences of taking the decision become apparent it is then possible for you to determine whether the decision that was taken and implemented was the most appropriate, or whether you need to reconsider another of the possibilities.

This will test your leadership skills, treading the line between rigidity or flexibility of decisiveness. In such circumstances you will have to decide the point of no return: the last stage at which you can change a course of action without impeding the achievement of your goal. Your responsibility for taking a decision includes the responsibility for changing it up to the point of no return.

If you follow this decision making process, it will lead you through a logical sequence of steps that will allow you to make a feasible decision. As with problem solving, you will need to use your intellectual skills to ensure that a rational decision is reached, based upon critical thinking.

After reading this chapter please complete the following learning activities:

Learning Activities

1. Explain what creative thinking is and how you can become a creative thinker.

2. What is critical thinking and how does it differ from creative thinking?

3. Describe the eight stages in the problem solving process.

4. Think of a major decision you have recently taken and write the process you went through to reach your decision. Now reflect on this process and critically evaluate your decision making skills.

Chapter Twelve
Project Management

After reading this chapter you will be able to:

1. Understand what constitutes a project.

2. Produce a network diagram, Gantt chart, and work out the critical path of a project.

3. Use an appropriate technique to make a decision within a project that constitutes the least risk.

4. Recognise the symptoms of stress.

5. Manage the key stages and tasks in researching and writing a dissertation.

This chapter focuses upon the subject of project management. Project management is something that is necessary to ensure that complex activities are successfully completed – on time, to the standard that is required, and within the budget that has been allocated to the project. As a student you will be required to manage a variety of different projects such as completing assignments or working on extended independent pieces of work – dissertations. Reading this chapter and carrying out the exercises within it will help to develop your project management skills.

This chapter will:

- introduce the concept of project management;
- look at the various stages of planning a project;
- examine project management techniques for 'mapping out' and timing change; and
- look at the management of people through the change process.

1.   Project Management Skills

Project management skills are transferable to your future career. They are required both in relatively simple situations, for example re-organising the layout of an office and also in complex tasks such as moving an entire company from one location to another. Managing a project is about evaluating what exactly needs to be achieved, as well as planning the various stages that go into this process.

1.1   Projects, Aims and Objectives

In order to manage projects effectively, it is necessary to properly plan the steps that are to be taken as part of your strategic journey. Projects are designed to bring about a different state of affairs or a new (and possibly unique) outcome. This projected outcome can be defined as your aims. With any project, in order to achieve your *aims* it is necessary to carry out steps along the way, these are known as *objectives*. It is the successful undertaking of your objectives that will eventually lead to your aims being attained. All projects will also have a start and an end date /time and at the end of the time period the pre-defined aims of the project should be met.

Some examples of projects include the following:

- Carrying out a piece of research and writing it up.
- Building a new road bridge over a river.
- Rolling out a new operating system to computers on a company network.
- Converting a loft in a house into a bedroom.

Consider any project, it could be one of those listed above, or it could be something different – consider the pre-defined aims of the project – what are they? In the example of the project to convert a loft into a bedroom, the aim is to create a new bedroom. This all sounds simple so far, however let us consider some of the objectives of this project:

- Laying electrical cables.
- Measuring the floor space.
- Insulating the spaces between the beams in the loft floor and the roof of the room below.
- Putting floorboards over the beams in the loft floor.
- Cutting boards to size.
- Putting plasterboard over the loft roof.
- Plastering breeze block walls.
- Painting.
- Carpeting.
- Adding lights, plug sockets and switches.

The list goes on, but what initially seemed like a straightforward project is certainly more complex than what was originally anticipated. The complexity of a project such as this one means that it must be properly planned in order for the outcome to be successful i.e. the aims to be achieved.

A valuable lesson to learn from this is that project management requires a full evaluation of what is required, along with carefully thought out strategies and plans as to what paths to follow and courses of action to take.

The next dimension to add to a project is that of timing – it is all well and good to be given a list of objectives or objectives to meet, but it is also necessary to know when these objectives should be carried out, including the order in which they should happen – and most importantly *when the deadline is.*

From what we have ascertained so far we can define a project as being a planned and complex sequence of objectives, that are undertaken according to a fixed time scale, the aims of which are to bring about a pre-defined state of change.

1.2   The Project Manager

Projects do not have to be large – as you will see later in this chapter even the simplest of projects can be broken down into component parts, that demonstrate the complexity of the project.

Due to the complexity of projects, and the many factors that may lead to the failure of a project, large scale projects are seldom carried out by one person alone, and therefore require effective people management, by individuals that possess a variety of interpersonal skills, including:

- Group working.
- Leadership.
- Motivation.
- Feedback and appraisal.

As well as interpersonal skills, a head for figures is an advantage so that monetary constraints and time scales can be forecast in advance, and re-calculated on an ongoing basis during the course of the project. The person in charge of doing this is often called a *project manager*.

A successful project manager has the ability to undertake a project and complete it successfully within the proposed time, and within the agreed budget – of course this is not always the case, especially with very large projects that are extremely complex in nature, and that have a variety of factors that may impede upon the timing of the project, which can often result in over expenditure.

Famous examples of projects running over time and budget include the UK Air Traffic Control Centre in Swanick, Hampshire, which ended up being six years late and £273m over budget, and the Jubilee Line extension on the London Underground that ended up being almost two years late and £3.5bn over budget (BBC News, 2000). Of course, not all major projects finish late and over budget, the largest construction project of its day – the Hoover Dam was actually completed two years early and well under budget!

Smaller projects that may not require a team of individuals to carry them out, and indeed may be undertaken by one individual, can also be benefited by applying careful planning in the early stages. Within Higher Education most Honours Degrees culminate in a dissertation being produced – often over the course of the final year. How many students at university apply project management techniques to their own dissertations? The honest answer is of course – *not many!* However, if students appreciated how useful careful project planning could be to a dissertation, not only might they find the task of undertaking the dissertation more manageable – they may also achieve better grades having planned the objectives that go into producing a dissertation more carefully.

There are several stages that go into the management of projects; these are outlined in the following diagram:

The Stages of Project Management

```
        ┌──────────────────────┐
        │      Definition       │
        └──────────────────────┘
                   │
                   ▼
        ┌──────────────────────┐
        │   Detailed Planning   │
        └──────────────────────┘
                   │
                   ▼
        ┌──────────────────────┐
        │        Start         │◄───────────┐
        └──────────────────────┘            │
                   │                         │
                   ▼                         │
        ┌──────────────────────┐   ┌──────────────────┐
        │      Influence        │──►│      Amend        │
        └──────────────────────┘   └──────────────────┘
                   │
                   ▼
        ┌──────────────────────┐
        │        Finish         │
        └──────────────────────┘
```

The definition stage highlights the aims of the project, estimating the risks and the level of commitment required for the project to be a success.

The detailed planning stage of the project is where the various objectives that need to be undertaken within the project are mapped out, or sequenced along with the estimated times that each objective will take. It is at this stage that tools such as network diagrams or Gantt charts are used (to be covered shortly). The final draft of identified risks and costs is also produced at this stage to ascertain whether or not the project is viable. Risk is covered in further detail later in this chapter.

Every project has a start and an end – at the start stage, the objectives of the project are implemented in the correct order. Communication between all concerned is vital at this stage in order for the objectives to run on time and in sequence within the project.

The influence stage is where finances, quality, and time are identified. It is at this stage that it needs to be decided whether or not the project is running to plan. If a project is not running to plan corrective action needs to be taken within the amend stage. It is here that timings may be changed, plans redrawn, and resources utilised in different ways. If the project is running to plan, time, and budget at the influence stage no amendment is necessary.

The finish stage is where all of the objectives within the project have been completed – and if successful the aims of the project have been reached.

1.3   Project Planning Techniques

Projects can be broken down into objectives. Objectives are activities which must be completed to achieve the project's overall goal. Each objective has an estimated time duration – it is the accuracy of these timings, along with unforeseen external forces such as the weather, staff illness or problems with suppliers (risk) that can have an impact upon the success of a project.

Projects are planned using Network diagrams and Gantt charts. When producing network diagrams and Gantt charts, the first objective is always to *start* and the last objective is always to *finish* – these represent the start and end points of the project. The rest of the objectives that go into the project appear between the start and finish.

Within a project, objectives can run in sequence or in parallel to other objectives. Those objectives that run in sequence are reliant on a previous objective having already taken place. For example when producing a dissertation, the results cannot be written up until the research has been carried out.

At the same time there are objectives that run in parallel with other objectives, this means that they are not reliant on another objective having taken place, and may therefore occur at the same time as another objective. In the above mentioned dissertation project another objective may be to prepare a map for an appendix – this objective is not reliant on either the results being written up, or the research being carried out – so it *may* occur at the same time – or in parallel to those objectives.

You need to be aware that certain large projects are carried out by teams of individuals – these teams are divided into smaller teams often that are specialists in a particular area – the teams are sometimes referred to as resources. An example of this could be in a construction project where there may be teams of bricklayers, labourers, plumbers, electricians, and plasterers (amongst others). Dividing a team into groups allows for the team to work on several objectives at the same time.

In order to properly plan a project, techniques are used that can visually map out and mathematically time the collective objectives of the project. The techniques that will be examined in this chapter are network diagrams, critical path analysis and Gantt charts. For a project management beginner, these techniques may seem complex, so in order to make them appear more understandable a very simple project has been chosen on which to base these techniques – making a cup of cocoa.

2.   Network Diagrams and Critical Path Analysis

Network diagrams are maps of projects that are created in order to work out the sequence and scheduling of objectives within a particular project. Network diagrams are used to work out the *critical path* of a project, which will be covered shortly.

The concept behind network diagrams is that you cannot commence certain objectives within a project until others are finished. These objectives need to be completed in a sequence, with each stage being completed before the next stage can begin (sequential objectives).

Other objectives are not dependent on completion of any other objectives. These may be carried out at any time before or after a particular stage within a project is reached (parallel objectives).

In order to demonstrate the project of making a cup of cocoa in either network diagram or Gantt chart form, it is necessary to list the various objectives that go into the project. These are as follows (please note that all projects have a start and a finish, and that these have been listed at the beginning and end of the objectives):

A   Start.
B   Fill the kettle with water.
C   Boil the water.
D   Find the cocoa, sugar, cup and spoon.
E   Add two teaspoonfuls of cocoa to the cup.
F   Add two teaspoonfuls of sugar to the cup.
G   Pour the boiled water into the cup.
H   Get the milk out of the fridge.
I   Pour some milk into the cup.
J   Stir.
K   Finish.

In the list each objective is given a corresponding letter – although you may use a number instead of a letter, but for the purpose of clarity, this example will use letters. The next step is to put the varying objectives into a table, along with a column in which *predecessors* are listed: Predecessors are the objectives that must have been completed before another objective can actually take place. The following table identifies this along with a fourth column (which would not normally appear) that has been included to explain the rationale for the preceding objectives.

Objective	Name	Predecessor	Description
A	Start		Project begins - the start is the only objective not to have a predecessor.
B	Fill the kettle with water	A	Filling the kettle with water is the first objective in the project. Its only predecessor is the project start.
C	Boil the water	B	The water cannot be boiled until the kettle has been filled, so the predecessor for this objective is listed as B.
D	Find the cocoa, sugar, cup and spoon	A	Finding the cocoa, sugar, cup and spoon - this is not reliant on any of the previous objectives having been completed, therefore its only predecessor is the project starting so it is listed as A.
E	Add two teaspoonfuls of cocoa to the cup	D	In order to complete this objective, you must have found the cocoa, the cup and the spoon, so this objective is therefore preceded by D.
F	Add two teaspoonfuls of sugar to the cup	D	In order to complete this objective, you must have found the cup, the spoon, and the sugar, so this objective is therefore preceded by D.
G	Pour the boiled water into the cup	C,E,F	Before the boiled water is poured into the cup, the water must have actually been boiled, and the cocoa and sugar must have been put in the cup, therefore this objective is preceded by three objectives - C,E,F.
H	Get the milk out of the Fridge	A	Getting the milk out of the fridge, again this is not reliant on any of the previous objectives having been completed, therefore its only predecessor is the project starting - so it is listed as A.
I	Pour some milk into the cup	G,H	In order to put the milk in the cup the boiled water must already have been added, at the same time the milk must have been found, so the objectives are G,H.
J	Stir	I	Once the milk has been added, the drink is stirred, the spoon has already been found and used, so there is no need to link that objective into this one, therefore the only preceding objective is I.
K	Finish	J	The cocoa has been made, and the project is over - so J is the predecessor.

What the above demonstrates is that even the smallest and simplest of projects can be complex in their nature. The next stage when making a network diagram is to put each objective into its own box, and then connect them with arrows, so that the map of objectives demonstrating sequential and parallel objectives can be clearly seen. This has been done below, study the diagram below and compare it to the table above, see how each objective is represented by a box with an identifying letter in. Take note of the following:

- Where an objective is preceded by another objective e.g. C is preceded by B there is an arrow from B to C.
- Where an objective is preceded by more than one objective it may have more than one arrow feeding into it from other objectives, e.g. G has arrows leading to it from C, E and F.
- Where an objective is followed by more than one objective there may be more than one arrow emanating from an objective, e.g. A has three arrows going from it, to B, D and H.

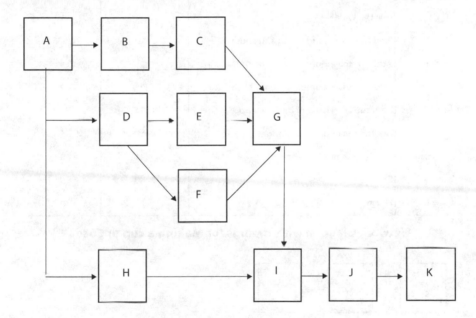

Network Diagram for Making a Cup of Cocoa

What the above diagram allows us to do is to map out the ordering of objectives allowing us to visualise which objectives must be carried out prior to following objectives, and which ones may be carried out at the same time as other objectives. The diagram also shows us several paths from A to K that may be taken. Following only the order of the arrows, the paths are as follows:

- A,B,C,G,I,J,K
- A,D,E,G,I,J,K
- A,D,F,G,I,J,K
- A,H,I,J,K

A point to note about network diagrams is that every box that represents an objective should feed into another box or boxes – apart from the Finish objective. If you produce a network diagram and this is not the case, you will need to re-look at what you have done, and amend this.

What needs to be established at this point is the actual path that the project should follow. In order to be able to do this one more piece of information is required about each objective – the time that they take.

The following table is the same as the previous table that identified the various objectives that went into making a cup of cocoa – with one significant difference, the description column has been replaced with a column that identifies how long each objective will take in seconds. Please note that both the project start and finish do not take any time, and are represented by a zero.

These timings can now be added to the network diagrams as below:

Objective	Name	Predecessor	Duration (seconds)
A	Start.		0
B	Fill the kettle with water.	A	10
C	Boil the water.	B	110
D	Find the cocoa, sugar, cup and spoon .	A	25
E	Add two teaspoonfuls of cocoa to the cup.	D	3
F	Add two teaspoonfuls of sugar to the cup.	D	2
G	Pour the boiled water into the cup.	C,E,F	5
H	Get the milk out of the Fridge.	A	5
I	Pour some milk into the cup.	G,H	2
J	Stir.	I	5
K	Finish.	J	0

Network Diagram with Timings for Making a cup of Cocoa

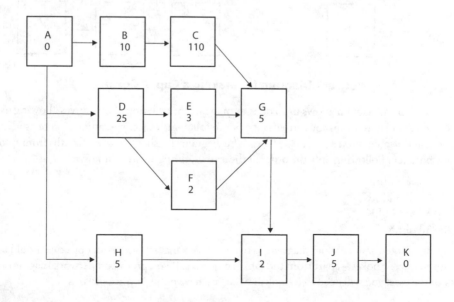

It has already been established that there are four different paths that this project may take – the next stage is to add the timings to each path, and then add them up, as below:

- A+B+C+G+I+J+K = 0+10+110+5+2+5+0 = 132 seconds.
- A+D+E+G+I+J+K = 0+25+3+5+2+5+0 = 40 seconds.
- A+D+F+G+I+J+K = 0+25+2+5+2+5+0 = 39 seconds.
- A+H+I+J+K = 0+5+2+5+0 = 12 seconds.

The next thing to decide is which of these paths should be taken in order to carry out this project – the tempting answer is always to say the shortest path, but this is actually wrong. If we chose the shortest path of twelve seconds the project would fail as some objectives take much longer than twelve seconds. The term for the path to choose for the project is the critical path. This is the longest path in a network that contains the critical objectives from a project that must be done exactly on schedule and to plan. Other objectives within the project may be carried out at the same time as the critical objectives, but the route the project should adhere to is the one along the critical path.

Critical path analysis (CPA) is used to organise and plan projects so they are completed on time and within budget. Objectives along the critical path cannot be delayed or take longer than their estimated time, without having an effect on the overall duration of the project.

There can be flexibility with objectives that do not fall along the critical path, for example if objective H (get the milk out of the fridge) took thirty seconds it would not impact upon the timing of the project overall, however if objective I (pour milk into the cup) did take longer than was estimated it would have an overall impact upon the length of the project as objective I is within the critical path. The flexibility that may be allowed to the timings of objectives that are not on the critical path is known as float.

For objective H to have an impact on the overall length of the project it (along with other objectives along its path) would have to exceed 132 seconds which is the current length of the critical path. Therefore if objective H took 126 seconds instead of 5 seconds the length of the project would be impacted upon (126+2+5+0 = 133 seconds).

The current critical path is 132 seconds, if we deduct from this the other objectives along the path that objective H follows I+J+K (7 seconds) we are left with 125 seconds (132-7=125). If we then deduct H from this figure (5 seconds) we are left with a float of 120 seconds. This means that the flexibility in the timing of H is 120 seconds before an impact will be had on the overall length of the project. We can therefore say that objective H has a float of 120 seconds. We cannot do this with any of the activities that follow the critical path, as their timings are crucial to the overall length of the project.

A successful project manager ensures that the timings of critical objectives are strictly adhered to, otherwise projects run over time, and possibly over budget. This represents the influence/amend stages of the 'Stages of Project Management' model.

As the project of making a cup of cocoa is a relatively straightforward project it is easy to work out the critical path. However large and complex projects such as construction projects may contain thousands or even millions of objectives – suddenly working out the path is not as simple. Many people now use software applications such as Microsoft Project for this purpose. To do this manually involves carrying forward the various paths mathematically to gain the total timings for each possible path of objectives. The highest total is then subtracted backwards along every possible path in order to verify which one is critical to the project. The critical path is the one that finishes with zero as the number.

This technique will now be applied to the various paths that go into making a cup of cocoa as below (please note that now the objectives appear in reverse order as we are subtracting backwards):

- Highest total minus (K-J-I-G-C-B-A) = 132-(0-5-2-5-110-10-0)= 0.
- Highest total minus (K-J-I-G-E-D-A) = 132-(0-5-2-5-3-25-0)= 92.
- Highest total minus (K-J-I-G-F-D-A) = 132-(0-5-2-5-2-25-0)= 93.
- Highest total minus (K-J-I-H-A) = 132-(0-5-2-5-0)= 120.

It is clear to see where the critical path lies, by the deducted sum equalling zero, this is now identified in the diagram below. The critical path route is now in bold.

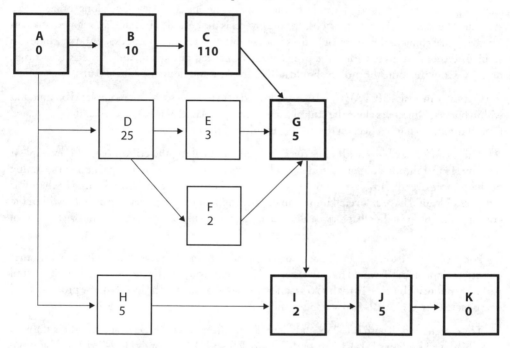

Network Diagram Featuring Critical Path

This is a *micro-project* that consists of *micro-tasks*, in practical terms projects that use these techniques take days, weeks or months. These types of project are not broken down into such small stages, as it would make them far too complex in nature. Typically the shortest length task that you would include in a project would be one that takes half a day.

3.   Gantt Charts

Gantt charts were developed during the first half of the twentieth century as a visual tool to show scheduled and actual progress of projects.

Like network diagrams Gantt charts allow analysis of the ordering of the objectives that make up complex projects, and feature a time scale that allows the scheduling of objectives within projects to take place. Unlike network diagrams Gantt charts commonly require the start date/time of a project so that timings can be placed against actual dates.

Gantt charts are used to try and work out the duration of a project. This is done by listing how long each objective that goes into a project will take. It is also necessary to establish which objectives are reliant on other objectives (predecessors).

Objectives are plotted along a horizontal time scale with a project starting date, which allows for the project planner to be able to work out the project end date from plotting on the duration of the various objectives within the project. Objectives are plotted in sequence to the objectives that they rely on (predecessors) and in parallel to other objectives that they do not rely on.

When producing a Gantt chart, the first objective is always to 'start' and the last objective is always to 'finish' – so these must be added to the above list. As well as this, each individual objective is given a unique identifier – commonly a number or a letter. For this example the previous project of making a cup of cocoa will not be used because it would be difficult to fit the timescale in seconds on a page! Instead a table will be given with eight objectives listed within, each objective has a predecessor (or predecessors), along with a time duration given in days. For the purpose of the example the project is set to start on the 20 July 2005.

The table of objectives is as follows:

Objective	Duration (days)	Predecessor(s)
Start - A	0	
B	2	A
C	1	B
D	3	A
E	2	D
F	4	C
G	1	E,F
Finish - H	0	G

From this table the Gantt chart below can be drawn:

Sample Gantt Chart

Note that the duration of each objective in days 'maps' against the timescale at the top of the diagram, for example objective B is two days long and commences on the 20 July and finishes at the end of the 21 July. The overall length of the project is eight days with the finish taking place at the end of the eighth day.

In the Gantt chart the preceding objective of a following objective has an arrow going from it to the next objective e.g. B to C, and an objective that has more than one predecessor has more than one arrow feeding into it e.g. G has arrows leading into it from E and F. Please note that all objectives should lead to other objectives until the finish has been reached. A Gantt chart with objectives that do not lead to other objectives is incomplete.

A Gantt chart can easily be created using either a table in a word processing application, or by using a spreadsheet application, and simply shading in the cells where an activity falls – as has been done with the above example. If you are able to get hold of dedicated project management software such as Microsoft Project, this will often plot both a network diagram and a Gantt chart for you, all you would need to do, would be to enter the objectives, duration, and predecessors, and the software would do the rest. The critical path can be worked out in the same way.

4.   Risk Management

Risk is the possibility that your project may not run to plan, budget or schedule because something that is unexpected happens. All projects have a degree of risk – it is being able to forecast risks, and make contingency plans should risks occur, that will aid you as a project manager – this process is known as *risk management*. The likelihood of risk occurring increases under the following circumstances:

- If a significant amount of time passes between the detailed planning and start stages.
- When new methods of working are being used in your project.
- When those undertaking the project are inexperienced.
- If your project takes a long time.

Techniques that may help to minimise the impacts of risks include the following:

- Thorough planning, this will help to identify risks.
- Not ignoring what might prove to be a risk.
- Properly assessing the extent to which risks may impact upon a project.
- Making sure that key project stakeholders are aware of any risks.
- Not denying that risks exist!

There is no substitute for experience when forecasting risk. For example if you have carried out similar projects in the past, you will be more aware of any future possible pitfalls – or risks. Here is an example of this in action:

Tom works in a position whereby he produces questionnaires for corporate clients. He has produced 250 different questionnaires over the past year, of which forty questionnaires were rejected by the client as not being suitable for the purpose. By looking at what has happened in the past, Tom can deduce that there is a 16 per cent risk that each future questionnaire will be rejected by the client – or to put this another way, there is an 84 per cent chance that each future questionnaire will be accepted by the client. This is worked out by dividing the rejected questionnaires by the total number of questionnaires produced, and then multiplying the figure by 100 e.g. (40/250) X 100 = 16.

A lesson to learn from the above scenario is that maintaining records and gathering all relevant data that may have an influence upon risk is a prudent action to take for any project manager.

4.1   Decision Trees

During any project, a time will arise when it is necessary to make a decision between which of several courses of action you should take. In order to do this it is necessary to base the decisions that you make upon estimated risks – more often than not against the financial cost (or benefit) of each course of action. A useful tool for doing this is called a decision tree. These offer a valuable composition that allows you to lay out options and explore the potential outcomes of choosing each option. Decision trees are also useful in giving a fair portrayal of the risks and rewards associated with each possible course of action, see the following example:

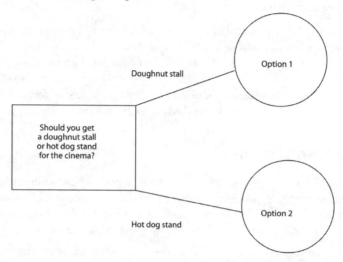

In this example, the decision being made is whether to get a doughnut stall or a hot dog stand for a cinema. The decision that needs making is written in a box, emanating from the box are two paths, each of which points to an option, which is represented by a circle, option 1 being the doughnut stall, and option 2 being the hot dog stand.

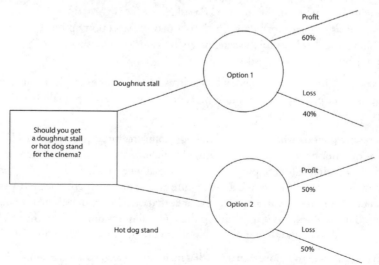

The next step is to assess the likely outcome of each option being either a success or a failure. In this case a success is represented by a profit, and a failure is represented by a loss. A further two branches are added to the tree diagram from each option to represent the probability of each outcome, which is expressed as a percentage – the total of the percentages for each option must always equal one hundred per cent. For the doughnut stall, the likelihood of it showing a profit is sixty per cent and the likelihood of it making a loss is forty per cent these added together equal one hundred per cent. This information is based on research that has already been carried out looking at what has happened in the past when a doughnut stall or a hot dog stand has been built into other cinemas.

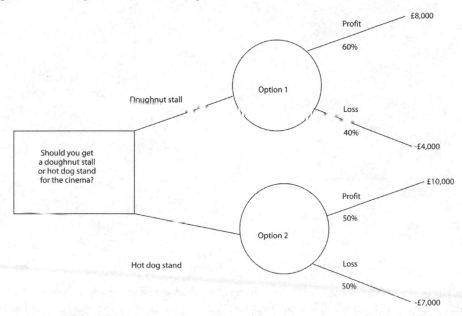

At the end of each of the branches of the decision tree, a figure is entered that represents how much revenue will be generated or lost (over a specified period e.g. one year) if either option succeeds or fails. In this example, if the doughnut stall succeeds it is projected to generate £8,000 over the first year, if it fails it is projected to lose £4,000 over the first year. If the hot dog stand succeeds it is projected to generate £10,000 over the first year, if it fails it is projected to lose £7,000 over the first year. Again all of this information is based upon prior experience from past projects – or the most educated guesses that can be made.

The next step is to multiply the profit or loss for each projected outcome, by the percentage that represents its likelihood.

For the doughnut stall to be a success this is worked out as follows:
£8,000 X 60% = £4,800

For the doughnut stall to be a failure this is worked out as follows:
-£4,000 X 40% = -£1,600

For the hot dog stand to be a success this is worked out as follows:
£10,000 X 50% = £5,000

For the hot dog stand to be a failure this is worked out as follows:
-£7,000 X 50% = -£3,500

The figures for both options are then added together as follows:

Doughnut stall: £4,800 + -£1,600 = £3,200
Hot dog stand: £5,000 + -£3,500 = £1,500

These figures represent the projected financial outcome of each option, taking into account the risk involved, they are then added to the decision tree to the right of the option circles.

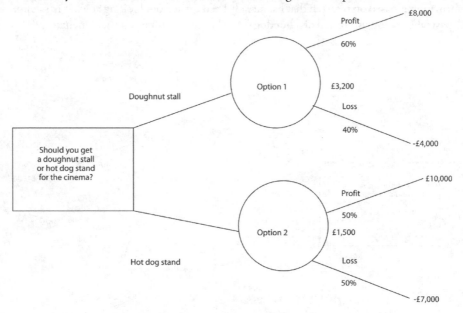

The next aspect to take into account with regard to which decision to make is how much each of the two options will cost to implement, in the case of the chosen example the doughnut stall will cost £1,700 to set up, and the hot dog stand will cost £1,900 to set up. These figures are then added to the decision tree.

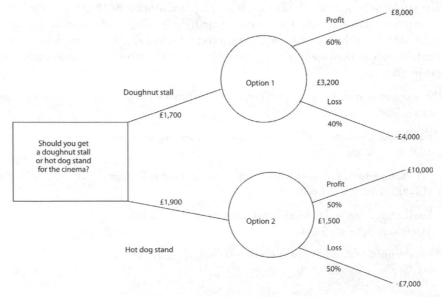

The penultimate stage of using a decision tree is to deduct the cost of each option from its projected financial outcome:

Doughnut stall: £3,200 - £1,700 = £1,500
Hot dog stand: £1,500 - £1,900 = -£400

These figures are placed within the appropriate option circle.

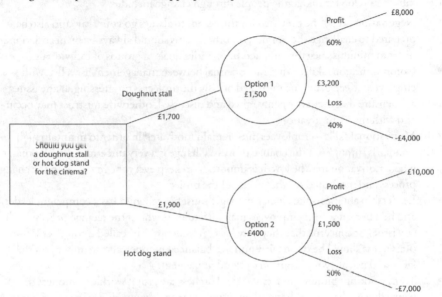

The final stage of using the decision tree is to make the decision as to which of the options to choose. The decision tree in this case tells us that taking into account the risks involved, that the doughnut stall is likely to make a net profit over the first year of £1,500, and the hot dog stand is likely to make a net loss over the first year of £400.

The decision tree allows us to easily work out the option that presents the least financial risk, which is the doughnut stall – so this is the option that is chosen.

A decision tree is only as good as the information that goes into it – it is up to you as a project manager to gather information about projects on an ongoing basis, and to thoroughly research what has happened in other projects before undertaking any project of your own. The more accurate information you have gathered, the better that you can prepare yourself for risk, and any negative impacts that risk may present to your project.

5. Managing People Through Change

The outcomes of most complex projects involve some form of change – whether it be change to working practices, changes to job roles, and even changes to the number of people employed by the organisation. People frequently find 'change' difficult to cope with. The uncertainty of the future causes anxiety and stress. When there is poor communication and a lack of information about the future, rumours can spread and this compounds the feelings of unease and uncertainty.

It is true to say that people who are managed well are themselves capable of managing change and its effects more effectively. Organisational change requires the cooperation and commitment of key stakeholders including management and those persons trusted with delivering change. In order to manage this process key interpersonal and management skills are required. As a student your first introduction to this will be in the form of group work assignments. Refining these skills whilst studying will certainly go a long way in the workplace, as being an effective manager of people through times of change is a very desirable attribute for an employee to possess.

Key skills to develop for managing people through change include:

- Negotiation skills – be prepared for things not to always go your way, and also be prepared to challenge the opinions of others. This should always be by negotiation in order to minimise negative impacts upon individuals or groups of individuals.
- Communications skills – these are essential between management as well as with employees. Keep everyone informed of how the project is progressing, if any issues arise ensure that they are openly raised and discussed, otherwise mistrust may occur – and with that demotivation.
- Motivational skills – employees must remain motivated in order to maintain high standards throughout the change process. Change is a very uncertain time for many when motivation may be low, it is important to keep everyone involved in the change process and motivated for the success of the project.
- Leadership abilities – the change manager must be recognised as a competent leader and be a person whom employees may turn to throughout the change process with any issues or concerns that they may have. A leader may be called upon to criticise or praise, this should be done fairly and in a balanced manner, acting only upon the facts, and not allowing emotion to cloud judgement.
- Team working abilities – to facilitate and orchestrate group working amongst the teams that are handling change. Few people manage change alone. In reality it is teams of individuals who work on the process of change – therefore team working and team leadership are important traits for those who manage the change process.

As has already been mentioned, change may be opposed by those who are against it, indeed resistance to change by those who are afraid of the unknown and the effects of change is commonplace, especially when the comforts of familiarity are lost. In the developmental stages of project management when changes are being proposed, resistance is minor due to the limited immediate effects of proposed changes. However when the process of change begins, and differences in results become visible, resistance increases as detractors step in. It is during this time that it is most important to maintain effective communication channels in order to keep everybody informed of the wider picture, rather than let those who criticise one part of the picture have an influential voice. Resistance to change occurs for a number of reasons such as new working practices that may require a personal investment of time in order to become familiar with them.

Change is a positive thing as it confronts apathy. All too often people do something because it has always been done like that without stopping and asking themselves – should it be done like that? Is this the best way to do it? What other ways can we do it? What would happen if we stopped doing it? Change is a good way of challenging how knowledgeable individuals are about what is actually being changed.

6. Stress Management

With change comes resistance, and with resistance comes stress – or rather distress. This is the fear of the unknown, and the ability or rather perceived inability to cope with it. Stress is a natural bodily reaction that we have had within us since the dawning of time. Once upon a time stress was a life saver – today it can be a killer – but what is stress?

To put it simply stress is a chemical reaction that takes place within our bodies when adrenaline surges, cortisol levels increase, the heart beats faster, breathing becomes more rapid, and blood pressure rises, which has an impact on cardio vascular well-being.

A long time ago before man was at the top of the food chain it was stress that allowed man to out run his predators. If you have ever been chased you will know the feeling that is stress as your body works overtime to try and save you from the unknown… But what about in the workplace?

Consider a typical office, you are given a new task to do in a very short space of time, yet you are working on other projects, and you feel that this is going to be a disaster, nobody listens to your objections and the success of everything lies with YOU. What happens? Adrenaline flows, the heart beats faster, breathing becomes more rapid – yet you have nowhere to run as you are sat in your chair at your desk – this is when stress related illness can occur.

Even managers can feel stress! The pressures of ensuring a project runs to time and budget can be causes of stress – but how do we see signs of stress within ourselves and others – and what can we do to combat this? Signs of distress include:

- Being out of breath.
- Being aware of your own heart beat.
- Back pains, and muscle aches.
- Tiredness, not wanting to get out of bed to face what is causing the stress.
- Being unable to sleep for thinking about what is causing the stress.
- Sudden changes in diet such as binge eating, or starvation for long periods.
- Continued worried and anxious feelings, and a general feeling of nervousness.
- Impatience with other people and things.
- Loss of interest in appearance.
- Obsession with what is causing stress.
- Abusing alcohol or drugs.

When people feel distress during a period of change it can be for many reasons, but when analysed in their most basic form these reasons are often because those who are stressed believe that they cannot cope with the changes that are taking place.

A good manager of change should be able to recognise symptoms of stress amongst themselves and others – and should act upon this, below are listed some ways that levels of stress may be relieved:

- Support those who seem to be stressed – if necessary bring in additional staff to provide cover. This is certainly cheaper in the short term than sickness cover for stress related illness in the long term.
- Once it becomes clear that an individual is susceptible to stress, the demands that are placed upon that individual should be carefully monitored, and adjusted as necessary.
- As has been mentioned people are afraid of the unknown – so make sure that lines of communication are open at all times and that everybody involved in change is informed about what is happening.
- Learn to be a delegator – stressed managers often have difficulty letting go, and many will want to prove that they can do everything themselves. An admirable attitude? No – a foolish one? Yes. Learn to trust other people with tasks – and learn to say 'No!' yourself. Another point here is not to be somebody who delegates a task, and then stands over the shoulder of the person who is doing the task – this is micro

management which is ineffective time management, and does not help to make the person undertaking the task feel valued or trusted.

- Prioritise the workload – if something does not need to be done today – can it be done on a different day? Those who do not prioritise will suddenly find themselves with much work to be done, and no time in which to do it.

It is not only of benefit to the individual to effectively manage stress, it is of benefit to the organisation. Knowledge about the symptoms of distress, and how to best manage this, are essential skills for those who wish to manage the change process.

If you are feeling stressed, the following points may provide some useful tips, which should help you to alleviate the symptoms of stress:

- Take a break – at lunch time, do not work through your lunch break, get up and go for a walk away from your work place. The exercise will help to alleviate some stress symptoms, and the change of environment will help to relax your mind – even if it is only for a short period.
- Eat healthily - don't be tempted to eat snack or convenience foods, which are usually high in salt and fats. Fresh fruit and vegetables will help to keep your body in good working order – something which is important during stressful times.
- Get plenty of sleep – don't have late nights, your body under stressful conditions needs all the rest it can get.
- Don't turn to alcohol – this will have a negative impact upon your body, and will only exacerbate the symptoms of stress that you experience.
- Progressive muscular relaxation (PMR) – this is useful if your muscles are feeling tense under times of stress. Take any muscle and tighten it as much as you can for several seconds, then allow it to relax, and then consciously make it relax even more than what it would normally be. This technique requires practice, but if used upon different muscles in your body, can allow you to feel physically more relaxed, which is useful in times of stress.
- Be active after work - don't sit at your computer or in front of the television when you get home after a stressful day. Your body would benefit from some gentle (or rigorous) exercise. Under such circumstances, go for a walk, ride a bike, join a gym – a little exercise will leave you feeling refreshed – and ready for bed, which is important in order to get a good night's sleep.
- Build exercise into your day – have you considered walking or cycling to and from work? This extra exercise will certainly help to make you feel more refreshed once you arrive at work, and when you get home, and is especially beneficial if it can be built into your daily routine, as in this example of commuting.
- Don't bottle it up – talk to people about how you are feeling, this can often act as a 'release' and leave you feeling less stressed than what you would have been if you hadn't talked about it.
- Deep breathing – this is a very simple yet effective way of relaxing your body. All that you need to do, is find somewhere quiet, close your eyes, and taken ten deep breaths, in through the nose, and out through the mouth. This allows your body to relax, and whilst basic, is an effective relaxation technique – try practicing this several times a day to help relax your body and mind if you are feeling stressed.

If symptoms of stress are recognised, and positive action is taken in order to combat them, both in the workplace with regard to workload, and personally by utilising the above techniques, individuals will ultimately become less stressed. If left unchecked however, stress can in extreme cases be a killer. If properly managed, the negative health impacts of stress can be vastly reduced, benefiting not only individuals, but also the organisation to which they belong.

Managers of change, should take note of the above. The success of any change that you are trying to implement, will ultimately hinge on the wellbeing of those who are a part of your project teams. As a project manager the importance of effective stress management should not be under-estimated.

7.   Preparing and Writing a Dissertation

Most degree level courses culminate with a major project in the final year. For those studying on Honours degrees this usually means a dissertation. A dissertation is an extended piece of academic study (in the order of twelve thousand words) completed individually by each student. It is a thoroughly justified piece of research that studies in-depth a current professional issue or academic concept.

- A dissertation involves the following tasks:
- Recognition and examination of a current issue, problem, or academic concept.
- The setting of aims and objectives for your study.
- A thorough literature review (secondary research) to establish current thinking on your topic. This will look at arguments from differing perspectives, and to present a well balanced critique of the views of other authors using a variety of research materials.
- Implementation of an appropriate primary research tool(s), for your own scientific investigation of the problem. Your primary research will be informed by your literature review.
- Collation and presentation of your primary research results in a variety of statistical and graphical forms.
- Analysis and interpretation of your findings, reflecting on the views of other authors presented in your literature review.
- A justified conclusion that states what has been achieved through your study with suggested future actions in the form of recommendations.

7.1   The Project

A dissertation or any other kind of major final year project is something that needs to be thoroughly planned before it is implemented. Such an undergraduate or postgraduate academic project should be seen as the culmination of your years spent at university, and as such is something that you should take pride in, and strive to achieve the best possible mark for. In order to help you achieve the highest possible marks in your dissertation or indeed any other kind of major academic undertaking, you should thoroughly plan what you are going to do – and how you are going to do it.

This section will use project management techniques that have been covered previously within this chapter, and apply them to writing a dissertation. It will also look in detail at the various stages that go into writing a dissertation, and offer advice on techniques for carrying out these stages. The advice given by your university on dissertation writing with regard to format and structure should supersede the advice in this chapter (as this often varies from institution to institution). However the project management techniques used in this chapter should help you to plan your dissertation to great effect.

For the purposes of this chapter, it has been assumed that the dissertation is to be handed in mid-April, and that the person undertaking the project has begun planning their dissertation at the beginning of September the year before. Tutor contact will not occur until the beginning of October (which in your final year at university is very often the case), but in the month leading up to that, you have the opportunity to begin some primary preparation for yourself – this is a prudent undertaking.

It is envisaged that the total time taken for the dissertation will be two hundred and sixteen days. A word of warning, if your dissertation is due before mid-April, and you do not begin to plan it by September, the timings for the various stages of this project will need amending so that your work is completed on time.

Nine key stages have been identified in preparing and writing a dissertation, and each of these key stages contain a number of objectives. The key stages in undertaking the dissertation project are as follows:

- Proposal.
- Literature review.
- Methodology including research.
- Results.
- Discussion.
- Conclusions and recommendations.
- Final additions.
- Final amendments.
- Completion.

In order to plan the project properly it is necessary to analyse the various stages, and populate them with objectives that should take place during each particular stage. It is then necessary to work out the order of the objectives, as well what preceding objectives must have taken place for another objective to take place. The following table is designed to achieve this aim. The left column contains numbers that can be equated to objectives and project stages; the second column from the left contains a list of project stages in **bold** with the objectives for each particular stage listed beneath them. The third column from the left contains the timings for each objective. The column on the right of the table contains the preceding objectives that certain other objectives are reliant upon having taken place. Please note that predecessors have not been given to project stages, or the overall project. The first objective listed is actually number three in the table, which is the starting point for the work undertaken in the project.

	Project Stages and Objectives	Duration	Predecessors
1	Dissertation	216 days	
2	**Proposal**		
3	Consider general subject and gather information	10 days	
4	Initial reading and research	14 days	3
5	Choose specific subject	5 days	3,4
6	Consider aims and objectives	3 days	5
7	Consider and choose research methods	3 days	6
8	Choose title	1 day	5,6,7
9	Ongoing Discussion with tutors	7 days	5
10	Write proposal including aims and objectives and submit	2 days	9,8
11	Await Return	7 days	10
12	Amend as necessary	7 days	11
13	**Literature Review**		
14	Gather and read literature	20 days	12
15	Prepare literature review and submit to tutor for feedback	10 days	14
16	Await return	7 days	15
17	Amend as necessary	7 days	16
18	**Methodology Including Research**		
19	Prepare research mechanism and submit to tutor for feedback	10 days	12
20	Await return	7 days	19
21	Amend research mechanism as necessary	7 days	20
22	Carry out primary research and collect data	30 days	21
23	Data entry	7 days	22
24	Data analysis	7 days	23
25	Data representation	7 days	24
26	Write up methodology and submit to tutor for feedback	10 days	23,25
27	Await return	7 days	26
28	Amend as necessary	7 days	27
29	**Results**		
30	Write up results section and submit to tutor for feedback	7 days	24,28
31	Await return	7 days	30
32	Amend and complete results section as suggested by tutor	7 days	31
33	**Discussion**		
34	Write up discussion and submit to tutor	7 days	17,32
35	Await return	7 days	34
36	Amend and complete discussion section	2 days	35
37	**Conclusions & Recommendations**		
38	Consider and write conclusions and recommendations and submit to tutor	2 days	36
39	Await return	7 days	38
40	Amend as necessary	2 days	39
41	**Final Additions**		
42	Write summary	0.5 days	12,17,21,32,36,28
43	Prepare bibliography and appendices	2 days	25
44	Create contents pages	0.5 days	39,38
45	**Final Amendments**		
46	First print	0.5 days	40
47	First proof read	1 day	42
48	Edit and amend	1 day	43
49	Second print	0.5 days	44
50	Second proof read	1 day	45
51	Second edit and amend	1 day	46
52	**Completion**		
53	Final print	0.5 days	47
54	Bind	10 days	49
55	Submission	0.5 days	50

The Gantt chart below demonstrates when the project stages occur during the project. It is evident that some stages are dependent on other stages having taken place, and must follow certain stages. For example the discussion stage is reliant upon the results stage. Other stages though will have no reliance on certain other stages having taken place, and may occur at the same time as another stage. An example of this is the literature review and the methodology including research – which partially both occur at the same time during the project.

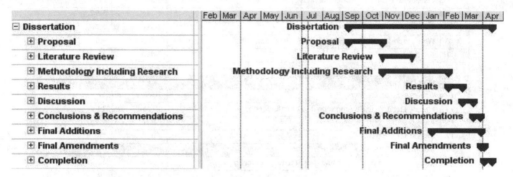

7.2   Proposal

This is the first major stage of the project, and should ideally begin BEFORE you return to university during the summer vacation, before commencing your final year. The final year at university will certainly be very challenging for most students, with other modules and work to complete as well as a dissertation – so getting a head start during the vacation period is a great advantage.

The objectives for this stage of the project are as follows:

- **Consider the general subject and gather reading materials.** The subject that you choose for your dissertation or major project is very important. You should ideally choose something that is of interest to you, as this is a piece of work, that you will be living, breathing, eating and sleeping with over the next eight or nine months. For example if you were studying Events Management, and had a personal interest in technology, computing and the internet, then choosing a dissertation subject that involved these would seem a logical thing to do. You may well choose to do a study that explores website design, establishing from the academic literature how to design a successful website before critically evaluating the websites of a selection of events companies. Whatever general subject you choose, it is at this point that you should begin collecting articles from newspapers, journals, the internet, and looking at relevant book titles that may prove to be of use, as well as past dissertation titles from your university library.
- **Initial reading and research.** Once you have gathered your initial materials, you need to read through them to see what existing studies are available on your chosen subject area. Make referenced notes, and use tools such as mind maps to help you mentally picture who has said what about the various components of your chosen subject area.
- **Choose a specific subject to investigate further.** After your initial reading you need to choose a specific subject, this should not be too broad, indeed a more focused narrower subject is better, than something that is vague and without focus.
- **Consider the aims and objectives.** Once you have decided upon the subject of your dissertation, you need to decide what the eventual aims of it will be. Ask yourself – what is it that you are intending to achieve? When you have decided this, you then

need to analyse the steps that need to be taken in order to achieve the aims – these are your objectives.

- **Consider and choose a research method**. A dissertation frequently involves your own primary research or scientific investigation. You need to decide upon the research method that you would like to use; questionnaires; interviews; focus groups; observations. Read Chapter Ten – there are a great many ways by which you can carry out primary research. You need to choose a method that is both suitable and achievable. In the example above, of critically evaluating the websites of a selection of events companies, the primary research tool could be actually visiting and using the websites from a consumer's perspective, and awarding marks that are recorded in a matrix. You also need to consider your sampling frame. In the given example, how many websites should you look at – and how would you go about selecting them? Will you do this on a geographical basis, on the type of events company – or both? Whatever you do, you need to justify your decision. This is a very important part of your dissertation and should be given thorough consideration.

- **Choose the title**. The title should be a reflection of the topic, your aims, and the research method – it should be ten words or less, and not sound like a newspaper headline, for example 'A Critical Evaluation of UK Special Event Companies' Websites'.

- **Ongoing discussion with tutors**. Your dissertation tutor is the person who will act as your mentor and guide throughout the entire dissertation process. Every aspect of what has so far been covered should be discussed with your tutor, so that the benefit of their expertise can be used to guide you in an appropriate direction. Remember, though, that the dissertation is your project, not your tutors, so most of the creative and academic input will have to come from you.

- **Write the proposal including aims and objectives and submit**. When you have had the benefit of tutor feedback, the next task is to write up a proposal or brief of what your dissertation will be. The proposal should cover the aims and objectives of the study, a review of the literature that you have already studied, a bibliography of suggested sources, an overview that justifies your chosen research method, and your proposed dissertation title.

- **Await return**. Your dissertation tutor may not always be able to return your proposal straight away, it is reasonable to expect them to take a week to look through it and make comments, or suggestions for improvements.

- **Amend your proposal as necessary**. Any amendments that have been suggested by your tutor should be implemented to the proposal. If you follow your tutor's guidelines, the amended proposal should then be accepted; once acceptance has been made formal, it is time to move on to the next stage of the project.

As can be seen a considerable amount of time and effort needs to be injected into the proposal for your dissertation. This will be time well spent as it should ensure that you have a clearly focused dissertation from the outset, allowing you to progress to the next stage with confidence and enthusiasm.

A Gantt chart of the proposal stage follows, this compares with the proposal stage from the table of project stages and objectives given earlier.

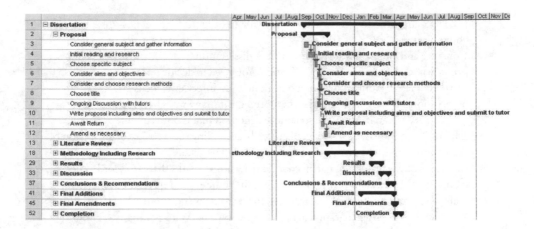

7.3   Literature Review

The literature review is designed to demonstrate your reading around the general subject area being studied, and is a write up of your findings from other sources such as books, journals, websites, newspapers and television. This stage of the project is important, as it introduces the reader to the subject area, and should give them a balanced view of any major issues, as well as a profile of any specific bodies that may later come under investigation within the primary research for the dissertation.

The objectives for this stage of the project are as follows:

- **Gather and read literature**. You should have already collated much of your reading material (books, journal articles, newspaper articles, video tapes, leaflets, pamphlets, web pages, current research papers and reports around the subject area), and already made some notes. This process should be extended until you have enough information on your subject area, to write a thorough and balanced literature review. Read Chapter Ten for guidelines on how to undertake a literature search.
- **Prepare literature review and submit to tutor for feedback**. Formally write up your notes, so that they clearly identify the issues and problems that are to be the focus of your dissertation. You do not need to call this section 'Literature review' but instead use headings and sub-headings that are suitable for the subject area – once completed submit to your dissertation tutor for feedback. In writing your literature review be analytical rather than descriptive. What this means is that you should comment critically on the views of other authors, rather than just describe (or repeat) what they say. Interpret the views of other authors in your own words and comment on the relevance of their work for your dissertation. Read Chapter Eleven to learn more about being a critical thinker.
- **Remember that you have to reference fully your literature review**. Normally using the Harvard Style of Referencing – see Chapter Four. If you do not reference fully your text you will be accused of plagiarism. This is a very serious charge and could result in your dissertation failing – being awarded zero marks.
- **Await return**. Await the return of your work; whilst doing so have a look to see if there are any other items that you think should have been included in the literature review. A word of warning here – know when to stop! Sometimes it can be too easy to carry on adding material into your literature review. The danger with this is that the word limit for your dissertation might be exceeded, and your dissertation may lose focus, digressing away from the central theme of your study. Thus, be selective when

undertaking your literature search. Always ask yourself the question – will this article help me address the aims and objectives of my dissertation?

- **Amend as necessary.** Your tutor might have made comments, and asked questions of your literature review on issues that may be unclear to them. Ensure that you consider any amendments that are suggested – your tutor will have had previous experience of supervising dissertations and their guidance will be of value.

The following Gantt chart of the literature review stage compares with the literature review stage from the table of project stages and objectives given earlier.

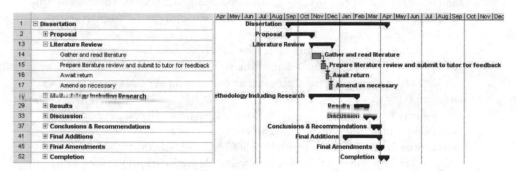

7.4   Methodology Including Research

Your dissertation methodology is the planning and write-up of the primary research that you might undertake as part of your dissertation. This is an extremely important part of your dissertation, and therefore careful consideration needs to be taken during this stage.

This stage should normally take place after the literature review has been completed. This is because your research should be informed by the research that other authors have conducted on topics similar to your own. However as demonstrated in the Gantt chart, this stage could actually begin much earlier – which may be beneficial in the long-term. The planning for the methodology is most important, as the more considered and planned your methodology is – the more likely it is to prove to be an effective research tool for your dissertation.

The methodology section should include a reflective section, that outlines any problems that you experienced when conducting your primary research, and if this had an impact or influence upon the results.

The objectives for this stage of the project are as follows:

- **Prepare the research mechanism and submit to your tutor for feedback.** Choosing the right research tool for your dissertation is essential. Do not underestimate the importance of this objective. Once you have decided upon how you are going to collect data, you must thoroughly prepare your research tool, taking into account best practice techniques from literature on the subject of research methodology. Many students choose to implement a questionnaire survey, but do not properly consider what questions are going to be used on the questionnaire – and how they will be analysed. Are you taking a qualitative or quantitative approach to data collection? Are you intending to scientifically analyse your data? If so, make sure that your questionnaire contains the correct type of questions for this purpose. You also need to pilot your research mechanism once it has been prepared, this should be done on an audience who are similar to those that will be the subjects of your investigation (not family and friends). The results of your pilot should also be submitted to your tutor, along with your thoughts thus far. Read Chapter Ten for information relating to conducting research.

- **Await return.** Your tutor should have a good idea as to whether your research mechanism is suitable or not, and should be able to provide guidance as to changes to increase the effectiveness of what you are doing. Whilst you are awaiting your tutor feedback, concentrate on your literature review.

- **Amend your research mechanism as necessary**. Discuss with your tutor any suggested amendments and changes that he/she has made, along with what you have learned by piloting your research mechanism. Make the suggested changes, before preparing to undertake your research.

- **Carry out primary research and collect your data**. Once your research tool is complete, it needs to be put into action. This is your one and only chance to undertake this activity, so careful planning up to this point to ensure that all goes well is essential.

- **Data entry.** This is the point within the project when the results from your research tool begin to materialise. Whether you are entering data into SPSS (a statistical software package) or writing up interviews DO NOT underestimate how long this stage will take – it can be VERY time consuming. Be prepared for some long hours, sat in front of a computer screen, carrying out a repetitive activity.

- **Data analysis** – or the science bit! This is the part of your dissertation that often involves statistical analysis of your results, which should help to 'paint an overall picture' of what you have found. Typical analyses include mean, median, mode, standard deviation, skewness and kurtosis. You will need to read up on research methods and statistical analyses in order to use the correct techniques properly. Chapter Five will help you with this.

- **Data representation.** Not all of your data will by represented numerically, in fact it can sometimes be preferable to graphically present your data in histograms, pie charts, scatter graphs, line graphs and a variety of other charts. Typically you would use a selection of charts and statistics to summarise your findings in both empirical and graphic form. Read Chapters Four and Five for guidelines on the presentation of data.

- **Write up your methodology and submit it to your tutor for feedback.** The method by which you have collected your data including the pilot survey and any amendments that you have made to your primary research is recorded in the methodology section. Provide as much detail as you can about when, where, how and with whom you conducted your primary research. Keep accurate records of the process by which you implemented the research as your tutor may wish to contact your interviewees to confirm that you did actually interview them. This section will also explain in detail the rationale behind your chosen research tool (for example the design of your questionnaire), and will break down into detail each individual question with the reason for its inclusion. To justify your research methodology and your research tools you will need to reference your text to authors who have written research methods textbooks. Your tutor should then review this, and whilst they will not be able to make many suggestions for amendments (as your methodology is a review of what has already happened), they should be able to point out any errors or omissions on your part.

- **Await return.** Whilst doing so start to think about what you have learned from your methodology.

- **Amend as necessary**. Make any amendments as suggested by your tutor.

The following Gantt chart of the methodology including research stage compares with the methodology including research stage from the table of project stages and objectives given earlier.

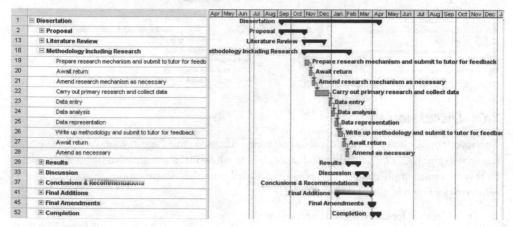

7.5   Results

This stage symbolises the beginning of the end of your dissertation. By now you have completed the secondary and primary research. You are now left to summarise your findings, and to provide the rationale for these. The results stage is a written summary of the main findings from your primary research – this stage will include your graphs, charts and statistics from the previous section.

The objectives for this stage of the project are:

- **Write up the results section and submit to your tutor for feedback**. The results section is a written summary of the findings of your primary research. It should include relevant statistics and other numerical data, as well as a *selection* of graphs and charts - but not pages and pages of them. If you have many graphs and charts, it is better to use them as appendices to your dissertation – and to refer to them from the results section. This helps to prevent your results section becoming too disjointed. When writing up your results be careful not to simply describe your graphs and charts in written text. What you should be doing is interpreting your data for the reader, explaining the significance and the meaning that can be derived from them – see Chapter Ten. After writing your results submit them to your tutor for feedback.
- **Await return**. Your tutor may spot mistakes, and or omissions made or seemingly important results that are missing. Whilst you are waiting for the return of your results consider their meaning along with the relationships you can make to the information gained in your literature review – this will contribute to the discussion stage.
- **Amend and complete the results section**. Reflect on the feedback you receive from your tutor and make any changes that you feel are relevant.

The following Gantt chart of the results stage compares with the results stage from the table of project stages and objectives given earlier.

1	⊟ Dissertation		
2	⊞ Proposal		
13	⊞ Literature Review		
18	⊞ Methodology Including Research		
29	⊟ Results		
30	Write up results section and submit to tutor for feedback		
31	Await return		
32	Amend and complete results section		
33	⊞ Discussion		
37	⊞ Conclusions & Recommendations		
41	⊞ Final Additions		
45	⊞ Final Amendments		
52	⊞ Completion		

7.6   Discussion

This is your opportunity to analyse and discuss your findings. At this stage in your dissertation you are required to give your understanding and rationale as to why your results are what they are. In order to do this, you must apply thought and reasoning gained from the information within your literature review to your own findings.

The objectives for this stage of the project are:

- **Write up your discussion as mentioned above.** Do not underestimate how important this section is as it really does demonstrate how much you have understood the topic on which your dissertation is based. Consider what your results are telling you – and WHY this is. Your discussion should use the information that you have gained from your own secondary research in the literature review to explain your own results from the primary research that you have undertaken. You might find that your research findings confirm the results gained by other authors, or indeed you might find that your findings contrast with the views of other researchers. This section should make up a significant proportion of your dissertation. At this stage you will have to utilise fully your critical thinking skills to draw out the key lessons that can be learnt from your research – see Chapter Eleven for guidelines on this.
- **Await the return of your discussion from your tutor.**
- **Amend as necessary.** Discuss your tutor's feedback with your tutor before making any suggested changes.

The following Gantt chart of the discussion stage compares with the discussion stage from the table of project stages and objectives given earlier.

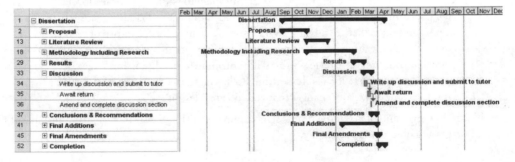

7.7   Conclusions and Recommendations

At this stage in your dissertation no new material can be introduced. Your conclusion summarises the main points that are made in your dissertation and demonstrates how you have attained the aims and objectives that were set in your proposal. The conclusion is designed to let the reader know overall what has been gained from this study. The conclusion must be entirely supported by evidence from within your dissertation.

After you conclusion has been written, you must then write a separate section that recommends future action to be taken, as a result of your study.

The objectives for this stage of the project are as follows:

- **Consider and write conclusions and recommendations and submit to your tutor.**
  Your conclusion should answer any questions that were posed at the beginning of your dissertation – with justification linked to your discussion. It should also state how closely the aims and objectives of the dissertation have been met. Once your conclusion has been written, your recommendations must be made, these may include suggested future actions – such as further research, and the application of accepted best practice techniques to the subject area on which your dissertation is based. This is your final tutor submission, before the official hand-in of your dissertation.
- **Await return.** Whilst you are awaiting the return of your work, start to edit your entire dissertation, so that it appears as one document, instead of a series of disjointed documents. Ensure that you have linking sentences and paragraphs at the beginning and end of each main section and chapter. These linking sentences and paragraphs help to guide the reader through your dissertation showing how the various sections and chapters support each other.
- **Amend as necessary.** Discuss your tutor's feedback with your tutor before making any suggested changes.

The following Gantt chart of the conclusions and recommendations stage compares with the conclusions and recommendations stage from the table of project stages and objectives given earlier.

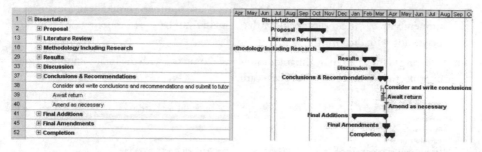

7.8   Final Additions

Almost there – the hard work is now over, and what you have left are a series of predominantly administrative tasks, that are still important and need carrying out in order to bring your dissertation to completion.

The objectives for this stage of the project are as follows:

- **Write the Summary** (sometimes referred to as the synopsis). The summary (or synopsis) goes at the beginning of your dissertation, usually after the contents page (check with your university's specified guidelines in case they differ from this). The summary is usually one side of paper that outlines the subject area, main aims and objectives, the research method used, the main findings and any major conclusions and recommendations made from these. It is basically the key points from your dissertation condensed and summarised into one page. You may also wish to write a page of acknowledgements to go at the front of your dissertation. You will also need to write an introduction to your dissertation, it can be a good idea to do it at this point if you have not already done this, looking at what your proposal states, and what you have achieved. Your introduction will provide a brief outline of the subject matter of your dissertation and your personal motivation for undertaking it. Then you should specify the dissertations aims and objectives before introducing the chapters – explaining briefly what each one contributes to your dissertation. If there have been any factors that have affected the completion of your dissertation you should explain these also in your introduction.

- **Prepare the Bibliography and Appendices**. Formally write up all of your references in a Harvard style bibliography (see Chapter Four), this goes between the main body of your dissertation and the appendices. The appendices go at the back of your dissertation, and are typically lettered Appendix A, Appendix B...etc. If you go beyond Appendix Z (which is uncommon) you have the option of then going back to Appendix A1, Appendix B1... or simply numbering your appendices Appendix 1, Appendix 2. Your appendices will typically consist of graphs, charts, maps, tables, diagrams, transcripts of interviews, and other supporting text, that would make the dissertation too disjointed if they were contained within the main body of the text. Your appendices pages do not need to be numbered. Ordinarily the Bibliography and Appendices will not be included in your final word count – double check this though, in case this differs to the practice within your own university.

- **Create contents pages**. Create a contents page of your entire dissertation – don't forget to number your pages, the correct ordering of sections is as follows: Acknowledgements; Summary; Contents; Introduction (to include aims and objectives); Literature Review; Methodology; Results; Discussion; Conclusions; Recommendations; Bibliography; Appendices. Page numbers should be in roman numerals up to the contents page, with the main Arabic page numbering (1,2,3) beginning with the introduction.

The following Gantt chart of the final additions stage compares with the final additions stage from the table of project stages and objectives given earlier.

7.9 Final Amendments

This is the penultimate stage of your dissertation, and involves, those finishing touches, to ensure that what you hand in is *perfect*.

The objectives for this stage of the project are as follows:

- **First print**. Once your dissertation has been completed, and all pages and appendices have been written, the entire dissertation should be printed off in order to proof read it.
- **First proof read**. DO NOT proof read from your screen, as it is easy to read over mistakes and skim read – take time proof reading, check everything including your spelling, grammar, punctuation, page numbering and referencing. Make sure that all references in your text appear in the bibliography.
- **Edit and amend**. Make any amendments as necessary.
- **Second print**. Print off a final draft for the second and final proof read.
- **Second proof read**. Try and give yourself plenty of time to read through this more than once. This is your last chance to spot any mistakes and to make any changes. Consider asking a friend or colleague if they will read through it for you – you may do the same in return for them. If a large number of errors are found you might want to consider a third proof read and amend.
- **Second edit and amend**. Make any final changes.

The following Gantt chart of the final amendments stage compares with the final amendments stage from the table of project stages and objectives given earlier.

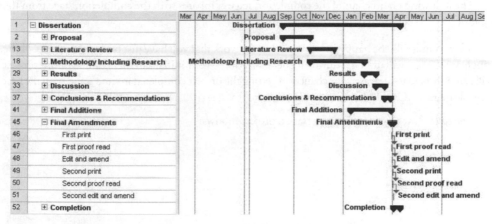

7.10 Completion

You are almost there – the project that you have lived with for the previous eight or nine months is almost at closure.

The objectives for this stage of the project are as follows:

- **Final print**. First impressions count, so investing in decent quality paper is a must, make sure that you get the correct type for your printer – i.e. ink-jet or laser. Make your final print a colour one, to highlight graphs, and images within your dissertation. It is important to print TWO COPIES of your dissertation – both of which are usually submitted.

- **Binding**. Your completed script should either be comb bound or hard bound – check with your university if there is a preference. Also check if there is a specific colour for the cover of the dissertation for your school/faculty. You may be able to hand one copy in hard bound, and one comb bound.
- **Submission**. Try and submit your dissertation before the deadline date, so as not to put unnecessary pressure on yourself – who knows what may happen on the way: the bus or train might not turn up; the car may break down – it isn't worth taking the risk. Make sure that you have your dissertation inside a waterproof carrier bag, inside your normal work/university bag (in case it rains).

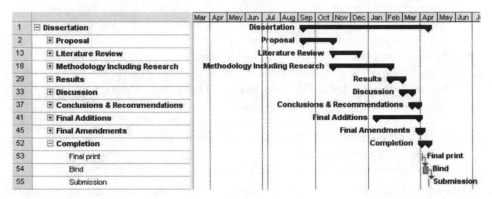

The following Gantt chart of the completion stage compares with the completion stage from the table of project stages and objectives given earlier.

After completion, be happy in knowing that the work that you have just undertaken is one of the toughest tests you will undergo during higher education – your initial careful planning of this project will certainly help to increase your chances of getting the project completed in time – and with the best possible marks. GOOD LUCK.

The full Gantt chart for this dissertation project follows:

#	Task	Duration
1	Dissertation	216 days
2	Proposal	52 days
3	Consider general subject and gather information	10 days
4	Initial reading and research	14 days
5	Choose specific subject	5 days
6	Consider aims and objectives	3 days
7	Consider and choose research methods	3 days
8	Choose title	1 day
9	Ongoing Discussion with tutors	7 days
10	Write proposal including aims and objectives and submit to tutor	2 days
11	Await Return	7 days
12	Amend as necessary	7 days
13	Literature Review	44 days
14	Gather and read literature	20 days
15	Prepare literature review and submit to tutor for feedback	10 days
16	Await return	7 days
17	Amend as necessary	7 days
18	Methodology Including Research	99 days
19	Prepare research mechanism and submit to tutor for feedback	10 days
20	Await Return	7 days
21	Amend research mechanism as necessary	7 days
22	Carry out primary research and collect data	30 days
23	Data entry	7 days
24	Data analysis	7 days
25	Data representation	7 days
26	Write up methodology and submit to tutor for feedback	10 days
27	Await return	7 days

#	Task	Duration
28	Amend as necessary	7 days
29	⊟ Results	21 days
30	Write up results section and submit to tutor for feedback	7 days
31	Await return	7 days
32	Amend and complete results section	7 days
33	⊟ Discussion	16 days
34	Write up discussion and submit to tutor	7 days
35	Await return	7 days
36	Amend and complete discussion section	2 days
37	⊟ Conclusions & Recommendations	11 days
38	Consider and write conclusions and recommendations and sub	2 days
39	Await return	7 days
40	Amend as necessary	2 days
41	⊟ Final Additions	73 days
42	Write summary	0.5 days
43	Prepare bibliography and appendices	2 days
44	Create contents pages	0.5 days
45	⊟ Final Amendments	5 days
46	First print	0.5 days
47	First proof read	1 day
48	Edit and amend	1 day
49	Second print	0.5 days
50	Second proof read	1 day
51	Second edit and amend	1 day
52	⊟ Completion	11 days
53	Final print	0.5 days
54	Bind	10 days
55	Submission	0.5 days

After reading this chapter please complete the following learning activities:

Learning Activities

1. From what you have read in this chapter, write a short piece on what constitutes being a project – apply this to a project that you have been involved with, highlighting each of the key stages of the project.

2. From the table below, draw a network diagram, Gantt chart – and work out the critical path of the project.

Objective	Time Duration	Predecessors
A	0	
B		A
C	6	B
D	12	A
E	10	C
F	2	D,E
G	9	F
H	1	E
I	5	F,H
J	7	G.I
K	0	J

3. You are working as an advisor to a company that produces specialist table sauces. The organisation is only small, and can only afford to develop one new sauce each year. You have been asked by the organisation to help them decide which of three sauce flavours they should develop over the next year. Taking into account the volume of produced sauces, and the revenue that they are likely to generate, you have researched how each of the proposed flavours have sold when introduced by other companies. You have also ascertained how much each of the sauces will cost to develop. You have placed all of this information in the following table.

Sauce Flavour	Cost of Development	Likelihood of Success	Likelihood of Failure	Estimated Revenue if Successful	Estimated Loss if a Failure
Garlic Chilli	£20,000	45%	55%	£80,000	-£10,000
Tangy Oriental	£18,000	50%	50%	£60,000	-£5,000
Onion and Chive	£16,000	40%	60%	£90,000	-£15,000

Using the information in the table, draw a decision tree – which of the above sauces should the company produce based on the results of the decision tree?

4.   What makes you stressed? From the information within this chapter on stress and stress management consider five separate times that you have been stressed. Write a short reflective piece that demonstrates how you know that you were suffering from stress, and the symptoms that you suffered. After you have done this write a stress action-plan against each of the times that you were stressed. Implement your stress action plan if you face any of these challenges again in the future.

5.   Apply the knowledge that you have gained from section 7 into planning your own dissertation or major project. Carry out the work for your dissertation, then critically review how effective planning has assisted the undertaking of your dissertation or major project.

Chapter Thirteen
Consultancy Skills

After reading this chapter you will be able to:

1. Understand the stages in the consultancy process.
2. Appreciate which ES are essential for consultancy work.
3. Establish a professional relationship with a client organisation.
4. Present consultancy findings in a competent manner.

We have decided to include consultancy skills as part of the ES programme because managers at work, and students at college and university, are increasingly being required to act as consultants to colleagues within their own organisations, or to other organisations as part of special projects.

To be a successful consultant you must master the full range of ES discussed in this book, from verbal and non-verbal communication skills right through to critical thinking and information gathering skills. The purpose of this chapter is to highlight the stages in the consultancy process, developing further special applications of ES already mentioned and providing guidelines for additional ones that need to be developed.

Consultants are recruited by organisations to carry out a wide range of functions such as:

- Solving specific problems.
- Providing specialist advice.
- Providing special skills that are not available 'in house'.
- Carrying out ad hoc studies and research.
- Assisting with the selection and recruitment of staff.
- Providing training courses.
- Implementing specific courses of action.

The range of skills and functions that consultants offer clients is increasing and so too are the number of consultants available. To act as a consultant you must be aware of the distinct stages of the consultancy process.

- Pitching for the Account.
- The Administrative Arrangements.
- Maintaining a Good Relationship with the Client.
- Undertaking the Work.
- Presenting the Work.
- Follow-up Procedures.

1.   Pitching for the Account

The first stage in the consultancy process is gaining the client's account. Frequently this will involve competing against other consultants. The client will probably require each consultant to make a brief presentation covering how each intends tackling the work involved. This is known as 'pitching for the account'. When pitching for the account you need to bear in mind all the points raised in Chapter Seven on Presentation Skills, and in Chapter Eight on Selling and Negotiating skills. In particular you need to stress to the client the benefits that will be gained from awarding you the contract. The presentation should be viewed as a means of establishing your credibility – a major factor when the client decides who will be awarded the contract. Following the guidelines below will help to establish your credibility:

- Research the clients, their business, their needs, problems and expectations.
- Prepare thoroughly for the first meeting with a client.
- Look smart and efficient – dress in a proper business-like manner.
- Be honest, and avoid exaggeration and claims that you cannot substantiate, do not make promises that you cannot keep.
- Listen attentively to what they say.

2.   The Administrative Arrangements

If you win the account it is important to clearly specify at the outset all administrative arrangements of the consultancy:

- A formal, legal agreement should be drawn up that specifies:
  - who the client is;
  - a full description of the nature of the work and what achievements (reports, training, recommendations, etc.) by the consultant for   the client will constitute fulfilment of the contract;
  - the timescale involved in completing the work;
  - the fee to be charged, plus expenses, plus VAT, and when fee payments are to be paid;
  - the liability of both parties;
  - how the contract can be terminated if either party wishes to do so.
- Your terms of reference.
- Where the work is to be carried out e.g. the physical working conditions.
- Reporting procedures if you have to work off-site.

3.   Maintaining a Good Relationship with the Client

At all stages during the consultancy process it will be important for you to maintain an impeccable relationship with all members of the client's organisation. To do this:

- Keep the client fully informed of the progress you make, the successes you achieve and difficulties you encounter. Be totally honest about these. Never make false claims.
- Arrange for regular meetings with the client to discuss the progress you make.
- Ensure that all work that you give to the client is meticulously presented – the client will be judging your ability to complete the contract at all stages of the process.
- Establish an informal relationship with clients, getting to know their interests, hobbies, likes, and family relationships. This gives you conversation topics other than the work, and will be helpful for developing a long-term association.

The relationship that you establish with the client is clearly an essential ingredient of the consultancy process and every effort should be made to nurture it into a friendly, yet business-like one.

4.   Undertaking the Work

You will have been recruited because of your specialised skills. The client will naturally have certain expectations that you will wish to meet. To achieve a successful outcome you need to bear in mind those points raised in Chapter Eleven – Thinking Skills, as this really is why you have been recruited:

- Clearly define the problem or nature of the consultancy at the outset, and establish mutually agreed objectives.
- Use divergent thinking skills to develop creative solutions to the problem – the client will be looking for new ideas, ones perhaps which have not already been considered.
- Adopt professional and ethical standards when collecting data e.g. follow the Market Research Society's Code of Conduct when undertaking questionnaire research.
- Follow logical problem solving and decision making steps.
- Critically evaluate all possible solutions to the problem.
- Draw reasoned conclusions, and produce data that are academically sound and free from ideological statements.

In undertaking the work you will have to manage your own time effectively to ensure that all deadlines are met.

4.1   Time Management Skills

In consultancy work time is of the essence. You should have worked out beforehand how long you expect to be involved with the client, and your fee will have been based on this. If you overrun, then you are unlikely to be able to charge a higher fee. The client will expect to see the results of your labours as soon as possible – profitability might depend upon it. Thus, you must be able to plan your working schedule effectively. This involves the following:

- Arrange the work into order of priority. You must decide at the outset what are the most important tasks that need to be carried out, and the least important. The tasks should be listed, and ranked in order of priority.
- In arranging the order of priority for the work you should take a long term view. You must think and plan ahead. For example if certain information is required in two weeks time, and that information has to be collected, then the research process to obtain the information needs to be instigated immediately.

- If interviews are to be conducted with colleagues of the client, or other people, these should be arranged well in advance to allow all concerned to prepare for them.
- On a daily basis, a plan of action should be drawn up – 'things to do today', once again in order of priority. Time should be set aside each day for making telephone calls, for dealing with unplanned events, and for writing up the progress made to date.
- Ensure that all working time is constructively used.

In thinking about managing your time, you must work out what you have to achieve in the time available, then consider how much can be achieved day by day, and translate this into a diary of activities and a Gantt chart – see Chapter Twelve. During the course of the consultancy you can check with this diary to see whether you are on schedule. The key to successful time management is to have a realistic plan of action that sets out all the steps involved in completing the consultancy work. Set targets that have to be met if the work is to completed on time. You should ensure that each of these 'incremental' targets is attained.

When such an approach is adopted, you know precisely what has to be achieved each day and each week.

5.   Presenting the Work

If you manage your time efficiently then the work will normally be completed to schedule. Your presentation of the final work needs to be meticulous. If you produce a written report then follow all the guidelines given in Chapter Four – Written Communication Skills. In particular, though, you must remember to:

- Be concise, clear and to the point. Follow all the conventions in writing academically sound data discussed in Chapter Four.
- Structure the report and make sure that there is an 'Executive Summary' at the beginning – this provides an overview of the key points raised and is useful in giving the reader a picture of the report's content.
- Pay careful attention to the front cover – remember this will be the first thing the client sees and so it must create a favourable impression.
- Provide a title page that indicates the title of the project, who has completed it, their qualifications, and the date.
- Check to make sure that there are no grammar or spelling errors. Have the report word-processed and printed using a high quality printer. Use a desk-top publishing programme to produce diagrams/tables/pie charts/histograms etc.
- Thoroughly proof read the report to ensure that all typing errors have been corrected.
- Find out how many copies of the report the client requires, and arrange for these to be printed or photocopied.
- Check to make sure that all the pages are in the correct order and then have the report bound.
- Retain a personal copy as a permanent record of the work.
- Present the report personally and discuss the main findings with the client.

In addition to the report the client may also require you to make a formal oral presentation. It is likely that the presentation will involve communicating data, and their interpretation, to the audience. In particular you should:

- Produce a handout of the key data being referred to and distribute this to the audience prior to the presentation, giving them the opportunity to digest the information.
- Prepare effective visual aids for communicating the main points that are raised – use PowerPoint for maximum impact.
- Do not spend too much time describing the data, concentrate on their interpretation – what do they mean for the client?

If you follow the above points then you will have completed a successful piece of work and hopefully created a good impression with the client.

The true test of your ability is how far you met the objectives that were initially set. This, plus the ability to deliver on time, every time, are the hallmarks of a competent consultant.

To foster a continuing relationship with the client, you should maintain regular contact, commencing with the 'CSQ', the client satisfaction questionnaire. Soon after work has been completed questionnaires should be sent to clients asking them to formally evaluate you and the work that you completed. Not only will this provide valuable feedback to you about the client's satisfaction with your work, but will show the client that you do care about your customers.

Thereafter, visit the client from time to time to see what progress is being made, and to further the personal relationship that will have developed. Indeed, the client might have additional consultancy work, or may refer you to other business associates.

Consultancy skills, therefore, draw upon all the ES mentioned in this book. In the discussion above it has been implied that you are working by yourself, but on many occasions you might be leading a team, or working as a group member requiring you to use your group work skills. The consultancy might involve implementing decisions for the client. Your full range of personal skills, assertive and affective, will be required here, as well as selling and negotiating skills to convince others to change their behaviour. Following all the guidelines detailed in this book will strengthen your skills and increase your chances of confirming success as a consultant.

After reading this chapter please complete the following learning activities:

Learning Activities

1. Describe in your own words the six stages in the consultancy process.

2. List all the ES you will need to use to be a competent consultant.

3. Explain how you can establish a professional working relationship with your client.

4. Upon completion of a consultancy project explain how you would present the findings to the client – what will be important for creating a positive impression of yourself?

Chapter Fourteen

Reflective Skills and Personal Development Planning

After reading this chapter you will be able to:

1. Reflect on your portfolio of ES and identify those skills where you are competent and those skills you need to develop further.

2. Develop a Personal Development Plan for your ES.

3. Create your own Progress File.

4. Understand the importance of continually reflecting on your portfolio of ES.

1. Reflective Skills

This final chapter of the book will explain how you can reflect constructively on your ES and from such reflection develop a personal development plan that will help you to continually develop your personal skills. To develop your ES you must be able to reflect upon your current abilities and identify your weaknesses as well as your strengths. The development of your reflective skills helps to improve your ES because only through experimentation and evaluation will you learn. This reflective process requires you to be objective and rational when considering your own skills and this necessitates a systematic approach.

Reflection can be structured and unstructured. Unstructured reflection is when you think about a situation where you have used your ES and after the event or situation has ended you think about what you did successfully, as well as highlighting the ES that you need to develop further. This unstructured reflection might occur simply by reviewing the situation in your mind, and then identifying what you feel went well, and which aspects of your ES you were not so happy with. In certain circumstances other people might provide you with unstructured feedback. After an oral presentation one of your colleagues might compliment you on your verbal presentation skills, or your colleague might suggest that certain aspects of your presentation could have been better. Unstructured reflection is very important as it can occur after every occasion when you have used your ES. Such reflection helps to identify how your ES can be developed further. To record your unstructured reflections carry a small note-book or diary with you at all times, and after a social encounter, or a situation where you have used your ES write down the ES you used effectively, and those you would like to improve.

Structured reflection is also very important for your personal development. Most students at college or university are now required to develop a progress file. Progress files provide you with the opportunity to formally record your achievements and to formally identify how you need to develop further. In your progress file you will record the formal feedback that you have received from your tutors on the development of your ES. Read carefully the tutor feedback and appreciate how your tutor is suggesting you can improve your ES. Structured reflection can also come from other sources. When you attend a job interview it is likely that you will receive feedback on your performance from the interviewer. Listen carefully to this feedback and incorporate any suggestions to improve your interview skills, into your next job interview.

When you have reflected on your current level of competence against certain ES you can then produce a personal development plan that indicates how you are going to improve further your ES.

Developing competent reflective skills is important because they allow you to:

- Identify your ES strengths as well as those ES you need to develop further – without such reflection learning and personal development will not occur.
- See yourself as other people do – this is essential when developing ES because in certain situations this gives you more control over your behaviour, enabling you to achieve your desired outcome.

Reflective skills are high order ES because you are required to be evaluative, to reach a judgement on your level of competence against certain criteria. At college and university students are increasingly encouraged to be independent learners, to use their own judgement. The previous chapters in this book have identified a range of ES and have indicated what constitutes a competent level of performance for each of these skills. When you reflect on your own ES, use the guidelines and bullet points presented in previous chapters as a frame of reference to evaluate your own competencies. Also when reflecting on your own ES take into account the following guidelines:

- Be honest in your reflections and evaluations. You will only develop further your ES if you are prepared to identify those skills you need to improve. Your tutors will expect you to be honest and will not penalise you in any way if you are critical of your current level of competence.
- Read through the guidelines presented in previous chapters of this book when reflecting on your ES. These guidelines indicate what a competent level of performance is for each of the ES considered. Then use unstructured and structured reflection to rate your level of ability against each of the ES.
- Be positive throughout the reflective process – remember that ES are developed over time and that we are all life long learners. If you feel that you have been overly critical in your reflections ask for additional feedback from your tutor or a friend. You might actually be surprised when you do receive such feedback – other people frequently see us in more positive ways than we do ourselves.

1.1 Reflection in Action

In order to identify those ES that you currently use, first of all appraise the activities you follow or are engaged in. After identifying these activities you can list the ES you use in these activities, before evaluating these ES to spot where your ES strengths lie and your weaknesses exist. The clearer the picture you draw of the activities you follow the easier it will be to assess your ES.

(i)   Activities

Some activities you pursue will be obligatory, such as attending college or work, while others will be freely chosen – leisure activities. It is important to recognise from these activities where your ES strengths lie.

The starting point is for you to list activities you frequently undertake. We give an example of this in the table below. We list activities that are both obligatory and are freely chosen in column one. The ES that you use in each of these activities is then noted in column two. You can then undertake some simple self-evaluation and enter your assessment in column three. Base this on a rating scale from '1' (not competent in the skill) to '5' (highly competent in the skill). Be honest in your evaluation – use both structured and unstructured reflection to arrive at your rating. Read the skills covered in previous chapters to determine how effective you are at using each of the ES listed.

Column One	Column Two	Column Three
Activities	ES	Rating 1 (low) - 5 (high)
Attend lectures	Note taking	4
	Thinking	3
	Listening	4
Part-time job	Working with others	4
	Conversation skills	2
	Being assertive	1
	Numeracy	1
	Writing letters	5
Scout Leader	Leading others	4
	Planning events	4
	Time management	3
	Oral communication	5

Completing a table like this which covers all the activities you undertake will provide you with a clearer picture of some of the ES you are currently using, and is a start in identifying where your strengths and weaknesses lie. The table will also give you a view of those ES that you enjoy using, because these will generally be the ones with the higher scores in which you are competent.

(ii)   Interests

Like your activities, your interests also give an insight into your ES. By analysing what you like doing, and the ES involved, you can shed further light on your capabilities. For example, if you enjoy playing chess it might be because you enjoy competing against other people (an enterprising skill). That you like to study others' approaches and styles of play (requiring the use of intellectual skills); or it gives you a sense of purpose and achievement in trying to improve your performance (personal skills). Your interest may be less in the game itself than in the satisfaction associated with it.

To translate these likes and satisfactions into ES, you should list the interests you enjoy and then say why you think you like them. The next stage should be to rank these interests in order of enjoyment, and then to state explicitly the ES that you use successfully in each of the interests, together with an evaluation on the rating scale of 1–5 of each of the skills:

Emerging from the analysis is a profile of those interests that you have and the ES that you most commonly use.

Rank Order of Interests	ES	Rating 1 (Low) - 5 (High)
1. Playing chess	Intellectual skills	4
	Oral communication skills	2
	Reading body language	5
2. Reading books	Intellectual skills	3
	Reading skills	5
3. Socialising	Leadership skills	5
	Conversation skills	5

(iii) Achievements

Just as the activities and interests you enjoy shed light on your ES, so too can your achievements. Achievements do not have to be headline making events, simply successes you have enjoyed, or about which you feel pleased.

A useful starting point is to list the achievements you consider are important. These achievements may be connected with work or in your social life. For each one, you should write down why that achievement is important to you. Emphasise those achievements that were difficult to attain successfully.

Once you have completed the list, evaluate the ES revealed. Listing achievements in this way, gives insight into your ES. For example:

Achievement	ES	Rating 1 (low) - 5 (high)
Winning the football competition	Working with others	4
	Leading others	3
	Oral communication skills	4
Attaining top mark in the examinations	Working under pressure	5
	Working to time constraints	4
	Self-motivation skills	4
	Self-discipline skills	4
	Intellectual skills	5
	Written communication skills	3

The achievements listed and their ES' evaluation will help to identify your capabilities. The person profiled above is able to accept pressure and to work well within constraints. To achieve examination success the individual must have been motivated to undertake all the necessary preparation, which has required a self-disciplined approach prioritising examination revision above other interests or activities. You could summarise this individual as being determined and dedicated.

Your personal competencies and capabilities, though, are made up of many elements and, importantly, develop over time.

(iv) Satisfactions

Your self-awareness will be enhanced by assessing your satisfactions.

Everyone gets satisfaction from some activity or event in which they participate. ES can be assessed in terms of the satisfaction they give. Listed below are a range of ES. Against each skill you can indicate whether or not you generally feel satisfaction when using it. The ability to use the skill can be evaluated in the third column.

ES	Gain Satisfaction/Dissatisfaction	Rating 1 (low) - 5 (high)
Conversing with friends	Satisfaction	5
Conversing with strangers	Dissatisfaction	2
Making a presentation	Dissatisfaction	1
Selling	Dissatisfaction	2
Negotiating	Satisfaction	3
Being interviewed	Dissatisfaction	2
Interviewing others	Satisfaction	4
Writing reports	Satisfaction	5
Writing business letters	Satisfaction	4
Using body language	Satisfaction	3
Reading body language	Satisfaction	4
Solving problems	Satisfaction	4
Taking decisions	Satisfaction	5
Working with others	Dissatisfaction	2
Leading others	Satisfaction	4
Chairing meetings	Satisfaction	4
Attending meetings	Satisfaction	3

The above list of ES is not exhaustive but it does cover a wide range of activities. By deciding whether or not you get satisfaction from using each of the skills, will give you insight into where your strengths lie, and which weaknesses need to be overcome.

(v) Personality

Your personality profoundly influences how you behave, react and feel towards other people and towards different situations. In turn, how other people react and respond to you will be determined partly by your personality. Knowing and understanding your own personality is of great importance when evaluating ES. Such a knowledge and understanding helps you to identify personality characteristics you might have that either support or hinder your ability to interact effectively with other people.

Listed on the following page are a number of adjectives that describe various personality characteristics. Read the list ticking those that you recognise in yourself. Put a cross beside those that you do not think describe you. Leave blank those which are indeterminate:

Adaptable	Aggressive	Amiable
Aloof	Ambitious	Assertive
Assured	Caring	Cheerful
Co-ordinated	Competitive	Confident
Considerate	Creative	Daring
Decisive	Dependable	Determined
Easy-going	Emotional	Enterprising
Extrovert	Fickle	Forceful
Friendly	Gregarious	Hard-working
Honest	Humorous	Introspective
Judicious	Lazy	Mild-mannered
Objective	Obstinate	Open-minded
Orderly	Overcareful	Persistent
Prudent	Reliable	Reticent
Self-conscious	Self-reliant	Shy
Sincere	Systematic	Tactful
Tenacious	Tense	Trustworthy

When you have done this look at the personality traits you have ticked and assess how you come across to others – how do friends think of you, do they see you as being assertive, tactful, or a supportive person, for example? Ask your friends how they see you. Ask colleagues at work. What are their perceptions of you? For instance, do they regard you as ambitious, reliable, decisive?

This analysis will increase your awareness of your 'personal' ES and give a picture of how you appear to others. To conclude this exercise you should try to summarise your evaluation of your own ES.

2.   Evaluating the Portfolio of Employability Skills

You cannot develop your ES if you are unaware of your current skills. The exercises you have completed in this chapter will be useful in starting this self-evaluation process by using reflective skills to highlight skills that have already been competently mastered, and those in which you have room for improvement. To draw all the previous sections together, you need to draw up a 'master-list' of ES, similar to that given below, which you can use to evaluate formally your own levels of competence.

A Compendium of ES

Read each skill statement and use the following rating scale to indicate your level of ability:

1. Not very good, and requiring considerable improvement.
2. Acceptable at a basic level but with need for improvement.
3. Not bad, but scope for improvement.
4. Reasonably competent, slight room for improvement.
5. Highly competent, scope for fine-tuning.

A   Oral Communication Skills

I am able to use:

> different tones of voice when speaking
> different speeds of speech
> emphasis in speech, stressing key words
> figurative language
> clear pronunciation

Skill Rating

B   Conversation Skills

I am able to:

> listen effectively to others
> start a conversation with friends
> start a conversation with strangers
> maintain a conversation
> conclude a conversation
> use the telephone efficiently
> contribute effectively to meetings
> chair a meeting
> give clear instructions to others

C   Body Language Skills

I am able to:

> use facial expressions appropriately
> use effective eye contact with others
> control my posture movements
> give appropriate gestures
> dress appropriately
> read the body language of others

D   Harvard Referencing Skills

I am able to:

> reference books
> reference journal articles
> reference data obtained from the internet
> produce a bibliography

E   Written Communication Skills

I am able to:

> write memos
> write business letters
> write business reports
> present data clearly using graphs
> present data clearly using bar charts
> present data clearly using pie charts

F   Employability Skills

I am able to:

> complete application forms effectively
> write an effective curriculum vitae
> create a favourable impression of myself at interviews
> interview others efficiently

	Skill Rating
G Presentation Skills	
I am able to:	
prepare for a presentation	
set explicit presentation objectives	
design an interesting message	
structure the presentation	
deliver the presentation competently	
evaluate the presentation	
H Selling and Negotiating Skills	
I am able to:	
present a persuasive message to a group	
explain the products benefits	
establish the needs of a customer	
handle objections to the sale	
close the sale	
negotiate with orders	
make concessions to reach agreement	
I Personal Skills	
I am able to:	
make a request of others	
cope with the refusal of a request	
refuse a request	
stand up for my rights	
show appreciation to others	
apologise to others	
reflect upon my own TPS	
J Group Skills	
I am able to:	
work in a group with other people	
accept the views of other people	
be sensitive to the vies of other people	
plan the work of other people	
motivate other people to work for the group	
K Thinking Skills	
I am able to:	
analyse a situation	
evaluate a situation critically	
interpret data	
identify weak assumptions	
solve problems systematically	
take decisions	
L Information Gathering Skills	
I am able to:	
use a library	
design a questionnaire	
conduct research interviews	
analyse research findings	
M Dissertation Writing Skills	
I am able to:	
produce a Gantt chart	
undertake a literature search	
manage my time effectively	
reference my dissertation	
structure my dissertation	
reach logical conclusions	

The checklist covers some of the ES in this book. When all the ratings have been given you will have a comprehensive profile of how you rate your own ES, identifying your strengths and weaknesses. The findings of the checklist can be usefully summarised as follows:

By explicitly evaluating your strengths and weaknesses and committing yourself to some form of skills development programme, you will be motivated towards converting weaknesses into strengths, thus developing well-balanced ES.

You need to develop reflective skills because much of the work involved in developing ES has to be done by yourself. If you follow no systematic process for reflecting upon your own skill levels then you will be less likely to master new skills and improve existing ones.

MY STRONGEST ES ARE:

MY WEAKEST ES ARE:

THE ES I NEED TO DEVELOP MOST ARE:

THE WAYS IN WHICH I WILL DEVELOP MY ES ARE:

3.   Personal Development Planning

The process that you have been following in section two is the start of personal development planning (PDP). PDP is a structured way of not only thinking about the ES you need to develop further but also the means by which such development will be achieved. All universities in the UK require their students to produce personal development plans.

The benefits of PDP are considerable:

▪   You will be able to clearly identify the ES you need to develop further.

- You will be able to devise a personal training or development programme that will enable you to improve your ES.
- The PDP should set objectives and time scales that will help to keep you motivated and will allow you to assess the progress you are making.
- You will be in control of your learning and personal development – the pace of learning and the ES you will be developing.
- Over time, your self confidence will improve as your ES develop.

3.1   What Does a Personal Development Plan Look Like?

There is no national standard for what a PDP should look like. Each university (and each employer) will develop a PDP that is appropriate for their own students or employees. What is important is that the PDP:

- should record your structured and unstructured reflections on your ES;
- should set personal development objectives for the future;
- should set out the development process that you will follow in order to attain the objectives specified above.

Most universities will devise a PDP pro-forma that each student uses to record the above. An example of a PDP pro-forma is given below. The PDP is produced in a two stage process. First of all you are required to look back and reflect on the ES you have developed to-date, and to write these down in the space provided. Then you look forward and identify those ES you need to develop further, specifying learning objectives that you wish to attain. The next stage in looking forward is to indicate how and when you will attain the learning objectives. The outcomes of this process are then recorded in a structured way:

Personal Development Plan for..   **Period 200..... - 200.....**

1. Looking back - record here the ES you are able to use competently, and record those ES you need to develop further.

    Remember to be honest and to use the reflective process specified previously.   .

2. Looking forward - indicate those ES you wish to develop further.

    Be very specific and provide as much detail as you can on the exact ES you want to develop further.

3. Looking forward - set clear personal development objectives for the ES you wish to develop further.

    Set one learning objective for each ES you want to develop further.
    Ensure your objectives are achievable, measurable and realistic.

4. Looking forward - devise a programme of self-directed learning that will enable you to attain your personal development objectives.

    Provide the time frame in which you want to achieve your learning objectives. Indicate very precisely how you are going to attain each of the learning objectives and the resources you will need for your personal development plan.

Summarise the responses you have given above in the following Personal Development Plan:

ES to be developed	Specific Learning Objectives	How the Learning Objectives will be Attained	Time-scale	Objective Met
1. Harvard referencing skills	Learn how to reference material downloaded from the internet.	Read Chapter Four on Harvard Referencing Skills.	Within the next four weeks	Yes
2. Group work skills	Learn how to be a team leader.	Read Chapter Nine on group work skills; attend a leadership course; practise leadership skills in social situations.	Over the next six months	
3.				
4.				
5.				
6.				
7.				

By working through the above process you will develop a PDP that is unique to your current stage in ES development. At regular intervals you should review your PDP to see how your skills development is progressing. When you feel that you have attained one of your learning objectives you should provide and keep the evidence that you have to show that the objective has been attained. Your PDP and evidence should form your progress file. Evidence that you can collate to demonstrate that you have met your learning objectives includes:

- assignment feedback sheets from tutors;
- appraisals from tutors at college or university;
- appraisals from employers;
- evidence from your own assignment work e.g. a report that you have referenced correctly;
- visual material – for example a video recording of you delivering an oral presentation.

Your progress file should be a formal file that you maintain throughout your educational and working career. It should be an evidence based document – not only should your progress file include your PDP it should also contain the evidence to demonstrate that you are developing your ES. When going for appraisals or attending a job interview you can take your file with you to demonstrate your competencies and achievements to your tutor or interviewer. Thus, you should keep your progress file up-to-date and ensure that it is presented and collated in a highly professional manner.

After reading this chapter please complete the following learning activities:

Learning Activities

1. Using the reflective exercises provided in this chapter evaluate your ES at this moment in time – which ES are you particularly competent in using, and which ES do you need to develop further.

2. Based on (1) above produce your own Personal Development Plan using the PDP pro-forma that is included in this chapter.

3. Create your own Progress File. Buy a hard bound file and store within it your PDP. As you develop further your ES update your file and include the evidence to show that you have attained your learning outcomes. Then write a new PDP and monitor your progress against your new learning outcomes.

4. Reflect on the content of this book and explain, once again, why it is important for you to be continually developing your portfolio of ES.

Conclusion

The purpose of the preceding chapters in this book has been to highlight some of the ES that individuals need to develop. This book will act as a reference text, informing you what a competent ES comprises. After reading it, you need to practise each of the skills discussed, in order to improve your level of competence. As mentioned in the Introduction, however, ES are not developed overnight. Their development is a life-long process, with each new business and social encounter providing you with the opportunity to try out new behaviours. It is this experimentation–experience process, followed by a time of reflection, which leads to successful ES development. Good Luck.

Index